THE ELEMENTS OF
UNIVERSAL JURISPRUDENCE

NATURAL LAW AND
ENLIGHTENMENT CLASSICS

Knud Haakonssen
General Editor

Samuel Pufendorf

Two Books of the Elements of Universal Jurisprudence

Samuel Pufendorf

Translated by William Abbott Oldfather, 1931
Revised by Thomas Behme

Edited and with an Introduction by
Thomas Behme

The Works of Samuel Pufendorf

LIBERTY FUND

This book is published by Liberty Fund, Inc., a foundation established
to encourage study of the ideal of a society of free and responsible individuals.

The cuneiform inscription that serves as our logo and as the design motif for
our endpapers is the earliest-known written appearance of the word
"freedom" (*amagi*), or "liberty." It is taken from a clay document written
about 2300 b.c. in the Sumerian city-state of Lagash.

Introduction, annotations, bibliography, index © 2009 by Liberty Fund, Inc.

09 17 18 19 20 c 5 4 3 2 1
17 18 19 20 21 p 6 5 4 3 2

The text of this edition is a reprint of the translation by William Abbott
Oldfather of *Elementum jurisprudentiae universalis libri duo,*
published in 1931 by Clarendon Press.

Frontispiece: The portrait of Samuel Pufendorf is found at the
Law Faculty of the University of Lund, Sweden, and is based on a
photoreproduction by Leopoldo Iorizzo. Reprinted by permission.

Library of Congress Cataloging-in-Publication Data
Pufendorf, Samuel, Freiherr von, 1632–1694.
[Elementorum jurisprudentiae universalis libri duo. English]
Two books of the Elements of universal jurisprudence/Samuel Pufendorf;
translated by William Abbott Oldfather, 1931; revised by Thomas Behme;
edited and with an introduction by Thomas Behme.
p. cm.—(Natural law and enlightenment classics)
Originally published: Elementorum jurisprudentiae universalis libri duo.
Oxford: Clarendon Press; London: H. Milford, 1931.
Includes bibliographical references and index.
isbn 978-0-86597-619-1 (hc: alk. paper)   isbn 978-0-86597-620-7 (pbk.: alk. paper)
1. Natural law. 2. Law—Philosophy.   I. Oldfather, William Abbott, 1880–1945.
II. Behme, Thomas.   III. Title.
K457.P8E42713 2009
340′.112—dc22   2008037404

LIBERTY FUND, INC.
11301 North Meridian Street
Carmel, Indiana 46032

CONTENTS

INTRODUCTION

Pufendorf's earliest work, the *Elementorum jurisprudentiae universalis libri II* (*Two Books on the Elements of Universal Jurisprudence*) marks the starting-point of his career as a lecturer on natural law and of the emergence of the modern natural-law tradition in Germany. Dedicated to Karl Ludwig, Elector of the Palatinate, one of the most splendid and enlightened rulers in seventeenth-century Germany, the work secured Pufendorf a professorship in international law and philology at the University of Heidelberg, the first professorship of that kind in Germany and one that included natural law in its brief. The subsequent establishment of natural and international law as university subjects in Germany had a strong impact on the development of enlightened despotism and on the great law codifications in Prussia and Austria at the end of the eighteenth century.[1]

Though overshadowed by Pufendorf's larger work on natural law, *De jure naturae et gentium,* and its textbook abridgement, *De officio hominis et civis juxta legem naturalem,* the *Elements* already contains essential features of his mature theory. What distinguishes it from those later works is the specific organization of the book, which methodologically follows the reformed, Euclidean Aristotelianism of his mentor Erhard Weigel, a mathematician and philosopher at the University of Jena (1625–99). Pufendorf's aim as articulated in the preface to the *Elements* was to develop natural law as a demonstrative science modeled after the mathematical disciplines. He saw the traditional denial that a moral science was possible as a misunderstanding of the Aristotelian doctrine of demonstration. In a scientific prop-

---

1. For further details and references, see Thomas Behme, *Samuel von Pufendorf, Naturrecht und Staat: Eine Analyse und Interpretation seiner Theorie, ihrer Grundlagen und Probleme* (Göttingen: Vandenhoeck und Ruprecht, 1995), 183ff.

osition, necessity does not refer to the subject of the proposition as distinguished from the predicate, but to the necessary connection of subject and predicate that can be demonstrated by some undoubted axiom or principle. This interpretation of Aristotelian *Apodeixis* as a universally applicable method of demonstrating necessary relations in any given field of knowledge—in contrast to its traditional limitation to the theoretical disciplines of mathematics, physics, and metaphysics[2]—is taken over by Pufendorf from Weigel's *Analysis Aristotelica ex Euclide restituta* (*Aristotelian Analytics as Restored from Euclid*) of 1658.[3] According to Pufendorf, the method is applicable also to human actions, for though they depend upon the free will, they can be an object of demonstration as far as the "rectitude . . . in their order according to laws" is concerned.[4] Like the *Analysis Aristotelica,* the *Elements* is arranged as a system of definitions and (rational and experimental) principles, from which propositions about specific matters and their relations are derived by syllogism.[5] To make the text more readable, Pufendorf did not introduce the propositions following the principles, as the order of logical inference would demand, but added them to each definition or principle as a kind of scholion containing a detailed exposition of particular matters subsumed under the general title.[6] Here Pufendorf often draws on sources that are not explicitly cited (especially Roman, Hebrew, and canon law) but that are discussed in a critical manner despite the syllogistic structure.

The *definitions* contained in the first book of the *Elements* concern basic moral and legal concepts that constitute the doctrine of moral entities [*entia moralia*]. In contradistinction to physical entities, which are qualities and processes resulting from the inner principles of natural substances (and thus ultimately from divine creation), moral entities are instituted by reasonable creatures who impose some rule on their freedom of acting. The authorship of such rules is twofold: on the one hand God who does not want "that

---

2. Aristotle, *Metaphysics* VI.I (1026a18–19). See Aristotle, *The Metaphysics,* trans. Hugh Tredennick (Cambridge, Mass.: Harvard University Press, 1933; repr. 1980).

3. See the preface, note 4.

4. Ibid., note 5.

5. See ibid., note 7, for the structure of the *Analysis Aristotelica.*

6. Ibid., pp. 9–10.

men should spend their lives like beasts without civilization and moral law" and on the other hand man acting according to convenience and human requirements.[7] Starting with the definition of human action as voluntary behavior whose effects are imputed to the agent, Pufendorf divided such action according to its object, principles, affections, and effects and thus developed a view of the moral world as a hierarchically arranged tree of definitions that embrace the central legal concepts in an allegedly self-contained and complete system. The most important concepts are "state" [*status*], that is, a configuration of rights and duties that constitute a kind of moral space for persons and their actions;[8] and the "moral person" [*persona moralis*], that is, one or more human beings considered under whatever state they have in communal life.[9] Like all moral entities, moral persons do not subsist in themselves but are "modes" that arise from voluntary imposition and are to be distinguished from their natural bearers. A man will therefore bear several moral persons or roles in social life.[10] Nonetheless, moral persons (like moral actions and things) are considered like substances (within the sphere of moral entities), for they themselves also bear other moral entities considered as moral "affections" [*affectiones*] or qualities.[11] The most important of these are the operative moral qualities of "obligation," "right," and "authority," which are correlated among each other and are ultimately grounded in "law" conceived as a decree of a superior who has the authority to direct the actions of his subjects.[12] While "obligation" [*obligatio*] denotes "an operative moral quality by which some one is bound to furnish, allow, or endure something,"[13] the corresponding quality arising in the person to whom one is bound is named a "right" [*ius*], an "active moral power [*potentia*], belonging to a person, to receive something from

---

7. *De jure naturae et gentium libri octo,* translated by C. H. and W. A. Oldfather, Carnegie Institution Classics of International Law 17 (Oxford: Clarendon Press, 1934) hereafter *JNG;* 1, 1, §3.
8. Def. 3, §1.
9. Def. 4, §1.
10. *JNG,* 1, 1, §14.
11. Def. 1, §8; *JNG,* 1, 1, §6.
12. Def. 13; *JNG,* 1, 6, §4.
13. Def. 12.

another as a matter of necessity,"[14] or—with a stronger emphasis on the person's ability of performing—authority [*potestas*] as "an active moral power by which some person legitimately and with a moral effect is able to perform a voluntary action."[15] All moral entities are ultimately rooted in natural law conceived as a divine decree imposed in accordance with created human nature and immutable as long as human nature remains unchanged according to divine will.[16] Thus the contents of natural law must be learned through a consideration of human nature, its desires and conditions, while the obligatory force of the law is solely derived from the divine will.[17]

Among the *principles* of the natural law system only two are considered as *axioms*, whose "certainty and necessity, flows from reason itself, without the perception of particulars," namely, the axiom of imputability of voluntary actions "that may be directed according to a moral norm,"[18] and the axiom of the obligatory nature of norms in proportion to the authority of the person prescribing them.[19] While *imputability* and the *prescriptive* nature of norms express formal requirements of morality, the material content of natural law is exclusively grounded in the other kind of principles—the *Observations*—whose certainty "is perceived from the comparison and perception of particulars uniformly corresponding to one another."[20] They concern the human intellect and its faculty of (moral) judgment (Observ. 1), the liberty of the will (Observ. 2), the natural sociability of man (Observ. 3), the harmony of self-preservation and society (Observ. 4), and the necessity to establish human sovereignty in particular societies (Observ. 5). Here Pufendorf mainly draws on the natural law writings of Hugo Grotius

14. Def. 8.

15. Def. 7.

16. Def. 13, §14; *JNG,* 2, 3, §§5, 19.

17. *JNG,* 2, 3, §14; 19–20; *Eris Scandica und andere polemische Schriften über das Naturrecht,* ed. Fiammetta Palladini, in *Gesammelte Werke,* vol. 5, ed. Wilhelm Schmidt-Biggemann (Berlin: Akademie Verlag, 2002) (hereafter cited as *Eris*), "Specimen controversiarum . . . ," c. V, §30, p. 186.

18. Axiom 1: "Any action whatsoever that may be directed according to a moral norm, which is within a man's power to do or not to do, may be imputed to him," p. 283.

19. Axiom 2: "Any person whatsoever can effectively, or with the obligation to perform them, enjoin on someone subject to himself those things to which his authority over the other extends itself," p. 295.

20. Axiom 1, §1, p. 284.

and Thomas Hobbes, whom he mentions in his preface. The basic anthropology contained in the observations emerges mainly from a critical
discussion of their natural law doctrines, resulting in an effort to reconcile
Hobbes's egoism and concept of human society as an artifact with Grotius's
doctrine of social appetite conceived as the *telos* of a rational and social
nature.

As a universal science of "law and equity, . . . by virtue of which the
duties of all men whatsoever . . . are governed,"[21] the natural law system
of the *Elements* also embraces matters belonging to international law, re-
flecting its growing importance in the emerging system of sovereign national states. In line with the Hobbesian identification of natural and international law,[22] the *Elements* does not treat these matters as a separate
body of law but subsumes them under the general definitions of moral
entities comprising items of natural, civil, and international law. Thus the
scholion to Def. 5 of a moral thing (§§7–10) also discusses a subject most
pressing for Pufendorf's contemporaries, the freedom of the sea. As the
citations of the relevant parts of *De jure naturae et gentium* reveal, Pufendorf was well acquainted with the writings of Hugo Grotius, John Selden,
and Alberico Gentili in that field.[23] According to Pufendorf's natural law
theory, property originates in negative community, that is to say, the natural
world is equally open to everyone and it requires contractual consent for
anything to be appropriated; but he leaves the concrete manner of con-
senting to be determined by the people involved. On this basis Pufendorf
argues for the possibility of exclusive dominion of parts of the sea, especially in coastal areas and straits. He rejects the Grotian view that the "un-
bounded" nature of the ocean argues for the impossibility of its exclusive
dominion (*De jure belli ac pacis,* 2, 2, §3). This issue and that of the invi-
olability of legates (Def. 13, §26) are closely related to the actual circumstances under which the *Elements* was written. As a member of the Swedish
diplomatic mission in Copenhagen in 1657–58, Pufendorf was arrested by
the Danes when the Swedes suddenly reopened the war against Denmark

21. Preface, p. 7.
22. Thomas Hobbes, *De cive,* vol. 2 of *Opera philosophica quae Latine scripsit omnia,*
ed. William Molesworth (London, 1839; repr. Aalen: Scientia, 1961), chap. 14, §§4–5.
23. For the details, see the editorial annotations throughout.

that had been suspended by the peace of Roskilde in 1658, a war mainly fought for the control of the Sund, the strait between Sweden and Denmark.[24]

Apart from the Euclidean methodology shown in the arrangement of definitions, principles, and propositions, the "geometric" nature of the *Elements* also manifests itself in a model illustrating moral degrees by spatial magnitudes. The basic idea of the "moral sphere" introduced in the scholion to Def. 18 (*The quantity of moral actions is the estimative measure by which they are said to be of a certain degree*) is to illustrate "divergence from law" by an angle, the first side of which represents the thing commanded by law, the second side the (actual or intended) action, and the angular distance the degree of fault. The indefinite number of possible deviations from law according to intention or execution corresponds (in the geometric model) to the infinite number of lines (and of the angles formed by them) intersecting in any point. So the complete quantitative aspect of moral actions is best illustrated by a sphere whose center forms the point of intersection of the sides of all moral angles. God is "conceived of as seated at the centre of the moral sphere, . . . as though in our heart, from which proceeds . . . the radius of the law . . . , the finger, as it were, of God, pointing out precisely to us the polar region," while he leaves "behind Him, as though He had turned his face away from it, the antipolar district . . . , opposite to this."[25] Of the sphere's three cardinal circles, the horizon represents the radius of execution and the meridian the radius of intention, while the equator separates the polar hemisphere of enjoined actions from the antipolar hemisphere of forbidden actions. An appendix added to the

---

24. See Detlef Döring's introduction to his edition of the "Gundaeus baubator Danicus sive Examen nugarum atque calumniarum quas Senator Regni Daniae Gundaeus Rosenkrantz in discursu De detentione legati Suedici Hafniae impudentissimi spargit" (Amsterdam, 1659), an anti-Danish pamphlet of Pufendorf dealing with the juridical aspects of that incident and answering to the legal opinion of a Danish councillor. Samuel v. Pufendorf, *Kleine Vorträge und Schriften. Texte zu Geschichte, Pädagogik, Philosophie, Kirche und Völkerrecht,* ed. Detlef Döring (Frankfurt am Main: V. Klostermann, 1995), 88–124; Ditlev Tamm, "Pufendorf und Dänemark," in *Samuel v. Pufendorf 1632–1982,* ed. Kjell Å. Modéer, Ett rättshistoriskt symposion i Lund 15–16 januari 1982 (Stockholm: Nordiska Bokhandolen i Distributien, 1986), 81–90.

25. Def. 18, §2 (p. 249).

Jena edition of 1669 (and all subsequent editions) enlarges the moral sphere by further concentric orbs arranged like the orbits of the Copernican system and representing the objects of moral actions (and the respective commandments of the Decalogue). It seems strange that this addition was made in 1669, the year when Pufendorf finished *De jure naturae et gentium*,[26] in which he dropped that geometric illustration of moral quantity and denounced the moral sphere as a product of juvenile subtlety [*argutia*].[27] Already in Pufendorf's lifetime Erhard Weigel was suspected of being the real author of the appendix.[28]

In his main work, *De jure naturae et gentium*, Pufendorf not only dropped the moral sphere and its geometric illustration of moral quantity, but also the Euclidean arrangement according to definitions, principles, and propositions. Though still committed to the program of a demonstrative science of natural law as articulated in the chapter (I.2) on the certainty of the moral sciences, the idea remained programmatic and no longer determined the organization of the book. As the methodological discussions in the *Dissertatio de statu hominum naturali* (Dissertation on the Natural State of Men) of 1675 and the *Eris Scandica* (Nordic Strife) of 1686 reveal, the model of demonstration was no longer seen in Euclidean geometry but in contemporary natural science and its method of resolution and composition that combined empirical and deductive procedures.[29]

---

26. Although the first edition of *De jure naturae et gentium* was published in 1672 in London, its manuscript had already been finished in 1669. See Pufendorf's letter to Johann Scheffer of December 18, 1669, in Samuel Pufendorf, *Briefwechsel,* ed. Detlev Döring, in *Gesammelte Werke* (Berlin: Akademie Verlag, 1996), 1:60–61.

27. *JNG,* 1, 8, §1.

28. See Leibniz, *Nouveaux essais sur l'entendement humain,* ed. André Robinet and Heinrich Schepers, in *Sämtliche Schriften und Briefe,* 2nd ed. (Berlin: Akademie Verlag, 1990), series VI, vol. 6, bk. IV, chap. 3, §19. For a more detailed discussion of the appendix and its authorship, see Thomas Behme's introduction to Samuel Pufendorf, *Elementa jurisprudentiae universalis,* in *Gesammelte Werke* (Berlin: Akademie Verlag, 1999), 3:xviii–xix.

29. See Wolfgang Röd, *Geometrischer Geist und Naturrecht: Methodengeschichtliche Untersuchungen zur Staatsphilosophie im 17. und 18. Jahrhundert* (Munich: Bayerische Akademie der Wissenschaften, 1970), 10ff, 88–89; Gerhard Sprenger, "Der Einfluß der Naturwissenschaften auf das Denken Samuel Pufendorfs," in *Samuel Pufendorf und seine Wirkungen bis auf die heutige Zeit,* ed. Bodo Geyer and Helmut Goerlich (Baden-Baden:

Like Hobbes in the preface of *De cive,* Pufendorf demands in the *De statu* that the state be considered like a body and explained by a hypothetical reduction to "prime matter," i.e., the condition of man outside of any society and devoid of arts and institutions, so that the nature, necessity, and advantage of civil society might be understood in terms of this "matter."[30] Accordingly, the doctrine of the natural state that only played a marginal role in the *Elements* gained a prominent place in *De jure naturae et gentium.*[31] The resolutive-compositive method shows us the "state of single individuals left alone by themselves" [*status naturalis in se*] as a counterfactual supposition [*fictio contrarii*] that demonstrates the necessity of social life and introduces "sociality" [*socialitas*] as the *fundamentum* of natural law.[32] In contrast to the plurality of principles discussed in the second book of the *Elements,* sociality figures as the unique principle of natural law in *De jure naturae et gentium,* a principle that "is not only genuine and clear, but also . . . sufficient and adequate [so] that there is no precept of the natural law affecting other men, the basis of which is not ultimately to be sought therein."[33] Although based on experience, it has methodological status as "principle" [*principium*], for while it corresponds to the hypotheses that the natural sciences gain from experience, once established it serves as the deductive basis for scientific theorems.[34] Accordingly, experience that already played a major role in the *Elements'* observations as foundation for that work's anthropology now gained preeminent importance. This is

---

Nomos, 1996), 165ff, especially 185–86; Hans Welzel, *Naturrecht und materiale Gerechtigkeit* (Göttingen: Vandenhoeck und Ruprecht, 1980), 112–13.

30. *Samuel Pufendorf's "On the Natural State of Men,"* trans. Michael Seidler, Studies in the History of Philosophy 13 (Lewiston, N.Y.: Edwin Mellen, 1990) (hereafter cited as *Statu*), §1.

31. *JNG,* 2, 2.

32. On the "state of single individuals left alone by themselves," see *JNG,* 2, 2, §2; Samuel Pufendorf, *The Whole Duty of Man, According to the Law of Nature,* trans. Andrew Tooke, 1691, ed. Ian Hunter and David Saunders (Indianapolis: Liberty Fund, 2003) (hereafter cited as *Off.*), 2, 1, §4; *Statu,* §§4–5; on its function as a counterfactual supposition see *Eris,* "Commentatio super invenusto Pullo," 280–81.

33. *JNG,* 2, 3, §19. Nevertheless Axiom 1 and the doctrine of imputation discussed in the scholion to it have also been retained in *De jure naturae et gentium.* See 1, 5, especially §5.

34. *Eris,* 280–81.

shown in the vast number of citations from manifold sources (ancient and contemporary philosophy, historiography and literature, legal texts, contemporary books of travel) that supplement the systematic approach to natural law by giving examples of concrete moral, legal, and social relations from different times and cultures.

In spite of the different methodological approach, the *De jure naturae et gentium* retains the essential features of the natural law theory already present in the *Elements:* the program of a *scientific* approach to natural law, a theory of the moral world grounded in a voluntarist concept of law, a concept of sociality as a basic obligation of natural law imposed by God and suited to human nature in all its rational and sensory aspects, natural equality as a basic feature of sociality leading to a contractual foundation of human society and the state,[35] and a contract-based and secular concept of sovereignty as a guarantor of order in a diffracted and confessionalized society.[36] Because the *Elements* lacks the copious citations of the mature work but treats matters in more detail than the textbook, the *De officio,* it offers a compact and readable introduction to Pufendorf's legal and political thought.

35. On Pufendorf's contractualism see the details in Behme, *Samuel von Pufendorf,* parts VIII and IX.

36. On the desacralization of political authority and the definition of a distinctive sphere of politics as a main aspect of Pufendorf's doctrine of sovereignty, see in particular Leonard Krieger, *The Politics of Discretion: Pufendorf and the Acceptance of Natural Law* (Chicago: University of Chicago Press, 1965), 104, 117; Ian Hunter, *Rival Enlightenments: Civil and Metaphysical Philosophy in Early Modern Germany* (Cambridge: Cambridge University Press, 2001), 148ff.

A NOTE ON THE TEXT

During Pufendorf's lifetime seven editions of the Latin text appeared: The Hague 1660, Jena 1660, Zwickau 1668, Jena 1669, Cambridge 1672, Frankfurt and Jena 1680, and Frankfurt 1694. The only modern translation is the English by William Abbott Oldfather based on the text of the Cambridge 1672 edition. Supplied with scanty philological notes and a photographic reprint of the Latin text, it was published in 1931 in the Classics of International Law Series by the Carnegie Endowment for International Peace (vol. 15). Parts of the *Elements* were also translated in a selection of texts edited by Craig L. Carr and translated by Michael Seidler.[1] I was responsible for a definitive Latin edition published as volume 3 of Samuel Pufendorf, *Gesammelte Werke* (general editor Wilhelm Schmidt-Biggemann). It is based on the Latin text of the first edition (1660) and supplemented by the appendix on the moral sphere that was added to editions since 1669. Like all of the *Gesammelte Werke,* this is a critical variorum edition that is primarily directed to a scholarly audience well acquainted with the Latin language.

The present edition is a revision of Oldfather's translation from 1931, which has been checked for mistranslations of the Latin text of 1672.[2] A great part of my revisions concern inconsistencies in the translation of technical terms, which I have standardized to their proper English equivalents. Where a term requires deviation from the standard translation, the Latin original is added in square brackets. Thus Oldfather translates *potestas,* an active moral power to perform a voluntary action legitimately,[3] as "au-

---

1. Samuel Pufendorf, *The Political Writings of Samuel Pufendorf,* ed. Craig L. Carr and trans. Michael Seidler (New York: Oxford University Press, 1994).

2. I am grateful to Prof. Michael Seidler, who has checked my revisions of the English translation.

3. See p. xii.

thority" in most instances but sometimes switches to "power," even in contexts where *potestas* has clearly been used in the normative sense. Here the translation has been standardized to "authority," while *potentia,* a (natural) power or potency, is translated throughout as "power." In those few instances where *potestas* has been used in the sense of a natural power, it will be rendered as "power [*potestas*]." In the instances where the Latin *auctoritas* (or *autoritas*) had also been translated as *authority,* I have added the Latin in brackets. In the case of *imperium,* which denotes an "authority over the persons of others,"[4] Oldfather's translation switches between "command," "authority," and "sovereignty," according to the different contexts. Since Pufendorf primarily uses *imperium* as a technical term for the highest authority in the state, the translation has been standardized to "sovereignty" in most instances. In those few cases where *imperium* denotes the authority of commanding in a more general sense or a subordinate authority (for example, of a commanding officer), "command [*imperium*]" is used.

Oldfather's annotations, which predominantly deal with misprints in the Latin text, have for the most part been dropped in favor of new annotations by the present editor. Readers interested in philological aspects of the Latin text are referred to the philological annotations to my critical Latin edition. Those Oldfather notes that have been retained are preceded by an asterisk and have "Tr." (translator) at the end of the note. The new annotations give short explanations on background and on items dealt with in the text that might be strange to modern readers. In particular, they identify allusions and references not made explicit by Pufendorf in the *Elements.* Sometimes this identification requires a consideration of sources cited in *JNG* that might also be seen as probable sources of the *Elements* insofar as their publication dates preceded that of the *Elements.* When the annotation refers to sources cited in *JNG,* their citation follows the English Oldfather edition of *JNG.* For the reader's convenience modern editions of these sources are given in the bibliography.

Page breaks in the 1931 edition are indicated in the present edition by the use of angle brackets. For example, page 112 begins after <112>.

Thomas Behme

4. Def. 7, §3.

ABBREVIATIONS

WORKS OF SAMUEL PUFENDORF

Eris   *Eris Scandica und andere polemische Schriften über das Naturrecht.* Edited by Fiammetta Palladini. Vol. 5 of *Gesammelte Werke,* edited by Wilhelm Schmidt-Biggemann. Berlin: Akademie Verlag, 2002.

JNG   *De jure naturae et gentium libri octo.* Translated by C. H. and W. A. Oldfather. Carnegie Institution Classics of International Law, edited by James Brown Scott, 17. Oxford: Clarendon Press; London: Humphrey Milford, 1934.

Off.   *The Whole Duty of Man, According to the Law of Nature* (*De officio hominis et civis*). Translated by Andrew Tooke, 1691. Edited by Ian Hunter and David Saunders. Indianapolis: Liberty Fund, 2003.

Statu   *Samuel Pufendorf's "On the Natural State of Men."* The 1678 Latin edition and English translation. Translated, annotated, and introduced by Michael Seidler. Studies in the History of Philosophy 13. Lewiston, N.Y.: Edwin Mellen, 1990.

OTHER WORKS

Dig.   Justinian. *Digests.* Vols. 2–11 of *The Civil Law, Including the Twelve Tables, the Institutes of Gaius, the Rules of Ulpian, the Opinions of Paulus, the Enactments of Justinian, and the Constitutions of Leo.* Translated by Samuel Parsons Scott. Cincinnati and New York: Central Trust Company, 1932.

Inst.   Justinian, *Institutes.* Vol. 2 of *The Civil Law, Including the Twelve Tables, the Institutes of Gaius, the Rules of Ulpian, the Opinions of Paulus, the Enactments of Justinian, and the Constitutions of Leo.* Translated by Samuel Parsons Scott. Cincinnati: Central Trust Company, 1932.

JBP   Hugo Grotius. *De jure belli ac pacis libri tres.* Translated by Francis W. Kelsey. Edited by James Brown Scott. 2 vols. Carnegie Institution Classics of International Law 3. Oxford: Clarendon Press, 1925.

W.A.   Martin Luther. *Werke.* Weimarer Ausgabe. Weimar: Böhlau, 1883–2005.

THE PRESENT WORK

Def.   Definition

Observ. Observation

THE TWO BOOKS

OF

THE ELEMENTS OF

UNIVERSAL JURISPRUDENCE

BY

SAMUEL PUFENDORF

Together with
an Appendix on the Moral Sphere
and Indexes

Latest and most accurate edition

CAMBRIDGE
FROM THE HOUSE OF JOHN HAYES
Printer to the most Celebrated University
1672

At the Charges of John Creed, Bookseller, Cambridge

TO THE MOST SERENE PRINCE AND LORD, THE LORD
KARL LUDWIG, COUNT OF THE RHENISH PALATINATE,
LORD HIGH TREASURER AND PRINCE ELECTOR OF
THE HOLY ROMAN EMPIRE, DUKE OF BAVARIA, ETC., MY
MOST CLEMENT LORD.

Most Serene Prince Elector, Most Clement Lord, Bold indeed is the undertaking of this book, which, without any confidence in its own merit, ventures to approach so great a Prince, and is not ashamed to draw upon itself by its own act those eyes before whose radiance they who appraise themselves according to the consciousness of their own insignificance cannot but blush. And to some it might have seemed more modest to inscribe a less august name at the forefront of so slight a work, were it not a well established fact that those lofty minds beam more blandly upon many men, the more unaffected they perceive to be the estimate which the same have made of their humanity. Your far-famed benevolence towards letters and those that cultivate them, MOST SERENE PRINCE, makes us believe that to have made what is no more even than an effort in letters has the value of a commendation in Your eyes; and, although we cherish Your greatness with a religious veneration, we have no fear that the same will suffer any diminution in accepting these meagre offerings. Indeed, You increase the glory of Your eminence rather than diminish it, in that from time to time You condescend to such interests of ordinary men, just as the sun, which does not disdain to pour forth his light even for the low-lying lands of earth to use, retains his glory none the less undimmed on that account.

The kind of portrait of a great Prince which others industriously limn,[1] this we may behold at close range most felicitously expressed in You. The

---

1. Pufendorf refers to the traditional ethics of the "mirror for princes," which develops an ideal of the ruler and outlines the virtues and duties required of him. It aims at the ruler's self-perfection as the basis of good government.

blood descended through so many heroes and the dignity but one removed
from supreme, together with all the other characteristics which have been
set forth as the sole ground for laudations in the case of those whom blind
fates, as it were, seem to have thrust forward to such position, we may regard
as residing properly and preeminently in You, abounding as You do in Your
own resources. You can of Yourself bestow something upon Your ancestors,
because through You they have been the glory not of their own ages only;
and so easy is it for You to clear Your name of indebtedness to fortune, that
fortune herself would be in debt to You, if, indeed, it might please her to
bestow her blessings in proportion to each individual's deserts. Your glory
springs up for You out of Your very self. A mind sublime, elevated, of which
fortune herself should stand in fear, penetrating <xxvii> moreover, pro-
foundly versed in law human and divine, and one which, if any can, in
itself meets the measure required of a Prince. This mind of Yours it is which
the age admires in You beyond all else, and proudly displays among its
ornaments. And yet that same mind, when it has fulfilled the duty of a
Prince, turns aside also to the pleasures of study, and applies with the utmost felicity that well-known vigour to every kind of Wisdom. You could
not fill the intervals in Your occupation with a more holy pleasure, nor
ought the leisure moments of a mind so noble to be otherwise employed.
Here You discover with what sincere veneration the memory of men like
Yourself is cherished by those who have no further profit from flattery; and
while You hear and see those silent ones, You cease to have need of the ears
and eyes of others through which full often facts are presented to Princes
in a distorted manner. Nay more, by Your patronage no less than by Your
example You cause these studies to flourish among Your friends. The shattered shrines of Wisdom You restore with a most liberal hand,[2] and, that
nothing be lacking to their splendour, You do not regard it as beneath Your

2. Pufendorf alludes to the reconstruction of Heidelberg's university after the Thirty
Years' War, one of the most successful aspects of Karl Ludwig's consolidation policy in
the Palatinate. A liberal policy in appointments and the statute reform of September 1,
1672, led to a quick revival of academic life and a growing attraction of Heidelberg for
students and scholars. See Ludwig Häusser, *Geschichte der rheinischen Pfalz* (1845; repr.
Heidelberg: Winter, 1924), vol. 2, pp. 599ff; Meinrad Schaab, *Geschichte der Kurpfalz*
(Stuttgart: Kohlhammer, 1992), vol. II, pp. 139ff.

high estate to grant them also the favour of Your presence. By such an honour You give courage to the timid Muses,* nor can their own fortune fail longer to satisfy them after the favour of so great a Patron dispenses itself upon such terms of intimacy.

I too have been persuaded by that humanity of Yours, although I have never yet experienced it, to feel that I should be doing no wrong against Your dignity, if I should venture to offer you this little book with all seemly veneration. While according to the scanty measure of my ability I have striven to set forth in this the principles of universal justice, I foresee for it an approach to Your presence, which, by virtue of the very subject-matter, is the more easy, the more confident Themis† is in claiming by her own right admission to the inmost audience of Princes.

Your Serenity's
most devoted
SAMUEL PUFENDORF. <xxviii>

LEYDEN, *September 1, 1660.*

---

* The word is here used in the rarer sense of men of letters themselves. Cf. Milton, *Lycidas:*

> So may some gentle Muse
> With lucky words favour my destined urn;
> And as he passes, turn
> And bid fair peace be to my sable shroud.— *Tr.*

† As the personification of Law and Justice.— *Tr.*

PREFACE

The science of law and equity, which is not comprehended in the laws of any single state, but by virtue of which the duties of all men whatsoever toward one another are governed, has hitherto not been cultivated, to the extent that its necessity and dignity demanded, by those who have extolled the study of universal knowledge under that designation. Among the chief reasons for this state of affairs the following also seems to belong, namely: A common conviction has prevailed down to the present among the learned that in matters of morality, by their very nature, there is no firm and infallible certainty, and that all knowledge of such matters rests upon probable opinion only. Hence it came about that they gave as it were but a light touch to what in their opinion rested upon so slippery a foundation; and herein the negligent found the plausible excuse, that such matters were not embodied in sure demonstrations, but could be treated only in a crude sort of way. The common run, indeed, felt the less shame in offering this excuse, because Aristotle himself, who, by some almost fatal partiality, has hitherto appeared to the majority of mankind to surpass the summit of human genius, prefixed it to the frontispiece of his work on ethics,[3] as though it

---

3. Aristotle, *Nicomachean Ethics,* ed. William D. Ross, 2nd ed. (Oxford: Clarendon Press, 1931), I, 1094b11–14: "Our discussion will be adequate if it has as much clearness as the subject-matter admits of. . . . Now fine and just actions, which political science investigates, admit of much variety and fluctuation of opinion, so that they may be thought to exist only by convention, and not by nature. . . . We must be content, then, in speaking of such subjects and with such premises to indicate the truth roughly and in outline, . . . for it is the mark of an educated man to look for precision in each class of things just so far as the nature of the subject admits; it is evidently equally foolish to accept probable reasoning from a mathematician and to demand from a rhetorician scientific proofs." Pufendorf epitomizes and translates that passage in *JNG,* 1, 2, §1. According to Aristotle, science in the strict sense (*epistéme*) deals with the necessary and

were some proud ornament. Now, of a truth, aside from the fact that it
appears utterly absurd for men to be denied sure knowledge of those things
which they were enjoined by the authority [*autoritatem*] of their Creator
to put into action, while at the same time one may have definite and clear
knowledge of things which can be safely ignored, this whole error has hitherto been so persistently nourished by the false interpretation of no more
than three or four words in Aristotle. When you restore them to their proper
sense, even by the decrees of the Stagirite, Law will be allowed to claim its
place among the sciences which are called demonstrative. For what he had
said about demonstration from which comes true and certain knowledge,
has been explained in this fashion, namely, that it was denied a place among
questions of morals because these latter were contingent entities produced
by free causes. But, as a matter of fact, in that passage he observes that the
subject of the demonstration [*subjectum demonstrationis*] is a declaration or
proposition (by no means, however, the subject in a demonstrative proposition, as distinguished from the predicate), which must be demonstrated,
that is, one in which a necessary connexion of the predicate with the subject
must be shown by virtue of some *principle* or very general declaration,
which contains the reason for that connexion.[4] Whence it follows that it is
sufficient for a demonstration, if some thing or action have an attribute
<xxix> whose necessary connexion with the subject one can directly or in-
directly demonstrate by some undoubted axiom, whether the action or
thing itself does or does not depend upon necessary causes. And thus, just

---

universal (*Posterior Analytics* I.2 in Aristotle, *Analytica priora et posteriora,* ed. W. D. Ross
(Oxford: Clarendon Press, 1964). Human actions dealing with variable particulars are
not the object of science but of prudence that takes into account individual circumstances (*Nicomachean Ethics* VI, 1140a1, a24–b30).

4. Pufendorf refers to Aristotle's *Posterior Analytics* and its doctrine of demonstration
as the basis of exact science. His interpretation of Aristotle's *subject of demonstration* as
the necessary relation expressed in a demonstrative proposition (and not as the single
subject in a demonstrative proposition) follows Erhard Weigel's *Analysis Aristotelica ex
Euclide restituta* (Jena, 1658; modern edition by Thomas Behme, 2008). See in particular
sect. I, chap. ii "De natura subjecti formaliter spectati" (On the nature of the subject
formally considered). Oldfather's translation is misleading here because he translates *effatum* as *declaration or proposition.* But *effatum*—a technical term in Weigel's *Analysis
Aristotelica*—means a complex entity or necessary relation founded in the nature of
things and existing independently of the speech expressing it (see *Analysis Aristotelica,*
sect. I, chap. ii, §14).

as it would be ridiculous if one should wish to demonstrate in some body of doctrine that, for example, "Seius is here and now committing theft, Titius is committing highway robbery," so no prudent man would dare deny that, when we assert "Seius is committing theft, Titius is committing highway robbery," a demonstration can be given that these same persons are sinning against the Law of Nature;[5] at all events, that one would be any less certain about this point than about that which is inculcated *ad nauseam* in the bodies of doctrine which by universal consent rejoice in the certainty of sciences, to wit, that "man is risible, because he is rational," and that "a sparrow is one, true, and good, because it is an entity."

All this was set forth not long since in a special treatise[6] in the most clear and reliable manner by that illustrious man, Herr Erhard Weigel, Professor of Mathematics in the University of Jena, a respected friend of mine. He it was who first exhorted me to attempt something in this field, and his genius has supplied me with a most helpful torch in matters not a few. This task, furthermore, I have undertaken with the greater zeal, because also by a special inclination I felt disposed to studies of that kind, and because it seemed to be worth making the effort to prove that what is handed down on this matter does by no means all rest upon vacillating opinions, but flows clearly enough from fixed and first principles.

And now, as to the method of this book, reason herself, indeed, makes it sufficiently clear that a man who is about to set forth some discipline must at the outset explain precisely what is meant by the subject-matter which he is about to treat; then he must seek for fixed principles from which

5. According to Pufendorf, this distinction of (demonstrable) knowledge of relations and (nondemonstrable) knowledge of facts makes it possible to treat natural law as an Aristotelian *epistéme,* notwithstanding the freedom of the will and contingency of human actions. While particular human actions (as matters of fact) are nondemonstrable, their moral qualities may be demonstrated from their agreement or disagreement with the (demonstrable) principles of natural law. This constitutes a distinction between two fields of moral philosophy: "one of them concerns the rectitude of human actions in their order according to laws, the other concerns the successful management of one's own actions and those of others, with an eye to the security and welfare primarily to the public" (*JNG,* 1, 2, §4). That distinction has also been taken from Erhard Weigel. See *Analysis Aristotelica,* sect. III, membrum II, chap. vii, §10.

6. The already mentioned *Analysis Aristotelica.*

necessarily true declarations concerning these matters may be deduced. Hence, any doctrine ought to be complete in three parts, the first of which comprehends the Definitions, the second, the Principles, and the third, the Propositions or Conclusions derived from the principles; to these, if it appear necessary, a fourth is to be added, into which may be gathered those topics in which certainty does not clearly appear.[7] For all that is commonly said about the difference between the synthetic and the analytic method is nonsense.[8] However, it has seemed best to us not to assign a special book to the Propositions, but to subjoin each proposition forthwith to the definitions or the principles on which it primarily depended; for there is a certain aridity which seems to deform the body of doctrine in question if it be set forth divided up into minute parts in the fashion of the mathematical sciences.

One other thing should be noted here. We have drawn much <xxx> from that marvellous work, *De jure belli ac pacis,* by the incomparable Hugo Grotius. Although appearing to treat merely a part of universal jurisprudence, he has, nevertheless, touched upon most of its parts in such wise that scarcely anything can be written in this field without his name appearing either as authority or as witness.[9] No small debt likewise do we owe

7. This method of science agrees with Erhard Weigel's reformed Aristotelian methodology based on Aristotle's *Posterior Analytics* and Euclid's *Elements.* Following the *Posterior Analytics* (I.2), the *Analysis Aristotelica* makes a threefold distinction between (1) *suppositive principles,* that is, the definitions of the subject (of the proposition) and its properties, plus the hypothesis of the subject's existence (hypothesis demonstrativa); (2) *perfective principles,* that is, the axioms, to which Weigel adds observations (experimental principles) and Euclidean postulates; and (3) the *practice of demonstration or method* (*Analysis Aristotelica,* sect. II, chap. i, §§5–6; sect. III, membrum II, chap. xiii, §§1–2). From those *essential parts of a discipline of study* Weigel distinguishes a fourth part of still unproved propositions which are based on probable principles, thus referring to Aristotle's *Topics* (*Analysis Aristotelica,* sect. III, membrum II, chap. xiii, §37).

8. The statement reflects Weigel's identification of Aristotelian analytics and Euclidean (synthetic) method. See ibid., §§31–32.

9. According to its title, Grotius's work aims only at an exposition of international law. That, however, requires an exposition of all possible legal controversies in order to show the possible reasons of war; consequently it amounts to a doctrine of universal natural law. See *De jure belli ac pacis libri tres,* trans. Francis W. Kelsey and ed. James Brown Scott, Classics of International Law 3 (Oxford: Clarendon Press, 1925) (hereafter cited as *JBP*), I.i.1–2: "War, however, is undertaken in order to secure peace, and there

to Thomas Hobbes, whose basic assumption in his book, *De cive,* although it savours somewhat of the profane, is nevertheless for the most part extremely acute and sound.[10] These two authors we have preferred to cite here once for all, as it were, and have refrained from mentioning them in the body of our work whenever their opinion is followed, because, aside from the tedium of frequent citation, we have followed rather their arguments than their authority [*autoritatem*]. For whenever the zeal for truth has compelled us to disagree with them and others, we have withheld their names, so that we should not appear to be eager to win a petty glory for ourselves by plucking at the blemishes of great men. And we have always regarded it as foolish, when you know yourself to be a man by no means free from errors, to incite others by harshness of criticism to subject you to the same treatment. We feel the greater confidence that this modesty on our part will meet with favour among the prudent, seeing that it has too frequently happened among those who have professed the study of the humanities, that they have inhumanely attacked others not without words of contumely. <xxxi>

---

is no controversy which may not give rise to war. In undertaking to treat the law of war, therefore, it will be in order to treat such controversies, of any and every kind, as are likely to arise. War will finally conduct us to peace as its ultimate goal" (I.i.2). "As we set out to treat the law of war, then, we ought to see what is war, which we are treating, and what is the law which forms the subject of our investigation."

10. The basic assumption in question is Hobbes's fundamental hypothesis of the natural state of man as *bellum omnium contra omnes.* See *De cive,* preface to the reader: "in the first place I set down for a principle, by experience known to all men and denied by none, to wit, that the dispositions of men are naturally such, that except they be restrained through fear of some coercive power, every man will distrust and dread each other, and as by naturall right he may, so by necessity he will be forced to make use of the strength he hath, toward the preservation of himself." Notwithstanding the substantial differences concerning the principle and content of natural law (see bk. II, Observ. 3 and 4), Pufendorf appreciated Hobbes's methodological contribution to the natural law discussion. See in particular *Eris,* "Specimen controversiarum . . . ," chap. i "De origine et progressu disciplinae juris naturalis," §6, pp. 126–27.

INDEX OF DEFINITIONS, AXIOMS, AND OBSERVATIONS[1]

1. The page numbers given here are those from the present Liberty Fund edition.

Book II

THE ELEMENTS OF
UNIVERSAL JURISPRUDENCE

BY

SAMUEL PUFENDORF

BOOK I

✠ DEFINITION I ✠

By human actions are meant the voluntary actions of a man in communal life regarded under the imputation of their effects.

1. Of a voluntary action which is also moral.
2. The material element.
3. The fundamental element.
4. The formal element.

5. That which is a positive entity.
6. The division of actions.
7. The natural action.
8. Plan of the first book.

1. We call voluntary actions those actions placed within the power of man, which depend upon the will, as upon a free cause, in such wise that, without its decision setting forth from the same man's actions as elicited by previous cognition of the intellect, they would not come to pass; and, indeed, according as they are regarded not in their natural condition, but in so far as they come to pass from a decision of the will. Now a voluntary action involves two things: One is, as it were, the material element, which is the exercise regarded in itself; the other is, as it were, the formal element, which is the dependence of the exercise upon the decision of the will, and the reason, operating with a kind of freedom of choice, by which the action as decided by the will is conceived.[1] The exercise itself, considered apart

---

1. Pufendorf considers the moral action (just as the moral person and the moral thing) like a substance (within the sphere of moral entities), which is understood as a whole of matter and form in accordance with the Aristotelian tradition (see Aristotle, *Metaphysics* VII.3). "Although moral entities do not exist of themselves, and consequently should in general not be classified as substances, but rather as modes, we nevertheless find many of them considered like substances, because other moral things appear to be directly founded in them, in the same way that quantity and qualities inhere in physical sub-

and in itself for the sake of distinction, is better called an act of the will, or one coming from the will, than voluntary. Now, in truth, an action of the will is further regarded either in itself and absolutely, according as it is a certain physical movement undertaken by a previous decision of the will; or reflexively, in so far as its effect is imputed to a man. Voluntary actions which include this reflexive aspect are, by a special use of the term, designated *human.* And since imputation regards first and foremost the inclinations of the mind and the habits of life, which are listed properly under the designation *morals,* it comes about that human actions themselves, by the figure of synecdoche, are called *moral.*

2. The essence, therefore, of a human or moral action consists in these three elements, one of which is, as it were, material, the second, fundamental, and the third formal.[2] The material element is a certain physical motion of physical force, for example locomotor force, that of the sensitive appetite, of exterior and interior senses, and of the intellect as far as the exercise of apprehension (for judgement so necessarily depends upon the quality of the object that concerning it there is no room for the direction of the will),[3] nay even of an act of the will itself, when the act is considered in its natural being, that is, according as <4> it is regarded absolutely as a certain effect produced by a force as such imparted by nature. Also the deprivation of a certain physical motion which a man was able to produce

---

stances" (*JNG,* 1, 1, §6). The "formal element . . . from which, as from a root, spring those affections, properties and consequences" is the imputativity of the action, presupposing "reason acting with freedom of choice" as its (natural) foundation (see §§4–5, p. 22).

2. Instead of this threefold distinction, the major work *JNG* makes only a twofold distinction of the material element and the formal element of the action (1, 5, §2), while "reason acting with freedom of choice" is attributed to its material, psychic element. See *Eris,* "Specimen controversiarum . . . ," chap. v "De origine moralitatis et indifferentia motus physici in actione humana," §2, p. 165; Hans Welzel, *Die Naturrechtslehre Samuel Pufendorfs: Ein Beitrag zur Ideengeschichte des 17. und 18. Jahrhunderts* (Berlin: De Gruyter, 1958), 22.

3. The parallel section in *JNG* (1, 5, §2) adds: "although in forming that judgement there are some opportunities for our own choice and activity." Pufendorf's anthropology makes a distinction between a natural and a free side of each of the central human faculties *understanding* and *will.* While the representative faculty of the understanding by no means is subject to man's free choice, the faculty of judgment depends to some extent on the will (see bk. II, Observ. I, §§1 and 3, and *JNG,* 1, 3).

either in itself or in its cause may be regarded as the material element; likewise the inclinations of natural powers toward definite objects, produced by preceding voluntary actions; as also a man's acts or habitual performances consisting in certain usages introduced by the human will, by which, due to the mere opinion of men, a certain moral effect is indicated. Not only can actions of my own which are of such a kind be the material element of my moral actions, but also actions of this sort on the part of other men, and instances of depriving them of actions, when these can be directed by my will; nay even the actions of brutes, of plants, and of inanimate objects, which are capable of a direction that proceeds from my will. So, in the divine law itself, injury done by a goring ox is imputed to the master, if he knows the ox to be of that kind.[4] So the vinedresser is himself held responsible, when, as a result of his neglect, the vine pours forth all its fecundity into its branches. He also who set the fire pays for its voracity.[5] Although about all these matters, in order that the actions of others can be reckoned as our own, there must have been some neglect on our part of an action due, or else an action must have intervened on our part, without which the other could not have taken place. Indeed, the material element of moral actions may even be instances of the admission or reception of another's actions, which, to be sure, considered in their natural being, are passive states, and yet, when one adds the element of imputation, which arises from the fact that they might have been prohibited or warded off, they are reckoned as actions.

3. The fundamental element of a moral action is reason acting with freedom of choice, by which reason the physical motion just described is perceived as produced by a decision of the will. Now this reason, acting with freedom of choice, presupposes or includes that faculty of man in which is placed the capacity to produce or to omit those motions.

4. The formal element of a moral action consists in the imputation, or rather in the imputativity, by which the effect of a voluntary action can be imputed to the agent, whether the agent himself has produced the effect in a physical way, or has had it produced by the instrumentality of others.

---

4. Exodus 21:29ff.
5. Ibid. 22:5.

Now it is from the formal aspect of an action that the agent himself, indeed, shares in the designation of morality and is called the *moral cause*. From this it is readily understood that, speaking properly and strictly, the formal reason of the moral cause consists in the imputation, but this terminally considered, and that this formal reason is nothing else than the voluntary agent to whom the effect is, or ought to be, imputed, because either in <5> whole or in part he has produced (expressed more effectively in German by *verursachet*) the effect, and turned out to be its author. And, therefore, if any good comes it must be entered to his credit, if any evil, it must be charged against him; so the very agent himself is bound, as it were, to stand in the place of the effect and to answer for it.

5. As for the rest, the formal element of a human action, that is, the imputativity, has the nature of a positive form, from which, as from a root, spring those affections, properties, and consequences of which we must treat here. Hence a moral action can be called a positive entity (in the class of things moral, not of things in nature), whether the material element be a physical motion or the deprivation of such a motion. For to the essence of such positive entities in the class of things moral it is sufficient if they establish something from which true affections in the same class result, since just as there are no affections of a non-entity, so that which has definite and positive affections can by no means be called a non-entity absolutely speaking.[6] What these affections are will be shown below.

6. Now moral actions are here distinguished primarily as follows: (1) By reason of the cause, into *immediate* actions, namely, those which some one has personally produced of himself, and *mediate* actions, those which he has caused to be produced by another. (2) By reason of the act itself, they are divided into *pure* actions and *mixed* actions.[7] Pure actions are those which are completed by a certain movement of some force directed to an object with a definite purpose. Such are the recognition of God and worship of Him, the exhibition of honour and of veneration, reverence, af-

---

6. See bk. I, Def. 1, note 1.

7. According to Aristotle (*Nicomachean Ethics,* II, 1105a32ff), the virtuous action takes place for its own sake (for an immanent end obtained by the action itself), while the mixed action takes place for an end different from itself (for example, fear of a greater evil).

fection, aversion, consolation, praise, vituperation, &c., whose effect consists in this, that the object is affected from the action in a certain fashion, or is felt to have been affected in the direction of being favourably or unfavourably disposed to one. Other actions, however, are, as it were, mixed, for they bring a certain real advantage or disadvantage to some one's person or property. Instances of these mixed actions are a gift, a loan, a theft, murder, &c., whose effect consists primarily in a certain deed that in a real way either helps or injures another's person or property. (3) By reason of the object, moral actions are divided variously, on which see below.

7. In contradistinction from moral actions are *natural actions,* or actions of any forces whatsoever, in so far as they are considered in their natural being, as movements produced by powers which are in one by nature, but without respect to the decision of the will and to imputativity, and therefore are deprived of the foundation as well as of the formal element of morality. And such are the actions not merely of the necessary powers which, granted all things requisite for action, cannot help but act, but also those of the free powers which, granted all things requisite for action, can act or not, if, indeed, they be <6> considered in the manner just mentioned. Among these, nevertheless, there is this difference, namely, that the former in themselves and directly are not capable of the foundation of morality, but the latter are.

8. Moral actions, moreover, can be considered either in genus or in species. In genus according to (1) the *object,* (2) the *principles,* (3) the *affections,* (4) the *effects.* <7>

⚘ DEFINITION II ⚘

By the object of moral actions is meant all that
with which they deal.

1. The morality of the object from imposition.
2. Division of the object.

1. In the next place, this object itself partakes of the designation of morality, and, considered in this respect, is itself also called moral. Concerning this in general it must be noted that its morality depends on *imposition,* that is, on the decision of free agents as such, and these free agents either of their own free will, or from some congruence of the nature of a thing with imposed morality, together with a tacit or expressed mutual agreement which has been entered into, have imposed morality upon things and persons, and have determined that definite effects should follow it.[1] And this is a consideration which can be applied even to the morality of the actions themselves. But there due note must be made of the fact that, when morality is said naturally to inhere in a certain action, this is not to be understood as though it meant that the morality results from the physical principles of the thing or from the very nature of the action in itself; but that it does not derive its origin from the arbitrary imposition of men, but only from the disposition of God himself, who has so formed the nature of man that particular actions of necessity are or are not congruent with this na-

---

1. Pufendorf's distinction of natural and moral entities and his doctrine of the latter's production by imposition goes back to Erhard Weigel. See *Analysis Aristotelica,* sect. I, chap. iii, §2.

ture.[2] And, of a truth, that He made man in this fashion and not in another depended entirely upon His own will. But if the morality of actions which are called naturally honourable or base were to derive their origin from the nature of these acts in themselves, and not from the will of the Creator, to which, nevertheless, the nature of the rational creature has been attuned, no reason could be given why particular acts may be moral for men, although they are not moral for brutes. So, moreover, that state of man which is called a state of nature is in fact so from imposition, yet not the arbitrary imposition of men, but that of the Creator himself, who destined men thereto at their very creation.

2. Now one object of moral actions is *suppositive,* the other *positive,* at least in a moral sense. The former is called *status;* the latter is divided commonly into *persons* and *things.*[3] <8>

2. Pufendorf here turns against the doctrine of *perseitas,* that certain actions are noble or base in themselves without any antecedent imposition, a point advocated by Hugo Grotius in *JBP,* I.i.10. That subject also plays a major role in Pufendorf's struggle with Protestant orthodoxy. See his criticism of Valentin Veltheim in *Eris,* "Specimen controversiarum . . . ," chap. v.

3. This threefold division originates in Roman law. See Justinian, *Digests,* vols. 2–11 of *The Civil Law,* trans. Samuel Parsons Scott (Cincinnati: Central Trust Company, 1932), I.v.1 (hereafter known as *Dig.*): *"Gaius, Institutes, Book I.* All the law that we make use of relates either to persons, things, or actions."

ᖭᖬ DEFINITION III ᖭᖬ

*Status is a suppositive moral entity in which positive
moral objects, and, above all, persons, are said to be.*

1. Analogy of status with space.
2. Natural status of place.
3. When it begins.
4. Can an irrevocable right be sought for him who does not yet exist in nature?
5. Peace.
6. War.
7. Liberty, Servitude.
8. Adventitious particular statuses.
9. Status from location.
10. Admonition concerning expressions for statuses.
11. Obligations accompanying a definite kind of status can be derived from different principles.
12. Status of time.

1. STATUS is called a suppositive entity because it is made the basis, as it were, of positive moral affairs, so that on it they rest such moral existence as they have, and erect their actions and their effects. And thus it has a certain analogy with space, because space is likewise made the basis, as it were, of things natural, so that in it they rest such natural existence as they have and exercise their own physical motions.[1] And yet it differs from space

---

1. Pufendorf's analogy of *status* with space resulted from his division of moral entities according to the classification of physical entities that originated with Erhard Weigel. Weigel conceived the *moral world* in analogy with the natural world as a *second creation* but constituted by the will. It consists of persons and things understood as moral substances to which other moral entities pertain as modes and accidents. Their abstract relations form a moral space in which persons and things are understood to have position and to be mutually correlated according to their respective value. See Erhard Weigel, *Corporis Pansophici Pantologia,* in *Universi corporis Pansophici caput summum,* ed. Thomas Behme, Clavis Pansophiae 3.1, eds. Charles Lohr and Wilhelm Schmidt-Biggemann (Stuttgart–Bad Cannstatt: Frommann-Holzboog, 2003), 155ff; idem, *Arithmetische Beschreibung der Moral-Weissheit von Personen und Sachen,* ed. Thomas Behme, Clavis Pansophiae 3.2 (Stuttgart–Bad Cannstatt: Frommann-Holzboog, 2004), 13.

in this respect, that space is a certain kind of substance, immovable and extended from the beginning and of itself, which exists even though things natural be removed; but status (as do also all moral affairs considered under their form and as such) possesses only the characteristic of quality and attribute, so that if physical things be removed, it can by no means preserve its existence.

2. Now status can be divided according to the analogy of space into status of *place* and status of *time*. The former is status which involves respect to some moral position, and it can be considered either *indeterminately* or *determinately*. Indeterminately considered, status is either *natural* or *adventitious*. The natural status of man, since it has no special designation, we shall for the time being call humanity, or human life. It is that condition in which every man whatsoever, by virtue of the very fact that he is a man, is constituted. It also involves the obligation of observing the law of nature both towards himself and towards other men, and of living with them on terms of social intercourse; as, further, the right of enjoying from any and every man the offices due by the law of nature, and of exercising other privileges which universally attend human life; as also the capacity of acquiring special rights for himself among men. To this is opposed the status or life of brutes which are united by no mutual bond of right, so that <9> they inflict upon one another whatever they can or will, even by violence, yet do no wrong thereby.[2]

3. Therefore, inasmuch as that obligation of which we have spoken, as also the rights, attend the natural status of man, it is not inappropriate in this place to inquire into the limits of this status, that is to say, when it takes its beginning, and when its end. The former seems to be placed rightly at the moment when an individual can be properly called a human being, even though there be still lacking those perfections which come to man only after some passage of time; and so, when he begins to live and feel, although he

---

2. The characterization of the natural state of man as "humanity" corresponds to what is later called the "natural state with respect to God" in Pufendorf's threefold division of the natural state into that with respect to God, that with respect to each person by himself, and that with respect to individuals' relations to each other. See *Off.*, 2, 1, §§2ff; *Eris,* "Specimen controversiarum . . . ," chap. iii "De statu hominum naturali," §3, pp. 134–35.

has not yet left his mother's womb. Obligation, furthermore, since it requires for its consummation the recognition both of itself and of that
which is being done, displays its efficacy only when a man knows how to
compare his actions with a given norm and to distinguish them from one
another. Rights, however, which cause to arise in others who already rejoice
in the use of reason the obligation of performing something, and can profit
those who are even ignorant of what is done, are in full force the instant a
human being begins to exist.[3] Wherefore, without doubt he does a wrong
who takes away from one who is still in the womb that which was left him
by testament or assigned him by some other title, even though it may happen that this right has accrued to him within the very first days of conception; and so, when he comes of age afterwards, he will be justified in vindicating that right.[4] Moreover, it is sufficient for him to testify, at the time
when his age enables him to do so properly, that wrong was done him
against his will, especially as his dissent always ought to be presumed; just
as he who has taken away or ruined my property in my absence has immediately done me a wrong, although I may find out about the damage
only after an interval upon my return. A wrong, however, cannot be done
to the body of an infant unless it actually has a body, or has its material so
disposed, that, from an injury done to it in the process of formation, harm
comes to the body. Therefore, if one has wrongfully violated a mother, so
that her offspring is thereby born disabled in some member, we think that
this offspring on reaching maturity can bring an action for injury against
that individual, unless the latter can establish effective ignorance. However,
since the shapeless seed within the first few days of conception can be called
properly neither a man nor a human body, we are of the opinion that, if
any one compass its corruption or abortion, it cannot be said that a wrong
has been done against that seed; although, in fact, the individual in question
is sinning against the law of nature by depriving human society of a member, and is doing a wrong both to the state, which he is despoiling of a

3. Here Pufendorf follows Roman law. See Paulus in *Dig.,* I.v.7: "A child in its
mother's womb is cared for just as if it were in existence, whenever its own advantage is
concerned; although it cannot be of any benefit to anyone else before it is born."
4. Cf. *Dig.,* I.v.26, XXXVII.ix.7, and L.xvi.231.

citizen, and to the parents, whom he is despoiling of a hoped-for offspring.
<10>

4. But the further question is raised, namely, whether a right can be acquired by one person for another even before he exists at all in nature; and with this effect, namely, that, if this right be alienated from him by another, or in any manner whatsoever diverted, he may, upon his birth in after time, be able to complain of a wrong, as it were, done to himself, and to demand complete restitution. Laying aside the fictions of the civil law, by which in certain cases the law sustains the person of those who are not yet in existence, we are of the opinion that no right can be claimed by one who is not yet in existence, except indirectly through the person of one who is now in existence, through whom that right will be transmitted to the one who is to be born thereafter; in such wise, however, that this right will not have its effect with regard to the one to be born, until after he has been born.[5] And this situation arises when something is acquired by some one or is handed down to some one, to be kept in such a mode of possession that he lets it pass on down to his successors also. Here, however, a certain difference is found; for some things are conferred upon another in such wise that it makes no difference to the donor whether the property goes to the other's descendants or not, although the recipient, so far as he is concerned, has the power to transmit it to his descendants. But some things are conferred in such wise that the donor retains for himself a certain right over the manner of possession that has been determined by himself, in such a way that the other cannot part with it except with the donor's consent. In whichever fashion something may be possessed by the predecessor of the one not yet born, to be transmitted to him, if in any way whatsoever it be diverted or alienated before the latter's birth, wrong is by no means done to the one born thereafter, unless his predecessor left him at least a claim to it by way of inheritance. For, in the former case, because the property, together with the manner of its possession, is entirely within the power of the possessor, if now he has alienated it or in any way whatsoever caused it to be no longer in his possession, absolutely all right to the same is extinguished; and therefore it cannot be transmitted to the one not yet born,

5. Cf. *JNG,* 4, 12, §10, and Grotius, *JBP,* II.iv.10.

who can claim no right to such possessions of his ancestors except that right
which is turned over to him by the same, from hand to hand, as it were,
when he is already in existence.[6] And, in the latter case, since authority over
the manner of possession still remains with him who bestowed some property upon another, the possessor assuredly accomplishes nothing to the prej-
udice of his successors if he alienates it, or treats it as derelict in whatever
way it may have passed out of his hands, unless the donor consent. And
therefore, if the people have bestowed upon some one the throne to be
continued for ever in the line of his descent, the king's act will be of no
avail if he alienate the throne against the will of the people; nor can that
act of the parent redound to the injury <11> of his offspring, even though
yet unborn, if, indeed, the people wish the throne to inhere according to
the manner in which the possession of it was once established. But if, on
the other hand, that be done with the consent of both parties, of the one
who possesses the property, as well as of the one who has the right to settle
the manner of its possession, that right likewise is utterly extinguished before it can come to those who are born thereafter. Nor do the people by
changing the manner of possession do wrong to the latter. Because not for
the sake of these, but for their own sake did the people reserve to themselves
the right concerning the manner of possession; and therefore it was for no
one in this case except themselves that they sought or retained the right,
and if they abdicate, or change it, no one else has any ground for complaint.
From all this it is clear how one must decide the otherwise thorny question,
whether it be possible for the not yet born tacitly to give up their right owing
to the dereliction of their ancestors.

Now human status comes to its end through death in the course of nature, after which the reverence and honour accorded to remains and reputation is exhibited primarily for the sake of the survivors. What, furthermore, we believe from the Christian religion concerning the status of men
after death may be secured from the Sacred Scriptures.[7]

6. Cf. *JNG,* 4, 12, §10, where Pufendorf refers to *Dig.,* I.ix.7, §1.
7. According to Pufendorf's distinction in *Off.* between natural law and moral theology on the basis of their respective objects, ends, and sources, the discipline of natural
law remains within "the Compass of this life only" and of reason left alone by itself,

5. Subordinate to the natural status of man and proceeding immediately from it is *peace;* for every man whatsoever, just because he is a man, is under obligation to cultivate peace with every other man whatsoever, so long as care for his own safety does not persuade him to a breach thereof on account of the wrongs done him by others. Now peace is either *universal* or *particular.* The former extends to all men whatsoever who use the law of nature in their dealings with us, and consists first and foremost in this, namely, that no one injure another unjustly, and, if by chance controversies arise, that he be at pains to have them adjusted by a mutual arrangement or by arbitrators. This peace stands solely by obligation of the law of nature, and unless the parties to the agreement come together into one body or society on that account, it is useless to fortify it by a pact or by treaties. For by a pact of that sort nothing is superadded to the obligation of the law of nature, nor does it become thereby a firmer bond, and violence is done to a man in this connexion with equal injustice whether a pact has intervened or not. It is also alien to the custom of men to enter into such a pact whose headings or conditions would contain nothing else than the mere direct non-violation of the law of nature. For in any pact whatsoever something is placed as a condition or a heading which another would not otherwise be able to demand of me by the law of nature, and therefore something which I did not owe him fully <12> on the basis of the law of nature; just as I am not bound by the same law to enter into a pact with another, although in due consequence, and assuming my consent, I would bind myself in the matter of furnishing another with some matter that was otherwise not his due, because I would be unwilling to violate that law of nature which bids pacts to be preserved. For just as the one who assigns another his services does by no means expressly and immediately agree under the headings of the pact that he will not act towards the other as, let us say, a traitor, a thief, a rascal, &c., even if, in due consequence, all of that is involved in the pact; so that would be a covenant which deserved to be blushed at, if a man should bind himself to another for nothing further than that in his treatment of him he would not violate universal peace, that

---

while the particular offices of the Christian aiming at "the Reward of his Piety after this Life" are to be derived from the sacred scriptures (*Off.,* "The Author's Preface").

is, would not use toward him the right which is commonly employed against beasts. But what they call the pacts of friendship do superadd something to the universal peace. For assuredly we do owe something more to a friend than to any other man whatsoever, as being such, and not an enemy. Moreover, those pacts or instruments and documents by which passage is made from a state of war to mere universal peace, contain nothing else than the public attestation that there will be on both sides a cessation from war, and the conditions to be fulfilled by both or either side, if arms are to be laid down; after all this has been done, then universal peace proceeds from the sole obligation of the law of nature.

Particular peace is either *internal* or *external*. The former obtains among those who have come together into one body or society, when they supply that for the sake of which the society has been instituted, and do not violently resist the authority which the society rightfully exercises over them. This peace is not disturbed by every exercise of force whatsoever, but only by the exercise of that force against the exercise of which provision was made in the agreement to establish the society. Thus, for example, internal peace is not disturbed in the state when the magistracy forcibly restrains and punishes evildoers; but civil war arises only when others attempt by the exercise of violence to save those men from punishment and to resist the magistracy in the exercise of its right. External particular peace is that which is fostered with other societies, consecrated and fortified by special treaties. In this class, after a treaty of friendship comes a treaty of commerce, granting the right to enter the territory of the other party, to act, to conduct business, to make contracts and accounts, to engage in export and import trade, to enjoy the same rights in these matters as do the citizens of the other state, &c. For it is not required by the law of nature that I should allow another to conduct business in my country, especially if some danger threaten me therefrom, or advantage be lost thereby; and therefore such liberty of commercial intercourse must <13> be sought by a pact. The same is true of treaties of alliance and mutual aid, and that either against assailants alone, or against any one whatsoever, even the one whom we assail. Peace of this kind is broken when one party by the exercise of force attempts to inflict anything upon another which the other repels by force, or when a wrong that has been inflicted is avenged by force.

6. But, in truth, since the obligation of observing the law of nature toward another ceases when that other does not observe the same law toward me (in Book II we discuss this subject in greater detail), there arises thence, as a sort of subsidiary status for man, *war,* when our safety cannot be secured except by force. Although this status must necessarily be entered upon from time to time, to wit, when, because of the perversity of men who reject pacific measures, we can defend or obtain our rights only by arms, nevertheless it cannot properly be called a natural method of securing one's rights, for the reason that nature has not directly destined man to employ this method, but has merely allowed him, in defect of a more appropriate means, to take refuge in war. Now war can be divided in the same way as peace into *universal* and *particular.* The former is the immediate consequence of the status of wild beasts, when no one exercises any right toward his fellow, but the conduct of all is governed by force alone. Such would have been the status of men had they not been bound by the law of nature to foster social relations with one another.[8] Particular war is either *internal* or *external.* The former exists between those who have come together into one particular society, when they break the bond of that society and rise up in arms against one another. Such war when it burns out within the period of what might be called its first effervescence, and without elaborate preparations on both sides, is called *sedition.* When the subjects of a prince take up arms unjustly against him, it is *rebellion.* In democracies, however, and in aristocracies, when the people and the nobles separate into parties which act in hostile fashion against one another, it has become customary to call such a state of affairs properly *civil war.* External war is war between those who are not comprised in the same state. This is commonly wont to be divided into *formal* and *less formal.*[9] The former is also called a regular war according to the law of nations (by that meaning of the word regular whereby a regular army is opposed to some irregular troop of bandits), and is war which is carried on by the authority [*autoritate*] of the highest power

---

8. For a more detailed exposition of Pufendorf's criticism of the Hobbesian conception of the natural state of "war of everyone against everyone" see bk. II, Observ. 3, §6, and Observ. 4, §5; *JNG,* 2, 2, §§5–9.

9. Cf. *JNG,* 8, 6, §9, and Grotius, *JBP,* III.iii.1–6; for the origin of that distinction in Roman law see *Dig.,* XLIX.xv.24 and L.xvi.118.

[*potestatis*] in the state, following a declaration. The purpose of this declaration is not that the enemy may have time to prepare himself for resistance, but to make clear that the war is not being conducted as the private venture of a few, but as a public enterprise, and that the enemy may accordingly know with whom he will have to deal. As for the rest, wars that are destitute of such requisites <14> are less formal. But when others are attacked in secret raids and by an irregular band, upon no public authority [*autoritate*], without declaration and without just cause, this is called *freebooting.*

7. The Roman jurisconsults, furthermore, formulated as the broadest and most general statuses of men (of course as men were regarded in the Roman state or a state similar to it), *liberty* and *servitude.*[10] To understand the nature of these more accurately, it must be known that liberty is commonly conceived as a status in which one has the faculty of undertaking something upon one's own free will; servitude, on the contrary, as a status in which it is necessary to do things at the desire of another. Now there are two kinds of impediments which limit the faculty of undertaking; physical impediments, as bonds, fetters, prison, guards; and moral impediments, as obligation, law, sovereignty, authority. These being assumed, it is clear that liberty is either *of all kinds,* or *limited.* The former is that which is circumscribed by neither natural nor moral impediments. Such liberty we believe that no one but God enjoys absolutely. But among men, those enjoy the highest grade of liberty who have been exempted from civil laws, or those who rejoice in the supreme authority in states. For these, although they are subject to the Divine sovereignty and the law of nature, recognize nevertheless the sovereignty of no man, nor, so long as they are such, can they be coerced through the means of punishment by any one whatsoever. Of limited liberty there are several species and grades. By a special meaning of the word, "liberty" is ascribed to those who live in an aristocracy, and particularly to those who live in a democracy. In general, however, liberty denotes the status of those who serve merely the state, and not a fellow-citizen in addition; who may of their own free will direct any actions whatsoever

10. Justinian, *Institutes,* vol. 2 of *The Civil Law,* trans. Samuel Parsons Scott (Cincinnati: Central Trust Company, 1932), I.i.3 (hereafter referred to as *Inst.*).

of their own about which there has been made no disposition by general laws. This liberty is the more restricted the more numerous are the particular obligations by which one is held. Thus, he who is his own master in the state and has not assigned to another a definite portion of his services, enjoys much more ample liberty than he who is under the authority of his father or guardians, or who has assigned his services to a fellow citizen, whether these services be more dignified, that is to say, intellectual, or more humble, that is to say, physical; under which latter class in our society come labourers and household servants. It is servitude, however, in general, when a man is bound to direct his actions about which there has been made no disposition by general laws, not merely according to the will of another, but even entirely to that other's advantage, in such wise that there redounds to himself directly as a result of his own actions no extrinsic utility, except in so far as the other wills by an act of grace. A further characteristic is that these men are understood to have no citizenship in the <15> state and are enrolled under the head of things, and not of persons. In former times quite generally, and among some nations even to-day, prisoners are reduced to such servitude by a certain mixture of humanity and cruelty, in such wise that those who might legally have been put to death were to do lifelong service to their captors in return for the privilege of enjoying life. Some states used to leave to masters the right of life and death over these slaves, because it seemed to them not unjust that the life which had once been in their power [*potestate*] should remain so. The children of slaves enter upon the same status, and those who of their own accord descend to that condition. On some persons also servitude is imposed by way of punishment. The lowest grade of servitude, however, is endured by those who are restrained also by physical bonds, as those who have been cast into workhouses or prisons, condemned to service at the oar, who are loaded down with shackles, or are compelled to work behind the barrier of walls. As for what the jurisconsults say, namely, that by the law of nature all men from the first are born free,[11] this must be understood ἀποφατικῶς [negatively], not στερητικῶς [privatively], as some express it,[12] that is, by the precept of

11. See Ulpian in *Dig.,* I.i.4.
12. Grotius, *JBP,* II.xxii.11.

the natural law no man's liberty has been taken away absolutely and without some antecedent action of his own; but the same law has by no means prevented the possibility that an individual might be carried off into slavery for some definite cause. And by the very act the status of servitude and its conditions have been introduced of the free will of men. But as for the fact that philosophers commonly call certain men naturally slaves, to wit those who are of a somewhat sluggish intelligence and are unfit to govern themselves, this must not be understood as though men of that kind are placed by nature in a state of slavery, or are necessarily to be carried off into it, as though it would be contrary to nature if they should remain free, but that their intellects have been so formed by nature that they can bear servitude with equanimity, and neither understand the blessings of liberty nor know how to use them aright.[13]

8. Furthermore, those who live in states, especially Christian states, are divided commonly into three statuses, *ecclesiastical, political,* and *economic.*[14] The first two are called *public,* because ordinarily men, by the authority [*auctoritate*] of a civil society, or by the authority of those men as such by whom that society is governed, are placed in them, and because these tend immediately and directly to the good of society as such. The last is called a *private* status, because it depends upon each individual's own free will, and tends immediately and directly to the advantage of individuals as such. In the political status matters directly concerning men's civil society as such are handled by public authority [*autoritate*]. The ecclesiastical status claims as its own the service of the <16> divine, which is to be exercised especially for the welfare of society. For although ecclesiastical persons care

13. Cf. the detailed exposition and criticism of the ancient idea of slavery by nature in *JNG.* Pufendorf concedes that there are considerable differences in the endowments of different people and resulting aptitudes for ruling and serving (*JNG,* 3, 2, §8), but he stresses the impossibility of directly deriving a right to rule or an obligation to servitude from it (*JNG,* 1, 6, §11).

14. According to the Lutheran doctrine of three estates, God has established three orders: the household, the political order, and the order of grace, and has warranted a peculiar office for each of them. See, for example, Martin Luther, *Werke,* Weimarer Ausgabe (Weimar: Böhlau, 1883–2005), 2. dept., vol. 5, pp. 453–54 (hereafter referred to as *W.A.*).

also for the salvation of individuals, nevertheless it is for the good of society, or the commonweal, that a particular status has been assigned them.

The economic status handles, for the advantage of individuals as such, matters which have their use in communal life. The common seed-bed, as it were, of these is the scholastic status, in which minds are imbued with a liberal culture. Entering into details one meets a number of particular statuses, which any one will find easy to reduce to their proper classification.

Determinately considered, a status is either *honourable* or *less so.* The former we commonly call *office;* it is that status in which a person, primarily by an intellectual effort, and accompanied with a certain degree of dignity, is expected to accomplish something for another's advantage. The latter we call *service;* in it a person, without an accompaniment of dignity, and primarily by a physical effort, is expected to furnish something for another's advantage.

9. A special status, moreover, is produced either by the mere place in which a person lives, or by the condition under which he lives. For he who engages in life's activities in his native land, or in the land where he has fixed the seat of his fortunes, enjoying full rights of that place, is called a *citizen;* he who enjoys partial rights, a *resident;* he who has established a less stable and a temporary seat of his fortunes in some place or other, is called a *sojourner.* He who goes about on a foreign soil, intending to remain but a short time, is called an *alien,* and his status *alienage.*

10. In general, however, one ought to be advised that sometimes because of the poverty of language, and sometimes because of the carelessness of philosophers concerning moral entities, we are frequently compelled to use one and the same word to express both the status and the attributes, as well as the quality proper to the status. And yet these are in fact distinct, and are differently conceived. Thus, for example, liberty as a status is conceived after the analogy of space; as a faculty of action it is conceived in the manner of an active quality.[15] So nobility sometimes denotes a status, and sometimes the attribute of a person, because it is conceived in the manner of a passive quality.

15. *Liberty* as a faculty of action denotes authority over one's own person and actions; see bk. I, Def. 7, §3.

11. But there is yet another point which must not be passed by, and this is that just as several statuses can exist concurrently in the case of a single person, so the obligations which accompany a certain status may be derived in parts from diverse principles.[16] Hence it follows, that he who gathers together the obligations which flow from some one principle, disregarding all others, does by no means forthwith establish for himself a status of that same kind, to which, beside those obligations which he himself bears in mind, no other obligations can <17> or should attach themselves. Thus, he who from the Sacred Scriptures alone gathers together the separate parts of the duty of priests, does not by any means deny that these same priests are bound to perform also those duties which are required by the ecclesiastical constitutions of individual states. So we also, who are devoting ourselves here merely to those duties of man, the necessity for which can be gathered from the light of reason, do not by any manner of means insist that the status of men ever has been, or ever ought to be, such that those obligations alone belong to it.

12. *Status of time* is that which involves respect to the question when, or to time considered in a moral light, and it can be divided into (1) *juniority* and *seniority.* Both of these expressions are used either in respect to duration in human life, and are called *age,* whose grades are infancy, childhood, boyhood, youth, man's estate, old age, and decrepitude; or in respect to duration in some adventitious status, as that of raw recruits, of veterans, of the honourably discharged at the expiration of service, &c. In the former class can be included, perhaps, even primogeniture, a status in which one has no elder brothers by the same parent.

Status of time can also be divided into (2) *majority,* a status in which someone is reckoned as being able to attend to his own affairs in his own way; and *minority,* in which one has need of a tutor or guardian. The limits of this status vary among different peoples. <18>

---

16. According to his different statuses man can bear different moral persons. Cf. *JNG,* I, I, §14, where Pufendorf refers to the Stoic role-theory in Cicero, *De officiis* I. See also Weigel, *Arithmetische Beschreibung,* chap. XIII, §8, which employs the concept of person in a similar manner.

A moral person is a person considered under that status which he has in communal life.

1. The variety of moral persons considered
   separately. Public persons.
2. Private persons.
3. From the union of several persons there comes
   about a composite person called society.
4. Its divisions.

1. This is the most general definition of a moral person. Otherwise, primarily among the jurisconsults, a person is said to be that which possesses a civil condition [*caput*], that is, personal liberty; a signification by which slaves are listed under things. Now moral persons can be considered either *separately* or *collectively*. Separately considered, according to the difference of their statuses, there are *public* persons, those, namely, who are situated in a public status; and *private* persons, those, namely, who are in a private status.

Public persons are either *ecclesiastical* or *political*, and these are either *principal* or *less principal*. Among principal persons some rule the state with supreme authority, such as emperors, kings, princes, or by whatever name they are listed in whose hands is supreme sovereignty. Some exercise a part of sovereignty, by an authority delegated by majesty, and these are called by the general word *magistrates*. Their names are different in different states. Less principal persons are those who, without exercising authority, let out their services to princes or magistrates; among these, attendants and bailiffs occupy the lowest place, and last of all come executioners. From association with these last, although they are not branded with any legal infamy, even men who are but slightly more worthy commonly turn away; and this they do primarily because the habits of these men are very generally apt to correspond to their ministrations, which are associated with a certain degree of severity and unseemliness, or else because only mean spirits betake themselves readily to that kind of life.

In war officers of higher and lower rank correspond to magistrates. Under them are private soldiers who are also listed among public persons, because by the highest civil authority they are directly or indirectly authorized to carry arms for the state. This is understood to be the case when they take the oath of allegiance or are sent forth by the special command of their superiors to undertake the operations of warfare.

A special kind of political persons also can be constituted of those <19> whom you might call *representatives.* These are equipped with power [*potestate*] and authority [*autoritate*] to act by some one in whose place they transact affairs with another to the same effect as though they had been handled by the same person himself. Such are ambassadors, vicegerents, plenipotentiaries, and likewise syndics. Among private persons trustees and guardians occupy an equivalent position.

As for the ecclesiastical persons, to the extent to which any one has been brought up in some religion, it will be easy for him to take cognizance of their variety; nor can scholastic persons fail to be recognized by the learned.

2. Among private persons distinctions are drawn from (1) *sex,* whence are male, female, and hermaphrodite. Although these distinctions are properly physical, they nevertheless belong here because of a certain moral respect, in so far as the sexes are differently treated in civil life. For we both regard most women as beneath the dignity of a man's wrath, and we treat their insults as of less account than those of men, nor do we set so high a value upon their judgement and testimony, and, as a general thing, we do not admit them to public office, however capable otherwise they may be. And as for the hermaphrodite we turn away from one as from a monstrosity of nature.

(2) Distinctions are drawn also from *moral status in time,* whence it comes that the treatment of a young man is different from that of an old man, and an old man may do what does not become a young man, and vice versa. So also the authority [*autoritas*] of an old man is different from that of a young man.

(3) They are drawn also from the *moral position in the state.* Hence one man is a citizen, another a sojourner, another a resident, another an alien. As these men are bound in different ways to the state, so also they are not rated in the same way in regard to the distribution of advantages and the imposition of burdens.

(4) Distinctions are drawn also from the *moral position in the family,* whence we have husband, wife, father, children, master, slave, who are as it were ordinary members; to their number the guest is sometimes added, outside the regular order.

(5) Also *from lineage,* whence we have the nobleman who may be descended from an illustrious or a less illustrious family, or the plebeian. These are differently distinguished in different states.

(6) Also *from occupation,* that to which each individual devotes his efforts. This is either liberal or illiberal. Here belong merchants, who make their living by the exchange of goods. In this class hucksters bring up the rear. Here likewise belong all those who attend to land, plants, or domestic animals; such as countrymen, vine dressers, market gardeners, herdsmen, &c. <20>

3. Considered collectively persons constitute a *society* or an association when several persons are so united that both their action and their will are regarded as the action and will of a single individual, and not of several. It is understood that this takes place when individuals coming together into a society so subject their will to the will of a single individual who is the head of that society, or to the whole association, that they are willing to recognize and have regarded as their own will and action whatever the head, or the majority of the society, has decided or done in matters concerning the society.[1] Hence it results that, whereas before, whatever several desired or did was regarded as the desires and actions of as many as was the number of physical persons there, now that they have been united in a society, but one will is ascribed to them, and whatever action proceeds from them as such is adjudged to be the action not of many but of one, even though a number of physical individuals have concurred in it. Hence also a society acquires its special rights and goods, which cannot at all be claimed by

---

1. For a more detailed treatment of Pufendorf's doctrine of union of wills, see bk. II, Observ. 5, §2.

individuals, as such. Here must be made the further observation, that, just as individual persons remain the same, although in the passage of time the body undergoes marked changes through various additions and losses of particles, so through the particular succession of individuals a society does not change but remains the same, unless at a single time such a change befall that it utterly destroys the true character of the former body or society.[2]

4. We can divide societies or moral persons, furthermore, like individual persons, into *public* and *private.* The former, again, are either *sacred* and *ecclesiastical,* or *political.* Among sacred societies some are *general,* as the Catholic Church, so likewise particular churches bounded by the definite limits of regions and states, or distinguished by public formulae of confessions. Some are *special,* as a council, either oecumenical, national, or provincial, a diocesan synod, a consistory, the gathering of a cathedral chapter, or a presbytery.

In the same way a political society is either *universal,* as a state which is divided into different species, for example monarchy, aristocracy, and democracy, according to whether supreme sovereignty is in the hands of an individual, or a council composed of a few citizens, or of all the citizens; or *particular,* as a senate, a cabinet, a tribe, &c. A scholastic society exhibits the same diversity. *A society in military uniform* is called an army, and its parts are the legion, the troop, the cohort, the decury, the maniple, &c. *Private societies* are not merely families, but also what are called guilds of merchants, and of craftsmen, and the like. It would be a long task to enumerate these one by one. Let it suffice us to have touched merely upon the most salient features. <21>

2. For the origin of this analogy, see *JNG,* 8, 12, §7, where Pufendorf refers to contemporary medicine (Thomas Browne, *Religio medici,* sect. 36), to Roman law (*Dig.,* V.i.76), and to ancient authors (for example, Seneca, *17 Letters,* 58, 102; Plutarch, *The E at Delphi,* 392; id., *Theseus,* 23; and Lucretius, *On the Nature of Things,* III.860).

ᛝ DEFINITION V ᛝ

A moral thing is a thing regarded in respect of its pertinence to persons.

1. How manifold is the respect of the pertinence of actions?
2. Eminent domain, and direct ownership both ordinary and for purposes of utilization.
3. Plenary ownership, and limited.
4. What is one's own, and what is common property.
5. The proper goods of societies.
6. Whether it be possible for a state to exclude outsiders from things of innocent utility.
7. Is the sea subject to claims of proprietorship?
8. The sea which is very close to the coasts is private property.
9. The wide spaces of ocean seem to have been regarded by the nations as derelict.
10. How navigation and commerce upon the ocean are free.
11. Possession is a complement of proprietorship.
12. The origin of ownership over things from the divine law.
13. How far the ownership of man over brute creation extends by divine law.
14. How far it extends by the law of nature.
15. Origin of proprietorship.
16. Occupation the original mode of acquisition.
17. How property has passed from the first owner to later owners.
18. How are goods to be divided among sons?
19. Lucrative modes of acquisition.
20. Burdensome modes.
21. Returns and profits of a thing are acquired for the owner.
22. Should species follow matter, or matter species?
23. False modes of acquisition.
24. Whether a fault in acquisition is eliminated through passage of time.
25. Whether it passes over to a third party.
26. How proprietorship may be lost, as also about wills.
27. Insanity does not destroy proprietorship of property.
28. No man's property; different kinds of property.
29. Corporeal property.
30. Incorporeal.

43

1. The respect of pertinence, considered *indeterminately* and absolutely, as it is the formal reason for moral things, is either *affirmative* or *negative*. Affirmative respect extends to proprietorship and common ownership, whence moral things are called *proper* or *common;* negative respect is uniform, as it were, and takes on the aspect of neutrality, whence moral things are called *no man's.* Now considered *determinately* respect of pertinence has established the significance of *mine* and *thine.* Considered materially, moreover, and in themselves, things are divided into corporeal and incorporeal.

2. Men divide ownership commonly into three species, which you may call modes of possession; that is, *eminent domain,* and direct ownership both *common* and *for purposes of utilization.* By the first is meant that authority which belongs to a state or its head over the property of citizens for the commonweal. Its effect is, that it can effectively <22> restrain, as far as it may seem advisable to do so for the common good, the force of ordinary ownership. By ordinary ownership private persons possess their goods, in regard to which they have full faculty of making disposal, except in so far as that faculty is restrained by the eminent authority. There, if the usufruct be with another, it is called direct ownership, such as that which the owner has of a piece of land given in implantation. Finally we are said to have ownership for the purposes of utilization over those goods whose usufruct alone belongs to us, but the direct ownership to another; such as what we possess as lessees in the tenure of implantation.*

3. Ownership is also either *plenary* or *limited.* It is plenary when the same person actually possesses both the proprietorship of the thing and of its usufructs. In this way are possessed not merely those things over which we have eminent domain united with ordinary ownership (just as sometimes a certain region is acquired by a prince or a people together with every kind of ownership rights, over parts of which afterwards a limited ownership is granted to individuals), but also those things over which we have merely ordinary ownership, from which the usufruct has not been separated except

---

* I have translated this paragraph (and its heading) literally, but the logical division seems to be at fault. The author clearly wants to make a threefold division. That is possible only thus: (1) eminent domain; (2) ordinary ownership; (3) limited ownership: (*a*) direct ownership, (*b*) ownership for purposes of utilization.— *Tr.*

temporarily by way of a revocable benefaction. Ownership is limited when either the usufruct of my property belongs to another, or, on the other hand, the usufruct of another's property falls to me by right of inheritance. In this latter fashion should be regarded those thrones which are not the ruler's patrimony (having been granted originally by the consent of the people), and which must be transmitted to his heirs. For that this is a limited mode of possession is proved by the fact that the whole or a part thereof cannot be left by testament to any one whatsoever, or alienated by donation, or in any other fashion, by the king's individual authority [*autoritate*], without the consent of the people. By that fact, however, the force of sovereignty is not at all diminished, because, of course, it is merely the authority of alienating it that has been taken away, which does not in itself affect the faculty of exercising sovereignty. Property is held also in a limited manner, when ownership of it, of whatever kind that ownership may be, is circumscribed by a definite length of time, after the lapse of which it expires. From these propositions it is obvious just what sort of limitation must be added to that well-known rule of the jurisconsults, namely, that "A man's own property can never become any more his own"; from which they conclude that neither pledge, nor deposit, nor purchase, nor lease of his own property can stand; likewise, that a legacy is of no avail, if any one has bequeathed the property of a legatee to the legatee himself, likewise that it is of no <23> avail to stipulate that his own property shall come to that condition in which his property already is.[1] The limitation, of course, is: "Unless it so happens that a limited measure of possession be extended to one that is fuller." This happens, for example, if what was formerly held in feudal tenure begins to be possessed for the future as an absolute and independent principality.

4. Those things, therefore, which belong to us as *our own,* whether in the ordinary fashion, or even in eminent domain (the way in which states or their heads possess their goods), we can enjoy according to our free will, and we can keep all other persons whatsoever away from them, unless by covenanted pacts they have sought for themselves a special right which supervenes upon our right, and, in the same manner, while these things are

---

1. *Inst.,* III.19: "Concerning Inoperative Stipulations" (subparagraph 22).

ours they cannot be wholly another's.[2] *In the same manner,* I say, for there is nothing to hinder the same thing from pertaining to different persons according to different modes of possession, and this is a very common occurrence. Thus, with reference to the same piece of land the state has eminent domain, the owner of the land direct ownership, and the lessee in tenure of implantation has ownership for purposes of utilization. The expression *wholly* was also used, for it is also true that several persons can hold a thing in the same manner of possession, yet not wholly, but each in proportion to a fixed share. This happens in the case of those goods which are possessed indivisibly by several, who appear possessed of the same kind of ownership with reference to the same thing. These things are called *common,* seeing that they belong indivisibly to a number of persons in the same manner of possession. For common ownership differs from proprietorship not in regard to the manner and force of ownership (for a number have, of course, the same right to a common thing that one man has to a thing which is his own, and just as proprietorship of a certain thing which pertains to one man excludes the right of all other persons whatsoever from that thing, so also from a thing in common possession all others are excluded who are outside the number of those for whom the thing is called common), but only as far as the limit of pertinence, because his own property pertains to one person, whereas common property pertains to several. Since none of these obtains to the thing a right which extends, as it were, to cover the whole, but a right which is valid only to a part thereof, it is perfectly patent that a single individual cannot dispose of that whole thing in his own right, but only of his fixed share in the same; and if some decision has to be made regarding the whole thing, the agreement and authority [*autoritatem*] of each of those to whom it pertains is required.

5. Now not only those things which belong to single individuals are our own possessions, but also those which belong to moral persons in conjunction, or societies as such. For these are a certain kind of unit. <24> Thus they have also their own goods and their own rights, which, wholly

---

2. Cf. *JNG,* 4, 4, §2: "Furthermore, proprietorship or dominion is a right whereby the substance, as it were, of something belongs to a person in such a way that it does not belong in its entirety to another person in the same manner."

or in part, not only no one outside the society, but not even the members which are included in the same society, in so far as they are not conceived of as the whole society, can claim as their own in that manner of proprietorship which the society enjoys.

Now things which belong to a public society or state come under what is essentially a threefold classification. For over some the state exercises merely eminent domain, but has left or assigned ordinary ownership to individuals. Such are territories, provinces, cities, countrysides, fields, &c.; likewise any kind of property of private persons, which is possessed, indeed, by individuals on share, in the ordinary manner of ownership, but still in such a way that the state retains eminent domain over it. The force of that eminent domain expresses itself in this, namely, that individuals are bound to pay assessments or taxes imposed on these things, nay more, to yield the whole of them to public uses, if, indeed, the Commonweal demand that. From certain things, moreover, the state has removed absolutely all ownership on the part of individuals as such, and has reserved the disposal and utilization of the same wholly to itself. Such are the public revenues, tolls, the treasury, the privy purse, and the like.

The use of certain other things, finally, the state has left to citizens indivisibly, and has assigned ordinary ownership to no one in particular. And these are otherwise listed under the head of *public property,* to the use of which, if, indeed, there are not enough portions of them to go around, his claim is the best who was the first to put them into actual use. Thus, for example, the seat which any one has occupied in a theatre he retains by right against the late comer, unless it so happens that some particular disposition has been made about such matters. In this class are public buildings, public places, markets, theatres, streets, &c.; likewise seas, rivers, and public pools, the use of which is granted to any citizen whatsoever. Here also belongs sacred property, like temples, sacred utensils, ornaments and revenues of churches, and the like. For they are not the property of no man, but in fact belong to the state, nor are they entirely removed from human authority or uses. But they are called sacred from the end to which they are destined by the state, which is that they may especially serve the exercise of divine worship until some different disposal be made of them. Thence it comes about that, when necessity presses upon the state, if other means are unavailable, a state may, for example, melt down chalices and other utensils or sacred ornaments, sell the bells, use the revenues of churches, &c., without the obligation of restoring the like thereafter; and this the state can do by the same right by which it can lay hands upon money in a treasury whose funds are reserved for a very pressing emergency, or can sell public lands to private citizens. All this, <25> however, rests on the proviso that this right is to be utilized only under the pressure of extreme necessity, so that no suspicion of irreverence towards the Deity be incurred in the minds of the common people.

What has hitherto been said about the goods of the state can be applied by analogy also to the goods of other societies which do not constitute states.

6. Here, however, it must be further noted concerning the possessions of a state, that some are so appointed as to make it possible for their use (whether that use be of all kinds or only restricted) to be free promiscuously even to non-enemy outsiders, without detriment to that state. These are called things of innocent utilization, as are fountains of water, rivers, straits, seas, royal roads, &c. The faculty of conducting commerce with foreign nations includes the employment of these for the purpose of travel. Since generally the more civilized states grant promiscuously to non-enemy outsiders the use of these things, upon this fact some have based the claim that they are not subject to any proprietary right, moreover that the law of nature altogether forbids proprietorship in them, and enjoins that an unlimited use of the same should be granted to all men; and that therefore those are violating a law of nature who, claiming for themselves proprietorship in these things, have desired to put restriction upon their use by outsiders, or to shut them off entirely from such use.[3] It is quite certain, however,

---

3. Pufendorf refers to Hugo Grotius and Francisco de Vitoria. According to these authors the use of the sea, rivers, and highways for passage and trading, the right to settle, and even (in *JBP,* II.ii.17) the use and appropriation of uncultivated soil by strangers belong to the common right of mankind and must not be denied anyone. Cf. *JNG,* 3, 3, §§5ff, where Pufendorf emphasizes against Grotius (*JBP,* II.ii.13) the right of the state (or the proprietor) to regulate use by strangers according to its (or his) own security and interest; see also (*JNG,* 3, 3, §9) his harsh criticism of Vitoria, *Relectio de Indis* pt. I, sect. 3, according to which the denial of that use by the Indians gave the Spanish the title to conquest.

that those who put forward this claim are in error. Moreover, as far as public roads are concerned, it is well established that the owners of a region can keep absolutely any outsider from passing through it, or else can refuse to grant passage except on a definite regulation, or a definite charge. For, inasmuch as no one would deny them the proprietorship over the region, a part of which consists of public roads, it is clear that the same persons have also the right of disposition regarding roads, and that therefore they have the right of interdicting to others the use of these roads, if, indeed, it appear to them that such an action is in their own interest. Although, as long as the use keeps within the limits of innocent utilization, that right should not be exercised, because of the common obligation of men toward one another, by which any person whatsoever is bound to relieve the needs of any other person whatsoever, as far as that may be done without injury to himself. And yet nothing but extreme necessity gives one the authority to assert a claim to the use of such a road by violence;[4] since, on the other hand, if all had an equal right to the road, whoever was prohibited from the use of it on any cause whatsoever would have just cause for war. Thence it follows that Dido acted properly and within her rights when she refused the comrades of Aeneas a reception <26> to her shores until it was well established that from them there boded no evil to the new state.[5] So it was no act of injustice when the Edomites refused the Children of Israel, who promised indemnity merely on their word, a passage through their country, on the not unfounded fear that the latter would be compelled by their toilsome wandering to choose the land of the Edomites themselves.[6] The same Israelites, also, were not given just cause for making war against Sihon and Og, kings of the Amorites, by the refusal of a passage through the territory subject to these kings, but by the fact that Sihon and Og, beyond what was right, crossed their own boundaries with an army to meet them, and pro-

---

4. Cf. Grotius, *JBP,* II.ii.6, according to which urgent necessity may return things to the original common ownership.

5. Virgil, *Aeneid,* ed. George P. Goold; in *Virgil: Eclogues, Georgics, Aeneid* (Cambridge, Mass.: Harvard University Press, 1999), I, verse 543.

6. Numbers 20:14–21.

voked the Israelites to battle.[7] For here there is no need of taking refuge in an extraordinary command of God, as in those wars in which the same nation attacked the Canaanites. For these wars would otherwise have been most unjust, had not a special mandate of God authorized the Jews to destroy nations which, although they were exceedingly contaminated with sins, had nevertheless not called upon themselves the arms of the Jews by any injury which they had done the latter.[8]

7. But whether the sea also be subject to the claim of proprietorship has been ardently disputed by the most illustrious intellects in our generation, some saying that it is so subject, and others denying it.[9] Yet one ought not to be regarded as having unjustly hurt the reputation of any of these men, if one say that each has had rather the advantage of his own state before his eyes, than the zeal for truth which is under obligation to no parties. We are of the opinion that this controversy can be settled clearly and firmly if we assume here (an assumption which will be developed at greater length a little later), that man's ownership of things, so that it is rightful by a positive divine law, arises from that concession of God by which He made man the master of the whole earth. In this concession, which has the character of a privilege and not a command,[10] since there is express mention

7. Numbers 21:21–35. Pufendorf is arguing against Grotius, *JBP,* II.ii.13, where the refusal of passage alone gave just cause for war.

8. Cf. Numbers 33:50–56.

9. Pufendorf alludes to the dispute about the freedom of the sea that took place against the background of the rival colonial and commercial interests of Spain, Portugal, the Netherlands, and England. Hugo Grotius wrote an extensive legal opinion for the Dutch East India Company entitled *De Indis* that was not published until the nineteenth century (under the title *De jure praedae*), but in 1609 he published one chapter, as *Mare liberum,* directed against the Spaniards. Its later use against the Stuarts' claim that the sea is subject to dominion was countered by John Selden in *Mare clausum seu De dominio maris* (London, 1635), written for Charles I. See Hugo Grotius, *Commentary on the Law of Prize and Booty,* trans. Gwladys L. Williams, ed. Martine Julia van Ittersum (Indianapolis: Liberty Fund, 2006); Grotius, *The Free Sea,* trans. Richard Hakluyt, ed. David Armitage (Indianapolis: Liberty Fund, 2004); Günter Barudio, *Das Zeitalter des Absolutismus und der Aufklärung (1648–1779)* (Frankfurt: Fischer, 1981), 330ff; and Martine Julia van Ittersum, *Profit and Principle: Hugo Grotius, Natural Rights Theories and the Rise of Dutch Power in the East Indies, 1595–1615* (Leiden: Brill, 2006).

10. Cf. *JNG,* 4, 3, §2; Grotius, *JBP,* II.ii.2, and Pufendorf's criticism of it in *JNG,* 4, 4, §9.

quite as much of the fish of the sea as of the beasts of the field,[11] whose ownership cannot be conceived unless at the same time there is the right to utilize the element which they inhabit as far as its nature admits—on this side, surely, there is nothing to prevent men from being able to claim for themselves dominion of the sea. That this same dominion is rightful by the law of nature results from the need and necessity of man, who, since he cannot maintain life without the utilization and consumption of other things, is recognized to have authority also to utilize and consume them. Seeing that the sea also is to some degree able to remedy that state of need, here also there will be nothing to prevent man from appropriating to himself any uses whatsoever of the sea that he can, after that he himself, a terrestrial animal, has learned to go to and fro upon an alien element. But that this pro-<27>prietorship be acquired in actuality and obtain its proper effects as much in due order toward the things themselves as toward other men, it is necessary that it be acquired in some way which is recognized among men, one, namely, which supposes or involves a pact by which other men are understood to have renounced their pretension to that thing. Whether, therefore, men wish to exercise proprietorship over the sea as they do over land, or, on the contrary, to regard it as derelict, the privilege of doing one thing or the other has been conceded to them by the law of nature and the law of God, and it has been placed within the range of their free choice. For the objections that have been raised to this conclusion, namely, that the sea is fluid, that it has capacity and is sufficient for the uses of all men, and that there is uncertainty as to its limits, pass for the most part into witticisms,[12] and it has long ago been shown by others that such objections do not at all stand in the way of proprietorship. Also one should well observe that the effects of proprietorship show themselves clearly or

11. Genesis 1:28.

12. This is directed against Grotius, *JBP,* II.ii.3: "There is, furthermore, a natural reason which forbids that the sea, considered from the point of view mentioned, should become a private possession. The reason is that occupation takes place only in the case of a thing which has definite limits. . . . Liquids therefore cannot be taken possession of unless they are contained in something else; as being thus contained, lakes and ponds have been taken possession of, and likewise rivers, because they are contained by banks. But the sea is not contained by the land, since it is equal to the land, or larger."

obscurely in proportion to the measure in which the physical nature of the thing under consideration allows them to show themselves; and that proprietorship does not, nevertheless, immediately expire, although it may appear that the utilization of proprietorship can be less conveniently compassed, as it were, by some one individual.

Hence it is sufficient for the sea or any part of it to be called some one's possession, if he has the right of so completely appropriating to himself the uses of it that, unless others are willing to recognize those same uses in the way of a benefaction of his own, he may be able with justice to keep them out; and this obtains even though the extent of the sea makes guarding and, as it were, exclusive possession of it difficult, and especially its superlative capacity for utilization makes such guarding and possession almost superfluous.

8. To this point, therefore, the essential controversy reduces itself: Whether, namely, as the nations have made portions of the earth their own, so they have also made portions of the sea their own. Or, indeed, whether by tacit consent they have treated the whole, or certain parts of it as derelict. For answering this question it is helpful to consider just what uses the sea furnishes to mortals, which uses are so appointed that, if they should be thrown open promiscuously to all men, the condition of some one state would be the worse. For from that it will be easy to judge as to just what parts of the sea should be regarded as occupied and under ownership, and just what should be regarded as derelict.[13] Laying aside, therefore, the use for purposes of drawing water and bathing, which is of no great consequence and is available only to those who live near the coast, there are found to be two reasons principally why a people cannot, without loss to itself, <28> allow others to go to and fro promiscuously on the sea that is close by; these are fishing and the defence of the region.

Now although fishing in the sea is far richer than in rivers or lakes, yet it is manifest that it becomes harder for those who live near the sea, or can

---

13. For the following, cf. *JNG,* 4, 5, §§6–8. Pufendorf argues against Grotius, *JBP,* II.ii.3, according to which the inexhaustible use of the sea makes it unnecessary to leave primitive community, and agrees with John Selden's and Alberico Gentili's argument for dominion of the sea (ibid., §8 referring to Selden, *Mare clausum* II, chaps. xx–xxii, and Gentili, *Hispanicae advocationis libri duo* I, chaps. viii and xiv).

be partially exhausted, if different nations desire to fish along the coasts of a certain region. Since the same sea, indeed, acts in the way of defence also (though an equivocal defence, whereby, although land ways are broken off, still there is wide open access by ships), it is of course plain that it is by no means to the interest of maritime peoples that any and every one should have the right to sail the sea which extends along their districts, without being on his guard against giving offence; no more so than that any and every one should be allowed to take short cuts across the moats and ramparts of cities. It is presumed, therefore, that every maritime state whatsoever has desired to reserve to itself such dominion over the sea which extends along its coast, as will suffice to prevent some peril being threatened against itself by ships which come too close. Thence it follows that, although otherwise the use of travel by sea is a matter of innocent and inexhaustible utilization (and it would be a matter of the utmost inhumanity to deny or to charge such things to any one, unless something else induce one to do so), still, for the aforesaid reason of defence, a certain people can rightly prevent any outsider from coming within a definite distance from its own shores, except by a previous announcement and with the consent of that same people, or else by giving a definite sign that the approach or passage is friendly. The distance out to sea which serves the function of this kind of defence, in respect to which ownership is exercised by some people over that distance, cannot be so accurately determined in general, but must be recognized from the accepted custom among different nations. But if a bay or a channel opens out between two peoples, their several sovereignty is understood to terminate in the middle of the bay or channel, unless one of the two, by pact or agreement on the part of the other, has acquired domain over the whole stretch of water. From this it is clear that that people or those peoples whose territory is washed by a bay of the sea obtain in due order sovereignty over that same bay. So it cannot be doubted that the Romans, when they held all the lands that bordered on the Mediterranean Sea, possessed such sovereignty over that same sea, or were properly able to exercise it, that they could prevent any ships whatsoever of outsiders from passing through the straits at Gades.

9. However, the dispute is not so much over these parts of the sea, as over that vast expanse of ocean. Its broad extent may, to be sure, not ab-

solutely prevent it from being subject to the claim of proprietorship, yet, on the other hand, it cannot be denied that its <29> possession will be practically useless, whether that possession pertain to one people only or to several. For those boundless stretches do not readily admit of fishing, or else this rewards the effort made; nor are those parts of the ocean which are very far removed from land regarded any longer as defences. For I should not believe any nation to be so timid that it regarded as a concern of its safety that no foreign vessel should sail, let us say, within two hundred miles of its coast; and therefore on this account it will not be able to interdict navigation thereon to any one, provided he does not come inside that limit within which he can effectively threaten peril. Hence the Spaniards or the Portuguese, for example, should no more be listened to, if under this head they should desire to interdict to the English or the Dutch navigation to the Indies, than, for example, the citizens of Cologne, if they should want to prevent any one at Speyer from crossing the Rhine. But if, in truth, it should be altogether expedient for the whole ocean to be under dominion, because of the convenience that would accrue to navigation, then assuredly not one people or another would be able to claim the ocean for itself, excluding all others, but all the peoples that dwell by the ocean ought to unite for its possession, each in proportion to its own region, unless it so happen that some one nation should yield its right and grant it to another. Since there is no record that such a division of the ocean among the nations has ever been made, and it would be useless to have it made, it is a correct judgement, that the ocean, if you except the portions adjacent to coasts, has been regarded by the nations as derelict, in so far as proprietorship is concerned; in such a manner, however, that no nation is able to appropriate to itself alone the use of it. And therefore no one ought to appropriate to himself beyond others a special right over it, for the reason that he was the first to cross it, any more than the men of Amalfi can exclude others from the use of the magnetic needle, because it was one of their fellow-citizens who is said to have demonstrated the use of it.

10. From all this it is clear that the navigation and commerce of all people whatsoever who dwell by the ocean, with all other persons whatsoever who likewise dwell by the ocean, is, in respect to a third party, mutually free, and that those who appropriate this navigation and commerce to them-

selves alone, are oppressing other nations with an unjust monopoly, unless they have acquired such a right for themselves by the consent of those other parties. Here, however, the observation must be made, that just as a prince can of his own right prevent any merchandise that is produced or manu-factured in his jurisdiction from being exported by outsiders, unless by a pact or by a generous concession on his part they have acquired that faculty (yet no one is bound by the law of nature to enter upon such a pact, or to grant this <30> favour to any one, unless perchance extreme necessity be pressing him, so that without commerce with the other the first would per-ish); so, if, for example, a European nation has made some region in Africa or India its own in the way in which it is customary among the nations to introduce dominion, it would be justified at its pleasure in cutting off all access thereto on the part of others, or else allowing access only on a definite condition or at a definite charge.[14] But, in truth, it is without all colour of right when one people presumes to interdict to another non-enemy people the passage across the ocean to a third people, likewise non-enemy, for the sake of carrying on commerce, and does so on this ground alone, namely, that thereby it would lose something from its own profits, unless it so hap-pen that the third nation desires to exclude the second on some definite grounds. And this conclusion is not affected by the fact that merely that nation alone, even though it be for a long space of time, has gone thither for commercial purposes. For unless this third people has specially granted another, to the exclusion of all others, the faculty of access to it, that other people will no more be able justly to keep the rest away by virtue of its priority, than he who was the first to buy wine from a wine merchant can keep others from buying there also.

11. Furthermore, that which is, as it were, the final complement of pro-prietorship, upon the establishment of which proprietorship begins fully to exert its effects, is *possession.* By possession a certain thing is, either by a man's own act or through another acting in his name, actually apprehended and occupied, as far as the nature of the thing admits, and the man so has it under his authority that he is able to exercise in action the force of own-ership over it, and to make disposition of it. This possession begins in the

---

14. Cf. *JNG,* 3, 3, §§6, 11, 12, with reference to Grotius, *JBP,* II.ii.13, 18–20, 24.

bodily act of seizure, and that it may produce some effect there ought to be not merely in the mind of the one who seizes, the intention of taking possession of the thing by that act, but the act of seizure must be so ordered that others may be able to presume that the thing has been apprehended with that end in view. Now apprehension is understood to take place not only when the body is brought in contact with a thing, but frequently even by a sign intended for that purpose, such as the acceptance of keys, when, for example, some one buys a house, or buys merchandise in a storehouse, and the like.

Furthermore, two kinds of possession are recognized: *legitimate* possession, when we have a right to the thing that we hold, and have also observed all things requisite in taking possession of it, if it so happen that some things are prescribed by positive laws; and *illegitimate* possession, when a man has no right, or no sufficient right, to that thing which he has brought under his power [*potestatem*].

This possession is again either *quieted,* when no one has called into <31> question any right whatsoever of the possessor; and *unquieted,* when the same right has been brought by protestations, or in other ways, into controversy. Now of whatever kind the possession be, this effect always follows it in states, namely, that the thing is regarded as belonging to the possessor until the contrary is clearly proven. Although sometimes an illegitimate possessor also is helped by this presumption, namely, when the owner cannot bring forward in court arguments that carry conviction with them, for there it is allowable to penetrate to the truth of a matter only by external indications; still, in general, it was to the public good to have that principle accepted, because otherwise any one whatsoever might at the pleasure of any one else whatsoever be exhausted in proving title to his own possessions. And yet among those who use the simple law of nature between one another, this presumption is not valid as long as they subject themselves to no arbitrator or judge, because they are bound to prove the strength of their right to no third person. Hence the position of the possessor in a court of law is always better than that of the claimant, because, of course, the bare proof of possession is all that is incumbent upon the possessor, and that is most plain and simple; but the claimant is bound to prove his right, which is a much more intricate and difficult process, ownership and use of the property remaining also meanwhile with the possessor until the claimant has proved to the judges the justice of his petition. This makes clear that famous dictum of the Roman jurisconsults: "It is worth less to have a legal action than to have the property."[15] For, of course, even if you should have a right, based upon firm proofs, to a thing which is possessed by another, and therefore it may be regarded to some degree as your own; nevertheless, aside from the fact that for the time being you are compelled to go without the use of the thing, in a state, at all events, there is incumbent upon you the labour of proving to the judge your right, and if he happen to be a corrupt judge and render an unjust decision, you will assuredly have to acquiesce in it. Among those, however, who use merely the law of nature among one another, the dispute must be committed to the uncertain dice of Mars.

On the other hand, what we wholly owe to another, although as long as we have not paid it, it has still to some degree a place among our goods, that is yet, in truth, not our own. Thus, he that has a thousand pieces of gold, but owes the same amount, has nothing; while it would be no absurd statement to make, that he who owes more than he has, has less than nothing. This throws light on the remark of a certain man who was in debt: "I need a number of talents, so as to have nothing."

12. The next point, therefore, is to examine into the origin of proprietorship, and the more ordinary ways of acquiring it. Here at <32> the beginning we lay as our foundation that statement of Sacred Scripture, namely, that it came to pass with the consent and will of the Deity, that man took to himself proprietorship and dominion over things not merely inanimate, but also animate.[16] For we read that those things which spring up out of the earth were expressly assigned to man for food, and that cannot be except the same be consumed. Nor did God any the less concede man authority over things animate that live in the air, on the earth, or in the waters. This concession, as we have already suggested above, does not have the force of a command, but merely the granting of a privilege which any one may use as far as it pleases him, and he is not bound to every kind of

15. *Dig.*, L.xvii.204.
16. Genesis 1:28.

exercise of the same. For otherwise man would be sinning against the divine law if he should let free any animal, let us say, a bird, a fish, or a wild beast, or should neglect an opportunity of bringing it under his power [*potestatem*]—a statement which no sane person would make.

13. Furthermore, it is not perfectly clear whether that concession of dominion over things animate grants man, from the very nature of dominion, an unlimited authority, so that he can kill them even for uses that are not necessary. For dominion does not involve the licence of killing with impunity and as a mere whim; nor would men have been able to complain that divine indulgence had been parsimonious toward them, or that their needs had been but ill provided for, even if authority over the life of animals had been denied them. For truly their service in cultivating the soil, and their products otherwise useless to themselves, like milk, or part of their eggs, wool, &c., could have sufficed men for maintaining life. Nor does it immediately follow from God's bidding them to be sacrificed as a token of divine worship, that man has acquired the authority to turn them to food at his pleasure. For it is possible that man, by a special command of God, has a right to do something which otherwise would by no means have been his right. Yet indeed, because we have observed that God has nowhere disapproved of such slaughter of animals for man's food, but rather has ordained definite rules for the same, we conclude correctly that it is not opposed to His will.

14. If, however, we consult the mere law of nature, since it assuredly would recommend to men that life be maintained, and it is impossible to preserve life without the utilization and consumption of vegetables, at least; it is understood that it has by all means granted the utilization and consumption of those things without which man is unable to preserve life. This is especially true inasmuch as most of them would either never have come into being without man's effort, or, apart from consumption by men, would also have perished otherwise, and that without being of use to any one. We must render the same judgement about most of the inanimate products of animals, like <33> hair, wool, milk, eggs, that are likewise not necessary for the propagation of the species. But, indeed, the right to bring animals to a violent death, and to turn them into food, is not so clearly apparent from the mere law of nature. This is the reason why not a few of the ancient

philosophers have disapproved of such slaughter. For why should a man take from an innocent animal, merely to please a superfluous desire, the life that has been given it by the same Creator? Especially since he cannot excuse himself by alleging the example of lions, indeed, or wolves, and other carnivorous animals. For nature has so formed these that they cannot preserve life except on their bloody diet, and they turn aside from the fruits of the earth; but that is not the case with man. Indeed, I should be inclined to believe that Pythagoras invented that fable of his about metempsychosis for no other reason than to frighten his own disciples away from the slaughter of animals, using this little bugbear, as it were, to make them afraid, forsooth, that in pork or in beef they were doing violence to kindred flesh.[17] And it is obvious that the truculence of men, originally irritated, as it were, or hardened by the slaughter of animals, burst forth afterwards upon men themselves; and those who took pleasure in slaying innocent animals found it easy to draw the sword upon weaker men and such as were exposed to injury.[18] Therefore the principal argument for defending the slaughter of beasts as being in accordance with the law of nature seems to be this, namely, that there is no mutual right or obligation between men and beasts, and, in the course of nature, there ought not to be, and this for the reason that beasts are not capable of an obligation, at least toward men, which must arise from a pact, this obligation being a bond of right that is common to a number. From this absence of a common right there follows a state of war between those who are able to do each other injury, and on grounds of probability are understood to be able to desire to do so.[19] In this status any one has the faculty of inflicting upon any one else with whom he is at war whatever he will and can. And this status, indeed, is very clear in the case of beasts of prey, which, whenever occasion is given, vent their fury not merely upon other brutes but even upon men themselves. If any one should wish them to be spared by men, he would be demanding that men

---

17. Cf. *JNG,* 4, 3, §4, where Pufendorf refers to Plutarch, *Symposiacs,* VIII.viii, and Diogenes Laertius, *Vitae philosophorum,* VIII.13.

18. See Pufendorf's references (*JNG,* 4, 3, §4) to Plutarch, *On the Eating of Flesh,* II, 998 B, and Ovid, *Metamorphoses* XV, fab. ii.

19. Cf. Thomas Hobbes, *Leviathan,* vol. 3, chap. 14, *The English Works,* ed. William Molesworth (London, 1841), and *De cive,* chap. 2, §12.

be in a condition inferior to that of those same beasts. As for domesticated animals, they give themselves to the uses of men not by some obligation, but because they have been caught by an enticement in the way of food, or have been subjected by force, and when you remove that, they will quickly return to their free state, and some will turn upon man himself. And this too seems not to be without bearing on the case, the circumstance, namely, that since otherwise those harmless beasts are exposed to the prey and the butchery of other beasts which are rapacious, their condition is rendered better, rather <34> than worse, by the fact that men have asserted so much power [*potestatis*] over them; for men both provide for their food as a kind of compensation, and protect them against the attacks of wild beasts.

15. For the rest, as the law of nature has given man the authority of appropriating and utilizing things which are necessary for life (and this authority is extended even to those things which in any way at all supply some use, provided only some right in the utilization of the thing, or a right existing in some third person, be not opposed); so it has left the measure of authority, and its intension and extension, to the free will and the disposition of men, to wit, whether they wish to circumscribe it with definite limits, or, indeed, with none at all; likewise, whether they wish any one whatsoever to have authority over anything whatsoever, or over merely some definite part of it, or, indeed, to assign to each man whatsoever his own portion, in contentment with which he may be unable to ascribe to himself any right over the rest; although the peace and tranquillity of the human race, which, beyond all else, the law of nature is intent upon, do by no means obscurely hint that whatever is instituted here by men should be to the highest degree consonant with nature. For the peace of the human race, at least after its multiplication, does not allow that any person whatsoever should be free to exercise equal authority over any things whatsoever, or that any thing whatsoever should be exposed to the use and disposition of any person whatsoever, or, what amounts to the same thing, namely, that all things should be common to all men.[20] Nay, the most ready occasion

---

20. This is an allusion to the Hobbesian right of nature as a right to everything and the resulting natural state of war of everyone against everyone; see *De cive,* chap. 1, §§6

of war is the simultaneous desire or need of the same thing among two or more persons, and practically no one would be willing to allow another person to seek to assert to himself as much right as the producer himself has to a thing which has been produced by his own pains; so I shall pass over the other difficulties lightly.

This, therefore, is what nature has been urging upon us, namely, that in order to preserve peace about those things from whose promiscuous utilization strife was very likely to arise, each man should have some definite portion assigned him, to which no other could assert any just claim. As for the rest of things, the utilization of which is limitless, nature left it to the mere free will of man as to what disposition he might see fit to make of them. And, in truth, no such state of affairs has ever existed, at least after men divided into several families, as one in which all persons had all things in common. For the fables which the poets tell us of the golden age,[21] have either been distorted from the state of man in Paradise, or else hint at the liberality and humanity with which primitive men gave freely to any one who needed it the use of their own possessions. In this way, even to-day, we say that friends have all things in common.[22] And again it was not necessary to mark so carefully the boundary of the field when the broad expanse <35> of the same abundantly sufficed the scanty number of men. In short, the sum of all that has been said comes to this, namely, that the first man, with the consent of God, and without the resistance of any obstacle in their nature, and furthermore under the pressure of necessity, took to himself things when they offered themselves, as it were, to him; that, after mankind multiplied, nature urged individuals to possess separately portions of the same, to the exclusion of other men, and this she has done in order to avoid the inconveniences which would arise from common ownership; that the actual division among individuals, which division confers ownership to a definite portion of these things, has been fortified by the tacit or expressed

---

and 10ff; *Leviathan,* chaps. 13–14, and Pufendorf's discussion of the Hobbesian theory in *JNG,* 2, 2, §§3ff.

21. See the references in *JNG,* 4, 4, §8.

22. Cf. Aristotle, *Politics,* trans. H. Rackham, vol. 21 of *Aristotle,* Loeb Classical Library (Cambridge, Mass.: Harvard University Press; London: William Heinemann, 1944), 1263a30.

pacts of men; and that therefore proprietorship, in so far as it introduces the division of things among several owners exclusive of others, is due to the suasion of nature, but that actually it has been established by the pacts of men.

16. From what has been said it is apparent that, if we should regard the mere law of nature, for the first owners of things the sole right of *occupation* was sufficient. For, inasmuch as no right hindered man from devoting things animate as well as inanimate to his own uses, there was nothing left for him to do but to assert his possession of them by an act. This mode of taking possession has place even to-day in the case of those things which are regarded as derelict, that is, things to which either no one has ever desired to assert a claim, or else those which a former owner has either thrown away, or else has lost by some accident, without the intention of recovering them. This intention is presumed from words and from deeds, as, for example, when a thing is thrown away (unless, perchance, because of some passing circumstance, and this has been done with the intent to recover it later); or when a person knowingly contracts, with another person who now possesses that which was formerly his own, for that same thing as though the other were its owner. The same is understood to be the case, also, from things which are not done, to wit, when a person for no probable cause neglects to do what he might easily do for the sake of recovering that thing. The reason why, however, other men also are not able to run in crowds to things of that kind, as to a common inheritance, lies in the fact that right to things which are about to pass to another in the way of inheritance, as it were from one hand to another, is passed on uninterruptedly from the former owner by his express or presumed desire; but in things of this kind, either no man's right at all exists in act, or, not having been derived from a former owner to another, has altogether expired, so that no one can in a special way assert for himself a right to them, except him who has especially sought it anew. For when posterity observed that an inheritance had been left by the first of mankind, aside from the original pact by which <36> any one whatsoever among a number of heirs has renounced his claim to the rest after accepting his own portion, they ought to be thought to have entered tacitly upon another pact also, to the effect that, inasmuch as they themselves had entered upon the universal inheritance of the world, as it

were, whatever had at that time not been expressly assigned to some one person, at all events in the way of universality, should fall to the one who afterwards was the first to take possession of it.[23] It must be understood that this pact had been made for the purpose of avoiding strife thereafter, which would otherwise certainly have arisen, although things which, by the tacit consent of the nations, have been so treated as derelict that no one is able to ascribe their possession to himself without consent on the part of the same, cannot at all be claimed by any one person through the right of occupation;[24] a view which we have set forth above in regard to the vast expanse of ocean far from coast-lines. It was, therefore, by title of occupation alone, if you remove from consideration the concession on the part of God, that the first man received his authority over all things, and he needed no further title, because there existed no one whose right could stand in his way. And he acquired dominion over all things none the less because he was unable by an act to take possession of all things, and apply them to his own use. For it is sufficient that, while he took possession physically of some portion of things, he had included others in his intent, and was going to take possession of them also when need of them arose; just as he who has entered merely one apartment of a palace, has occupied the whole,[25] and, in the case of things which, as a whole, have devolved upon some one, he who has taken hold of some portions only, is adjudged to have taken possession of them one and all. Yes, and the same right would have been sufficient, even if a number of men had been created by God at the same time. For the pact which under these circumstances they would

23. Cf. *JNG,* 4, 4, §§5ff; Grotius, *JBP,* II.ii.2: "At the same time we learn how things became subject to private ownership. This happened not by a mere act of will . . . but rather by a kind of agreement, either expressed, as by a division, or implied, as by occupation."

24. Cf. Grotius, *JBP,* II.iii.10: "it has resulted from established practice rather than from natural reason that the sea was not occupied, or could not lawfully be occupied, in the sense in which we have spoken. . . . But many things, which were permitted by nature, universal customary law, by a kind of common understanding, has been able to prohibit. Consequently, wherever such a law is in force, and has not, by common consent, been abrogated, a portion of the sea, however small and almost enclosed by shores, cannot become subject to the ownership of any people."

25. Cf. *JNG,* 4, 9, §7, with reference to *Dig.,* XLI.ii.3, §1.

have regarded as necessary to make about the division of things for the sake of preserving concord would not have given them a new title or a new right, but would merely have circumscribed within definite limits a right which was common, and would have assigned to each his proportional share; since, of course, such a pact about things does altogether presuppose a certain right to the same.

17. From the first man that dominion over things has been transmitted and conserved to posterity by various titles, in such a way, however, that in his case this dominion was undivided, and both unimpaired and unrestricted in every part, but in their case, because of the plurality of those who enjoyed an equal right, it was not at all possible for a single person to succeed to the whole inheritance, but the property had to be divided into several portions. And afterwards, when men multiplied and separated into states, it rested with these <37> same states to determine the effects of proprietorship and to include it within definite limits; for example, that it should not be permissible for any one whatsoever to turn to merely any kind of use a definite sort of thing; likewise, that it should not be allowed any one whatsoever to alienate his own property in any way he desired, and the like. Furthermore, of those titles by which property has been transferred from the first man to posterity as such, there are two of prime importance: *Donation made by a living person* and *succession to the right of a deceased person,* or entrance upon an inheritance, whether that be by testament or without a testament.[26] That a portion of goods was transmitted to children during the lifetime of their father is perfectly clear from the longevity of early man, which does not allow us to believe that sons lived such a space of time without possessions of their own, and the very authority of sacred history repeatedly declares. For we read that Abel and Cain sacrificed to the

---

26. For these derivative modes of acquisition see Grotius, *JBP,* II.vii, who reduced them to three legal sources (*lege naturae, aut lege gentium voluntaria, aut lege civili*). Pufendorf's exposition of that matter in *JNG,* 4, 10 (*On Wills*) and 4, 11 (*On Succession to a Person Intestate*) mainly draws on contemporary authors such as John Selden (*De successionibus in bona defuncti, ad leges Ebraeorum, liber singularis; accedunt eiusdem De successione in pontificatum Ebraeorum, libri duo,* [London, 1636]), Roman law (especially *Dig.,* V.2ff), the Old Testament (Genesis 21:8–12, 37:4, 48:22; Numbers 27:8–11; Deuteronomy 21:17; Judges 9:18, 11:1–2), and canon law (Gratian, *Decretum Gratiani,* prima pars, distinctio 56, first part, distinction 56, canon 3).

Lord of their own possessions.[27] So, afterwards, when dominion over the whole earth had returned once more to Noah, it is reported on good authority that he divided the three portions of the globe among his sons.[28]

18. Now, as regards this donation and, as it were, assignation of possessions of their own, it must be observed that it was not necessary for a father to grant exactly as much to one of his children as to another, and that he did not sin against a law of nature if he gave to one more and to another less, provided only that he gave to some particular one what might suffice for his needs; although it might have been proper to take into account the offspring of the one who is under consideration, in so far as the number of such offspring could be conjectured with probability, so that they might not think it necessary in after time to take violent measures in order to provide for their needs. Otherwise nature absolutely binds parents only to the point of furnishing necessary supplies to their children. But, for the rest, as it is, indeed, the most convenient means of preventing envy among children, if a father distribute equal portions among his children who are equal, and who have equal deserts; so, none the less, it could rightly be established in many states, that, in order to preserve the splendour of families, the larger part of the possessions should go to the first-born son alone, and that daughters, inasmuch as they pass over into other families, should not share equally with sons in goods of some particular kind, whatever that may be. And surely no wrong is done other children if a parent gives to one child or another some special gift in comparison with what he give the others, whether that be for definite grounds in the case of that child himself, or merely on account of a special inclination of the heart toward him. The same holds true also in the case of testaments; for, on the basis of the law of nature, no complaint against a testament as being contrary to one's duty has any grounds, <38> except when the father, without antecedent wrong on his son's part, has left him not even the necessaries of life. For children have, to the goods of parents, as long as the rights of the parents remain, not a right, but only a natural aptitude, at least as far as the requirements of their necessary sustentation, and this natural aptitude has the same effect

27. Genesis 4:3ff.
28. Genesis 9.

as a right when necessity urges, such as appears in this case, since otherwise this son would have to perish or live a life of misery. Therefore, by virtue of this principle, a son who has been passed by in a testament can recover from the other coheirs his portion, if he lives in a state, by process of law, or, if outside a state, by force. But if, indeed, succession must be entered upon without a testament, then, without doubt, those who stand in the same relationship to the deceased, receive also equal parts in his goods when positive laws do not establish something different. And as equal parts those things also are regarded which one has himself selected for his own portion with the consent of the others, or, when assigned him by his coheirs, has approved, or has received by lot, even if possibly they are not in themselves equal to the other portions in value.

19. There are, furthermore, several ways in which property passes from one person to another, not as though passing to a man's heir. These can be divided conveniently into means or titles which are *lucrative,* and those which are *burdensome.*[29] Among the former is donation. This is when, out of pure liberality, something is given another person which could have been withheld without doing him wrong, and is unaccompanied by the stipulation to furnish under compulsion, as it were, some other thing or service. A species of this is the alms or charity which is distributed among the poor and those who have been overtaken by calamity. Here belong also rewards, when something is given to some one in view, to be sure, of a bit of work which has preceded, yet not as it were for pecuniary compensation, but rather as though from a certain free munificence, in order to extol the recipient's talent and to stimulate his own and other men's talents to yet further achievement. In such a way also do all kinds of inheritances pass, whether with or without testament. You can, however, scarcely list among these inheritances the trusts [*fideicommissa*], and things which have a relationship to them, as, for example, when an entire inheritance must be expended for definite purposes designated by the testator;[30] for properly speaking nothing is acquired in these transactions, but only the burden of

29. For this distinction see Grotius, *JBP,* II.xii.2; see also the analogous division of contracts into beneficial and burdensome in bk. I, Def. 12, §§54–55.

30. In Roman law (see, for example, *Inst.,* II.xxiii) a *trust* [*fideicommissum*] was a kind of bequest obliging the heir to give the estate or a part of it to a third person.

a mandate is undertaken, seeing that the same things must be transferred to others. Here it must be noted that, just as by the law of nature no one is bound to assume an inheritance which is burdened with debts that exceed it in amount,[31] so, by the same law, if a man has assumed it, he is not bound to make up out of his own property that whereto the inheri-<39>tance does not suffice. But where civil laws bring the payment of all the debts of the testator upon the heir, the latter will be held bound to pay them, yet not on the basis of the testament and the wish of the deceased, but on the basis of his own consent;[32] although it is true that in the Roman law the slave of the master who died involved in debt was compelled to become his master's heir, not in order that he might be compelled to pay anything out of his own property, but so that he should sustain the ignominy of the auction being held under his name, in compensation for which ignominy he commonly enjoyed his liberty.[33] In this class belong legacies, when by testament a definite portion of goods is left to some one not a primary heir; likewise dowries which come to the husband through his wife on the ground of matrimony; as also bridal gifts which are given by the groom to the bride, and the like. In a like manner also are acquired those things which, after being treated as derelict by a former owner, are seized by the first finder.[34] Under this head come hidden treasures, wreckage which is thrown up on the coast, things which have been lost on the road and elsewhere, only so far, however, as the former owner has given up the intention of recovering them. For otherwise, although by some unforeseen accident or other the possession of my property has been interrupted for a time, nevertheless my right to it has not perished, unless by neglecting to look for it, or in some other way, I have signified my abdication of it, as it were. Hence they do well for their conscience, who are careful to make public announcement of the finding of that kind of thing which they cannot prove by definite circumstances to have been treated as derelict by its owner. This is particularly

31. Cf. *JNG,* 4, 11, §19, with references to *Dig.,* XI.vii.14, §1; XVI.iii.7, §1; and XLIX.xiv.11.

32. Cf. *Dig.,* XXIX.ii.8.

33. See *Inst.,* I.vi.

34. For the subsequent remarks on seizure of derelicts, cf. *JNG,* 4, 6, §§12–13; Grotius, *JBP,* II.viii.1–7; and (as source of both) *Dig.,* XLI.i–ii.

appropriate when things are concerned that have been lost by dropping, or by shipwreck, or on a journey. In treasure-trove, however, this is not so necessary. For he who digs up a treasure on his own land will be able rightly to retain it until such time as another has proved himself to be its legitimate owner, and has presented credible grounds for concealing it and keeping it hidden until that time. For he from whose possession a field or a house has passed to its present owner, who is the finder of the thing, is not presumed knowingly to have left therein a treasure which he had himself hidden away, when he was alienating the field or the house; just as also he who has hidden some such thing in another person's land without the knowledge of its owner, has not lost the chance of asserting claim to his own property, when there was the justifiable fear that it might fall into another person's hands. But, in truth, he who has discovered a treasure on another's ground, is altogether bound to declare that fact, at least to the owner of the land. For it is generally presumed that things contained in the ground belong to the owner of the ground. On these matters, however, positive laws in different places make different regulations. <40>

Finally, under the head of lucrative title is acquired the booty which soldiers, with the indulgence of their general, take from the goods of the enemy, in addition to their pay; for otherwise whatever is captured in war belongs to those who are principally carrying on the war; and it is incumbent upon them, moreover, to pay out of the booty for whatever damage was done to their own citizens by the enemy, either before the war or during its course. And soldiers ought to be content with their pay or with what takes the place of pay; if anything is given them out of the booty they will ascribe it to the liberality of the general.

20. In contrast with the preceding, however, that is to say, under a burdensome title, soldiers acquire their military pay, or what is assigned them in place of that pay; also all those things which come to us by burdensome pacts or contracts, for example, things acquired by payment of money, by exchange with a thing of equal value, by labour or effort, even though some element of profit be not altogether lacking here. Thus, it is by truly burdensome title that merchants acquire property, even though they sell their merchandise for more than they paid for it; since the labours and dangers of transporting and handling the merchandise are regarded as being equiv-

alent to the gain. For this reason even usury upon money let out at interest belongs here, for the obvious reason that, while this money is lent for another's use, besides the risk involved of losing the loan, it cannot be paid out for other profitable uses by its owner. Nay, even money or property which is acquired on wagers, by so-called urns of fortune, or by any kind of game, belongs here; for there was a contract also in the case of all those things, and my money was exposed to equal risk with that of another; although contracts of that kind have in some places been altogether prohibited by civil laws, or else the resources of legal action have been denied against those who are unwilling to abide by them. No less accompanied with burden is the income of princes which the privy purse receives out of the revenues of the state for the expenses of single individuals or their own household; for this is granted as some measure of compensation for the undertaking of cares and labours in behalf of the state. And as for the rest of the revenues, those, namely, which are spent upon public uses, nothing but the administration and distribution of these has been left to princes, and therefore, when these revenues are brought into the treasury, they cannot properly be said to be acquired for the princes.

Into this class falls also that which is seized from the enemy in a just war.[35] For although he who gives me a just cause for making war would also, as far as in him lay, be giving me the right of taking all that is his own, however far, perhaps, this would exceed the injury that has been done by him (as will be shown somewhere), and therefore, <41> assuming that I have a just cause for making war, nothing further is required for my laying hold of his possessions than the act of occupation; nevertheless, because, aside from the fact that these are imputed to the payment for damage which has been received, such occupation cannot take place without expenses, perils, and labours, not to mention the uncertain cast of the dice of Mars, property of this kind is regarded as passing from one owner to another under burden. In war, moreover, the property of the enemy becomes ours, his movable property, indeed, when it has been brought behind our outposts; but his immovable property, even though for a time it may be held under our power [*potestate*], becomes ours only when it has so been oc-

---

35. Cf. *JNG,* 8, 6, §20, with reference to Grotius, *JBP,* III.vi.

cupied by us that for the time being the enemy has left open to him no avenue of approach to it. Nevertheless, a quieted possession of the same is obtained only at the time when the enemy has either been utterly annihilated or scattered, or else has also by a pact given up his claim to such property. Here, furthermore, it must be noted that, if among the things taken from the enemy there be some which have been taken from some third party likewise, in case this third party has given up the effort to recover them, and has left them to the quieted possession of the second, then he cannot demand back that property from the last holder. For to property which has been taken away in a just war I am understood to have lost at the same time every right. The same thing happens when I suffer my right to a thing which has been taken away from me in any way at all, to expire by neglecting to recover it, or at least to protest against the wrong, or by entering into transactions with the one who took it away.[36] Also the obligation of restoring a thing which has been taken away unjustly does not pass from the one who took it away to the latest holder, and that because this obligation inheres in the person of the former, and does by no means attend the thing which the first possessor has already regarded as derelict. But if, in truth, the first possessor has preserved his right, then he will be able rightly to recover his property from the last holder, with this proviso, however, that he is bound to make good to the latter the effort expended in recovering it.

21. These are about all the ways in which, either as a whole or as individual items, things are acquired, as they exist at different times in the world. Furthermore, that method of acquisition is in the highest degree natural, by which the natural and artificial increments and fruits of our property or our industry and any or all improvements of the same, come to us. Now this means is extremely widespread, and it is the most frequent as well as the most fruitful of them all, especially inasmuch as most things either take on natural increments and produce fruits of the same kind, or are capable of being made better, larger, and more fruitful by human industry. Now increments and fruits of things are either merely natural, or merely artificial, or mixed. To <42> the first class can be referred trees and other plants which, without man's cultivation, grow out of the earth, and

---

36. Cf. Grotius, *JBP,* III.vi.3, and Pomponius in Ulpian, *Dig.,* XLI.i.44.

the fruits of the same which do not need the labour and industry of man for their production. To this class also you can assign alluvium, in so far as it is deposited without human effort, the violence of the stream adding to one man's farm a bit of soil which has been cut away from somewhere else, and the process being one of silent increments. It is recognized that this alluvial deposit comes to belong to the owner of the farm, principally for the reason that no one can positively prove that it was to this particular spot and nowhere else that parts taken from his farm had been added; and likewise that whatever has been placed there is from his land alone and from nowhere else.

To the third class belong those increments and fruits in which the operation of nature as well as the industry and effort of men concur. Such are all manner of crops which are improved through cultivation by man, trees which put off their sylvan nature as a result of ingrafting, and the fruits of the same; likewise the offspring and fruits of animals which are fed by men, or of those animals whose offspring and fruits are not produced at all without human effort, or else have to be sustained thereby. The fruits of animals I call milk, wool, hair, feathers, teeth, deciduous horns, and the like.

To the second class we assign those things which, due to human skill, put on a form that is fit for definite uses, such as are practically all things with which the industry of workmen and artisans is occupied. Their industry is accustomed to fashion these rude benefactions of nature, as it were, for the most convenient uses of human life.

22. Here also may suitably be placed that which otherwise is a common matter of dispute among the jurisconsults, whether, namely, in regard to the production of a species out of material belonging to another, the artificial form follows the material, or the material follows the form.[37] Although the civil law, by virtue of sovereign authority, might have settled this controversy by distinguishing between the species which can be reduced to their earlier form and those which cannot, so that in the first class the form yields precedence to the material, in the second class the opposite is the case; never-

---

37. *Dig.*, VI.i (various passages); X.iv.9, §3; X.iv.12, §3; XLI.i.9, §1; further, *JNG*, 4, 7, §§7–10, and Grotius, *JBP*, II.viii.19ff.

theless, for those who follow only the law of nature, the discrimination must be made as to whether a certain person applied his industry to the elaboration of material belonging to another either through error, or from a credibly presumed willingness on the part of the owner of the material; or rather did so with guile, and with the intention of defrauding him of the material by this means; and, in the next place, whether the material, or the value of the art employed, was the greater. For he who knowingly, and with malice aforethought, has given my material a new form so as to defraud me of it by this means, has neither acquired any right to <43> the material, nor is he any more able to demand from me the reward of his labour, than is the housebreaker, because with a great deal of trouble he has made a new entrance into my house. But if he has acted through error due not to absolutely heedless negligence, that is, if otherwise that material might easily have been replaced from elsewhere, or was not so very necessary to the owner, or under other circumstances he would have had it for sale, the option still remains with the owner as to whether he shall accept pay for the material and leave the product to the artisan, or prefers to pay for the effort and keep the thing himself. For it would be absurd that the error of another could produce a right to my property against my will, which would outweigh my own right to it, especially when the value of his effort does not exceed the value of the material. Thus, why should he who through an error has from my olives, grapes, or grain pressed out oil or wine, or has cooked bread, as though the materials had been his own, have a better right than I? Or why should he have the right of choice rather than I, especially when, as often happens, we neither can do without things of that kind nor desire to do so? But, indeed, where the cost of the material is out of all proportion to the form, as is the case in painted pictures, and in those articles which are manufactured out of less valuable materials, as, for example, bronze, iron, or wood, equity assuredly demands that the owner should yield the object to the artisan after receiving the value of the material, inasmuch as materials of that kind are generally of such a nature that, when their value has been restored, no loss redounds to the owner. But, whatever has been done under these conditions, on the credibly presumed consent of the owner, is just as valid as if the express consent of the owner had been given. Thus, for example, if I make a statue or anything else out of another's bronze which was otherwise for sale, after I have presented a credible reason why I made use of his property without his knowledge, and after I have offered him the money for it, he cannot rightfully compel me to yield him possession of the object. But, when some one has built a house on another man's land, or has sowed grain and planted trees, he has not thereby acquired any right to the soil, nor can he compel the owner of the soil to pay him any return at all for materials and labour, for the reason that an accident of this kind can scarcely happen except in consequence of utter and crass negligence. And, indeed, he who has built a structure can tear it down again and carry off the material, and claim that for himself; provided, however, that he is bound to repair whatever damage has been done to the land by that structure. But he cannot at all in the same way carry off a tree and a crop and keep them for himself, because they draw their nurture from the land, and the owner will have been prevented from having his own trees and crops put in their place. If, however, there was no <44> intent to deceive on the part of the other, it is fair for the owner of the soil to restore him as much benefit as has been rendered to his own land by the other's tree or crop.

23. It remains for us to examine into illegitimate modes of acquisition. They can be brought under two principal heads, *force* and *fraud;* that is to say, when some one destitute of legitimate authority either extorts by violence, or fraudulently and surreptitiously steals away from another, that to which he himself has no right, and in such a way that the other's right is injured. Here two things must be noted. (1) It frequently happens that a man has the right to a certain thing which is in the hands of another; as, for example, when that same thing or its equivalent value is owed him; and yet in states it is judged that he has not rightly taken possession of it, when he takes it to himself in private enterprise, violently or surreptitiously. For within states it is the established usage that no citizen should by his private authority [*autoritate*] extort from a fellow-citizen against the latter's will that which is owed him, but he should use the assistance of the magistracy; although, by the mere law of nature, I may by any means at all take to myself from him who refuses to give it to me freely, that which is owed me. And thence it comes about that he who herein exercises violence in a state, commits the crime, not of theft or robbery, but of a breach of the peace, and of extortion by means of threat. (2) One may have to the goods of

another a right which is either perfect, and, as it were, double, or a right which may be called one-sided (μονόπλευρον). It is the former, when, in very truth, my right to a certain thing has been acquired by some preceding act, in such wise that the other party also is under obligation to give it to me. It is the latter, when I, indeed, without doing injury, am able to appropriate something, in such wise, however, that on the other party there rests no obligation to give it to me. This is the case in war, where he who did the first injury is bound to make good nothing but the original damage which he did, and that which proceeds therefrom. Because, nevertheless, that same person, as far as he was concerned, broke the common bond of right with the other, and gave the injured party an unlimited authority over himself and what was his own (as will be set forth below),[38] the injured party can, without himself doing injury, appropriate by any means at all any goods whatsoever of the other's, although the other is by no means bound to offer them or to yield possession of them freely to him; I mean thereby, of course, those goods which are in excess of the damage which has been done by him. Exactly as between two persons who by mutual agreement have come to fight, each has the authority to inflict blows upon the other, but neither is bound to offer himself freely to the one who is aiming a blow at him. Although that mode of acquisition has not been associated with wrong, and therefore should not be pronounced <45> out and out illegitimate, nevertheless, nature grants no further use of it than in the case of war, which, in a subsidiary manner, as it were, comes to the rescue of the security of men, when it is not permitted to employ peace.

24. Now under the aspect of species, various names are given to illegitimate modes of acquisition. Under the former class are listed rapine, brigandage, piracy, driving off of property, &c.; under the latter class, theft, peculation, sacrilege, and all manner of defrauding in contracts.

But, in truth, the following point requires profounder consideration, whether, namely, the fault which adheres to a thing from the illegitimate means of acquisition may not possibly be corrected by a subsequent deed, or even by the mere lapse of time; and whether the fault remains even at

38. See bk. I, Def. 12, §22; bk. II, Observ. 4, §13.

the time when the thing comes to a third party by a good title.[39] Here this much is certain, namely, that as long as a thing which has been unjustly taken away remains in the hands of the first robber, the fault always adheres to it, as long as that fault has not been quashed by the former owner, and that no matter how long the robber has possessed the thing. For mere time in itself can neither eliminate a fault nor produce a right, because, of course, by time a fault or right which was originally inherent is merely continued. But by the usage of nations, there have been introduced, and in most states accepted, usucaptions and prescriptions, by the force of which a thing that has been acquired with a good title, and in good faith, and has been possessed in quiet, is regarded, after a certain length of time, as possessed by a good right, so that the otherwise legitimate claim of a third party no longer obtains. That is both because no one is presumed knowingly to have desired to have his own property remain so long in the hands of another, when he might easily have asserted his right to it (at least without having made any contest of his right, whereby a full right is preserved), unless he himself regarded it as derelict, and approved of the other's possession of it—and neglect so careless as that seemed to deserve the loss of such property; and also in order that the limitless crop of litigation should be suppressed, which litigation would necessarily be excited, when, after so long a lapse of time, the same property should be demanded from the fourth or fifth possessor, who had come into possession of the thing by a just, and possibly also by a burdensome title, especially since a number of accidents might happen by which this latter will be prevented from being able to demand restitution for the damage from the robber. And there is no obstacle to this conclusion in the fact that my property cannot be transferred to another without my own act, or that no one ought to be enriched by another's loss. For here a non-deed, that is to say, supine negligence in claim-

---

39. On the matter of usucaption dealt with in the present and subsequent paragraphs, cf. *JNG*, 4, 12, where Pufendorf treats that matter with reference to Roman law (in particular *Dig.*, XLI.iii, but also Gratian's *Decretum*, pt. II, cause XVI, question III, canon 13) and discusses contemporary authors (Grotius, *JBP*, II.iv; Hugo de Roy, *De eo quod justum est et circa id philosophiae, theologiae et jurisprudentiae syncretismo libri tres* [Hildesheim, 1653], bk. III, title iii–iv; and Jacques Cujas, *Observationum libri XXVIII* [Cologne: Hieratus; Oberursel: Iunghenius, 1618]).

ing one's own right, is regarded as a deed, and that is not regarded <46> as a loss, which one was willing to have inflicted upon himself. Now willingness here is presumed from such long-continued silence. Thence it comes about that he who has the thing in usucaption is safe in conscience also. For, before the time of usucaption, he possessed the property in good faith, as is supposed; and afterwards, if he live in a state, by civil law also the thing in question is adjudged to be his, which civil law utterly extinguishes the claim of the former owner. Among those who are not included in the same state, the same result is produced by natural equity itself. Furthermore, just as by the law of nature he who has done another damage by violence or by guile is bound to repair the same; so, since any one whatsoever can yield his right, the fault pertaining to the property expires, and the obligation of making restitution ceases with the one who did the damage, when he to whom it was done condones it voluntarily to the other, and does so, not from fear of further evil or molestation, or, as men commonly say, for the purpose of buying off trouble; and, indeed, so that the other may have the faculty of recovering his own property if he should so desire, and the robber may have the inclination not to defend by violence the thing which he is called upon to restore. And it makes no difference whether this act of condoning has been performed expressly or tacitly, that is, of course, by dissimulation, and, although you could do so conveniently, by not starting a controversy, or for a notable length of time making no signs as though you cared to put forward some legal claim to that property. Hence, if, for example, he from whom something has been taken away should die, and, when he was transmitting to his heirs the rest of his goods under express designations, made no mention of the property which had been taken away from him, it appears that he is treating that property as derelict, and therefore his heirs cannot recover it from the present possessor. However, in order for this act of tacit condonation to satisfy the conscience, it seems to be altogether required that it should somehow or other be brought to the attention of the former owner that the possessor is ready to restore his property if the former should demand it back.

25. But if, in truth, property unjustly taken away has come under a good title to a third party who is effectively ignorant of the fact that the second party is an unjust possessor of it (for he who knowingly, for example, has

bought stolen goods, brings upon himself also the fault attending the acquisition, and therefore is required to make restitution, and he from whom
the thing has been taken can appropriate it in the same way as he can appropriate it from the robber), and he from whom it had been taken chances
to light upon it, the question arises whether he may immediately lay hands
upon his own property and compel by litigation that third possessor to turn
it over, leaving it to him to bring against the man who had alienated from
the other faulty <47> property of this kind, an action for the reparation of
damage; or, indeed, whether, leaving out of consideration the third possessor, one ought to go after the robber himself, so as to make him restore
the property either in value or in nature, the transaction being instituted
with the third possessor. In this case, although in many places positive laws
favour the one from whom property has been taken, and grant him the
right of laying hold of it wherever it has been found, nevertheless, those
who follow the mere law of nature must carefully determine whether his
ignorance regarding the fault which adheres to this piece of property, has
been contracted by some negligence, or, indeed, not. For if the third possessor not only saw no fault adhering to the property, but, more than that,
neither from the condition of the property, nor from that of the vendor
could have suspected it with any degree of probability, as, for example,
when it is a public presumption that such and such a man can possess such
and such property with a good title, then it does not appear that the third
party must be dealt with directly, but that the inconvenience must be
brought upon the robber alone. For, inasmuch as the former had acquired
that property in a way which is commonly recognized, and he could not
have been aware of the fault, there is no apparent reason why he himself,
rather than the man who is trying to recover his own property, ought either
to be deprived of the aforesaid property without compensation, or weighed
down with the burden of extorting payment for the damage from the man
who sold it to him. For the faultiness in acquisition has not passed with
any effect to such a possessor, because faults of that kind adhering to things,
and obligations resulting to persons from them, cannot be derived upon a
third person without an act or culpable omission on his part, such as is not
found in the present case. The situation, however, is different when the
condition either of the thing or of the person produces the probable sus-

picion that the property in question has been faultily acquired, or else an edict has been issued that no one should buy anything from such persons, edicts of that kind being promulgated not infrequently in war with regard to soldiers; for here the fault of failure to make proper inquiry about the property leaves the third person no ground for taking exception to the first owner coming into possession of his own property by the shortest possible route.

26. Now we lose proprietorship and right to property when we either treat it as derelict, or by any means whatsoever alienate it, or transfer it to another. It is easy to infer from the modes of acquisition the number of modes in which this takes place. For whenever another person acquires in a legitimate mode that which was our own, or we in any way whatsoever irrevocably transfer to another our right to the property, then that property ceases to be ours. Now, although through death a person ceases to be among men, and by that very fact every <48> right of his over persons and things expires, nevertheless, because it seemed undesirable that that which a man had acquired with such labour throughout the whole course of his life, should be regarded as derelict upon his death, in such a way that any one whatsoever might have the faculty of appropriating it to himself, it has been introduced by the customs of nations that even those goods which a person, while he was yet among the living, had not yet transferred or alienated to another, should go to him to whom the deceased wished them to go. That wish is either expressed or presumed. The latter is the case in instances of intestate succession, when a person has died without a will. For then the presumption of the wish on the part of the deceased ordinarily favours those who are the next of kin, among whom the very next of kin are severally understood to have the strongest right. Now the expressed wish of the deceased is learned from the testament, the codicils, or by whatever name those final dispositions are listed, by means of which the property is alienated in the event of death; but before death this alienation is revocable, and in the meantime the full right to the property which obtained before is kept. Hence the effect of these dispositions is not that, as soon as they have been conceived and expressed in signs, proprietorship of the property passes over to the heir, and the usufruct remains with the testator during his lifetime, but that the entire ownership remains with the testator, while

the right of the heir begins only at the moment of the testator's death. The evident proof of this position is the fact that, even after the making of a testament, the testator is able to alienate the property, nay more, he can utterly change the heirs as well as the testament, without any complaint on the part of the previously recorded heir.

As for the rest, although natural equity and ordinary affection (which, however, does not render unavailing whatever has been done in its despite) has been wont to urge that a man should leave his goods to his children or to relatives, rather than to aliens, unless by some notable fault the former have rendered themselves unworthy; yet, since nothing is required from parents as a natural debt other than that they should be at pains, according to their means, to have their children well brought up until they may be able to look out for themselves adequately; it rests in the free will of any man whatsoever, quite apart from the disposition of civil laws, to decide what he chooses to leave his children beyond that debt, and what, if anything at all, he chooses to leave relatives, out of his own goods. To have this situation the more clearly recognized, a number of civil laws have ordered that certain formalities be observed, and that, if they are not in evidence, the testament should be void, and this for the reason that it is not presumed that this was truly his desire, which he did not express in that way in which alone he knew it could be valid. Although, truly, <49> civil laws can define what a man ought to leave and to whom, nevertheless, the very complaints about a testament which is contrary to one's duty do not so much raise the doubt as to whether the testator had the right to dispose of his own property according to his free will, as they seek from the judge that the reasons which moved the deceased be looked into, because he willed to do something which was contrary to common inclination, so that, if it be found that he had abused his authority [*potestate*], owing to the deception or fraud of others, the goods may by public authority [*autoritatem*] be assigned those to whom they would otherwise have come, if, indeed, he had brought reason to counsel rather than inconsiderate emotions. And the statement is not unqualifiedly true that parents acquire all things for the sake of their children, for each one primarily acquires for his own sake, and that which exceeds his own particular needs he is willing then to have go to those who are dearest to him, such as are ordinarily considered to be his children and his next of kin. But this is easily understood, namely, that he whose goods are held in a restricted mode of tenure can make no disposition of anything to the injury of the one who has had some superior or prior right in those goods; and this follows from the common axiom that no one can confer more right to another than he himself possesses.[40] Hence, in testaments, not only can no valid disposition be made which is contrary to the laws of the state, but even that which is owed to others by the testator, by contracts, or under some other head, must first be subtracted from his goods before anything comes to the heirs. For right had been acquired by all other creditors before the heir, his right beginning only after the death of the testator. And therefore a person is understood to be transmitting to the heir no more than is left to himself at the time of death, after subtracting that which is needed to pay his debts. There are, however, states in which a man by testament may dispose of only that which he has acquired by his own industry, but not that which he has himself inherited. Elsewhere there is even no such thing as the making of a testament on the part of citizens, but everything descends to the nearest blood relatives without testamentary disposition.

27. Properly, however, and by a certain necessity of natural law, ownership is not made void through defect of reason, as, for example, either childhood, or insanity which later supervenes. For property which is under ownership is for the most part subservient to the needs of the body, and since these needs rest no less heavily upon the aforementioned than upon those who are in possession of their reason, it would be absurd for the condition of age or for disease to be of any avail in taking away from them that ownership which has become a more precious thing to them because of the concomitant inability to acquire property. But, truly, because an intellectual defect prevents <50> them from being able to make a good use of their own property, in most countries civil laws out of humane consideration have entrusted the administration of their goods to others, in such a way that not the owners, who are not in full possession of their reason, but guardians can effectively dispose of that property, and this is done to prevent the owners from being dispossessed of their property because of

40. *Dig.*, L.xvii.54.

their own lack of prudence and through the fraud of others. For it was thought to be incongruous that those who cannot understand what is being done, and therefore cannot consent, should be able to alienate something; and to accept something from such a person in whose case there is presumed to be no rightly considered will to give, is not without the appearance of fraud. Besides it is also to the public interest that no one make a bad use of his own property. It is due to this consideration that guardianship is extended also over those years which already possess an understanding of affairs, but wherein, because of the violence of emotions, persons are regarded as incapable of guarding their property.

28. Things are no man's which pertain to no particular man, and to which no one possesses any special right for the present above others. Certain of these are absolutely incapable of proprietorship and have been excluded from interchange among men; to wit, those whose nature rejects every corporeal possession and seizure made by men, and those which admit no act out of which a special right can arise for some one above others.[41] To this class we are of the opinion that air, wind, heat, and light of the sun, so far as they inhere in the air that surrounds us, or in circumjacent space, are by no means so simply to be referred. For, since these things cannot, like others, be transferred by men from one portion of space to another (in which respect, that is, separately, they do not enter into exchange), they can assuredly, as things inherent in space, also come under an estimate of value, and therefore, as far as proprietorship is concerned, they participate in the nature of space. Thence it follows in due consequence that the man whom I can exclude from my space I can also prevent from enjoying the air, the wind, the warmth and light of the sun existing in my space. Thus it is not unusual to charge up to another the clemency of the air, and the convenience of wind and sun which is enjoyed by the farm that I am renting or selling him; likewise it is not unusual that over space belonging to me I leave a path, as it were, for wind or for the light of the sun to another's house, since otherwise I might shut out his light with a building.

41. In *JNG* Pufendorf deals with that matter in a more differentiated manner: "For, although the lack of a physical faculty does not immediately extinguish a moral one" (4, 5, §6), "the effects of proprietorship are maintained against others" the more easily, "the more closely a thing can be, as it were, shut in and surrounded" (ibid., §3).

Now certain things are for the present, indeed, no man's, although otherwise, by their nature they are capable of proprietorship and become in act subject to it when they are occupied by some person. Such <51> are the things which the nations have treated as derelict when they were appropriating other things to themselves as their very own. However, they have been unwilling for some among these to become the actual property of one or another person or people by act of occupation, but have ever tacitly agreed that they should be no man's property, as we said above on the topic of those parts of the ocean which are far away from the shore. But other things yield to any one whatsoever who takes possession of them. Such were, according to the view of the ancient Roman jurisconsults, fishes, birds, and wild beasts, which it was permissible to catch even on another's farm, although the owner of the farm might keep out any one who wanted to enter for the sake of hunting animals or birds.[42] And these things, when once become one's own property by right of occupation, became again no man's property and returned to a free state, when they had escaped the custody of men.[43] Into this class they put bees, doves, peacocks, tamed wild animals when they had run away and had put off the habit of returning; likewise property exposed to looting in war, missiles, treasures, things thrown up on the shore, and whatever else there is of that sort. But about many of the things just mentioned the peoples of the world to-day have made different dispositions. Certain things were even regarded as derelict, as it were, at least in respect to those persons whom the same state or the same society included, yet those who were outside the state or the society were excluded from participating in them; and this is certain in the case of booty, missiles, and some other things. For who could believe that the Romans ever granted also to outsiders the privilege of carrying off booty from cities which they had themselves given over to plunder? Although those things are less accurately listed among no man's property, when, in truth, they belong to the state, or to those persons by whom they are conceded, who by means of donation grant those same things, or symbols representing

42. *Dig.,* XLI.i.1 and 5; *Inst.,* II.i.12.
43. *Dig.,* XLI.i.3.

them, to the first who lay hands upon them. Under the heading of no man's property come also those things which are treated as derelict by a former owner, in that he either intentionally throws them aside and does not desire them to be his any longer, so that he transfers his right to no one in particular; or else, when they have been lost by some accident, he neglects to recover them. Whence it appears that those things are not listed here which are thrown overboard for the sake of lightening the ship, or have been swallowed up by the sea after shipwreck, and are cast up upon the beach;[44] likewise things which are lost by travellers. For the owners retain their right to these things as long as they maintain the purpose of hunting for them again; and to the finders of such things no more is due by the law of nature than is the value of their effort in gathering them up and preserving them. And there is a certain flavour of piracy about those civil laws which appro-<52>priate to the fiscus, or to those who live along the coast, the goods of shipwrecked men even after they have been recognized by their owners.

29. A *corporeal thing* is an extended substance considered in a moral fashion. It is divided commonly into *mobile* and *immobile.* Things mobile are those which, not being attached to the soil, can be transported from place to place, like money, clothing, cattle, utensils, &c. First among immobile things is space, which is immobile both in its proper nature and from the beginning; and it can be divided into common space and proper space. By common space are designated public places, for example, markets, theatres, temples, military highways, &c. Proper space is that which perpendicularly hangs above or lies beneath the area of the possessor, upwards as well as downwards. Now since the areas of the terrestrial globe possess a spherical convexity, any one understands that perpendicular lines meet below in the centre of the earth, but diverge and expand upwards to infinity.[45] Thence it follows that I might lawfully build a structure above my ground, even

44. See *Dig.,* XIV.ii.2 §8, XIV.ii.8, and XLI.i.9, §8.

45. Cf. Weigel, *Arithmetische Beschreibung,* chap. viii, §6: "On account of his land, each householder [*Haußvater*] owns the space that forms a pyramid or a cone whose apex reaches to the centre of the earth, while its sides go through the estate's circumference and diverge more and more upwards, until they strike a corresponding part of the outermost sky as the bottom that closes the pyramid shape."

beyond the lunar heaven, if that were possible, unless perhaps the territorial limits of the inhabitants of the moon were in my way; so, likewise, I might lawfully dig down until I reached only as far as the centre of the earth, even if it were possible to go farther. For that which in respect to us lies beyond the centre belongs to our antipodes. Yet in certain places positive laws assign not to the private owners of estates, but to the fiscus, that which is found in an area below such a depth that it cannot be reached by the ploughshare. Perpendicular lines, however, drawn in both directions, upward and downward from the circumference of my area, are to be observed carefully. For, just as my neighbour cannot erect a structure which overhangs my area, although it does not rest upon my soil, but is upheld by beams which project transversely from his own house; so, in turn, I have no legal right to pass beyond the pyramidal surface* by building on the sides, unless, perchance, an agreement has been made on that point by special pact.

After space as a thing immobile from the beginning, follows the natural substance of earth, which here appears under the name of land. After earth follow those structures attached to the earth, together with all things which are made fast by nails and bolts. Here can be referred not only windmills whose foundations remain firmly fixed to the soil, despite the fact that at a breath of wind the structure itself can be turned around to all points of the compass; but also floating mills, as they are called, which, although they admit a change of location, must nevertheless be firmly fixed to the land by means of <53> anchors or stakes, so that we get any good out of them. These are not built for the purpose of being in motion like ships, but for the purpose of being fixed. Although herein positive laws or customs of places differ, as they do also in regard to ships, which, although they have been built for the purpose of being in motion, and properly supply the use of vehicles and not houses, are in some places classed among immobile things.

---

* According to the author's view, *proper space* has the shape of an inverted pyramid, whose apex is at the centre of the earth and whose base is at an infinite distance therefrom. The edges of this pyramid are formed by the lines which start at the centre of the earth and pass through the points upon the earth's surface which mark the corners of one's property.— *Tr.*

30. An *incorporeal thing*,[46] which is a mode considered as a subject in respect to pertinence, can be divided into *qualitative* and *quantitative*. To the former belong primarily *titles, authorities* or moral powers, *rights, aptitudes,* and other things of the same sort, if there are any. To the latter pertains *value,* which is sometimes of persons, and is then called *esteem,* sometimes of things and actions, and those either good for man, and called *worth,* or bad for man, in which case there is no special word, unless one be willing to call it, after the analogy of demerit, an unworth (*depretium*). <54>

46. By an *incorporeal thing* the Roman law understands a thing "which cannot be touched, and is such as consists of rights; for instance, an inheritance, an usufruct, or obligations contracted in any way," but also "rights attaching to urban and rustic estates, which are also called servitudes" (*Inst.,* II.ii.2–3). While this relates to property, Pufendorf extends the meaning to any kind of moral faculty.

A title is a moral attribute by which distinctions are marked among persons in communal life according to their esteem and status.

1. The distinction between titles and their effect.

1. TITLES have primarily a twofold distinction. Some mark directly the intensifying of the esteem of persons in communal life, or their peculiar qualities, and connote and suggest their status more clearly or more obscurely in proportion as that title is wont to be granted to one status or to several. The extremely copious crop of these titles which has sprung up in this present age among certain nations is wearisome to gather together here. Now some directly denote the status, or position in status, as well as indirectly connote the intensifying of esteem which is wont to adhere to that status and office. Such are any and all names of moral persons, which are here regarded not so much in themselves, in so far as they are notions representing to the intellect of another the status and office of a certain person; as in regard to the degree to which they denote the rights, authority, and function of a certain person as fixed by the imposition of men. Hence it is not for nothing that sometimes titles are fought for with the greatest ardour among men, because, when the title is denied, it is understood that a person is denied also the status, authority, right, and office, which that title is wont to express or to connote. <55>

Authority is an active moral power by which some person legitimately and with a moral effect is able to perform a voluntary action.

1. Perfect authority and imperfect.
2. Personal and communicable.
3. Division of authority on the principle of the object, where also sovereignty is treated of.
4. Authority over alien things.
5. The effect of authority.

1. AUTHORITY, as it here comes into consideration, is either *perfect* or *imperfect*. It is the former when he who interferes with its exercise violently and illegally does wrong (which happens when that authority does not depend upon his own will), and it is this authority which gives the injured party ground for action in a human court against that man. War takes the place of this authority among those who are not subject to a common judge, unless one subjects oneself to the other as a supreme judge. Authority is imperfect when, if a man has been prohibited illegitimately and violently from the exercise of it, he is, indeed, inhumanely treated, in such wise, however, that he has no ground for action in a human court, unless, perchance, the accident of necessity has supplied that which is lacking to his right. Thus, for example, he who violently keeps me from entering my own land, does an injury which gives me ground for action against him; but he who denies me innocent passage through his land, a passage which must be sought somewhere else only by a troublesome, roundabout route, does, indeed, act inhumanely, yet I can by no means for that reason bring an action against him in a human court of law; except that, for example, when

an enemy is attacking me from the rear, I have the right to escape even by cutting down the man who hinders me, in order to save my own life. The former can, moreover, be called the right to bring action, the latter, the aptitude.[1]

2. In the second place authority is either *personal* or *communicable*. The former is that which one cannot transfer legitimately to another. In that authority itself, however, not a few differences occur. For some authorities are so closely united with a person, that their employment cannot at all be exercised properly by any other person. Such is the authority of a husband over the body of his wife, which the laws will by no means allow him to exercise through a representative. Among certain others, moreover, although they cannot be transferred from us to another, the employment can be delegated for others to exercise, <56> in such wise, however, that they have all their authority [*autoritatem*] from those in whom the authority [*potestas*] roots and rests. Finally, certain authorities can be indirectly transferred by us to another, while we abdicate from them in his favour and resign them, as it were, into his own hands; with the proviso, however, that this transfer is to be confirmed by the authority [*autoritate*] of a superior. Of this kind was the authority [*potestas*] of a father according to the ancient Roman laws, which, although it arose naturally from the fact of generation by a personal incommunicable act, a father was able to transfer to another, when, after abdicating his authority, he gives over his son to be adopted by another. This adoption, however, had to be confirmed by the authority [*autoritate*] of the praetor or of the people, and from this authority alone did it borrow its force.[2] For in a state no private citizen is able to give to another the right of life and death over a free man, except it be that he who holds the rights of majesty authorizes it.

That authority is communicable which one can transfer to another legitimately, and, indeed, by his own proper initiative.

---

1. The distinction originates from Grotius; see *JBP,* I.i.4: "a right becomes a moral quality of a person, making it possible to have or to do something lawfully. . . . When the moral quality is perfect we call it *facultas,* 'faculty'; when it is not perfect, *aptitudo,* 'aptitude.' To the former, in the range of natural things, 'act' corresponds; to the latter, 'potency.'"
2. Cf. *Inst.,* I.xi.1.

3. For the rest, it is permissible to reduce most authorities, from the point of view of their object, to four species primarily; for they regard either *persons,* or *things,* and both of these as either *one's own* or *alien.* Authority over persons and actions which are one's own is called *liberty,* which can be understood from what was said above, where we treated of statuses. Authority over things which are one's own is called ownership, which likewise has been explained above. Authority over the persons of others is called *sovereignty,* whereby another can be enjoined legitimately and efficaciously to supply something, that is to say, so that another is under obligation not to resist my order or not to refuse the same. Now sovereignty is either *absolute* or *restricted.* It is the former, when its acts cannot be rendered void by any third person who is superior, nor be refused obedience on the part of those over whom sovereignty is exercised, upon the basis of some right which has been sought or retained by a pact entered into at the time when the sovereignty was established. It is the latter, when one or the other, or both of these, can take place. For one's sovereignty admits of restriction in a twofold fashion, either when, by him who has a superior sovereignty, the power of the one who exercises his sovereignty is checked, or those who obey are absolved from the obligation of taking specific orders; or when those who have put themselves under some one's sovereignty, have by a pact made for themselves the express reservation that they are unwilling to be bound by his orders in certain things. Such a restriction is not at all repugnant to nature. For, since he to whom sovereignty is given possesses otherwise no right over me, and therefore holds by my mere free will whatever authority he has over me, it is assuredly patent that it rests with me how far I care to admit his sove-<57>reignty over me. And yet these restrictions ought not to be of such a kind that they overturn the purpose of sovereignty and reduce it absolutely to nothing, or render unavailing the pact between the ruler and the ruled. And the ruled are not understood to have the authority to refuse certain commands of the sovereign, unless there be the privilege of appealing to arbitrators or to a judge, or of coming together into a council where they may have the right of considering the deed of the sovereign; on which topic I shall have more to say elsewhere.

In the second place, sovereignty is either *private* or *public.* The former belongs to persons as private individuals for the use of each as such. Species of this sovereignty are the authority of a father, the authority of a master or owners of slaves, the authority of husbands over wives, preceptors over pupils, guardians over wards, &c. Public sovereignty is that which comes to persons in their public capacity for the use of civil society. If this sovereignty be supreme in the state it has an adjunct authority, which men call *eminent,* over the persons and property of subjects, an authority which is stronger than any rights whatsoever of individuals, but one to be exercised only for the public safety.

4. Finally, by authority over the property of others, we refer to those rights which have been secured by some one over the property of another, through the concession of the owner or through a pact, proprietorship over the property remaining with the owner. Here belongs usufruct, which is the right or authority to use the things of another, without doing injury to their substance. It is a matter of legal tradition that usufruct can be established in any useful things whatsoever, except those which are destroyed by the very use, or those whose use consists in abuse. Here belong the servitudes of estates in the possession of the inhabitants of cities, and of those in the possession of the inhabitants of the country-side. Among servitudes of the latter class are commonly enumerated a road, a cartway, a highway, an aqueduct, the drawing of water, the driving of cattle to water, the right of pasturage, &c.; among those of the former class, the right of setting beams in a wall, of drawing off rain-water falling from the eaves of houses, of keeping a neighbour from building his house too high, and the like. On these servitudes those whose commentaries have illuminated the Roman law are to be consulted.

5. The effect of authority is for obligation to be brought upon another to perform something, and either to admit, or not to impede, actions which are exercised by the force of the same authority, and to enable one to confer upon a second party the faculty of doing or having something, that faculty having previously been lacking. <58>

*Right is an active moral power, belonging to
a person, to receive something from another
as a matter of necessity.*

1. Ambiguity of the word.
2. Perfect right.
3. What sort of a right inheritance is.
4. Mixed right.
5. Imperfect right.

1. In addition to those meanings by which the word right (*jus*) is used for
law, and for a complex or system of homogeneous laws, as also for a judicial
sentence, or the sentence of laws applied to deeds, for example, when we
say that the praetor renders judgement (*jus*), or the jurisconsult answers
on a point of law (*jus*), the most frequent use is to employ it for that moral
quality by which we properly either command persons, or possess things,
or by which things are owed to us. Thus, under the name of right comes
commonly authority over persons as well as over things which are our own
or another's; and that authority which regards things is in a special sense
called "the right in the thing." Concerning these words, however, this discrimination seems to be observed, namely, that authority rather suggests
the actual presence of the aforesaid quality over things or persons, but more
obscurely connotes, and leaves almost undecided, the manner in which one
has acquired it; while right properly and clearly indicates that the quality
has been acquired properly and is now also properly held. But because a
number of species of the above-mentioned quality rejoice in special designations, which that quality, whereby something is owed us, lacks, we have
preferred to mark this quality here in a peculiar way with the designation

of right (*jus*), under the proviso, however, that we do not at all wish to be bound to accept this word always within these narrow limits.

2. Now right is either *perfect* or *imperfect.* He who has infringed upon the former does a wrong which gives the injured party in a human court of law ground for bringing action against the injurer. To this corresponds on the other side perfect obligation in him from whom that which is owed us is to come. Therefore, I am able to compel him, when he refuses to pay this debt voluntarily, either by directing action against him before a judge, or, where there is no place for that, by force. Rights of that kind, when they have not yet been deduced with sufficient clearness, or are disputed by him whom they regard, are commonly called pretensions. <59>

3. Furthermore, under the rating of rights, it is customary to bring *inheritance,* the word being taken not for the property, but for a definite mode of pertinence. Here it must be noted, that inheritance upon the end of the life of him from whom it descends, has the force of plenary right against all who in any way whatsoever have temporary possession or administration of that property. For, by the death of the owner, plenary right to the goods devolves upon the heir, whether he be the heir according to the testament and desire of the former owner, or by the laws of the state. But, so long as the testator is still among the living, there belongs as yet to the heir, no matter in what way he be called to succession, no right which is valid against the testator and can keep him from being able still to make disposal of his goods to please himself, notwithstanding the fact that he has once signified his desire; unless, perchance, civil laws should order that all goods, or a definite part of the same, should altogether be turned over to certain persons, and should not grant the free making of a testament, just as in certain states the authority to dispose by will is allowed in the case of no goods at all, in other states only in the case of goods which have been acquired by one's own industry. In this case inheritance comes very close to the efficacy of a right, even before the death of the owner, to such a degree that he may not transfer to another, on any ground at all, to the injury of his necessary heir, a notable part of his own goods.

4. It is customary, of a truth, for a number of things to come commonly under the rating of rights, which, if we should care to speak accurately, are a sort of composite made up out of authority and right, both properly so

called, involving at the same time either things which presuppose obligation and honour, or something of that sort. Of this kind is citizenship, or the right of citizenship. For this embraces the faculty of exercising with full effect the acts of that state peculiar to its members, and the right of enjoying advantages which are its very own, positing an obligation toward that same state. Thus also civil dignities, for example, nobility and its grades, likewise the honours of learned men, embrace the authority of exercising definite acts proper to that dignity, and the right of enjoying the advantages of that order, to which advantages there adheres in addition a certain honour and intensification of esteem.

5. Now it is an imperfect right, which is called by some an aptitude,[1] when something is owed some one by another in such wise that, if he should deny it, he would, indeed, be acting unfairly, and yet the injured party would by no means be receiving a wrong which would furnish him with an action against the injurer; nor would he be able to assert for himself that right by force, except when necessity does not admit of any other means to secure his safety. In regard to all those things <60> which others owe us on the basis of some imperfect obligation we possess only an aptitude. This is a topic which we shall have to discuss at greater length below. Thus, I am able neither to compel another to do me benefactions, nor to bring an action for ingratitude against another, although, in very truth, he is doing wrong who neglects an occasion for doing a benefaction to others, or does not return the favour as best he can in requital for benefactions received. The following case also frequently occurs, namely, that some one may be able to admit rightly, indeed, that something has been given him by another, in such a way, however, that there is no obligation upon the latter to give it, nor has the former a perfect right to possess it, but merely the bare ability. Thus, for example, when a number of persons equally fit contend for some post, and no one of them has any peculiar right to it before another, he who has the authority to confer the post can select whom he will at pleasure, without leaving at the same time to those who have been rejected any cause for complaint. <61>

1. See bk. I, Def. 7, note 1.

*Esteem is the value of persons in communal life
in accordance with which they are fit to be placed
upon an equality with other persons, or to be
compared with them, and to be rated either
above or below them.*

1. Simple esteem.
2. Intensive esteem.

1. ESTEEM of persons in communal life is either *simple* or *intensive*. The former is considered either outside of states or inside the same. Simple esteem of a man outside a state consists in this, that he is regarded as the kind of person with whom, as with a man who observes the law of nature, it may be possible to have intercourse. Hence it is clear that all those who use commonly against any men whatsoever, or at least against those who are outside their own fellowships, the same licence which they do against beasts, have no such esteem. Such are states with powers unimpaired, if there be any of that kind, by which all outsiders are regarded indiscriminately as enemies, and especially if they themselves attack these outsiders of their own volition. Likewise, pirates, brigands, highwaymen, assassins, cut-purses, and others of that ilk; whom, unless they are on the way to give up that life of rapacity, it is no more appropriate for others to spare, than to spare wolves or other fierce monsters; nor are the offices of humanity to be shown them, by which, forsooth, they are made stronger to inflict damage upon others; nor should any confidence be put in a pledge which they have themselves given, the value of which in the minds of others is destroyed by the wickedness of their life.

Now that is simple esteem inside a state, by which each one is regarded at least as an ordinary and a complete member of the state, or as one who has not been declared a defective member of the state according to laws and statutes. And any and all free men and respected, or those who have not been branded by disgrace in process of law, rejoice in that esteem. Furthermore, this esteem in a state fails one either from mere status or from misdeed. The former is the case among slaves, who are not regarded as civil persons, or are understood not to have the standing of a citizen. For that slaves, at Rome, for example, were formerly regarded as no persons at all, and therefore lacked civil esteem,[1] is perfectly clear from the fact that they had nothing of their own and acquired nothing for themselves; from the fact that anything could be inflicted upon them by their masters with impunity; moreover, that, according to the law of Aquila, an action <62> was brought against some one else who had done harm to slaves, just as though he had injured the cattle of another;[2] that no kinship among slaves was recognized, nor was cohabitation among slaves regarded as marriage, exactly as is the case among beasts; that no credence was given in a court to their testimony even when under oath; and by other facts of this nature.

This esteem is lost as a result of antecedent misdeed, when some one, in accordance with the laws, because of a definite kind of misdeed (for not all misdeeds extinguish esteem in a civil sense), is branded with infamy; and this consists either in his being eliminated at the same time from natural existence; or utterly ejected from the state; or else retained, indeed, in the state, yet not as a complete member, but as a defective member, so that he rejoices, indeed, in domicile within the state, and in the common protection of the laws, but is excluded from public official duties and honourable associations, and is disdainfully deprived even of individual intercourse with all but the base. Such infamy can be invoked only by those in whose hands is the execution of the laws. By the judgement of private persons no one is brought into infamy in such a manner before that fact has been declared openly by a competent tribunal. And much less can any obligation

---

1. See *Inst.*, I.xvi.4: "Servus autem manumissus capite non minuitur, quia nullum caput habuit." [A manumitted slave loses no civil rights because he did not possess any.]
2. See *Dig.*, IX.ii.2.

of true infamy adhere by virtue of the mere undertaking of private citizens, without the authority [*autoritatem*] of the magistracy, because of failure to perform some act, any more than those private citizens are able by their own authority [*autoritate*] to grant effectively the rights of citizenship to any one. For it belongs to the same authority both to give, as it were, civil life, and to inflict civil death.

2. That is intensive esteem, in accordance with which persons equally honourable in civil capacity are preferred one above another, in proportion as one has a larger share than another of those things whereby the minds of others are commonly moved to show honour. Now honour, which corresponds to the intensification of esteem, is properly the signification of our judgement concerning the superiority of another; and therefore, in truth, honour is not in the person honoured but in the person who shows honour, although by a certain kind of metonymy, esteem also itself, or that which deserves honour, is denoted by this word, and, in a special sense, definite statuses which honour is wont to accompany, are called honours, because in due course these statuses are bestowed only upon those who surpass others in some point of superiority. That same esteem, as far as it produces in others the opinion of a special prudence and wisdom regarding the determination of practical affairs or of theoretical truths, is called authority [*autoritas*]. And as far as it suggests the widespread recognition of that superiority among large numbers of men, it is called reputation. After the analogy of passive natural qualities, one might call these not incon-<63>gruously passive moral qualities, because, as the former are understood to affect the senses, so the latter in a definite way affect the mind.[3] Now one's esteem is apt to be magnified primarily by notable achievements and a life led with great regard for the laws; by those things which are called the goods of the mind, with which belong to an excessive degree in the thinking of the ignorant, also the goods of body and fortune; by the condition of status, as that is conspicuous and splendid beyond other statuses; by moral position in status, for example, whether one be the first or the last in the

---

3. The allusion is to Erhard Weigel's idea of different kinds and degrees of esteem in analogy to the perceptible qualities of natural bodies. See *Arithmetische Beschreibung*, chap. 11 "Vom Unterscheid derer Moralischen Elementar-Qualitäten" (On the division of elementary moral qualities).

same association; by the condition of public service, that is, in proportion to the distinction of the functions with which that service is performed; by age, because, forsooth, experience and prudence are judged to come from advanced years; finally, by lineage or family, because it is commonly believed that something of the worth of ancestors is transmitted to their descendants; and by such other things as are here valued. <64>

Worth is the moral quantity or value of merchandise or things, and of actions that are good for man in communal life, in accordance with which they are fit to be compared one with another.

1. What should be regarded in appraising worth?
2. The worth of incorporeal things and actions.
3. Common worth and eminent worth, as also about money.

1. The most natural foundation of worth in things is their ability to exhibit some use in communal life.[1] Hence things which are utterly useless we are accustomed commonly to call worthless. Now the use of a certain thing is defined not merely from the circumstance that it truly helps to preserve or to make pleasurable our existence, but in addition that it contributes some pleasure or ornament, even though this be in the sole opinion of certain men. Upon such things the luxury and the lustfulness of men have generally placed an inordinate worth. Now in comparing things with one another according to their worth, various considerations are commonly regarded. For here to such a degree does the necessity of a thing, or the nobility of its application, fail always to have chief consideration, that, by a singular provision of nature, those things which our life cannot do without are rather accorded the less worth, because nature presents a bounteous supply of them. Therefore it is rarity which is principally effective here, and this

1. The subsequent discussion of the foundation of price is largely based on Grotius, *JBP*, II.xii.14; cf. *JNG*, 5, 1, §4.

98

is held in an esteem none too slight when there are brought from far distant places things to which frequently the desires of men are violently drawn. For most men value chiefly those things which are to be had in common with a few; and, on the contrary, that thing is held cheap, whatever it may be, which is seen among the household goods of any and everybody.

Determinately, moreover, worth is commonly recognized from usage or custom, that is, a thing is commonly estimated at as much as is very generally offered or given for it.[2] This is scarcely so that it does not have some range within which more or less can be demanded, except when the law has fixed the worth of a thing at a definite point. Now in common worth the labours and expenses which merchants undergo are customarily taken into account. There may also be certain estimable accidents of a thing because of which it may be legitimately bought or sold above or below the common price, <65> for example, because of a loss which is to follow, deferred profit, peculiar affection, or if it be bought or sold as a favour to another, when otherwise it was not to be bought or sold. These same accidents are customarily pointed out to the man with whom a bargain is being made about a thing, and can properly be imputed. That deferred or increased gain also which arises from delayed or anticipated payment of the worth can be computed. For the day of payment is a part of the price, and it means more to give something immediately than after a time; since, forsooth, in the meantime profit might have been secured therefrom. Also there is not a little in the consideration of the place where the merchandise is produced or the worth paid. For the same thing is valued differently in different places, and the value of money, or the interest, is not the same everywhere, and the rates of exchange for forwarding money are different in different places. Moreover, it very frequently happens that the worth of a thing changes, that is, goes either up or down, this change being due to the large or small supply of buyers, of money, of merchandise, or because of impending peace or war, and similar chance happenings.

---

2. Cf. *Dig.,* XXXV.ii.63: "The value of property should be estimated, not by affection nor according to any particular advantage attaching to it, but for what it can be disposed of at an ordinary sale"; about that, *JNG,* 5, 1, §9.

2. Now not merely corporeal things have their own worth, but also in-corporeal things and the very actions of men, in so far as they can bring to others some utility or delectation. About these, however, it must be noted that, by the laws of God and of man, some of them have been placed outside of human bartering, to such a degree that man ought not to fix a price for them, and ought not in turn to supply or perform these actions for a price. Of this kind are those sacred actions to which a certain super-natural effect has been assigned by divine will and institution, for example, the remission, through priestly absolution, of sins and of punishment due sins, the application of spiritual benefactions through the exhibition of the sacraments, and the like, in regard to which, if a man supply them to an-other for a price, he is said to be committing simony. Thus the judge cannot rightly sell for a price the justice which he ought to administer gratis. Thus the plyer of the dagger, or the poisoner, does not rightly for a price sell his services in murdering a man, or the harlot sell her favours, or the man who disseminates lies to the injury of others, his stilus, or the man who sets out to help unjust causes, or to overthrow just ones by the perjuries of others, his honour; and so others of this ilk. Furthermore, the worth of useful or delectable actions is commonly estimated in proportion to the necessity, utility, difficulty, or delicacy of the action, or the multitude or scarcity of the artisans or workmen, the large or small number of contractors available, and the abundance or scantiness of their means.

In incorporeal things utility and splendour are principally regarded. And in all things corporeal as well as incorporeal, worth is <66> determined in particular cases by law or custom, or by an understanding between the par-ties to the agreement.

3. Now worth can be divided into *common* and *eminent.* The former is that which inheres, from the foundations already mentioned, in all sorts of things which enter into exchange. Before the use of money was introduced, men knew no other worth beside that, and even yet some barbarians do not know of any. Hence business intercourse on the part of such men consisted merely in the simple exchange of things, and they were not able to let or to hire one another's services except in return for a thing. Now, indeed, that was a highly inconvenient method of fulfilling contracts between men, since it is not easy for any one whatsoever to possess things of that kind for

which another is willing to give his own in exchange, or which have the exact value of the other's property; and in states where citizens are distinguished by different statuses, it is necessary that there be several classes of men which cannot at all maintain life with that kind of exchange, or else are able to do so with extreme difficulty. Hence civil life was rude and simple as long as that was the sole method which obtained of exchanging goods; and those who use it to-day are far removed from the customs of the more civilized nations. Having considered, therefore, the inconveniences of exchange, most nations agreed with one another to set a certain eminent worth, as it were, upon a definite thing, according to which as a standard the worth of other things should be exacted, and in which that same worth should be, as it were, eminently contained; and all that to such a degree that this thing could be used in exchange for any thing at all, and could be conveniently employed for conducting business and fulfilling all kinds of contracts. For this end the nobler metals, gold, silver, and bronze, were judged to be the most suitable, forasmuch as their substance is not too common, is durable, and is not clumsy because of its bulk; although a state might destine other substances also for this use, which would have to be employed by citizens in the place of money. These metals, in quantities of a definite weight, and marked with definite figures, are called coins, upon which the administrators of states, or the mutual agreement of the users, set a fixed value. Nevertheless, that increase or decrease of worth which other things undergo because of scarcity or abundance, money also itself does not entirely escape, as a coin made of the same material and with the same weight is worth now more and now less; although that variation is not as sudden or as frequent as the variations of value among other things. From what has been said in passing can be explained also the controversy among the ancient Roman jurisconsults regarding worth.[3] Sabinus and Cassius, of their number, affirmed that other things besides money had worth, and therefore they included exchange under purchase and sale. Both of <67> these positions were denied by Proculus and Nerva, because otherwise it could not be made clear, when things had been exchanged, just which would appear to have been sold and which to have been given under

3. *Dig.,* XVIII.i.1, §1.

the name of price. For it seemed to them to be absurd that both things had
been sold and both given under the name of price. Now, in truth, both
views can stand in a certain way. The first can stand, indeed, if we say that
the purchase was made at common or eminent worth; and that the price
in exchange appears to be the thing which is given by the one who started
the business transaction. For he appears to be the purchaser who asks that
something be given him in exchange for some property of his own. And
the latter opinion can stand if only that in which eminent worth appears
is called purchase. <68>

Principles of human action are those things from which it springs and upon which it depends, and by which a human action is brought to completion.

1. Division of principles.
2. What is the end?
3. What is the occasion?
4. What is an order, and what counsel?
5. The means?
6. What the habit?

1. The principles of an action are either *disposing* principles, by which it is merely begun, or *efficient* and *deciding* principles, by which a human action is brought to act.

Disposing principles are: (1) *Moving* principles, in part *indirectly* and that either naturally, as the *end,* or morally, as the *occasion;* in part *directly,* and that likewise either naturally, as *inclination,* or morally, and that extrinsically, as *persuasion, bidding, incitation,* or intrinsically, as *obligation.* (2) *Directing* principles, either in a moral way, as *law,* or in a natural way, as *discernment.* (3) *Assisting* principles, as *means* which are natural, like natural power, and that which chiefly manifests itself here, *the faculty of locomotion;* or else moral things, as *authority.* Efficient or deciding principles are immediate causes from which a human action has its being, and are such either simply, as *will,* whose respect to the directing moral principle is called *obedience;* or else they are combined with inclination, as *habit.*

2. The end is a certain good which is sought for its own sake, or because it has something in itself for the sake of obtaining which the action is undertaken; and it is either an *ultimate* end or an *intermediate* one. The greatest variety is found in this latter class. The former is called the *summum bonum,* which is either *imaginary* or what seems the *summum bonum* to

the corrupted judgement of men, as pleasure of the body, wealth, honour, power, fame, &c., or *true* and agreeable to reason, as the pleasure and repose of the mind resulting from the practice of the virtues and the contemplation of things. To this is opposed the *summum malum,* which again is either *imaginary,* as poverty, diseases, servitude, contempt, &c., or *true,* as disquiet and anxiety of the mind arising from the practice of the vices and ignorance of things. The leading place, moreover, among principles is assigned to the end, because it must be known and valued before the rational agent bestirs himself to perform an action, and it is abhorrent to the nature of the rational agent to move, as it were, toward a vacuum, that is, to undertake anything without a predetermined end.

3. Occasion is that by which is offered to any one equipped with a natural faculty, in a convenient place and time, an object of some <69> action. For, in order that a person be said to have an occasion for acting, it is essentially required: (1) That the object of the action be present, or that it can be secured with only a little trouble. (2) That there be ready at hand a convenient place where we can be unhindered by others in our action, or, after the action, may not be affected by some inconvenience. (3) That a convenient time present itself, in which more necessary matters do not have to be performed, and in which we and others who concur in the action are conveniently situated. (4) That there be a natural faculty or power to act. It must be noted, nevertheless, here, that in common speech sometimes he also is said to have an occasion, who has merely the first three requisites, although he be deprived of the power of action. But, since the rest are of no avail when this last is wanting, you will call that an imperfect occasion. Moreover, occasion is like a very effective spur to undertake good as well as bad actions, and thus the common expression, that "occasion makes the thief," is all too true.

4. An order is that whereby there is pointed out to some one, by virtue of the force of command [*imperii*], an action which he ought to perform. An action of that kind upon orders, undertaken as by that person who is subject to the orders of another, satisfies the obligation toward the giver of the order; thus, if neither the giver of the order has exceeded the limits of his authority, nor the other exceeded the limits of the thing commanded, it reflects, as it were, its effects properly and directly not back upon the

executor, but upon the commander, and therefore it is imputed primarily not to the former but to the latter. But, truly, he who has no authority over another, so that he may deal with him as under his command [*imperio*], is left only the faculty of persuading or dissuading, whereby, through the introduction of reasons, and by explaining the nature of the effects, he strives to induce the other to undertake something or to call him back from the same. But, if we confirm or drag back a man who has already determined upon a destination, or one who is already equipped for action, we are said to be inciting and deterring. And although there is by no means the force of obligation attached to cases of advice and incitation, and so he who lends an ear to them, since he admits them freely, is altogether exercising his own action and not that of another; since, nevertheless, they have great force, especially when dexterously applied, to make others undertake or cease from an action, or to be confirmed or weakened in regard to their undertakings, this is the reason why the effect of an action is in part imputed also against advisers and inciters.

5. Means are employed by an agent to attain a certain end, when the will is unable to achieve that end directly by its own motion, so that some end may, as it were, approach the agent, or the agent approach some end. The following rule must be observed with regard <70> to the end: He who justifies the end is regarded also as justifying those means without which the end cannot be obtained, for otherwise nothing would have been done. From this it follows that, if the means be illicit or impossible, I am not held to that end which cannot be obtained without them. And from this it follows that evil ought not to be done in order that good may result, because no one is regarded as being bound to that good which it is not given him to attain without wrongdoing.

Now among natural means the principal one is the faculty of locomotion, whereby a man is able to move his body from one place to another, to make a partial change in the position of definite members, and to impress movement upon things. This faculty slavishly obeys the will, that is to say, it can never refuse to do its commands, but rather, as far as in it lies, it performs them, unless either the members themselves are restrained by some intrinsic or extrinsic impediment, or the object is not so proportioned that movement can be impressed upon it by that faculty.

6. The second book will be the place for treating of the emotions, the intellect, and the will. Here must be noted, concerning the will, merely that it is called habit, in so far as it is conformed and enabled to handle expeditiously the moral object, under difficulty of abstention from, or vehement inclination toward, that object. Immediately upon the presentation of the object the will so disposed is swept away toward it with so great an impetus that it can scarcely abstain from it. Also this habit is directed principally towards any moral actions, and this for the reason that good and evil are measured principally according to the free choice of the agent's action, and this free choice is commonly regarded to have been scarcely complete, unless one has acted in accordance with one's habit. And so it is that he, and he only, who acts well by habit, receives the name of a good man, and he who acts ill by habit, the name of a bad man; not the man who once or twice by some chance impulse, or because he could not do otherwise conveniently, has done some good, or who through thoughtlessness, or the violence of emotion, has done some evil.[1] Moreover, in a special way there are listed under the designation of virtues those habits by which the mind is so ordered that it acts, in regard to the objects which move it, according to the dictates of sound reason. Reason prescribes, furthermore, that the sight neither of good nor of evil, when brought before the mind, should disturb and shake it out of its tranquillity;[2] just as, on the contrary, we say that he is suffering from a fault whose mind is so affected by the appearance of an object, be it harsh or pleasant, that his tranquillity is, as it were, agitated by violent waves and broken up.

Obligation, law, and authority require a more detailed discussion. <71>

---

1. For the connection of free choice, habit, and virtue discussed here, the primary source is Aristotle, *Nicomachean Ethics* III, 1113b3–1114b25; cf. *JNG,* 1, 4, §6.

2. These remarks on *tranquillity of the mind* derive from the Stoic doctrine of ἀπά-θεια; see Cicero, *Tusculan Disputations,* trans. A. E. Douglas (Warminster, Eng.: Aris & Phillips, 1985), 4, 37, where we first find the term *perturbatum* [disturb(ed)] that is used here (4, 11: *perturbatio* as translation of the Greek πάθος). See also the Neo-Stoic references (Pierre Charron, *De la sagesse livres trois* [Bordeaux, 1601], bk. II, chap. vi, nn. 1–2) in *JNG,* 2, 4, §§11–12.

Obligation is an operative moral quality by which some one is bound to furnish, allow, or endure something.

1. Obligation, congenital and adventitious,
2. Of equality and inequality,
3. Perfect and imperfect,
4. Perpetual and temporary,
5. Mutual and non-mutual,
6. Perfectly mutual and imperfectly mutual; where also of the obligations of princes toward their subjects.
7. What sort of obligation lies upon the promisor because of gratuitous promises?
8. How many kinds of promises are there?
9. Valid promises must be expressed in words about time present.
10. No valid promise is made by one against his will.
11. A pure promise and a conditional promise.
12. How do obligations perfectly mutual, or pacts, stand in mutual good faith?
13. What should be judged of partly fulfilled pacts?
14. What sort of efficacy comes from civil rights?
15. Obligations can be contained even in the sole law of nature.
16. Whence comes their validity?
17. No one is under obligation to himself.
18. Obligations which are to be contracted upon both sides require agreement.
19. On error in pacts.
20. To whom can a person obligate himself?
21. Should faith be kept with him who compelled me by unjust violence to make a pact?
22. Are pacts valid between enemies?
23. On tacit pacts.
24. On vows.
25. Can a man by his own act put somebody under obligation to a third party?
26. Pacts of societies.
27. By what kind of pacts are societies established?

1. With this definition agrees that common one of the jurisconsults in which they define obligation as a bond of right whereby we are bound by the necessity of furnishing something.[1] For it places, as it were, a kind of

---

1. *Inst.,* III.xiii: "An obligation is a bond of law by which we are reduced to the necessity of paying something in compliance with the laws of our state." In contrast to that original meaning limited to (monetary) debts and property, Pufendorf's concept of obligation as an *operative moral quality* embraces any kind of moral or legal bond. See Jean Barbeyrac's note to *JNG,* 1, 6, §5, in *Le droit de la nature et des gens* (Amsterdam,

moral bridle upon our liberty of action, so that we are unable rightly to
turn in a direction different from that to which obligation leads; although
no obligation has the natural efficacy of so binding the natural liberty of
our will that, at least in fact, it cannot go in another direction. Now obligation can be divided on the principle of origin into *congenital* and *adventitious.* The former exists in all men by virtue of the fact that they are such,
from the moment of birth onwards, showing itself to the full as soon as
through advancing years they begin to understand its force and to be able
to modify their acts by the use of reason. In this class there is listed that
obligation of all men towards God as the Supreme Lord of this universe,
by the force of which obligation we are bound to recognize and to venerate
His rule and to observe the laws which He has given us;[2] likewise, the obligation of all men towards all men whatsoever as such, by virtue of which
they ought to employ the law of nature in their relations with one another,
and to live a social life.[3] Adventitious obligations are those which are voluntarily assumed by men after birth, or else are enjoined by the command
[*imperio*] of a superior, or by law.

2. In the next place obligation, in consideration of the subjects, is either
of *equality* or of *inequality.* We call the obligation of inequality that which
makes him to whom something is owed by us in virtue of it our superior,
and brings some authority or sovereignty upon us. Such is subjection, or
that obligation by which a man is bound to furnish what has been enjoined
upon him by another in virtue of his sovereignty. This can be divided into
universal obligation, whereby every man whatsoever is bound to yield obedience to God, and particular obligation, whereby definite men are beholden
to definite men. This again is either public, whereby one is subject to the
public sovereignty of some one; or private, whereby we are placed under the

---

1706), vol. I, p. 81: "L'Auteur rend générale la définition des *Institutes,* qui ne regarde
proprement que les paiemens, ou tout au plus les engagemens où l'on entre de son pur
mouvement, par rapport à autrui." [The author generalizes the definition of the *Institutes*
that properly regards only payments or at most such engagements that are considered to
be voluntarily undertaken toward another.]

2. The obligation toward God which, according to Pufendorf, is fundamental to the
force of any other kind of obligation is treated at length elsewhere. See *Off.,* 1.4, "Of
the Duty of Man towards God, or concerning Natural Religion."

3. See bk. II, Observ. 4.

private sovereignty of some one. Both are either limited, as the subjection of a wife, a son, a ward, a hired servant, &c.; or unlimited, as the subjection whereby citizens are bound to the state,[4] and complete personal servitude, <73> whereby a man is bound to devote his profitable actions wholly to the use and pleasure of another. Both these obligations, however, yield precedence to the obligation towards God, and even to the obligation towards the state, when it is impossible to satisfy both at the same time.

3. In respect of the efficacy, moreover, which it exerts in human society, obligation is either *perfect* or *imperfect*. To the former, in the case of a second person to whom it pertains, corresponds perfect right, whereby he is granted an action against us in a human court of law; to the latter, in the case of a second person to whom it pertains, corresponds only an imperfect right, whereby he is not granted an action against us in a human court of law. Why that results we shall set forth a little later on.

4. Furthermore, as regards duration, certain obligations are *perpetual,* certain others *temporary.* The former cannot be done away with as long as the persons in whom they inhere exist. Such is the congenital obligation towards God and towards all men whatsoever as such, an obligation which no man can put off as long as he is a man. For, although, when another does not observe the law of nature towards me, I myself am not bound to observe it towards him, but may use force upon him, and therefore the law of war; and that because this obligation is mutual, and when it is broken on one side it is no longer binding upon the other, wherefore the exercise of that obligation, at least in regard to most of the commands of the law of nature, whereby it is commanded that duties to the other party be performed, is suspended (as we shall show at greater length in Book II); nevertheless, this stands forever, namely, that, as soon as consideration for our own safety allows, we ought to be ready once more to observe the law of nature and to cultivate peace with him.[5] This is the nature of all obligations

---

4. Strictly speaking, civil subjection is not unlimited either but bound to *peace and common security* (*JNG,* 7, 2, §13), an end requiring a stronger sovereignty than private subjection and including the right of life and death (*JNG,* 7, 6, §1).

5. Cf. Hobbes, *Leviathan,* chap. 15: *"The laws of nature oblige in conscience always, but in effect then only when there is security.* The laws of nature oblige in *foro interno;* that is to say, they bind to a desire they should take place: but in *foro externo;* this is, to the

which result from commands or affirmative laws, that they bid men be ready to perform their acts as often as there is occasion to put them into operation; but to cease from putting them into operation when either there is no object to receive them, or the object suffers from an evil disposition, or when a closer obligation leaves no place for one which is more remote; just as here the care of my own safety does not at all allow me to take account of the safety of him who is coming to attack it unjustly.

Now among adventitious obligations there can be listed here the debt of honour and gratitude on the part of children towards parents, which in due course does not cease as long as the latter are among the living, although it might appear that cases could arise in which that obligation would utterly disappear; that is to say, when parents, without any compulsion of necessity, cast aside all care for the child born to them and expose it destitute of all human aid; or when, in later years, they shamefully neglect its education, or are otherwise <74> heartlessly proceeding to destroy its well-being. For that obligation on the part of children proceeds primarily from the law of gratitude, and this regards antecedent benefactions. And, indeed, neither can parents impute to the offspring that bare act of generation, because, forsooth, in that act they were scarcely seeking anything else than their own pleasure; nor can a mother, although in gestation and delivery she has suffered great discomforts, be regarded as having done a benefaction if she brings forth a child merely to cast it away, or, by neglecting its education, to allow it to contract base habits. And I am regarded as remitting the debt of returning gratitude in the case of him with whom I myself strive to destroy the favour of my benefactions by harsh treatment.

But the bond of marriage has by the divine positive law this one peculiarity, namely, that, as long as the essence of the conjugal pact has not been violated, it cannot be dissolved, like other temporary obligations, by the consent of both parties. For otherwise it has this in common with other pacts, namely, that, if its essential feature be violated on one side, the other is no longer bound to abide by it. But the essential feature of marriage consists in this, namely, that the husband grants to the wife the right to his

_____

putting them in act, not always." For Hobbes—in contrast to Pufendorf—the latter is not possible until the erection of a commonwealth (ibid.).

body, and the wife to the husband, and she, besides, to no one else. When this feature has been violated even the divine law grants the right of divorce.[6]

Temporary obligations are those which can be ended while the persons in whom they inhere are still alive. How that may take place will be set forth below.

5. As for respect of obligations, whereby they correspond to one another, obligation is either *mutual* or *non-mutual.* It is non-mutual when one person, indeed, is bound to furnish something to another, in such wise, however, that in that other person to whom something is owed, there is no obligation corresponding to it, and binding him to furnish an equivalent. Such is the obligation of men towards God, whereby they, indeed, owe Him absolute obedience, but He is in no way bound to furnish them anything in return for that obedience, as on the force of some obligation which devolves upon Him from outside. For whatever He furnishes men comes from His own gratuitous benevolence.

Now of the obligations which obtain mutually among men, none seems to be of the character of the foregoing, and that because it is repugnant to the natural equality of men among one another for one to be bound to another in such a way that the latter is in his turn bound to the former in no way at all. That all men should, indeed, in actual fact be equal as far as their adventitious states and authority go, nature does not intend, as long as she destines man to life as a social being, and this kind of life cannot exist at all with that sort of equality <75> in all respects. Nevertheless, because the actual inequality of men among one another (for example, that Gaius is superior, Titus inferior, that Seius is prince, Sempronius subject) exists as the result of the mutual convention and the positive laws of men, it cannot be presumed that one man has been willing to bind himself to another in such a form that the other in his turn is bound to him in no way, at least by a different species of obligation. Add also that society could not exist unless each and all were united in a mutual bond.

6. Mutual obligation is that to which another obligation corresponds in that person to whom something is owed thereby. This again is either *im-*

6. See especially Deuteronomy 24:1–3; Matthew 5:31–32, 19:1–9.

perfectly mutual or *perfectly mutual.* That obligation is imperfectly mutual to which, indeed, an obligation in the second party corresponds, but one of a different kind; as, in case a merely imperfect obligation be referred to a perfect obligation. This comes about primarily from a twofold cause; either when the adventitious inequality of the persons between whom the obligation is found to exist is so great, that one has supreme sovereignty over the other; or when one person is himself unwilling to bind the other with an obligation equal to his own. The former is the case in obligations which lie between an absolute prince and his subjects, or between the state and a citizen. Their nature is of the kind that, in the citizen, indeed, or in the subject, the obligation is perfect, but in the prince and in the state it is no more than imperfect. There are, indeed, those who say that an absolute prince cannot be under obligation to a subject at all, or the state to a citizen, for the reason that subjects or citizens, by the very circumstance that they are such, resolve their will into the will of the prince or the state, in such wise that the will of the former is comprehended in the will of the latter, and therefore is the same as the latter;[7] but, now, no one can be under obligation to himself, because, since the one obligated and the one obligating are the same, and the one obligating could free the one who is under obligation, it would be in vain for a man to be under obligation to himself, since he could free himself from obligation according to his own pleasure, and he who can do that is in actual fact already free.

Of a truth, this reasoning, otherwise acute enough, reaches no other conclusion than that an absolute prince as such cannot contract with his subjects an obligation holding good in a human court of law, concerning the mode of sovereignty, so that, forsooth, this same prince remains absolute. However, it does by no means reach the conclusion that an absolute prince can in no wise be bound to exercise sovereignty aright, nor to anything else to which he has perchance agreed. To make that appear more clearly, it must be observed that he who subjects himself to a prince or a state in such wise that it has supreme sovereignty over him, does by that very fact recognize in it <76> the authority to make determinations, as it

7. The reference is to Hobbes, *Leviathan,* chap. 17 (at the end); cf. also the idea of authorization and representation, *Leviathan,* chap. 16 (at the end).

wills, concerning the public welfare, in which the welfare of individuals also is contained, so that he does not reserve to himself any authority in the matter. That is why there cannot be a case where the prince can contract with a subject any special obligation about those matters which properly concern the supreme sovereignty and its exercise. For it is implied that he has supreme and absolute sovereignty, and yet is entering upon a special obligation with his subjects, and one which would give ground for action among men, concerning the manner of exercising supreme sovereignty. For, if an obligation of that kind should rest upon any prince with this effect, namely, that an action could be brought against him by the citizens, or coercion applied, it is altogether obvious that such a prince does not have supreme sovereignty. The obligation, therefore, which obtains between a prince and his subjects about matters pertaining to the supreme sovereignty, stands in this wise, namely, that, upon the subjects, indeed, there rests the perfect obligation of doing the bidding of the prince, and that the prince has ground for action against the disobedient, and the authority to bring them to order. But upon the prince, by that very fact, as long as he bears himself as such, there rests the obligation of caring for the public welfare in the way in which he has promised though only an imperfect one. For it binds only by force of the divine and natural law, but not as by the force of some civil law, because, forsooth, there exists no court of law among men where an action can be brought against a prince of this kind, and the subjects themselves are not competent to take cognizance of and pass judgement upon the actions of a prince. And therefore the prince is under obligation to his subjects in regard to the exercise of the supreme sovereignty, but in this wise, namely, that if he use it less well, he sins against God, indeed, as the avenger of the law of nature; nevertheless, because a human court fails to exist, and because his acts are not liable, his subjects are incompetent to bring action against him, no matter if he may also have pledged his faith with an oath.

Thus, even if a prince yield a part of his supreme authority, or promise not to use it, still, unless he either resign that authority into the hands of another, with the effect that the latter have the right of maintaining it against any and everybody, even against the prince himself, and of repressing any and every one who is about to disturb it; or else the prince give to a council of peers, or the people, the faculty of bringing him to terms, if he should act against them, he will be sinning against the law of nature, indeed, if he should usurp that authority again, and yet he cannot be prevented by his subjects from doing so, and those acts of his will be valid which in this case are undertaken *de facto*. For that something in the state should have the effects of a <77> civil right depends entirely upon the pleasure of the supreme authority. It is no less true, that, if a prince should have some other business with a subject, which does not depend upon the force of supreme sovereignty, for example, if he should borrow money from a subject, or contract for another's services, the obligation is imperfect. And this is so, not so much by virtue of the power of eminent domain extending even to this right which has been acquired by the subject on the ground of a pact with the sovereign himself, by which power he can remove this very obligation if he should see fit to do so in the public interest (for by the very nature of the transaction it is understood in such a case that the prince has given up his right to eminent domain, so as not to have nothing done between them); as because of the absence of a court of law and of a superior authority among men. But if, nevertheless, princes, as frequently happens, grant their subjects action against themselves in their own court in matters of that kind, this action does not exist by virtue of the force of civil law, but by the force of natural equity, as if it were impossible for him not to be willing to pay that which he owes, when once his obligation is recognized; and therefore the purpose of that action is not to compel the prince to pay what he owes, but to let the subject show clearly that the prince has put himself under obligation to pay it to him.

The same must be judged of the obligations between parent and children, and master and slave, in regard to those things wherein civil laws leave the former absolute authority, and do not grant the latter action against the former in a civil court of law. Thus, for example, if a master has promised a slave a definite reward for some extraordinary service, and one which is not included under the object of obligation which flows from the nature of his status, if, now, the master should not pay the reward, he is sinning against a law of nature; but, since the civil law renders a slave herein no assistance, he will have no action against his master in a human court of law. Moreover, as for the pronouncement of Roman laws, namely, that a stipulation is of no avail, if he who is subject to your authority should stipulate for something from you, or you for something from him,[8] adding, as the reason therefore, that no one can be put under obligation to himself or transact business with himself; and that the master and the slave, the father and the son, in those things which are matters of right and can be acquired by the master and the father, perform the function of a single person; it does not follow from all this, that, between father and son, master and slave, there is no obligation, at least a natural one. But reference is here made only to a civil obligation, which could not arise between those persons in matters of this kind, because these same civil laws herein denied a son action against his father, and the son of a household (aside from what the special favour of laws had granted), or the <78> slave, had nothing of his own except such private property as the liberality of the former had granted him, which the former could rightfully take away, if, perchance, he had need of it; and therefore it was of no avail to seek to acquire for himself a right to those things by stipulation.

7. An imperfectly mutual obligation arises in the second way, when a person, while binding himself to furnish something to another, does not demand that this latter be put in his turn under obligation to him in the same way. This takes place principally in the case of gratuitous promises. For when I promise something to another, I myself contract the obligation to supply it, and this obligation gives the other ground for action against me even before a judge, when the stipulations have been ratified by civil law.[9] It is no less true that, when those stipulations are valid by the mere law of nature, I am able to demand the fulfilment of his promise from the one who made it, in that way in which I have a right by the law of nature alone, at least where it is clear that the man who made the promise is fraudulently and insolently trying to slip out of it, and I have based my calculations upon that promise, and would suffer some loss in consequence. However, the obligation of the man who makes a promise to keep his promise, and the obligation of the other to show his gratitude, are not equivalent,

8. *Inst.,* III.xix.6.

9. The Roman institute of *stipulation* consisted of a formal verbal promise to furnish something that gave the promisee ground for action against the promisor; see *Inst.,* III.xv (Concerning Verbal Obligations).

even if the promise also should stand by the mere law of nature and should not furnish action on the basis of the civil law. The reason is that when some one promises anything gratis, he indicates thereby that he does not desire to call upon the other one to furnish him any equivalent thing, as though it were an indebtedness, and for that reason he is not shaping his actions with a view to the other's gratitude, and, if that should fail, he is not suffering any injury or insult, as did he who had faith in the promiser as though he were an honest man, and arranged his plans with reference to the other's promises. Hence, although by the law of nature I can properly demand from him who has deceived me with his promises, at least the amount of injury which I have received therefrom; I do not by any means have the same right, if the hope which I had conceived of another's gratitude has deceived me; and that because, as has been said above, I have, as far as I was concerned, relieved him of that very obligation, and I have left it entirely to his sense of honour.

8. As for the rest, rightly to understand the nature and effect of a promise, it should be known that there are constituted three grades of speaking about the conferring upon another of those good things which are under our authority, or, we think will be; to wit, bare assertion, imperfect promise, and perfect promise.[10] It is bare assertion when we disclose our intention about the future, such as our intention now is, without the obligation of persevering in that inclination; for example, <79> if I should say to some one: "If I should feel the same way a month from now, I will give you a horse." From an assertion of that kind there is no effect. For it does not bring with it any obligation to persevere in the same inclination, and when the time mentioned has elapsed, or another added condition appears, it is altogether the first person's full right to decide whether he cares now to make a valid promise on the subject, or to furnish the thing referred to, or does not care to do so.

An imperfect promise is that whereby a person defines his inclination at some future time to furnish something freely to another, and accompanies that expression of inclination with a sign sufficient to indicate the necessity

10. The distinction of *three grades of speaking* and the respective *grades* of the validity of promises is taken from Grotius, *JBP,* II.xi.1–4; cf. *JNG,* 3, 5, §§5–7.

of persevering therein, and yet in such wise, that he to whom the promise is made, is granted as yet no proper right to demand the thing promised. This appears to be principally the case when he to whom something is promised, has, by reason of the authority of the latter over him, no action in a human court of law against the one who makes the promise; as if a master should promise something to a slave, a father to a son, a prince to a subject. The same is likewise true, when, in states where stipulations have been ratified by the civil law, a certain formula, or regular proceeding pre-scribed by law, has been omitted in making the promise. There the prom-isor, by virtue of natural equity, indeed, is bound to keep his promise, and yet, on account of the defect in customary usage, cannot be compelled by civil action to do so.

To this class also they refer a promise conceived in the following way: For example, "I have the intention of giving you a hundred pieces of gold, and I ask you to believe me." For in this case the first party confers properly no right upon the second, and he is bound to furnish what he has promised rather by virtue of the rule of truthfulness than that of justice.

Finally, a perfect promise is that whereby a person defines his inclination at some future time to furnish something freely to another, and accom-panies that expression of inclination with a sign sufficient to indicate the necessity of persevering therein, in such wise that the other party is also granted the right to demand the thing which has been promised.

9. It must be noted, furthermore, about promises, that right to the thing promised is transferred to a second party only by words regarding the pres-ent or the past, but not by words regarding the future, unless, in addition to the words, there are added also signs which declare that the promisor, in speaking of the future, wishes his words to avail also for the present and completed transfer of right. For otherwise, if any one should say, for ex-ample, "To-morrow I will promise," or, "To-morrow I will donate," he shows plainly that he has <80> not donated as yet, and so his right remains to him undisturbed the whole of to-day, as also to-morrow and thence-forward, unless, in the meantime, he has actually given it. For since by that kind of promise of gratuitous donation no piece of property has been, or is to be, acquired, he is not reckoned as having fully determined his desire as yet, or as being desirous of transferring his right to another, so long as

he is still speaking in the future tense, and that, because, in the meantime, either his state of feeling may alter, or a chance event intervene, which will give him reason for being unable to part conveniently with his property, or, finally, the reason in the second person for making the promise may cease to exist. And therefore, as long as he does not transfer a right in the present (for the present transfer of the thing is not required), he is understood to be yet deliberating, and to be reserving to himself the authority to change his mind; just as in the case of a testament the testator does by no means transfer to the heir a right in the present, but is always regarded as having added the clause, "Let this man be my heir, unless I change my mind before I die." And yet he who vainly deludes others by an empty hope of this kind, incurs the reproach of inconstancy. However, he who says, for example, "I give," or "I have given something which is to be had tomorrow," signifies that he is to-day giving the right to have a thing to-morrow, or he is to-day transferring to another the right to something, the transfer of which ought to take place on the morrow. And it makes no difference that, by a common habit of speech, practically all promises are expressed in words which de-note future time, if you consider the grammatical form of the words. For this has come to be customary because the giving over of the thing promised follows generally after an interval, nay more, that in which the intention of giving is manifested at the very same time that the thing itself is pro-duced, can scarcely be called a promise (since, forsooth, here it would ap-pear that either there had been no obligation, or else it has expired again immediately upon its being contracted); and, in truth, men commonly say that they "have" a thing only when they have acquired its possession. And therefore the proper sense of such words as occur in a perfect promise, as, for example, "Within six days I will give you one hundred pieces of gold," is this: "I give you now the right of having and demanding from me at the time stated one hundred pieces of gold, and at the same time I bind myself to turn them over to you at the expiration of the interval of time which has been fixed." It is apparent from this, that the words referring to future time in promises, as especially the word "give," regard either an obligation which is yet to be contracted, and by these words neither the thing itself nor the right to the thing is transferred; or else they regard a transfer of a thing which is to be made thereafter, the right to which thing is either now transferred, <81> or has been transferred, and these words do not prevent this from being a perfect promise.

10. Furthermore, in order to make a promise perfect, there is required not merely the willingness of the one who makes the promise, but also the willingness of him to whom the promise is made. For, where the latter is lacking, or where the second party refuses to accept the thing, even if I had made the promise under oath, complete right to the thing which is my own remains with me; and this for the reason that I was unwilling to thrust upon another, who did not want it, the thing which was my own, and that I based the whole transaction upon the condition, "If, indeed, he be pleased to accept it." Now I did by no means wish simply to renounce my own right, or to transfer it to another, or to treat as derelict that which I offered to a man who refuses it; for the cause that moved me to make the gift was in him alone, and not in other persons as well. But if, in truth, the will to accept on the part of the second party, to whom something is promised, has concurred with the will of the one who makes the promise (and this is understood to be the case, even if the second party had previously sought to have the thing promised him, and did not afterwards revoke it), then it is understood that at this same moment the right to the thing promised has passed from the latter to the former, and therefore the promisor has no longer the right not to fulfil his promise to the promisee against the will of the latter, and that for the reason that in this way his own right would be denied the latter, and his calculations would be upset, which the promisor himself wanted him to base upon his own good faith.

11. Now a promise is either *pure* or absolute, by which a man obligates himself to furnish something gratuitously to a second person, without supposing any thing, event, or deed; or else, *conditional,* which supposes a definite thing, fact, or event as far as concerns the bare adessence, and when this thing, fact, or event has been denied, there is no promise.[11] I say "as far as concerns the bare adessence," by which I mean that the bare supposition is made, that we will supply something, if this or that has taken place, or if this or that has been done by somebody, or has not been done.

---

11. The latter takes its bearings from the Roman *stipulation . . . under a condition* (*Inst.,* III.xv.4–6); cf. *JNG,* 3, 8 (On the Conditions of Promises).

For otherwise, if something of that kind be supposed as a cause which deserves the promise, or gives one a right to demand it, or if the promisor should make some express stipulation from the promisee, if only the mode of acceptation be in the highest degree definite, or if the supposition be a recognition, it will be a pact.

As for the rest, the obligation of conditional promises is in a state of pending efficacy, until the existence or non-existence of the condition be recognized by the promisor. When that has taken place obligations acquire the force of pure promises. But when the condition does <82> not appear, there is also no obligation, forasmuch as the obligation depended upon the condition. Thus, if a man has promised that he will furnish something, if some other person agree, he will not be held to his promise until that other person's willingness is definitely ascertained. But if, in truth, the matter is not now in the power [*potestate*] of the promisor, but may sometime be, the promise will be in a state of pending efficacy, because then the promise ought to be regarded as having been made on the condition, "If the thing come within his power." But if, in truth, the condition whereby the thing may come within the power of the promisor, be itself also a matter of power [*potestativa*], that is, if it be in the power of the promisor, that that condition come within his power, the promisor will be bound to do whatever is proper in order to have the condition fulfilled.

It must be observed, furthermore, that promises are unavailing and null, when the condition under which the promise is made has been put under our own mere pleasure, for example, "My slave will be the guardian of my children, when I am pleased to give him his liberty"; "You will have ten pieces of gold from me, when it pleases me." For this is just the same as if I had said: "It pleases me to give you nothing now, but when it has pleased me, then, and not until then, you will have it"; and yet I am not binding myself that it will please me at some time. Hence the jurisconsults were right when they said: "That which is in our power [*potestate*] ought not to be conferred on a chance."[12] Thus also an impossible condition makes no promise; for it is equivalent to the negation of a promise. When the mention of a place is added in a promise it involves the length of time necessary

12. *Dig.*, XVIII.i.7; XLIV.vii.8; XLV.i.17,108, §1.

to enable one to arrive conveniently at the place where some one has undertaken to fulfil his promise. Moreover, the addition of a definite time
brings it to pass that the effect of the obligation is not exerted until that
time has elapsed, or that the effect of the obligation cannot be demanded
except when the appointed day has arrived.

12. A perfectly mutual obligation is one which arises from the agreement
of two or more persons concerning the furnishing to one another of definite
things or actions, in such wise that on both sides there is an obligation of
the same kind regarding one another mutually. Obligations of that kind
are commonly listed under the name of pacts, or contracts, although by
the latter word are generally signified those which have to do with things
and actions which become matters of commerce. Furthermore, since these
obligations regard matters which have been agreed upon by both sides and
presuppose reciprocal good faith, it is readily seen that if one party has
broken its pledged good faith the other party also is no longer bound, and
therefore, he who does not stand by pacts already violated by the other party
is not perfidious. For one and the same covenant has separate heads different <83> from each other in the mode of the condition, as though it had
been expressed, "I will do thus, if the other also shall have done what he
promised"; and, indeed, regularly in such a way, that, if this same pact,
perchance, should contain several heads, when one head has been violated,
the whole pact is dissolved, unless it has been especially agreed that the other
heads will be none the less valid, even if, perchance, one head or another
has been violated. Here, however, it must be noted that most covenants
have been conceived in such wise, that one party is bound to do his part
before the other does his. Herein, although the former should do his part
on the condition that the other also would afterwards do the equivalent,
nevertheless his obligation thus far is absolute, because having trusted to
the other's good faith before a part of it was exhibited, he is altogether
bound to maintain his own good faith, unless, perchance, after the covenant
had been entered into, manifest signs should appear that the other party,
after receiving the thing, would deceive him. The obligation, moreover, of
the one whose duty it is to fulfil his promise second, depends in this wise
on the fulfilment by the former of his promise, so that, when the fulfilment
does not take place, this obligation immediately expires, and there arises

for him the right, if he so desires, of compelling the other by force to live
up to his pact. But if, however, the things are to be presented mutually in
succession and in portions, immediately upon one party ceasing to continue
to present that which is due, the other also will no longer be bound to
proceed further.

13. Now under these circumstances what will become of the things which
have been already in part supplied? Will both parties have just as firm right
to them also, as if the pact had been brought to full execution? Here we
feel that the question as to which of the two breaks the half-completed pact,
must be carefully considered. For if the other person should be the first to
violate a covenant which had been entered into with me, I, indeed, retain
full right to the part of the things already received; moreover, I am able,
should I so desire, to compel the other either to make up the remainder
according to the agreement, or else to furnish the worth of the same; and
the other has by no means this right against me. For the well-known principle obtains: As often as the fulfilment of the condition is prevented by
him to whose interest it was that it should be fulfilled, it is regarded as
though the condition had been fulfilled,[13] and if, afterwards, due to repentance, he should wish to continue the pact, I myself am not compelled to
accept it, seeing that the breach of the pact which he has once made, has
entirely absolved me from all obligation towards that same pact. The same
principle also holds, if that which I have received should be worth more
than that which I have furnished to the other party, in which case also I am
not bound to restore that which exceeded the <84> value of my own piece
of property. For he who was the first to break the pact is himself regarded
as removing the obligation upon me, and of being unwilling to furnish
anything further upon the basis of that pact. Thus, for example, if any one
should hire my services for a year and pay me my wages in advance, and
afterwards, before the expiration of the year, should dismiss me without
any fault on my part, I am not bound to restore to him the value of my
services during the remainder of the period.

14. Now the force of obligations arises either from the law of nature or
from the civil law. Also concerning obligations of the latter kind, indeed,

13. *Dig.,* L.xvii.161 and XXXV.i.24.

it is beyond controversy that the efficacy of the same in bringing to bear
upon both sides the necessity of furnishing that about which the agreement
had been made, ultimately resolves itself into the force or the faculty of
compulsion which inheres in that which wields the supreme authority in
the state; and therefore, because those things which are owed on the basis
of obligations which are legitimate in the civil law must necessarily be furnished, the ultimate reason in that kind of obligations is, that if men should
be disinclined to do this, they are compelled to do it by the authority of
the state. For from this very cause states have ratified, by their own laws
also, the majority of covenants in which otherwise there inhered the force
of obligation on the basis of the law of nature, and on the ground of their
own law they have granted action to the contracting parties, so that, if,
indeed, a man should be disinclined to furnish what he owed in due respect
to the law of nature, it might be possible for him to be compelled by the
force and authority of the magistracy. For, unless those covenants should
be kept inviolate, business intercourse between citizens, and a peaceful society, could not exist, and it did not appear that adequate provision had
been made for peace by leaving herein each man to his own conscience,
especially the common run of mankind, whose sense of the honourable is
dull, and yet the majority in states is composed of this common run. Now,
although in almost all covenants confirmed by the civil law, there inheres
a force of obligation deriving from the divine law also, and therefore, even
if one be unable by the assistance of the judge to come into possession of
one's own right, either because, as a result of lack of foresight, some error
has been made in the customary phrases of the formulae, or because the
judge has rendered an unjust opinion due to an imperfect perception of
the case or to some personal feeling, or has altogether refused to take cognizance of the affair, there remains none the less upon the second party, on
the basis of the law of nature, the obligation of furnishing that about which
the agreement was made. Nevertheless, he to whom injury has been done
is by no means left the faculty of obtaining what is owed him on the basis
of the law of nature, by means which are otherwise granted <85> through
this same law, for example, by private exercise of force, or by war. The
reason for this is that, through the act of civil subjection, individuals have
yielded up the authority of exacting from the unwilling in any other way

than by the assistance of the magistracy, that which is owed them by their fellow citizens, at least. And these conditions properly obtain when citizens of the same state have made a contract with one another, not merely according to the formula of civil laws, but even on the basis of the law of nature alone. For those pacts also about which the civil law makes no disposition do not give the citizens of the same state the authority to put forcible compulsion of their own proper initiative upon the violator of the same pacts. But if, now, the matter be between citizens of different states, it must be carefully considered whether some one state is willing and accustomed to give to strangers as well as to citizens the right of appearing in court, or not. If the former is the case, action on the basis of the civil law is proper against him who does not want to stand by his agreement, and this action must be instituted in the state of the defendant, if, indeed, the latter have his present residence here in regard to his person as well as his property. And if, in the state of the other, he either be as a stranger regarding his person, or else possess certain goods under the same state, the plaintiff does not need to institute the action in the state of the defendant, but may bring suit against him in the plaintiff's own state, if the defendant be present, or may ask to be allowed to lay hands upon the goods which exist there. For any stranger whatsoever, aside from those whom the usages of nations have especially excepted, is regarded as recognizing the jurisdiction and the courts of that state in which he sojourns, at least regarding acts performed in that state, or with citizens of the same. But if, now, some state is not accustomed to give foreigners the right to appear in court, or, if otherwise accustomed to do so, it has unfairly denied that same right to some definite person, then the agreements of citizens of that state with citizens of a different one will have efficacy on the basis of the law of nature alone, and therefore will give the authority to apply force, which authority, in defect of civil and pacific action, the law of nature has granted. Here, however, the following observation must be made: Just as a prince who is not such over me, when implored for aid against a subject of his own in obtaining my right, brings himself under the accusation of wrong-doing by denying me that aid, and therefore gives me the authority of pursuing my right, not merely in the primary debtor but even in the prince himself (if the obedience which I owed him while dwelling in his territory has expired by my change of location); so I cannot in private enterprise descend to violent means against the citizen or the prince of the other commonwealth, without the consent of my own state, but I ought to <86> implore its aid in securing my own right (to furnish which, if it conveniently can, my state is obliged); and that because states themselves can be implicated in war by controversies of this kind on the part of private citizens; unless, perchance, the state without sufficient reason should desert me, or I myself should be able to take adequate precautions for the state, that, from my violence, no inconvenience will redound to it.

15. Now among learned men it has been a matter of dispute, as to just what strength of obligation there be in pacts which have been joined upon the law of nature alone, such as are the pacts between those who do not recognize a common judge in a human court of law, or the pacts about which the civil law makes no disposition. For not a few have concluded that the efficacy of these same pacts is contained in the mere bond of the sense of shame and decency, especially when as yet no agreement (συνάλ-λαγμα) has been entered into, and nothing has been furnished on either side; while others vigorously attack this opinion as one which enervates the good faith behind all treaties. To us the matter does not seem to have so much difficulty about it, if you suppose at the outset, that men have been made by nature to cultivate society among themselves, and that no one at all ought to bring upon a second person that which can furnish a cause for discord and war. This is primarily the case when some one by whom no special right has been acquired by pacts, does not allow a second person to enjoy the same right with himself, and by his own efforts makes the condition of the second person worse. Now since society cannot be cultivated and conserved without mutual covenants, and it is the very greatest cause of irritation among men and of throwing them into discord, and without any doubt makes the condition of the first person worse, if he be frustrated by another whose good faith expressed in a pact he had accepted; it is certainly apparent that men are altogether bound by the law of nature to keep their pacts, and that men who violate those pacts are sinning against the same law. And this is by all odds most manifest in the case of those pacts in which each of the two contracting parties has already furnished that, or a part of it, about which the agreement had been made. But where, in truth,

on neither side has anything as yet been furnished, although the loss which is experienced be less than in the former case (just as also pacts of that kind, while matters are still untouched on both sides, can be very easily dissolved by agreement); nevertheless, here also there is quite as much sinning against the law of nature if that which was the subject of the covenant be not fulfilled. For this supplies me with a just cause for complaint, if my calculations, which I had based upon the good faith of the other, collapse upon his deceiving me, or at least if I be mocked by him undeservedly. And the other person, who, <87> according to the agreement, must furnish his part first, is not released from the obligation by the fear that if he himself have made good what he owes, I who follow him may not abide by the pact. For, by the very act in which, with deliberate intent, he made a contract with me, he renounced this exception, since, forsooth, otherwise there would have been no transaction between us; and it would be absurd for the fear, which could not prevent the making of the agreement, to hinder the furnishing of that about which the agreement was made. Nay, if that fear should prevail over good faith, no civil society could be formed or preserved, but life would have to be spent in perpetual warfare, and therefore in the status of brute beasts.[14] For those especially who unite to form a state ought to have good faith among themselves, because they, indeed, wish to procure public welfare, the rest of men to obey it. Otherwise they would never coalesce into one body, unless those who subject themselves to the other party should compose themselves to obey, content with the pledge of good faith which has been given by the one who is to bear authority. And a large

14. This is an allusion to Hobbes, *De cive,* chap. 2, §11: "But the Covenants which are made in contract of mutual trust, neither party performing out of hand, if there arise a just suspicion in either of them, are in the state of nature invalid. For he that first performs, by reason of the wicked disposition of the greatest part of men studying their owne advantage either by right or wrong, exposeth himself to the perverse will of him with whom he hath contracted . . ." Such a just suspicion requires "some new cause of fear" which was unknown at the time when the covenant was made, as Hobbes adds in a note. That reservation is missing in his early work *The Elements of Law Natural and Politic,* ed. Ferdinand Tönnies (London: Cass, 1969), part II: *On the Body Politic* (I.ii, §10), so that "the wicked disposition of the greatest part of men" seems to be a sufficient reason for not abiding by the covenant bringing about a general invalidity of covenants in the natural state. Cf. *JNG,* 3, 6, §9, where Pufendorf criticizes the argument of Hobbes's early work but takes the reservation of the "new cause of fear" from *De cive.*

part of the business transactions of men with one another would necessarily be destroyed, if Greek faith only should be current, and hands with eyes in them* should believe nothing but what they saw. But if, nevertheless, after a pact has been entered into, a new ground for fear should emerge, as when the second party has given manifest indications of a desire not to furnish what he owes on his side, after I have made good my part, then I also am not bound recklessly to furnish my part without taking precaution. For, inasmuch as pacts of that kind exist on the basis of mutual good faith, where that good faith is lacking on one side, the other side also will be absolved; and it appears that he who testifies in advance to his own perfidy has already excused me from my obligation. But that cause of just fear ought to be a new one, and it ought to come after the pact. For the cause of fear which preceded has been eliminated by the very pact; and that cause which does not specially regard my pact, as, for example, if he has not kept faith with others, or others in the meantime deceive my confidence in them, does not absolve me. For both the rascality of others ought not to cause loss to a third party, and, just as I cannot make complaint of him who has paid me my own, even if he does not pay others, so, as long as he shows no sign of employing perfidy in my case particularly, I am not released from the obligation of furnishing my part, because he has deceived others. For it is possible that he who has broken faith with a number of others, has a firm determination to keep faith with me.

16. But indeed, <88> to prevent a man from neglecting this obligation which has been contracted by himself, if perchance his will has been changed out of consideration for his advantage or through desire, the mere honor of having kept faith, the shame of having violated it, and the care for defending his reputation do not appear to have sufficient efficacy, even though they have no little importance. This is patent from the same reasons by which we shall show later on, that the law of nature in itself is not sufficient to maintain peace among men.[15] It is necessary, therefore, that there exist something which will bring it about that a man shall not lightly

---

* The reference is to Plautus, *Asinaria*, 202: *Semper oculatae manus sunt nostrae: credunt quod vident,* "Our hands have eyes always: seeing is believing with them" (Nixon).— *Tr.*

15. See bk. II, Observ. 5, §1.

dare to change the will which he has once expressed and obligated, and that he judge it to be better to maintain that will than to violate it, even though, perchance, an immediate advantage seem to urge the contrary. Now we observe that nothing has such effect except the fear of bringing upon oneself, from some one who is stronger, some evil because of the violation of the pact, so that, in the last resort, the efficacy of obligations is derived from force. This force is either in the one to whom injury is done, or in other men with whom, perchance, the perfidious person may have some dealings, or men to whom his perfidy pertains because of the common example, or else, finally, in the supreme governor of the universe, God. The force in the man with whom the pact was made generally has about the most present efficacy for constraining men not to depart from a pact. For the larger part of mortals is of such a disposition that, when a just cause for employing violence has been offered (such as the violation of pacts suggests), they rarely refrain from inflicting the most severe punishments without delay upon the perfidious. Nor are the rest of men not to be feared by the violator of pacts. For it is frequently known to happen that other persons come to the rescue of one who has suffered some injury, no matter for what cause, and with joint force attack the perfidious. And other more powerful persons with whom the perfidious has some intercourse, even if the efficacy of their pact with him does not depend on the observance of the pact which is made with a third party, do for the most part eagerly rejoice in seizing a plausible pretext, namely, that they are avenging the injuries of the weaker, for concealing their own passion. And pity commonly turns her back upon those who suffer the things which others may seem to have learned from their example. Finally, there is no mortal man whose safety is not bound up in the good faith of others towards him; and how can he have the face to demand that others shall hold this bond sacrosanct towards him, if he himself makes a jest of having violated this same good faith? To such a degree is that Palladium of human security to be defended by common consensus, and the perfidy which, perchance, in a definite case seems to be more profitable, turns out to be on the whole harmful. <89>

Now indeed, when the affairs of a man are in such a state that he feels he need not greatly fear any man, a persuasion which from a variety of causes very often steals into the mind even of those who are not extremely powerful, there yet remains the fear of God, the supreme vindicator of justice, who does not allow the violators of the law of nature to escape with impunity. Although this vengeance of the Deity walks often with a slow step, and others cannot always comprehend the way in which it acts; nevertheless, because frequent and famous examples occur of the perfidious being afflicted with the utmost misery, sufferings which all who are not atheists trace back to God as the avenger of perfidy, it results that the fear of the Deity adds finally the last element of strength to human good faith. From this fact also it is apparent, in passing, to what a degree it is a matter of concern to human affairs, that atheism should not grow strong. For, if you have removed God from the function of administering justice, all the efficacy of these pacts, to the observance of which one of the contracting parties is not able to compel the other by force, will immediately expire, and every one will measure justice by his own particular advantage. And assuredly, if we are willing to confess the truth, once the fear of divine vengeance has been removed, there appears no sufficient reason why I should be at all obligated, after the conditions governing my advantage have once changed, to furnish that thing, for the furnishing of which to the second party I had bound myself while my interests led in that direction; that is, of course, if I have to fear no real evil, at least from any man, in consequence of that act.

17. Now as for the persons between whom an obligation may exist, at the outset it is manifest that an obligation requires at the very least two persons, and that one person cannot, properly speaking, be under obligation to himself. Thence come those well-known rules of the jurisconsults: "When the debtor succeeds to the creditor, the debt ceases," or, in other words, obligation is removed by uniting.[16] Likewise: "When two persons become one, the contract is invalid." For although we are commonly in the habit of saying, for example, "Any one whatsoever is bound to save himself," nevertheless, that obligation inherent in man regards man himself only in so far as the exercise of an action which derives from that obligation ought to terminate in him; and properly this obligation is ascribed to God, the author of the law of nature, as to the one who is able to compel the

16. *Dig.*, XXXIV.iii.21, §1.

exercise of the obligation and to punish the neglect of the same. And therefore man is bound to care for himself only in so far as he is a servant of
God and a part of human society. Hence, just as one can rightly beat his
slave, if the latter has made himself too weak to endure labours; so a state
also rightly chastises a citizen who has made himself a useless member of
the state by self-mutilation. The Romans gave an <90> example of this
kind of punishment in the case of those who made themselves useless for
military service by cutting off a thumb. Otherwise, it is repugnant to the
nature of obligation for some one to be under obligation to himself. For,
since the obligation expires when the other party to whom it pertains wants
to free me from it, if I have been put under obligation to myself, I shall be
free as soon as I desire to be, and therefore I shall be absolutely free. And
this is not to mention the fact that there will be no advantage in an obligation of that kind, since nothing accrues to anybody by an act of furnishing, nor is anything lost by an act of intermission, as long as a person
is giving or denying something to himself, and therefore he is doing absolutely nothing. And this obtains even in the case of composite moral
persons, or societies, which cannot bind themselves as such. And so the
decrees or the laws of a certain society promulgated by itself for its own
members bind merely the members of the society as individuals, and by
no means bind the society itself as such. The reason for this is readily apparent. For, as an example, in a society constituted like a democracy, the
individual associates, in becoming such, bind themselves to the agreement
that they are willing to observe the laws and the statutes approved by the
consensus of the majority, or even of individuals; and by this circumstance
the whole body is given the authority of forcing them so to act, if afterwards
they should be disinclined to do so. Now by their vote individual associates
as such do not bind themselves directly, since, forsooth, even he who has a
different opinion is bound by the consensus of the majority; but they bind
themselves only as far as their vote, coalescing with the votes of the majority,
acquires, by the fundamental pact of the society, the force of sovereignty.
Now the society as a whole does by no means bind itself, nor can it even
bind itself, to the wish that it be bound by that decree for a longer time
than it shall find agreeable. The result is that decrees of this kind on the
part of societies, to which belong also civil laws, can be abrogated again by

the same societies whenever they desire. Also, in those pacts by which a society is established, it is not the society which obligates itself, but the individual members as such bind themselves mutually to the declaration that they wish to form a single moral body.

18. As for the rest, any man whatsoever can be under obligation to any man whatsoever, naturally, at all events, if not civilly. For the sense in which it is said that a prince cannot be under obligation to a subject, a father to a son, a master to a servant, has been set forth just above. Now it is pre-supposed, quite as much in the case of the one who ought to contract an obligation, as in the case of the one towards whom that obligation is di-rected, that he possesses the natural requisite for contracting an obligation, or for allowing an obligation towards him to be contracted by the other, and that is the faculty of <91> understanding the force of an obligation, and the matter about which the obligation is contracted. For, since in an obligation the right of having something from me is transferred to the other party, and it is fair that that act be valid because consent has been secured from me who am an interested party; it is, of course, patent that they who do not understand the matter under consideration, and therefore cannot agree to it, are unable to assume obligations. Such persons are infants, as long as they are destitute of the use of reason; likewise the insane and the mad; although these latter, as long as their madness is broken by lucid in-tervals, can validly put themselves under obligation, just as also no piece of business which was properly transacted is undone by subsequent mad-ness. To this class also are relegated those whose mind has been disturbed by drinking to excess, who, if, indeed, they reach such a stage of drunk-enness that for the time being they do not understand what is being done, are properly regarded as not having contracted an obligation, even if, per-chance, a second party has secured from them while under the influence of drink, symbols which otherwise testify their assent. But if, now, when their fit of drunkenness has been shaken off, they approve the same, they will be under obligation, because of what they have done while sober, but not because of what they did while drunk. And it does not follow, that, if a misdeed committed in a state of drunkenness can be charged against a man, obligations also can be contracted under the same. For the reason behind the former position is that it is incumbent upon a man to avoid as

far as he can any occasions at all which may very likely precipitate him into doing a misdeed, and every one knows that drunkenness is such an occasion. And so, when he has yielded to it, he is regarded as having yielded also to the things which were to result from his drunkenness. But this mode of reasoning cannot be extended to obligations, for the reason that, since no one is bound actually to contract or not to contract them, a man is also not bound to avoid such occasions as those in which some symbols which otherwise denote obligation can be enticed out of him while he does not understand what is going on. And therefore, since drunkenness had not been forbidden him as far as concerns contracting or intermitting obligations, it cannot be presumed from his yielding to drunkenness that he has therefore consented to an obligation; but the strength of the obligation depends upon the consent which obtained at the time when the symbols were executed. But, truly, that consent in such a state of drunkenness as thoroughly paralysed the use of his mind is regarded as no consent at all, for the reason that it is not understood what the matter is about.

Now that minors who already rejoice in the use of reason are unable to obligate themselves, if, indeed, that obligation is destined to be a burden to them in the future, does not come from the law of <92> nature, but has been introduced by positive laws only. And that is because such a time of life, commonly prodigal and not sufficiently attentive to its own affairs, is exposed to pillage by designing men; also because, being of changeable purpose and accustomed to rush ahead with inconsiderate ardour, it can readily be induced to agree to what is anything but conducive to its interests. For this cause the same laws have determined that such persons should make contracts under the auspices of their guardians or overseers.

19. Here where consent is being treated of, it is convenient to subjoin the topic of error in pacts; that is to say, if I have made a false supposition in some matter, in consideration of which I have committed myself to an obligation, is there for that reason no obligation? This question must be answered in the affirmative; and that because consent is founded upon a presumption regarding that matter, and if the matter turns out to be otherwise, there was no consent at all, and no obligation at all; since, forsooth, any and all things which are conditional stand and fall together with the condition upon which they are based. And this obtains not simply if the

error was in regard to the physical substance of a thing about which a pact is made, but even if it was in regard to a quality which I had especially before my eyes when I made the contract. Thus the contract is null, not only when, for example, I bought from another man Davus to be my slave, when I thought he was Syrus, but even, for example, when he whom I wanted to get especially for that service does not know how to cook, if, of course, I openly announced that I was looking for that kind of slave. For, although a quality of that kind does not belong to the physical substance of the thing, nevertheless, it happens very frequently in pacts that the quality of a certain thing is the principal consideration, and that its actual substance is regarded as nothing but an inevitable accessory. Therefore error has to do with the essence as such of the object about which the contract is made, and therefore a pact is rendered void when the motive, which influenced a man to make the contract, was based upon a false premise, whether that motive be the physical substance of the thing or merely a quality. But, truly, it can scarcely be said that an error has occurred when that does not appear which had not been presupposed as a condition, either expressly, or by the nature of the transaction. For such a matter is regarded as being, by the very judgement of the contracting parties, without effect upon the stability of the contract. But if, indeed, a man has been careless in looking into the matter and in correcting an error of a kind which he might have escaped, he is bound to make good to the other party the loss incurred by a vain promise or pact of that kind. Now, of a truth, errors of that kind can come about more frequently in promises and less frequently in contracts, because in the latter case the thing about which the agreement is made, together with its qualities, which the contracting party has before his eyes, ought to be expressed separately, or else they are understood to be presupposed by the very nature of the transaction, or by other circumstances. For, if these matters are unknown, assuredly the contracting parties cannot come to any agreement regarding the thing itself. Therefore, when those qualities, expressed or presumed, are not apparent in the thing agreed to after it has been delivered, the contract is not properly speaking void because of error on my part, but because of the fraud or lack of foresight of the one who delivered a thing deficient in the qualities which it ought to have had. This fraud results in making it lawful for me to withdraw from the contract, or else to compel the other party to make good the defect and to compensate for the loss which was suffered therefrom. And this obtains not merely if the contracting parties have expressly stipulated or promised good faith towards one another, as, for example, if an agreement has been made between persons who were not in one another's presence, or if the vendor has delivered, as though it corresponded to the terms of the pact, a thing which the purchaser had not examined; but even when the second party discovers only after an interval the absence of those qualities. This is particularly true when those qualities cannot be discovered from a glance at the exterior, or by one who is unskilled in the art in question. But when the absence of a certain quality has been discovered by the second party, and he none the less accepts the thing, he is regarded as having agreed also to that absence of the quality, and so for that reason the pact is not rendered void.

20. Now I can put myself under obligation, if, indeed, a stronger obligation has not thrown an obstacle in the way, to any one to whom my obligation can in any way become known, or who can accept the same. Nay more, I may do so even to those who for the time being cannot understand it. For no reason seems to prevent a man from binding himself validly to a minor even without the authority [*autoritatem*] of his guardian, if, indeed, the nature of the transaction by which his own condition is improved should furnish no ground for presuming that he himself, when he comes to understand the situation, will repudiate the same obligation. And if, perchance, moral failings be discovered in the man himself, they do not prevent him from being capable of admitting my obligation. For there are many faults which do not affect the obligation at all, and those which, perhaps, may bring his good faith under suspicion are judged by the very fact of the contract to be of no avail for hindering the acquisition of a right acquired by an obligation, since otherwise nothing would take place between the two contracting parties, did they not renounce those exceptions. But the reason why I too am no longer bound, when, in the same transaction, <94> the other party does not keep faith with me, is different. Because all pacts presuppose as a fundamental condition mutual good faith between the contracting parties, and when one has broken this good faith the other also is immediately released from obligation to the same.

21. But it is a little more difficult to make plain whether I am under obligation to him, who, by a crime on his part, has brought upon me the necessity of making a pact. Properly, indeed, the question here is not about those pacts which, for example, are made with a brigand, in so far as he is not such; for it can scarcely be doubted that these ought to be observed, and this is the sense in which it seems those should be understood who make the general statement that one's word when given to a brigand must be kept. But, in truth, it is our judgement that one must come to a different conclusion about those pacts to the formation of which with a brigand we are compelled by an unjust use of force on his part; for example, if we should promise a brigand, in order to keep him from taking our life, that we will pay him something, should we be bound to furnish what we have promised, after we have been brought to a safe place out of the reach of his violence? As for civil laws, indeed, there is no doubt that, even if they do not forbid the keeping of such pacts, at least they do not at all compel us to keep them; nor do they give the brigand ground for action, since, forsooth, he is an enemy of civil society, who, if he is caught, is customarily made away with like a harmful wild beast. Nor does it seem that there is here a natural obligation. For since, on the basis of the law of nature, he who has extorted something from another through unjust fear is bound to restore it, and so a brigand of that sort ought, on the basis of the law of nature, to pay me as much as he himself has taken from me by virtue of such a pact, it is understood that by compensation the obligation is, as it were, removed, if that which ought to be restored immediately is not paid;[17] and it would be foolish to pay voluntarily what had been promised as the result of force, of course after one has succeeded in reaching places of safety, and thereafter to desire to extort by violence from the same person rec-

---

17. Cf. *JNG*, 3, 6, §11 with reference to *Dig.*, XLIV.iv.8; Grotius, *JBP*, III.xix.4. Pufendorf principally regards pacts contracted under the impression of fear as valid because actions undertaken from fear of a greater evil are to be classed as voluntary (*JNG*, 3, 6, §10, with reference to Aristotle, *Nicomachean Ethics* III.1). It is not the victim's fear but the lack of a right of intimidation on the brigand's side that invalidates the obligation in the case mentioned here (cf. *JNG*, 3, 6, §12). See also 3, 6, §13, where Pufendorf—criticizing Hobbes, *De cive*, chap. 2, §16—distinguishes *fear* as a "safeguard against some" indefinite "evil" (when contracting the civil obligation) and *fear* as "terror" arising "from some serious present and threatened evil" (in the case of the brigand).

ompense for the loss he has suffered, especially since, by the very fact that he exacts a promise from me, he professes his unwillingness to make restitution for the damage which he has done me. Nor does it appear that he is any more bound, who, in a case of this kind, gives bail for a second person,[18] even if he does not properly bind himself as a result of fear. For, since giving bail is, as it were, an accessory support to the principal pact, it seems absurd, at least from the law of nature, for there to be more efficacy in the accessory than there is in the primary pact, or for the principal debtor to be under a looser obligation than he who has promised to undertake the obligation of the principal debtor, <95> in case the latter shall not have met it. And yet the situation appears to be different, if a third party contracts with a brigand an obligation of his own, and one which does not depend on the obligation of the one who has been captured, or support the same. For upon this third party neither has unjust fear been brought, nor can he borrow the excuses of the captured man, because he has bound himself not under the latter's name, but under his own name, nor has he based his obligation upon the latter's obligation, which was something that did not exist. But if, in truth, he gave hostages, or, after his capture, left some of his companions in the power [*potestate*] of the brigands until his promises were performed, he is bound, not by the pact with the brigand, but by the pact which exists between himself and the hostages. If, however, an oath has been given, we are of the opinion that the man captured is bound to fulfil his promises; not because the brigand wins a peculiar right therefrom, since, forsooth, oaths add nothing further to the substance, as it were, of the obligation, as far as concerns the man to whom the promise is made, and no special right arises from them in a human court of law, at least in this case; but because of the reverence due the Divine Spirit, whose mercy he has renounced unless he keep his promise.[19] And it is better to suffer loss of money than to have treated the Divine Majesty with a certain lack of respect.

18. The original note here read: "Probably we ought to read *altero* ('a second person') instead of *altore* ('sustainer').—*Tr.* "Altore" has been replaced by "altero" in the editions of Jena, 1669, and Frankfurt and Jena, 1680, but was retained in the editions of Zwickau, 1668, and Cambridge, 1672.

19. See Grotius, *JBP,* III.xix.5.

22. The following point also must be made clear, whether, namely, I can contract an obligation with an enemy as such, or whether pacts which are made with enemies be valid. These pacts are of two kinds, for they have to do either with bringing war indirectly or directly to an end, or else with furnishing certain things while the state of war endures. Now that the former create an obligation on the basis of the law of nature, cannot be doubted. For, since nature allows men war merely as a sort of extraordinary means of acting with one another, and bids us, as far as our safety permits, to avoid it, or to bring it to a peaceful conclusion, which cannot be without pacts; it is undoubtedly understood that the same law of nature also binds us to observe the pacts which are formed for the purpose of ending war. And this position, because of the favour extended to peace and the necessity of it, has been extended by the usage of nations so far that in solemnly establishing peace both parties are generally put on an equality as regards the justice of the war which had been undertaken, and the excuse of the unjust application of fear is not allowed to be extended to pacts of that sort; because, otherwise, there would be no end or limit to wars of that kind, which are assuredly frequent enough as it is. Under pacts of this kind is included the pledge of one's good faith which has been given for the safe access and return of those who are going to transact the negotiation of the peace. Likewise the pacts of truces by <96> which the exercise of hostility is completely suspended, if, indeed, they look to the restoration of complete peace. This is understood to take place if it has been expressly agreed, that, while the truce lasts, the means of composing peace are to be employed. But, indeed, it seems to be otherwise with those pacts which neither end a state of war or hostility, nor look towards ending it. For, since a state of war as such recognizes violence as a proper mode of action, just as good faith is the instrument of peace among men, no obligation at all can be contracted between enemies on the basis of the law of nature (forasmuch as obligation rests on good faith), unless both sides call men to witness that they are going to embrace peace when the war is finished. And it is of no avail to have signified that one is not going to use the licence of hostility herein, for this implies the demand that the other party follow my pledge of good faith, as is the case in pacts, while implying none the less the profession that one desires to remain an enemy, that is, one who wishes to do

him harm in any way whatsoever. And, as we said above, the fact that those who make the contract have by that very act renounced the excuses which, drawn from the person of the other, might cause fear, does not prevent the other party from deceiving his confidence. For that presumption cannot obtain among those who still expressly profess the continuance of hostilities between one another, and it is rather to be presumed that they want to deceive one another by fictitious proposals of that kind. Nay, not even to the other party who is deceived by a pact of that kind can any new right arise against the deceiver, since, forsooth, hostility itself already furnishes the right of exercising violence to an unlimited degree against the enemy, at all events without impediment to some right which exists in the very enemy.[20] And thus, if we should follow the law of nature alone, we shall assign no efficacy to pacts of that kind, except the amount shown by the immediate exhibition of the thing agreed upon, or the ready faculty of returning to the deceiver like for like. Nevertheless, as the usage of the more civilized nations has brought into being a number of things favourable to martial fortitude, so it has also brought it about that such pacts as do not pertain to ending a state of war, ought to be valid. Of this kind are a truce of a few days for burying the dead, pacts with the presiding officials of cities which are surrendering, pacts for sending off to their own side persons with the faculty of immediately taking up arms once more against us, a promise about granting the right of passage through our lines to definite enemy persons, and the like. So, likewise, it has come about also from that same usage, that enemies can validly make a convention on the subject of a restriction of hostilities and of an exercise of hostilities with a definite degree of moderation, as, for example, that specific places, seasons, and

20. Cf. *JNG*, 8, 6, §7. Pufendorf's characterization of war as a state of necessity annulling any legal relation and furnishing a "right of exercising violence to an unlimited degree," though with an obligation to restore peaceful legal relations as soon as possible, shows obvious similarities to Hobbes's characterization of the natural state and its right to everything. Grotius, on the contrary, emphasizes an obligation to good faith toward the enemy while the state of war endures (*JBP*, III.xix.1) and makes detailed regulations for warfare as such (*JBP*, bk. III). Such regulations don't have any obligatory force according to Pufendorf (bk. I, Def. 13, §25); nevertheless, he recommends their observance for reasons of humanity, when it is possible to abide by them without endangering the pursuit of one's right or the ending of the war (bk. II, Observ. 4, §18).

persons should be immune from hostilities, either <97> altogether, or at least from some definite kind of injury, likewise that specific instruments of doing injury should not be employed, &c. For it seemed to be expedient to human interests to establish certain kinds of arrangements, as it were, in war, after it appeared that, as a result of the lust for warfare, the number of those who were destined to suffer what they had not deserved, would be no smaller than that of those who were going to inflict it.

23. Now, although in order to contract an obligation between men it is in due course required that the consent of both parties to the agreement be expressed by customary signs, nevertheless, it is usually the case that a pact is made without the expression of agreement in signs to the form of the pact, but simply on the presumption of willingness which is drawn from the nature of the transaction that takes place between the contracting parties, and these are called tacit pacts. They are contracted in such a manner that they form either the principal transaction, or are understood to be accessory to an express pact, and to proceed from the same. To the first class belong such cases as the following: If, for example, some one should come as a stranger to a state which is in the habit of treating outsiders in a friendly manner, the stranger, although he has never expressly pledged his good faith, is, nevertheless, regarded as having pledged his good faith, both tacitly and by the act of coming, to a willingness to accommodate himself to the laws of that state in accordance with his status. And so he in his turn has tacitly stipulated for his own temporary protection on the part of the same state. Thus, when a man's business is carried on in his absence, there exists a tacit pact whereby, after one has accommodated one's services to the concerns of the other, that other is bound to recompense the services together with the expenses incurred. Thus, he who seats himself at a table in an inn, although not a word has been exchanged with the host on the subject of price, nevertheless, from the very nature of the case, is understood to have obligated himself to pay the price, because it is notorious that food here is not given gratis to any chance comer. To the latter class belong cases of the following kind: For example, if some one agrees with a second party about conceding the right of entrance to a certain place, he is judged to have made an agreement also about the right to return from the same place, although no express mention of this has ever been made; because otherwise nothing

would have been achieved by the former pact. Thus he who agrees to the pact that outsiders may purchase merchandise in his own state, is definitely understood also to have agreed that they should export the same. Just as also it is absurd, for example, to sell you a field, but not to be willing to concede that you should possess the same in that place, but to demand that you should transport the field to some other location. Thus he who rents me a room in his house is also <98> judged to have rented me the use of those parts which we cannot do without, that is, the door and the passage ways which lead to the room, as far, at least, as is necessary in order to go out of the house and to return. Now in tacit pacts of that kind we are bound to that for which those who expressly make a covenant about such things are commonly in the habit of contracting.

24. Furthermore, since in any and all obligations in the person whom they regard, or for whom some right is being sought thereby, is required the consent of the other party to accept the obligation or the right which has been transferred thereby, and that consent either in his own person, or as represented by another, has been expressed by signs attesting the feeling in his mind, it is obvious what should be thought of vows or obligations voluntarily undertaken towards God. Of course they cannot be undertaken validly unless either God himself has revealed that He will accept them, or some one has been appointed to take cognizance of them among men. For otherwise, a man cannot be certain whether God wills him to be under obligation, or, indeed, not; especially since vows ought to be taken relating to matters of a kind which God did not previously demand from us in the way of command, but which were subject to our own free will, whether, namely, we wished to do them or not to do them. For there is also implied a desire to impute to a second person that which otherwise must necessarily have been done, as a deed which he was not under obligation to perform, and we cannot be assured, except by divine revelation, that some act which was neither a prescript of the law of nature, nor otherwise a precept of God, will be grateful to Him. And so it is useless to take on vows about which there is no assurance that they will be grateful to God; and it will be permissible to observe or to retract such assumed vows, to the extent to which the tenderness or the firmness of each man's conscience persuades him.

Now the following is clear, namely, that towards brute beasts men cannot be under obligation, since, forsooth, there is no communication by signs of consent and of willingness with that which has no communion in right with us; for, as to the fact that a person is bound, for example, to care for the horse of a second person, to harness it, to feed it, not to injure it, &c., that obligation applies not to the animal itself, but to the man who owns it.

25. Another question must here be cleared up, whether, namely, by one's own act one can put somebody under obligation to any third person. Here we must proceed with careful distinctions. For there can be no doubt on this point, namely, that a man can validly put the person over whom he has sovereignty under obligation to furnish something to some third party, and to do this so that a perfect or an im-<99>perfect right to have that thing be acquired by this same third party; just as there is no doubt about this point also, namely, that one person can be put under obligation to a third by the agency of a second person who is legitimately conducting the first person's affairs, in such wise that every right is acquired by the third person and not the second person; and so, if the obligation be not fulfilled, the third person only, and not the second person who comes in between, secures ground for action. For those actions which we have openly promised to recognize as our own produce for us an obligation and a ground of action, and are regarded as our own actions. But if I confer on some one the authority [*autoritatem*] to transact my business under the general formula that I will accept whatever he has done therein, I am under obligation by that person's act, even if, perchance, he has done something beyond the private instructions which I secretly gave to him to be followed in that matter. For, by the former instrument, I put myself under the obligation of ratifying his acts to the third party with whom the contract must be made, but by the private instructions I bind only my agent to follow my instruction which is known to him and not to others, unless, perchance, it should be manifestly apparent that my agent has acted in bad faith and by nefarious prevarication has betrayed my interest. For, under those circumstances, I am not regarded as being under obligation by virtue of his deeds, for the reason that in conferring upon him authority [*autoritate*], the condition was tacitly supposed, that I did so only in so far as it might appear that he

was acting with good faith in the matter. Furthermore, since every one is presumed to have enjoined upon those persons placed under his authority that they make his own condition better, if they can conveniently, the reason is apparent, why, for example, it is to the advantage of a master or a father, if a slave or a son of a family make a stipulation, so that it be not sought from the father or the master. For such persons are regarded as making agreements by the authority [*autoritate*] of the head of the family, and so in his place. But the same situation is by no means presumed to obtain in matters disagreeable, or such as make his condition worse. However, it cannot be that I as an outsider should bind a second person to some third person under whose authority I do not stand, and in charge of the management of whose affairs I am not placed, and do so in such a way that I should stipulate no right also for myself. For thereby neither do I seek to acquire a right, as we suppose the case, nor does the third person who does not recognize my action as his own; and so, as a result of my action alone, he does not accept an obligation, without doing which no right can come to him. Hence it was that the Roman laws rightly declared unavailing pure stipulations (or those which were drawn up without the addition of a penalty) made for the advantage of a third party;[21] adding, as a reason, that stipulations have <100> been invented so that every single individual may acquire what is to his own advantage; if, however, something be given to another, it is not to the interest of the stipulator. But by a penal stipulation, for example, "Unless Seius give Titius one hundred pieces of gold, he shall pay me fifty pieces as a penalty," a right has been acquired by me, at least, if not by the third party, to such a degree, that, if he should not do his part first, I can bring him under my own name to the punishment specified, if that third party under his own name may be utterly unable to bring him to pay the former sum.

Now as for the common saying of the jurisconsults, namely, that the testator puts the heir under obligation to give certain legacies to a legatee, the expression is improper, arising as it does from the circumstance that, by legal fiction, all the goods of the deceased have been assigned the heir under the condition that he pay the legacies, or because the heir is the first

21. *Inst.,* III.xix.19.

person who is accustomed to act as the possessor of all the goods.[22] But, as an actual fact, legacies pass directly from the testator to the legatee, and this is apparent from the circumstance that the legatee, without the intervention of any act with the heir, can bring suit to compel him to pay the legacy, if, indeed, the heir be unwilling, after taking possession of all the goods, to fulfil the wishes of the testator.

But what should be thought about a pact of this kind, where, for example, when two parties are quarrelling with one another, two or more parties who had not been invited by the litigants, agree that they desire to offer themselves as arbitrators, and draw up definite terms in accordance with which the two parties first mentioned must make peace, announcing that they intend to treat as an enemy the one who refuses to accept these terms? Here this much is clear, that those persons who arrogate the function of arbitrators can validly put themselves under mutual obligations by an agreement that they shall not take part in that war between the former parties otherwise than as has been agreed, and that the rest acquire the power of forcibly compelling the one who acts contrariwise to abide by the pact. Although it is necessarily required among arbitrators of this kind, that there rest upon them no special obligation to render aid to either of the belligerents. For, when this obligation obtains, it is impossible for him who has taken sides to act as an arbitrator. But, in truth, it cannot by any means come about that these same would-be arbitrators by their decree put the parties to the quarrel under an obligation, and acquire a just ground for making war upon the recalcitrant. For, as the case is supposed to stand, the parties to the quarrel have never made any promise to them, or subjected themselves to their arbitration, from which acts, perchance, some colour could be derived for taking action against the recalcitrant.[23] Although there is this difference between a judge <101> and an arbitrator, namely, that the former, by virtue of sovereignty, enjoins upon the parties to a quarrel the

22. The reference is to *trusts* [*fideicommissa*]. See bk. I, Def. 5, §19, note 30.

23. Otherwise *JNG,* 5, 13, §7: "Nay, it appears that this further step can rightfully be taken. Two or more to whose interest it is for the war to cease, upon weighing the cases of both sides, may agree on what terms they feel peace can be most fairly secured; and then they can offer these to the warring parties with a threat that, against him who refuses peace on those terms, they are ready to join arms with him who accepts them."

acceptance of his opinion, and this faculty does by no means belong to the latter. Now to take upon ourselves the decision of a controversy in which there is involved a second party not subject to ourselves, and to desire to force him to follow our own opinion, is to usurp a sovereignty which neither the law of nature, nor the consent of the second party, or a pact with the same, has conferred upon us. And the second party is so far from being bound to recognize such sovereignty, that he has rather the right to bring action for injury against arbitrators of that kind, as against those who presume to limit his freedom. But, in truth, it would be utterly intolerable if they should deliver an opinion without first looking into and coming to know clearly both sides of the case, and without hearing the reasons and excuses of the two parties. For it is perfectly apparent that persons who act in this way are not interested in bringing peace, but are looking for a pretext to take part in the war.

26. It should be observed, furthermore, that several persons, as long as they have not united to form a single composite moral person, act and contract as individuals in whatever actions they take or whatever contracts they enter into, and so the number of separate actions and obligations is the same as the number of the persons. From this it follows that, even if a man be in some large group with which he has not joined so as to form one moral body with it, and in that group the majority, or even all the rest, are performing some act or entering into some contract, but he himself has not consented thereto, or otherwise taken part in the same, he should be regarded as not having acted. And so the stranger is not bound by the acts or obligations of that state in which he is living, such acts and obligations having been contracted by the same state as such, at the time when he was there, unless he has himself in a special way concurred in those acts and obligations. However, when a number of persons of that kind enter into a pact as individuals with individuals, to the effect that they desire to have their affairs of a definite kind attended to in common with the others, if, indeed, they have agreed to one single form of transacting these affairs, and afterwards, when some form has been agreed to all around, they have contracted with some definite persons for undertaking the oversight of the common property—pacts of that kind are equivalent to a bond whereby all those who have so contracted partake of the nature of one moral per-

son,[24] whether that be a family, or an association, or a state, or under whatever name it be listed. The result is that whatever action is taken or whatever
contract is entered into by those to whom has been entrusted the management of some common property, all those who are included in that society
are understood to have agreed thereto, and to have contracted an obligation
therefrom; <102> with this proviso, however, that all together are bound
by one obligation (not each by a separate obligation), which has the same
character as the obligations that have been contracted between individuals,
unless in some way an agreement among the nations has introduced some
special observances about the same.

27. There are, accordingly, two pacts which combine in the establishment of a society, and primarily of a civil society.[25] One is the pact of
individuals with individuals, to the effect that they desire to have their affairs which are mutually intertwined, administered by common counsel;
the other is the one which is made with those to whom the care of the
common welfare is entrusted. In the former pact the consent of each and
all is necessarily required, and the one who does not express his consent is
not at all bound by the plurality of votes to join himself to that group, but
remains outside the society. This pact, furthermore, is either absolute,
whereby a man absolutely binds himself to adhere to the group in question,
whatever form of administration may finally commend itself to the majority; or else it supposes as a condition the introduction of a form of government which the individual approves of. In the latter case, likewise, the
consent of individuals is required, and the one who does not signify his
consent is not regarded as a member of the society. Moreover, in the former
case the consent of the majority is accepted as the consent of all together,
and so, by the force of the former pact, even he who is not pleased with
the form of government will be put under obligation by the plurality of
the votes. For, since he who puts himself so absolutely under obligation to
some group cannot demand that all the rest should follow his opinion, he
is regarded as having obligated himself to ratify what the majority has ap-

24. On Pufendorf's doctrine of the compound moral person, see bk. II, Observ. 5,
§2, with notes.
25. On the contractual formation of the state, see ibid.

proved; since otherwise no method of transacting business could be found, and without that obligation of himself on the part of the individual, most pacts of that kind would amount to nothing. The result is that in almost all societies which are administered by a number of persons, it has been recognized that the votes of the majority have the force of the votes of all together, even if it should sometimes happen that the opinion of the minority is more conducive to the common interest and more reputable. For, about general arrangements of that sort, since practically no faultless means are found for conducting transactions, the most expedient is the one which should be followed. Therefore he must be extremely inexperienced who wishes to argue thus: "Since it is in accordance with nature that the policy which the more prudent propose should prevail over that which is proposed by the less prudent, it is repugnant to nature that the less prudent opinion of the many should prevail over the more prudent opinion of the few, and that therefore the former should be able to obligate the latter to undertake something less prudent."[26] And <103> it will be much more absurd if this contention be extended also to monarchs, and if their subjects should not be obligated by the less prudent pacts or commands of the same. For it implies that there is a monarch, and that his subjects have the faculty of judging whether his acts have been undertaken prudently or otherwise, with this effect, namely, that, if they seem to have been less prudent, the subjects cannot be obligated by them. Nor can the former position be admitted any more than this latter. For who will render the decision as to which of two opinions is the more prudent? Certainly not the dissenting parties themselves, for one side will not accept the judgement of the other, and how many persons are there who will not prefer their own judgement to another's? Therefore, one will have to abide by the decision of yet another party, a position which is involved in no fewer difficulties, since the prudence or the integrity of the arbitrator can readily be called into question, so that to settle this point one will need another arbitrator, and so on endlessly; not to mention the fact that generally those matters are so constituted that they cannot be laid conveniently before arbitrators outside the

---

26. Cf. *JNG,* 7, 2, §15, with references to Seneca, *De beata vita,* II.1; Plutarch, *The Education of Children,* IX.6b; Plato, *Symposion* 194b.

society. Accordingly, it has seemed best to adopt a method of a kind which
has no difficulty or obscure occasion for dispute about it, and that is the
number of the voters; especially since the presumption of prudence commonly militates in behalf of the majority, at least in regard to matters which
are open to the common perception of men. Nor does the law of nature
demand forthwith that those obligations be ineffectual which have been
undertaken by the less prudent, or in a somewhat imprudent fashion. For,
since the matter at stake is merely some advantage or disadvantage relating
to the good things of fortune (for that pact is properly said to have been
entered into imprudently which brings some disadvantage to the good
things of fortune), assuredly man has the authority to neglect some advantage or to allow some disadvantage in the case of those good things, and
so he will be able by the law of nature to obligate himself firmly by virtue
of such a pact which has been somewhat imprudently undertaken.

28. Now that it be possible to judge clearly just what obligations on the
part of the rulers of a society are binding upon the individual members,
and for what reason, and, on the contrary, what obligations from the acts
of members redound to the directors or the members themselves, three
things must first be noted. (1) Certain obligations arise from convention or
from some pact; certain others from a transgression.[27] (2) Among pacts
some are terminated directly and ultimately in the individual person, as it
were, of the party to the pact; and certain others tend indirectly or directly
to the society and its affairs, and exercise their ultimate efficacy therein. (3)
In a transgression there <104> is either guilt extending to the person of the
delinquent, or else obligation to make restitution for the injury done, which
comes upon the goods of the delinquent.

On the basis of these principles we make the following assertions: (I)
Obligations arising from a pact ultimately and directly terminated in the
person of some one, do not bind individuals other than the very person of
the party to the agreement. Thus, for example, a marriage pact is directly
and ultimately terminated in the persons making the contract with one
another, and so it will not bind other persons at all. From this it follows

---

27. The distinction originates from Aristotle, *Nicomachean Ethics,* V 1131a2ff (voluntary and involuntary transactions).

that if a prince has promised marriage to some woman, no one in the whole state beside himself will be bound to take her to wife.

(II) In transgressions guilt does not pass to other persons included in the society, unless they have themselves agreed to it by an efficacious consent, by rendering aid, or by some other means.[28] For it was not in the power of others to prevent them from happening, either in their own persons, or in their own cause. Not in their own persons, for that is the situation supposed, nor in their own cause, as, for example, by the force of a pact whereby they have merged into one moral body with the delinquent. For that pact on the side of the sovereign introduces, indeed, the obligation to prohibit transgressions on the part of the members of the society, in so far as that is necessary to the preservation of peace, but only in a moral way, that is, by promulgating laws, threatening punishments, and appropriately executing the same. Now he is by no means bound to a physical prohibition, that is, to bind the physical faculty of action in such a way that nothing at all can take place. For this is opposed to the nature of men, and utterly subverts the course of human life. So a prince or a magistrate, if he has not neglected to announce a moral prohibition, contracts no guilt from the fact that a transgression has been committed by an old subject or a new-comer, or by one who, after committing a crime in one state, flees to another. Nevertheless, it were well, if, on being advised thereof and entreated, as best he could, and, as in his judgement it was best for the commonweal, he shall have neglected to inflict punishment. Now a subject does in no wise participate in the transgression of another subject, unless he has in some way or other concurred therein. For both the faculty and the obligation to prohibit the misdeeds of a second party proceed from authority over the second party or sovereignty, and there is no such thing between subjects. For equality makes it impossible for one person to be responsible for the deeds of a second person, since, forsooth, the effect of a moral prohibition comes thereby to naught, as will be apparent from what we shall say on the subject of law. Nor, indeed, do subjects contract guilt from the misdeed of <105> princes, unless they themselves have directly contributed to it. For neither

28. On the concurrence of rulers with transgressions of the subjects and vice versa, see Grotius, *JBP,* II.xxi.2, 7.

by virtue of their present status can they or ought they to prevent it, not even in a moral way; nor, on the basis of that pact whereby they have bestowed such authority upon the prince that they cannot bring him to order, does his guilt redound to them. For by that pact they did by no means bind or impel him to do wrong; and much less have they acquired, after the sovereignty has been bestowed upon him, the authority to prohibit misdeeds, which, before that sovereignty had been bestowed, they did not have over him as an equal. For this latter clearly implies, as did also the former, that authority between a prince and his subjects is, as it were, reciprocal, so that he may or should restrain their transgressions, as they his. From all this it is patent that a magistrate cannot be punished, in the proper sense of the word, for the transgression of a subject, unless he has failed to perform something that he should have performed in prohibiting it; nor can a subject be punished, in the proper sense of the word, for the transgression of a fellow citizen, or of the prince himself, unless he has participated in it, either from the very beginning, or after its commission.

(III) Obligations arising from a pact made by the prince or the directors of a society as such, or obligations arising from a transgression of the same, bind the whole society and the individual members, each for his proper share, to the extent of making restitution for the damage done. The basis for this assertion is to be sought in the pact between subjects and their rulers. For those who commit to some person sovereignty and the care of the public welfare, as well as full authority to make disposition for the same, by that very act obligate themselves to contribute, each his own share, to what he has enjoined upon them as necessary or advantageous for the public welfare. Now all the obligations which the one who bears authority contracts with others relative to some public business are presumed to look to the public welfare; nay more, whatever their character be, they ought to be regarded by the subjects as such, forasmuch as the subjects do not properly have the faculty of taking cognizance of or judging about the means employed by the one who bears authority, in order to ensure the public welfare, that is to say, of taking cognizance or judging, with the effect that their obligation depends upon their own judgement. For the absolute right of sovereignty which we are here supposing altogether rejects that. From this it is clear that subjects are bound to pay any and all debts contracted by princes for the public good.[29] But as far as concerns the private indebtedness of the same, if, indeed, they have had definite revenues for their private expenses, on the basis of the law of nature it seems that subjects are not directly and immediately bound to pay such indebtedness, and that creditors have the right to bring an action only against the private property of princes. Nevertheless, since by <106> custom it has become recognized among the nations that all the goods of subjects are obligated to meet any debts whatsoever of princes, it will be permissible to lay hands upon these also, primarily because princes may, and do habitually, use the strength of their subjects to keep from being compelled to pay their own private debts. But if a prince has not rendered to a second person those things which he has obligated himself to render, the people will be bound not merely to pay the original debt to the second person, but also to make good the loss which results from the refusal to pay, although, perchance, as individuals they may never have approved that refusal. For the retention of the debt is adjudged to have been done likewise for the good of the state, and to be making for its advancement, since, forsooth, to retain what one was otherwise bound to pay, amounts to a gain, and all goods whatsoever of individuals included in a civil society are in a definite way reckoned also among the goods of the state. And this holds true, even though no one participates in the guilt of perfidy but the man who has especially made it his own.

29. However, obligations which individual citizens assume with fellow citizens or aliens do not directly bind the rest of the citizens or the directors of the state, unless they have drawn them upon themselves by some act of their own. And, indeed, from the obligations of individual citizens among one another the obligation is drawn upon the one who bears authority, in the following way: that is to say, when one of two persons on his own initiative refuses to render what he owes, and the one who suffers injury thereby has implored the aid of him who bears authority, by virtue of his office the latter is bound to the extent of his power to see to it that the injured party attains his right. When he neglects to do this, by the law of

29. For the discussion in this and the next paragraph of the liability of the property of subjects for the debts of rulers and fellow subjects, see Grotius, *JBP,* III.ii, "How by the Law of Nations the Goods of Subjects May Be Held for the Debt of Their Rulers; and Therein, on Reprisals"; cf. *JNG,* 8, 6, §13.

nature he himself is under obligation to make good the loss to the injured party. But, in truth, because of the force of sovereignty that obligation does not give the injured party the faculty of summoning the one who bears that authority before a human court of law on the subject of that debt. For this reason neither are the rest of his fellow citizens bound to render satisfaction to the injured party, nor can he under any title demand the same from them; since, forsooth, the citizens entered into a pact with one another to the effect merely that they were willing to refer their controversies to those who bore authority over them, and to obtain their right by the help of the same, and, moreover, have submitted themselves absolutely to their judgement, a thing which outsiders have not done. Thence it follows, that, if a citizen owing something to an outsider refuses to render it to him, and the injured party has in vain implored the aid of the rulers of the state in the matter, not only are the rulers of the state bound to make good that loss, but also, after them the whole state; since, forsooth, it is imputed as a profit to the state if some fellow <107> citizen has not paid what he owes to an alien. In cases of this kind, however, by the law of nature princes are put under obligation primarily and individual citizens after them, and the latter not for the whole debt but each for his share, just as those who unite to form a society obligate themselves to bear its burdens not as a whole, but each only for his own share. Hence the outsider suffering from the wrong ought first, indeed, to have sought his right in the prince and the prince's own goods, and could not exact the whole of that in which he had been injured from some one citizen, or a few citizens, but only what each man's share amounted to. But, of a truth, because it was most difficult for outsiders to attain their right in this fashion, by the usage of nations the custom has been introduced of understanding that all the corporeal and incorporeal goods of those who are under a society or a head are bound, and, as it were, tacitly pledged to meet the debt of such a state or of such a head of the state, whether that debt be original, or derived upon it by the denial to others of justice; and this holds to such a degree that not merely is each bound for his proper share, but even eventually for the whole, in such wise, however, that his own state ought to restore to him what he has been compelled to pay beyond his portion. Hence an outsider who cannot obtain from some state what is owed him, can lay hands upon the goods of any citizens whatsoever of that same state in an amount equivalent to the sum due him. Necessity has compelled the exercise of such a right, since, forsooth, frequently a man cannot lay hands upon the private property of princes as easily as he can upon that of ordinary persons, who are more numerous, and the members of some society can customarily obtain their right among one another more easily than can outsiders, of whom often very little account is made. Also there was this common advantage for all people from that obligation, namely, that those who were at present harassed by it, might at some other time be assisted thereby. Nevertheless, if a man care to examine into the question minutely, he will find the foundations of that matter in the very pact whereby states are constituted, and in consequence of the very law of nature. For although those who unite to form states do by no means destroy or confound the ordinary ownership of things, or introduce a community of goods (where that had been brought about, since everything which one had acquired by a pact with an outsider had accrued directly to the public property, without doubt also the same goods would be held by virtue of the fact that the second party in that pact had promised him an equivalent value, as it were), nevertheless, since all the possessions of individual citizens have been made subject to one person by virtue of eminent domain, they are understood to have coalesced also into one body, in so far as they contribute to the preservation of civil society. And so he with whom rests the <108> power of eminent domain, that is to say he who has supreme authority in the state, can order the citizens to contribute the amount which each one ought to contribute in order to meet the public expenses, or, when necessity does not admit of delay, he can order them to take as much as the situation demands from a few persons where it is most convenient, on the understanding that restitution is to be made afterwards to these few by all the citizens together. Furthermore, since that same eminent domain has been established also for the purpose of preserving the goods of individuals, and the more extensive these are, the more easily individuals endure public burdens, and so whatever goods come to the members of that state, they redound in some measure to the advantage of individuals; it results that individuals also can be bound in a definite way on the basis of the obligation which follows all goods whatsoever which are included under that society. This happens primarily when some outsider cannot attain by an ordinary

road to that which is owed him by some member of a second state. For
under those conditions the favour accorded me by the law in my effort to
secure what is owed me, seems to grant me the right to appropriate to myself
that which is my own out of the goods of any person whatsoever belonging
to that society, by the strength of which, arising as it does from the union
of individuals, my debtor is protected. This same position the usage of
nations has approved. And from these sources the right of reprisals is to be
derived.

30. Furthermore, the following general observation must be made in the
matter of obligations which bear upon the property of the man who contracts the obligation, namely, that together with the goods they are transmitted to the heir of the original debtor. Such are the obligations which
have to do with rendering to another some property which is commonly
the subject of commercial transactions among men. For, in the case of
these, there is primarily given to the second party the right and ground of
bringing action, to the amount of the debt, against the goods of him who
puts himself under obligation. The result of this is, that, although the heir
is not bound by the transgressions of his predecessor, nevertheless it is possible to reach some agreement concerning his debts, since, forsooth, the
creditor had a prior right to those goods before the heir.[30] Now in societies,
and above all in the state, debts always adhere to the society until they are
paid, although the individual members of the society have been changed,
nay more, even if, perchance, no one still remains alive of those who originally contracted that debt; yes, and even though the accidental form of
the state may have been changed, for example, if it has been transformed
from a monarchy to a democracy, or vice versa.[31] For all who unite themselves to that society are understood to be obligating themselves to endure
its present burdens, quite as much as stipulating for the <109> acquisition
of its present and subsequent goods, and so he who is now a citizen is bound

30. Cf. *JNG,* 4, 11, §19, with references to *Dig.,* XXIX.ii.8, and Quintilian, *Declamationes* CCLXXIII.
31. The "accidental form" of the state arises from the particular bearer of sovereignty,
whether a monarch, an aristocracy, or a democratic assembly. This is in contrast to its
"essential form," which is the "community of right and sovereignty" (*JNG,* 7, 5, §1; 8,
12, §§1, 9).

to pay also his proper share of the debt which the state contracted many
years before. States, too, have this in common with other societies, namely,
that although different members succeed one another individually, and
change, nevertheless the states themselves remain perpetually the same, as
long as they retain the bond and continuity as well as the unity of the community.[32] But if, in truth, the citizens have divided to wage civil war, and
so have broken up into two parties, then it is certain, that, as long as dissension remains, one part is not affected by an obligation contracted by the
other part. But when those who have been at variance return once more to
concord and form a single state, it must be carefully decided just which part
retained the equivalence of the commonwealth, and which part had the
appearance of rebels, or of the seditious. The former is adjudged to have
done all things in due order and as on the basis of legitimate authority, and
it imposes on the other part the necessity of approving the things which it
has done, and so after secession the seceders, once more united, are obligated to pay the debts contracted during the interim, even though contracted with the purpose of bringing the seceders themselves back into line.
This situation does not obtain in the case of the seceders. For they are adjudged to be acting as private citizens in whatever they have done, and so
their debts do not devolve directly upon the state, unless either there has
been some special agreement to that effect, or else they themselves have
vanquished the rest and taken to themselves by force the supreme [sover-
eignty] of the commonwealth. But when it is difficult to determine, the
dignity of the two parties remaining equal, just which part retains the
equivalence of the commonwealth, the question will have to be adjudicated
by agreements, if, indeed, they have had their difficulties composed by
peaceful means (when the equality of the parties urges the creation of an
equal obligation, in such wise that all together pay the debts of both); or
else, if an end is put to the dissension by the sword and by force, victory
will show which part is to be regarded as the commonwealth. But if, in
truth, some one has seized upon the state by the right of war, none the less

32. On the continuity of the state and its debts through changing generations and
constitutions, see Grotius, *JBP,* II.ix, "When Sovereignty or Ownership Ceases"; cf. Pufendorf, *JNG,* 8, 12, "On Changes Within States and the Dissolution of States."

may they to whom that state had been under obligation of indebtedness, demand the payment of their debts out of the possessions of the state, from the one who has seized it, if, indeed, they have been outside that state and were not the enemies of the one who has seized it. For there is here no reason why his right ought to be taken away from a third person, a right which, based upon property of that state, can be made good against any possessor whatsoever, in so far as the latter has not alleged a more valid right. But if the creditor be <110> included in that state, such right on his part will redound to the victor by virtue of his victory.

31. From the same principles also it can be deduced that the treaties formed by a people among whom the supreme authority is in the hands of more than one, are real, as they say, or last continuously, even if the persons administering the commonwealth have changed; since, forsooth, as has already been said, however much the persons may change, the state is regarded as being always one and the same, composed of men now present and their successors. But, in truth, in a monarchy it is more difficult to make clear whether a successor to whom the supreme authority is transmitted directly of full right, is bound by the treaties of his predecessor, when they have not been expressly restricted to the predecessor's person.[33] Here the question is not properly one of pacifications, nor of pacts of the kind whereby a certain right has been transferred from one of the parties in an agreement to the other, as is the case in gift, sale, and similar contracts. For by pacifications previous injuries which furnished a cause of war are utterly extinguished, conditions being satisfied on both sides; and by pacts of the latter kind, he who transfers something retains for himself absolutely no right in it. That is why the successor can neither do away with a peace which has been made by his predecessor, unless some new cause arise, nor take up anew contracts or donations, unless, perchance, these were invalid in some point of law. Nor is there properly any doubt about a case of this kind, whether, namely, after the obligations of a pact have been met by one party, and the other party had died before he could meet his obligations also, the successor is bound to render equivalent value. For,

---

33. On the following discussion, see Grotius, *JBP,* II.xvi.16, "What Compacts Are to Be Considered Personal, and What Real, Is Set Forth, with Distinctions."

since that which was rendered on condition of recompense has gone to the use of the commonwealth, or at least was turned over with that intention, it is, of course, patent that, unless an equal amount be repaid, the second party retains a right to the property which was conditionally turned over, and so he who has succeeded to authority over it is bound to restore the thing turned over, or what was mentioned in the agreement as its equivalent value.

There remains, therefore, only the question whether, on the basis of an agreement which had been entered into by one's predecessor (having to do with a mutual rendering of things previously not owed), whereby either nothing had been rendered as yet by either party, or else what had been turned over between the two parties was equal, the successor also is obligated, before he has bound himself to that agreement by his own consent. Here some others have found it most convenient to decide the case on the basis of the exact form of the agreement; to wit, that it is regarded as a real pact, if the proviso has been added that it is to be permanent; if it has been made for the good of the kingdom, or been made with the prince and his successors, or for <III> a limited time; likewise, that there comes to be a basis for conjecture in the material itself, to the effect, namely, that agreeable pacts are believed to be real, but disagreeable pacts to be personal. But, in truth, after a very careful inspection of obligations of that kind, it is perfectly plain what in general must be laid down as a definition here. It is certain, therefore, that obligations are primarily binding upon those very persons who contract them, or in any fashion whatsoever make them their own. And so, on the basis of the law of nature, there results from all obligations the right to bring action against a person. For the rest, in due consequence, obligation carries over also to the property of the man who obligated himself, to wit, that I can acquire what is due me on the terms of the obligation by laying hands upon the property in question. And so any one whatsoever in obligating himself is understood to be giving a second person the authority to lay hands upon his own goods, if, indeed, he does not render what he owes. And this happens in a twofold respect, either because his own property has been increased by that which the second party has already rendered, or else because he can be compelled by his love for his own property to render what he owes so as to avoid an invasion of his goods. The result of the first respect is that, even after the original person is no more, the obligation inheres in his property, so that even though those goods of his may have devolved upon an heir, nevertheless the second party may out of them appropriate to himself what is owed him. But the second respect disappears with the person himself, because the reason for it is based merely on the fact that a person is rendered wretched by the invasion of his property, and so can in this manner be impelled to pay his debts. Now since the kingdom is counted among the goods of the king, it is readily apparent that, in the case which we have assumed, upon the death of the king the obligation is no longer based upon the kingdom, and so he who succeeds to that possession is not bound, at least on this consideration, by the compact of his predecessor. There is left, therefore, the case that the predecessor himself has directly and expressly transmitted his own obligation to the successor. But, in truth, it is obvious that a second person cannot fasten upon me an obligation, which is to be valid even after his death, unless the authority to exact that obligation from me has been conferred upon some one of those who survive him, and that either a man, which cannot be the case among those who rejoice in supreme authority, or else God, as comes about by a sworn oath. The conclusion from this is that a successor is not bound by the agreement on the part of his predecessor, being of the kind just described, before he obligates himself by his own consent, unless he has made promise under oath to his predecessor that he will continue to observe that agreement; although on this score the obligation is destined to be valid, not so much on the basis of a proper right <112> resting upon the agreement of his predecessor, as because of reverence towards the Divine Spirit.

32. As concerns their material,[34] obligations can be contracted about any matters whatsoever, which we have either the faculty or the authority to furnish. For, when something has been put within my power, and I have the authority to dispose of it, then nothing keeps me from binding myself by a certain bond of necessity to turn it over to a second person. From this it follows that it is impossible for any one to obligate himself effectively

34. On §§32–37 see *JNG,* 3, 7, "On the Subject-Matter of Promises and Pacts," and Grotius, *JBP,* II.xi.8–9.

with regard to a thing which is put beyond his own power, or has not been placed under his authority, or in regard to which he fails to have a natural or moral faculty. Here, however, should first be noted in regard to the former condition, that it can happen that an obligation about a matter which for the present is put beyond a man's powers, may not lack all efficacy, when, to be sure, either a possible thing has been entrusted by one of the two parties to the agreement, or else it is due to a man's own fault that it cannot be discharged by him. For he who has made a promise about something which he thought was possible, after it has been found to be impossible, is certainly bound to furnish it as far as his strength admits in that case, at least when time has, perchance, brought him the faculty of furnishing it; or else to make up in some other way what is lacking, for example, by offering an equivalent value, or by remitting what corresponded to that matter in their mutual relation of furnishing things to one another. For he who enters upon a pact with a second person about any matter, considers primarily, indeed, and directly, the matter which has been mentioned in the pact, and indirectly some other good for himself which has the same value as the matter expressed in the pact. For, of course, a person in a pact furnishes one thing altogether with the purpose of acquiring something else which is of advantage to himself. Therefore, it is understood that, when he cannot secure what he has expressly designated, he desires to have furnished him something else of equivalent value, so as not to be suffering loss himself while the other party is making gain. And this holds, unless something impossible was promised with the intent to deceive. But, if both parties know that the thing is impossible, and if each knows that the other knows it, they are judged merely to have been jesting, and so not to have concluded any contract. But he who promises something which was possible at the time of the promise, but has since become impossible, if, indeed, that change came about without any fault on his part, nevertheless owes it to put forth his utmost effort; but when this change has been brought about by his own fault, he renders himself liable also to punishment. Thus, he who by some unforeseen turn of fortune is unable to pay, is bound to labour to the utmost extent of his powers, indeed, so as to discharge the debt, <113> taking also some time to do so; nevertheless, he cannot be subjected to punishment on that account. But he who has wasted his resources by his own fault, beside being bound to do his utmost to pay, is also making himself liable to punishment.

33. Now a number of men have raised here the very thorny question, whether, namely, a man can obligate himself to endure evils which commonly surpass our fortitude of spirit, for example, whether a man can be obligated by his own pact not to resist one who is inflicting death or wounds upon him. And to this question they answer, No, for the following reasons.[35] Because, out of a certain natural necessity, it is not possible that any one should fail to avoid these evils, and no one is bound to the impossible. The same is found to be true in the case of those who are being led away to punishment, and who are under the compulsion of attendants or bonds, but we trust the man who is bound by a pact; therefore, it does not appear that those persons have been adequately obligated to non-resistance by pacts. They contend, furthermore, that such a pact is unavailing; for in a state it is sufficient if the state should stipulate by a pact that no one should defend the man upon whom punishment is to be inflicted. Now outside the state, since such a pact is referred to another pact which comes into play if the first be not fulfilled (for example: "This I will do, and unless I do it, I promise that I will not resist the one who comes to put me to death"), it likewise will be unavailing. For, if the second party has violated the former pact, the parties to the pact have already come to be in a state of war with one another, whereupon the latter pact also immediately expires. Finally, by a pact of that kind, not to resist evil, we are obligated to choose of two present evils that which appears to be the greater; for certain death is a greater evil than a fight; and yet of two evils it is impossible not to choose the less. Therefore, by such a pact we would be bound to do the impossible, and that is repugnant to the nature of pacts. The last reason, however, can scarcely be allowed, because it might appear possible to infer from it, that the force of all obligations whatsoever expires, as often as a man has come to the conclusion that it is worse for him to stand by the obligation than to withdraw from it, and on that reasoning the whole efficacy of obligations would depend upon each individual's good pleasure, not to mention that, for an obligation to be binding, it is not required that its violation may not

---

35. The author in question is Hobbes; see *De cive*, chap. 2, §18; cf. *JNG*, 3, 7, §5.

sometimes appear more desirable than its fulfilment. On the contrary, the efficacy of a contract still persists after it has been judged to be preferable to violate it, with the result, namely, that the second party, by virtue of the same, has the authority to secure his right from the other by force. But, of a truth, it is readily apparent from the nature of pacts, what judgement should be rendered upon this question. For the force of pacts ultimately comes to this, namely, <114> that the obligator has the authority to exercise forcible compulsion upon the obligated when he goes back on his promises, or even to inflict evil upon him directly or indirectly for this reason. To enter upon a pact about suffering this evil without reluctance is utterly absurd. For, since there is no efficacy to an obligation except a person be restrained, as it were, by the fear of some evil which is to arise from its violation, the said pact would again have to be buttressed up by another penal pact, and this again by yet another, and so on endlessly. And, truly, it is quite useless to desire to bind some one twice with the same kind of bond in regard to the same thing. For, if the first be broken, the second also falls immediately. Therefore, there is no reason why a second person should be bound to suffer a penalty without any reluctance on his part.

From this it follows also that no one is bound to accuse or to inform upon himself. For the tortures which are applied to the accused are properly neither accusations nor testimony, but are aids in extracting the truth. And so men are not customarily submitted to investigations unless there already exists some pretty clear evidence as to their misdeeds, and that is because judges are commonly unwilling to condemn any one, unless he himself admits that he is not being wronged thereby. Nor should he be judged to have broken his obligation who under torture has denied his deed, or has made no answer at all. Now in oaths of clearance, which are treated as the equivalent of moral torture in cases that are not capital, one may not, because of reverence for the Divine Spirit, conceal the truth, although the judge, as far as he is concerned, may seem to be giving the man to whom he administers the oath, the choice either of confessing as true that which will bring some inconvenience upon himself, or of renouncing claim upon the divine mercy. The latter, however, no one is presumed to do.

34. We are unable also to contract an obligation about those things, over the disposal of which we have lost the moral faculty or authority. Of this

sort are matters forbidden by the laws. For he who by law forbids any one
an action, takes away from him, of course, the authority to undertake it,
and, in consequence, the faculty of obligating himself to another to perform it. Therefore, he who has covenanted to commit a sin, sins twice if
he should keep his pact, even if he has also interposed an oath. Here, however, it should be noted that certain things are forbidden by laws, and yet,
when a contract has actually been made about them, the obligation is not
rendered invalid, even if the contracting parties be generally subjected to
some punishment or fine therefor. And this is almost the usual thing in the
case of acts which are in themselves licit, but in which the contracting parties have neglected some circumstance that is necessary merely in the civil
law. Here, even though, perchance, the obligation be invalid on the basis
<115> of the civil law, nevertheless it will be valid on the basis of the law
of nature. Thus also, on the contrary, many things which are done against
some duty of the law of nature, because civil laws make no regulation concerning them, are not immediately held invalid or null in a human court
of law, although there be a sin against the law of nature, quite as much
when a man obligates himself to such pacts, as when he performs the same.

35. Furthermore, just as there is no doubt that a pact about an illicit thing
ought not to be observed, and he does well who withdraws before that illicit
thing has been fulfilled; so, if that base deed has been performed, the question arises, whether a man be altogether bound to pay the reward for which
the other had bargained to commit the act. Some say that he is, because a
reward of that kind itself, or a promise before the crime, carries with it the
discredit of being an incitement to evil, but that this discredit begins to
pass away after the crime has been performed, when the force of the obligation which hitherto lay in pending efficacy, discloses itself, inasmuch as
it had not been intrinsically lacking from the beginning, but was impeded
by an added fault. But we are of the opinion that the law of nature has
declared such pacts to be invalid; so also that the same law does not at all
obligate the parties to an agreement to pay the reward for the performance
of a base service about which they had made an agreement. For, on this
score, that prohibition about not entering into pacts on illicit matters,
would be of no avail, if by the law of nature the pact would be valid after
the deed had been performed; since that would amount to saying: "Theft

should not be perpetrated; but, if a man has stolen something, he can properly retain it." And if the promise of a reward had a discredit about it before it was kept, because it was an incitement to evil, it will also not be without a discredit after the crime has been committed, because the rewarding of wrong is also the incitement to further evil. But if, therefore, a man has voluntarily, recognizing the turpitude of the crime, offered his services, and has stipulated for the receipt of a definite reward, you cannot at all believe that the law of nature is concerned to see that his wickedness should not have to go without its reward. For they allege the example of Judah's being willing to pay Thamar, whom he thought to be a harlot, the promised reward as a thing which was due her; to which the answer can be made that, in this region, the carnal intercourse of an unmarried man with an unmarried woman was regarded as licit, and accordingly it was possible to make a contract about it that was valid, at least in civil law.[36] But if with his promises and other solicitations a man has corrupted some one who was otherwise averse to crime, of course he is bound to pay him at least as much as he promised, not by the force of the pact, but on the basis of the law about making good the injury which <116> has been done to a second person. Thus, for example, he who has induced a virgin to lie with him by promise of matrimony, is bound to marry her, not as the reward of lying with him, but to compensate her for the injury done to her chastity. And yet pacts of that kind have this effect, namely, that, because there has been agreement to them on both sides, if, indeed, one of the parties to the agreement has been compelled by the other through the exercise of force to fulfil his engagement, or because of failure to fulfil the same has suffered some ill, he has no just cause for making complaint on that score, nor is he properly regarded as having suffered injury, since the evil for which a man has given cause by his own fault, is not judged to be coming upon a person against his will. For by his own consent he brought it about that he cannot employ the protection of the law of nature, whereby no one is forced to a thing which is not due, and no one may be subjected to evil because of failing to perform a thing which is not due; and he renounced the favour

36. Genesis 38.

of this law at the same time, that, as far as in him lay, he gave another the
authority to demand something of that sort from him.

The same condition obtains in states where duels have been prohibited;
for there neither can I rightfully challenge another, nor am I bound myself
to answer the challenge of a second person, even after I have once given
my word of promise to do so. And yet, if any man voluntarily enters a fight
which is forbidden, and is wounded therein, he has none whom he may
rightly accuse but himself, and he cannot complain that a wrong has been
done him, or demand of the man who wounds him compensation for the
injury. Thus, for example, if, contrary to the interdict of the civil laws, two
persons fight to a conclusion with arms over an inheritance, on the condition that the victor receive the whole, if, now, the victor appropriates the
inheritance, the vanquished has not experienced a wrong which enables him
to lodge a complaint; nor is the judge bound to restore him to his full right,
but he may mete out to both a suitable punishment, and besides, as it seems
to him, he may either leave to the victor the property about which they
fought, or else take it entirely away under the guise of a fine, unless it please
him better to restore the property to its former condition.

36. Moreover, since the things and the actions of others are beyond our
authority, it is readily seen that I cannot make a contract about them with
a second person, so that the other by my act acquires a right to them. But
when I make a contract in this wise with a second person, as, for example,
that I will see to it that a third person furnishes a definite thing or performs
a definite action for him, I am obligated to expend every effort morally
possible to impel the third person to furnish that thing; but the second
person does by no means <117> acquire therefrom a right to the property
of the third, nor can he demand it of him as though it were due the second
person on the basis of that third person's obligation. But if, now, I make a
pact in this wise, namely, that, unless the third person supply something,
I myself will be bound to supply it or pay a definite fine, it is manifest that,
if I cannot obtain it of the third person himself, I ought to make it good
to the second person. This is very much like the provision of the Roman
laws, whereby, if any one, knowing it to be such, bequeathed property
which was another's (because no one is presumed to have desired his action
to have no effect), the heir was compelled to purchase and turn over that

property, or, if he could not purchase it, to give its equivalent in value.[37] But if any one simply promises that a second person will give, he obligates neither himself nor the second person. Nevertheless, the things and actions of those over whom we exercise sovereignty are not regarded as belonging to others, as far as that sovereignty extends. For I can contract effectively about these, as about my very own, so far, indeed, that I am not merely bound myself to observe the pact, but also the second person, whose deed or property I engage for, is obligated by the force of the authority which I properly have over him, to fulfil my promise, in such wise, that, not from me alone, as the original promisor, but also from that second person, after my will became known to him, the third person may be able to claim his right. But I cannot also make a valid pact with a third person about my own things or actions over which a second person has already acquired a right, unless, perchance, this latter be willing to yield his right. For he who by former pacts had transferred his right to another, has himself, assuredly, no longer any such right left to himself which he can confer upon a third person. Also in that way all pacts could be evaded without any trouble by entering upon another pact, in which arrangements were made contrary to the former. And so, in this case, the later pact is rendered invalid by the earlier, or rather the earlier shows that a later cannot exist. And in this sense is to be accepted that trite dictum, "The prior in time is superior in right," namely, not that time in itself confers any right, but because the prior in time has already acquired some right which prevents the later in time from being able to acquire a right to the same thing. On the same foundation rests also the principle, that, by the Roman laws, a servant could not be obligated to his master (aside from that general obligation which accompanies his own status as a slave);[38] since, forsooth, already all of his useful actions and property were under the authority of his master; but neither could he be obligated to any one else, because the slave had no right of his own, but was under the right of a second person, and so he could not make

37. The reference is again to the Roman law institution of *trust* [*fideicommissum*]. See bk. I, Def. 5, §19, note 30.

38. See bk. I, Def. 12, note 8 (§6), p. 116.

any effective disposition about himself, as being the property of another.
<118>

37. On the same principle we are to understand also the following dictum, "A laxer obligation yields to a stricter, when it is impossible to satisfy both at the same time." That is true because, of course, I am more obligated to one thing than to the other, when it is impossible to act upon both obligations at the same time, and so it follows that one person to whom I owe something, or who has fastened an obligation upon me, has an authority over me which the other either does not have at all, or else does not have with an equal effectiveness. And so when a man who is under a second person's authority obligates himself to furnish something to a third person, it is always understood that he has added this limitation, or ought to have added it: In so far as it may be possible without infringing upon the obligation by which he is bound to his superior. But if, now, neither party with whom I am making the pact, has rightfully more authority over me than the other, that obligation which is prior in time prevails; and this is so because I can no longer make a valid disposition about the action or the thing which I am now owing to a second person. From this it is understood how questions should be decided when a man has been bound to two confederates.[39] If, namely, both at the same time should demand his promised aid, which he cannot furnish at the same time, that is, let us suppose, the presence of the promisor, or all his forces of a definite kind, for example, all his ships, all his cavalry, &c., to which of the two should he rather furnish aid? For here the earlier alliance takes precedence, because in the later it is understood that only those actions which were free from the former obligation have been obligated. And this obtains not merely when the confederates have to do with a third person, but even when they have to deal with one another, if, indeed, by the prior treaty of alliance confederates-to-be are not expected thenceforward. But the nature of the prior treaty of alliance does not even allow one to produce that which can be furnished to both at the same time. For to do so implies that he who has stipulated for assistance from me has left me at liberty to furnish assistance likewise also

---

39. On the following discussion of how to deal with conflicting obligations from different alliances, see Grotius, *JBP,* II.xv.13.

to him against whom he is imploring my assistance. For in this way the effect of the aid promised to the former would amount to nothing, inasmuch as things added to one side are of no moment if the same amount be added to the other. Nevertheless, the justice of the cause of those who are waging war should here be well considered. For since no one is obligated to support the wrongs done by a second person, it is surely patent that, if the earlier ally does wrong to the later ally, I can also give help to the later against the earlier (unless it has been agreed that I am bound not to give aid against him on any score at all), since, forsooth, the assistance promised to the earlier ally presupposed the justice of his cause.

38. For the purpose of confirming obligations, and especially pacts, <119> there are added instruments, oaths, pledges, hostages, and suretyships. As regards the first of these, it is necessary in contracting mutual obligations among men that the will be expressed by signs, since, forsooth, there can be no effect mutually among men of the acts of their will as long as these acts are not manifested in signs. Now the more imperfect signs, indeed, are gestures, which it is proper to employ in making commercial transactions between those who do not understand one another's language; and the more perfect are words which are understood on both sides. That these words, furthermore, should express more clearly and more firmly the will, it has been instituted both that at pacts of greater moment there should be present witnesses, to whose memory and conscience an appeal may be made, if, perchance, the pact itself be denied by either party to it, or if some doubt arise about the words of the pact; but especially that the terms of the pact should be expressed in writing. For the memory of even a number of men is defective, or their good faith wavering, but things written are by no means so subject to forgetfulness or perfidy. Bare words also are frequently frustrated by the excuse that they were proposed hurriedly, or without a careful consideration of the matter; and this exception also is excluded by things written, for, assuredly, while these are being drawn up, they present the matter with the utmost clarity and not without some delay to the mind of the contracting party, so that, if, indeed, he has approved the things written, he should altogether be judged to have consented fully to the matter itself. Nor can things written be so easily distorted by cunning interpretations as can words, in which some trickily inserted particle that was

not noticed in hurriedly pronouncing the words, can upset the whole matter, an inconvenience to which things written are by no means so liable.

As for the rest, although the obligation of pacts does not in itself depend upon things written or instruments of that kind, for, assuredly, an obligation can be contracted without them, and, as far as the law of nature is concerned, persist, even if, perchance, they have perished by some accident; nevertheless, in a human court of law whose finding rests only on the most manifest signs, these instruments are to the very highest degree heeded, and more confidence is felt in them than in any other kind of evidence at all. And if they cannot be produced, the plaintiff is ordinarily rejected, unless he has proved by satisfactory witnesses that he has lost those instruments by some accident. Hence also it follows, that, if the creditor has knowingly given back the instrument of the obligation, or has knowingly destroyed it with the knowledge of the debtor, he is regarded as having absolved the latter from his debt. Nevertheless, if the debtor should by any means secure possession of the agreements (suppose that he has stolen them, or extorted them in some other way) he will not at all have been released <120> from his obligation, at least on the basis of the law of nature, although, perchance, in a human court of law an action against him might fail.

39. An oath is customarily administered for what is essentially a threefold purpose, either that we should deny that we are guilty of some crime or privy to it, or that we should confirm our intention to speak the truth about a matter known to us, or else that we should bind ourselves to furnish something. We can call the first an oath of clearance, the second an oath of testification, the third an oath of promise. An oath of clearance is customarily offered by those who have the authority to exact punishment, or who wish to accuse us when some indications, indeed, of crime point to us, but nevertheless do not constitute complete proof, and where it is impossible to get the truth in the case by other evidence or testimony. Now we cannot be compelled to take such an oath except by those to whom properly belongs the authority to inflict punishment upon us, and this principally because the one who refuses such an oath is regarded as being convicted of the crime and as having confessed it; although when others demand an oath of us we can rightly refuse it, unless, perchance, they are bringing an action against us, and then it appears more convenient to avoid in this way a trial,

than to plead our case with danger, or at all events with annoyance. And yet such an oath is not customarily offered in a case where the confession of the truth is followed by capital punishment. Indeed, just as no one is commonly presumed to renounce the divine mercy in order to avoid some inconvenience which falls short of danger to his own life, so only a few have such strength of character that they prefer to meet death rather than commit perjury, especially since after perjury they are by no means interdicted from appealing once more to the divine mercy, and the hope is not precluded that it can once more be prevailed upon. Very much the same obtains in regard to the oath of testification. For this also can be forced upon me only by those who have sovereignty over me, and to the rest of men I can impute it as a free service. Also in cases involving capital punishment it is not appropriate for it to be taken by men who are united with those against whom testimony is to be given, by a certain kinship, which produces a strong effect upon the emotions, for, of a truth, they are commonly judged to put personal considerations before religious scruples.*

40. Now, in general, an oath is a religious assertion, by which we forfeit the divine mercy, or call down upon ourselves the divine punishment, if we do not speak the truth, or fulfil our promise. For that this is the meaning of oaths is readily indicated by the formulae which are customarily employed: "So help me God," "God be witness," and the like, which amount to much the same thing. For when a superior, <121> having the right to inflict punishment, is called in as a witness, at the same time vengeance upon perfidy is demanded from him. And so those asseverations which cannot be reduced to this meaning do not possess the character of oaths. Here can be set forth in passing, also, what we should think about the custom of the ancients who attributed equal or almost greater force to oaths sworn by the safety, head, and life of the prince, than those sworn by God.[40] For this, properly speaking, was not done because they thought there was a divine spirit in their princes, or because they were calling down upon

* By an obvious slip the text has *gratiam post religionem habere,* for *religionem post gratiam habere.* Cf. also the *De jure naturae et gentium,* bk. IV, chap. ii, §20, where the same topic is discussed.— *Tr.*

40. Cf. *JNG,* 4, 2, §3, with references to Pietro della Valle, *Viaggi* pt. II, ep. I; Augustine, *Sermones,* CLXXX.

themselves the wrath of their princes, if they broke faith; but because most of them wished it to appear that they cared more for the safety of their princes than for their own safety, and so would have greater scruples about turning the wrath of God upon the heads of these princes, than in bringing it down upon their own heads. Of course the meaning of oaths of that kind was properly this: "I so hope for the safety of the prince, as I shall do this," that is to say, "Unless I do this, I call down the wrath of God upon the prince." This makes it clear that in former times men who swore falsely by the head of the prince were, not without reason, punished more severely than those who swore falsely by their own heads. For in this latter fashion they were believed to be calling down the punishment for perjury merely upon their own persons, but in the former way, to be calling it down even upon the prince, with whom the safety of the state was bound up. Also from the purpose of these same oaths the meaning is gathered, and this purpose is, that men should be more firmly bound to tell the truth and to fulfil their promises, out of fear of the Divine Spirit, omnipotent and omniscient, whose wrath, if they should knowingly practise deceit with an oath, they are calling down upon themselves, where otherwise the fear of others appeared to be a less effective bond of faith, as they hoped to be able either to escape their power or else to avoid detection. For where the violator of pacts cannot either elude us or avoid our punishment, it seems superfluous to demand an oath. Now, although all non-atheists assume that God punishes the violation of pacts, even though they are not confirmed with an oath; nevertheless, it is a common and no vain persuasion, that he who has provoked the anger of God, and, as far as in him lay, voluntarily by his own perjury shut off the way of access to His mercy, will be more severely punished.

41. Now it should be well observed that the swearing of an oath does not properly produce a new obligation, but supervenes as a kind of accessory bond to the obligation which was in itself firm. For something is always presupposed, failure to furnish which calls forth divine vengeance by virtue of the oath. But this would be absurd unless it were illicit not to furnish that which is presupposed, and so we were already under obligation. The result is, that those pacts which other-<122>wise in themselves, on the basis of the law of nature, give the second person no right, do not supply it,

indeed, even when an oath is added, as happens in the case of those who through unjust fear have given cause for a sworn promise. For on such men there remains no less an obligation to restore the thing promised which was extorted by violence, even when the promise is accompanied with an oath, than when it is not; on the topic of compensation for which, as overriding the obligation of fulfilling the promise, we have spoken above. Nevertheless, in honour of the Divine Spirit, such promises ought, in our opinion, to be kept. For since, in consideration of having taken an oath, you have escaped an evil greater than the promise was, it would be particularly irreverent to have retracted, as it were, so effective an invocation of the Deity, after having escaped the peril. Nay more, we are not under obligation also concerning matters about which in themselves we could not be obligated, even if an oath were added. Such are matters which are forbidden by enacted laws, for it is absurd to invoke the divine vengeance in case you fail to do something, when, if you did it, you should be punished by the same Deity, and so be abusing the reverence for God for the sake of ignorance of him, as it were. And oaths have been introduced so as to add strength to the licit and good actions of men among one another, not so as to render assistance to crimes. Thus they also are right who say, "Vows taken upon oath, which impede another greater good, are invalid." Such was that usage among the ancient Jews whereby they swore that they would never do any good to this man or to that; since, forsooth, we cannot at all forbid ourselves to do a benefaction which has been ordered by the Deity.[41] It is clear that the same holds true of what is absolutely impossible, although it be beyond doubt that he who thus recklessly treats the religious scruples invoked by the divine name is grievously sinning. In the same way the addition of oaths does not change a conditional promise into an absolute one. For the oath no less stands and falls with the condition, because it presupposed one, than does the promise. Thus, also, if it be certain that the one who swore an oath supposed that something had been done which had in fact not been done, and if he had not believed such to be the case, he would not have sworn the oath, then the oath will not be binding. But if there be doubt

41. See Grotius, *JBP,* II.xiii.7, who refers to Philo Judaeus, *De legibus specialibus,* cf. *JNG,* 4, 2, §10.

whether he would not have sworn the same oath even without the supposition, he will have to stand by what was promised, because, out of reverence for God, the most simple interpretation ought to be applied in the
case of oaths. Similarly, from the nature of pacts a judgement should be
reached as to whether an act committed contrary to an oath be merely illicit,
or rather invalid also. For, unless the promisor has under an <123> oath
yielded his right to the property and transferred it to a second person by
his sworn promise, the act will not be invalid, if afterwards he bestow the
same right upon a third person. Thus, for example, if one has sworn that
he will bequeath a definite thing to somebody, and afterwards sells the same
to a third person, the sale will not be invalid at all, although the seller has
contracted the fault of perjury. Finally, an oath will have efficacy, on the
basis of the law of nature or the law of the state, according to the nature
of the pact or promise to which it is added. For the oath in itself does not
cause the promise or the pact, otherwise valid in itself on the basis of the
law of nature alone, to obtain the efficacy of a civil right, unless, perchance,
the civil law regarding certain pacts has especially assigned it this force.

42. Furthermore, that formula in oaths under which God is invoked as
witness or avenger, is to be adapted to the persuasion or the religion cherished by the one who takes the oath. For no one supposes that he is swearing
by God under any other formula or any other name than that contained
in the precepts of his own religion, that is to say, in the opinion of the oath-
taker, the true religion. So he who has sworn by false Gods, whom he, nevertheless, believes to be true ones, will be obligated; and if he has committed
perjury, he is guilty of perjury against the true God, because, under any
conception whatsoever, he has, nevertheless, before his eyes the notion of
the Deity, and if he have knowingly perpetrated deceit after calling upon
Him, he has been irreverent to the divine majesty, as far as in him lay.

Now, for the rest, the words of an oath are to be taken, and are valid, in
the sense in which he to whom the oath is given professes that he takes
them. For the oath is taken for his sake principally, and not for the sake of
the one who swears the oath. And so, although there will by no means be
an obligation upon him, who, by mere recitation, has pronounced the
words of some oath, as the poets tell us about Cydippe;[42] yet, if a person

42. Ovid, *Heroides* XXI.135ff.

wishes to swear either in such a way that he is not obligated, or in mental reservation takes the words in a sense different from that in which the other person, the one, namely, to whom the oath is being given, understands them, he will altogether be obligated by his oath. And this is not so much because, out of reverence for the Deity, he ought to exclude from this act all cavilling, but, more than that, because otherwise the whole transaction would come to naught. For oaths have been introduced with this purpose, namely, that, so far as possible, a person be made secure on the subject of a second person's good faith relative to a thing promised, or his veracity in response to interrogations, and this purpose is utterly overturned, if that exception is allowed to obtain. And the necessity by which signs of that kind have been instituted among men for the sake of preserving society, altogether required that the signs should be valid in such a way that <124> they could be discerned by the judgement of those for whose sake they are employed. But it is quite impossible for this condition to obtain, if these signs are to be valid, not according to the understanding of the one who receives the oath, but according to an interpretation on the part of the one who takes the oath, which is secret, and at the same time contrary to common usage.

43. Pledges are commonly added to pacts when either the good faith of that party, which, according to the terms of the pact, performs its obligation last, does not appear to be sufficiently certain, or else so as to enable us to be spared the trouble of extorting our right before a tribunal. And on that account a pledge is also commonly wont to equal or to surpass the worth of the thing owed, so that if we be deceived in the faith of the other party, we may have at hand a source from which we can get what is our due. Now pledges are either productive or sterile. The former, by the product which they bear in the meantime, can compensate for the loss which comes to us by a deferred payment of the debt, and accordingly it is not so necessary to have a definite time set at the expiration of which the pledge becomes the property of the holder, unless it has been redeemed in the meantime, inasmuch as delay does not cost him anything. But, because the opposite is the case in sterile pledges, men have for the most part adopted the custom of fixing a definite length of time, at the expiration of which the pledge is appropriated in cancellation of the debt. But if this fixed time has not been expressed, then the redeeming of the pledge after any lapse of time is not

prevented, unless, perchance, sufficient indications appear that it has been abandoned by its owner. Now a pledge is to be restored when the debt is paid, before the pledge be lost in cancellation of the debt after the time-limit has expired. In the meantime the creditor owes the pledge no less care and attention than he gives his own property, since it was given, of course, primarily for his own advantage. And if it suffer any harm, or be utterly lost through the bad faith of the creditor, or any failure on his part to man-ifest at least ordinary diligence, the risk and the loss fall upon him.

44. It is customary to give hostages[43] primarily for the sake of confirming public pacts, when we feel at the same time that mere good faith is not a sufficient guarantee; to wit, that a second party may be prevented by fear from violating the pact, the fear, namely, that some very severe measures will be adopted against those whom he has put under our authority; es-pecially since it is customary not for persons of low estate to be given as hostages, but for those who are highly regarded by the rest. Now hostages are given either by one party alone, or by both parties. The latter course is taken when it equally concerns both parties to keep their agreements, or both are equally able to do <125> harm, or, finally, in war, when it is not definitely established whether the matter is being taken up in all serious-ness, or, under the pretence of a pact an opportunity is being sought for treachery. But the former is pretty apt to be taken when the party which is inferior in strength is forced to enter into a pact upon somewhat severe conditions.

Now the otherwise extremely intricate question which has to do with the obligation of hostages, and what it may be licit to do to them, if that for which they were given has not been observed, seems to admit of set-tlement most conveniently in the following way: If, namely, a distinction be drawn between that which they can suffer without being subjected to a wrong, and that which can properly be inflicted upon them on the basis of the law of nature. For, since hostages are added for the purpose of strength-ening pacts, on the violation of which a war arises, it is clear enough that, on the rupture of the pacts, the hostages also, just as the whole state to

---

43. On the following §§44–47 on hostages as accessories of pacts, see Grotius, *JBP,* III.xx.52ff; cf. *JNG,* 8, 2, §6; 8, 8, §6.

which they belong, pass over into the category of enemies, against whom one may lawfully do whatever one will, at least as far as concerns the absence of any law preventing it which exists in the enemy himself. For by that very pact, when they become enemies, they retain no right which prevents them from suffering every extremity at the hands of him whom they have injured, as we shall set forth at greater length below. There is added the further circumstance, namely, that those who gave them over appear to have granted that same legal right. For the giving over of hostages amounts to this, namely, that one has no objection to make against the foe treating them in any way that he sees fit, in case it so happens that good faith is not maintained. Nor does this legal right remain within the limits of keeping custody merely over hostages. For they undergo this custody in either a stricter or a laxer form, to the degree that it appears necessary, as long as they remain hostages, even when the pact is observed. And so, when pacts are violated, it is well understood that it is possible to go farther, that is to say, to torture and to death, which are next in order after custody. Thus, even when hostages have been given on both sides, if one of the contracting parties has without any just cause maltreated or killed its hostages, the other will be doing no wrong if it treat in the same way the hostages which it has, and this from the bare right of war, and not from some right of talion, although it very commonly happens that this latter is alleged in deeds of that kind: in order to avoid the reputation of cruelty among men. Since, forsooth, by the usage of nations it is regarded as talion, not only when there is visited upon the person who has done wrong, the very evil which he himself did, but even when the same evil is visited upon others in the same moral body, particularly those who are of the same condition. For no one regards an enemy as having been harshly treated when his own practices are visited upon him. But, in truth, <126> since the law of nature bids us to temper those evils which are inflicted upon an enemy, according to the mode of punishment otherwise customarily employed among peaceable men, as far as military considerations and the necessity of defending ourselves and attaining to our right admit, it is readily apparent, that, upon the violation of a pact, innocent hostages cannot rightly be killed or otherwise cruelly handled, unless, perchance, they have done something worthy of death, or have consented to the violation of the pact, and have ordered the violation as at their own peril. For in this case it is beyond doubt that they can be punished even with loss of life.

45. Now here arises a no less thorny question, whether, namely, they who have given a hostage be doing a wrong to him whom they expose in this fashion to the wrath of the enemy. That question we wish to be understood of those who have supreme sovereignty over the hostages whom they give. For if a man, in behalf of persons other than those who have supreme sovereignty over him, has offered himself as a hostage, there is no doubt that he is entering upon a pact with them that they are not to make his condition harder for him by their perfidy, and so the violators of the pact are altogether doing a wrong to the hostage. This question depends on the one, whether he who enjoys the supreme sovereignty has authority to expose, for the public welfare, the life of a subject of his to the immediate or probable peril of death, and whether there devolves upon the subject the obligation of undergoing peril of that kind, if he be ordered to do so. It seems to us that the answer must be, Yes, although there are those who deny this, for the reason that God alone has reserved to himself dominion over life, and man does not have over his own life that right which he has over other things which come under proprietorship, and so this right could not come to the state by the express or tacit consent of individuals. Certainly the common saying, that a man does not have dominion over his own life to destroy it, allows of this limitation, namely, unless it is to be spent for the safety of a number. For the social nature of man seems not merely to permit, but frequently even to persuade, a few to purchase by their own death the safety of very many. And so, since frequently, especially in war, occasions arise in which a multitude cannot be saved unless a few perish for them, we see in all states those in whose hands is the supreme sovereignty, exercising this authority, that, namely, when the safety of all, or of a large number demands it, some few be sent to the immediate peril of their lives, with the effect, that, if they do not obey, or are too slow in submitting themselves to the peril, they are visited with the punishment of death. And it is not probable that they would win praise with such common consent for putting into execution their orders with vigour and meeting death with intrepidity, if in so doing they were sinning against the law of <127> nature. From this it follows, that, just as in war a state can oppose a certain few, at

the probable risk of death, to the onslaught of the enemy; so, if a second party, trusting to the hostages which he has, should decide to vex with new wrongs those who gave the hostages, and do so in such a way that it would be more expedient for the state to lose its hostages than to allow such wrongs, it appears that the state may altogether rightly abandon its hostages at the probable risk of death or serious misfortunes, so as to ward off those wrongs from itself. And a wrong is no more done the hostages because they in particular are exposed to peril in behalf of others, than a wrong is done those, who, at the express bidding of the sovereign, are sent to face the enemy where the most violent assault is making headway. Nevertheless, in our judgement, the same assertion cannot be made, if he to whom hostages have been given, has suffered wrong in the following manner; suppose, that is, that after leaving hostages with him, those who gave the hostages should break the pact in which otherwise there was no inherent defect on the basis of the law of nature. For it is not to be believed that a moral body can enjoin upon a member, because he has been united to it by the bond of supreme sovereignty, the necessity of suffering some misfortune visited upon his own person, yet not as by way of punishment, and this for the sake of giving that moral body the opportunity to do the other party a wrong.

46. The remaining moot points about hostages can be easily explained. The question, namely, "Should hostages still be retained after the death of the king with whom the treaty was made?" is to be decided on the basis of what we said a little above about real treaties and personal treaties. For if by the treaty the obligation passes directly over to the successor, the hostage will still be altogether bound; if otherwise, he will be free. But if some hostage be given merely to redeem a second person who is a prisoner, upon the death of that second person the hostage is not immediately set free, if, of course, he has been given because a certain sum of money had been promised the captor. For since in this way the captor has acquired a ground for action against the goods of the captive, the hostage will be held until what is owed the captor has been paid out of the property of the captive. Otherwise, if the captor regarded nothing but the person of the captive, the hostage will certainly be set free on the latter's death. But if a man has allowed himself to be given as a hostage so that another hostage may be set

free, at the latter's death he will be free, if the second person wished to acquire security primarily in the person of the first hostage; but not if it is a matter of indifference to the second person as to just what individuals should be given as hostages, provided only a definite number of hostages of a definite social station be main-<128>tained. But if it should happen, as we read that it took place more than once among the ancients, that a hostage be the heir and successor of the one who gave him, we are of the opinion that, after this latter has met his fate, the hostage is no longer bound, even if the treaty has not expired at the other's death. For it is understood that this eventuality is tacitly excepted, namely, that he be no longer a hostage if he has changed to the person of the principal debtor; in such wise, however, that he ought to substitute another in his place, if that be demanded.

Now it is not permissible for a hostage to flee as long as the state desires to perform that for which he was given. But when the state has now broken its pact, the hostage becomes a prisoner, who has the right to flee, unless, in order to secure greater freedom of action, he has pledged his good faith not to flee. Thus we are of the opinion that those hostages also who were called to succeed someone upon the throne were justified in fleeing, and this because of the very natural fear that they would be forced to accept unfair terms, if they had openly demanded their dismissal.

Finally, since the obligation of hostages is an odious one, and so demands a strict interpretation, those who have been given for one reason cannot be retained for another, if, of course, something else has been promised without the additional provision for hostages. But if in another case good faith has been violated, or a debt contracted, the hostage may not be retained as such, but on the ground that all citizens are bound by the deed and debt of the state; unless, perchance, the agreement has been expressly reached that hostages be restored altogether, if that for which they had been given has been performed, even if afterwards some controversy arises between the contracting parties on another score.

47. It is a case of suretyship when we show by signs that we are willing to take upon ourselves the obligation of a second person, so that if, indeed, he does not perform his obligation, we ourselves will satisfy it. Now suretyships can be interposed in any pacts dealing with things and actions which

can be redeemed for a price, with this effect, namely, that, if he who bound himself in the first instance should not produce what he owes, the giver of the surety is bound to pay it, in such wise, however, that he has recourse and action against the one for whom the surety was given, in order to recover the loss suffered on his account. Nor is it merely in private contracts, but also in public pacts between such as do not recognize a common judge among men, that givers of surety are introduced, and those primarily by whose interposition the pact was entered into. Their obligation is of the kind that, if one man breaks the pact, the others are bound to give aid whereby he may be forced to furnish once more what he owes. Furthermore, since suretyship is an accession to the principal obliga-<129>tion, it is readily apparent that the giver of surety cannot owe more than he for whom the obligation is assumed. Although, according to the Roman laws, the condition of the giver of surety was in a certain way worse than that of the original debtor, because it was allowed the latter to clear himself of the whole debt by yielding up his property, even though the debt was greater than his property, a favour which was not granted to givers of surety, since, forsooth, givers of surety were provided with the purpose, that, if the debtor should be deprived of his property, the creditor should altogether get his due through the givers of surety. But, of a truth, the law of nature, which knows nothing of that favour of the yielding up of one's property, puts them on an equality as far as the degree of obligation is concerned. And yet, it can very well be that the giver of surety owes less, supposing, for example, if he obligated himself to furnish merely a part of what was owed; if, instead of making an out-and-out promise, he took the precaution of adding a condition (now that, instead of a conditional promise, he should make a pure caveat, to wit, that he does not add and presuppose the condition which the original debtor presupposes, is repugnant to the nature of suretyship); if he undertook to make payment himself only after some interval of time; and if there are other means whereby the obligation becomes less binding.

48. Now in a case where a crime has been committed, suretyships can be brought in only to the degree that either the giver of the surety may promise the magistrate to whom belongs the prosecution of the wrong, that he will himself make good the loss incurred by the wrong, or else he will

guarantee that the accused will appear in court. This interposition commonly takes place either in order to free the accused, who has been arrested already, from the distress of imprisonment, or else to keep some action from being taken against a man who is absent and undefended, as though he were convicted. For, otherwise, the man who gives security cannot at all obligate himself to undergo punishment, properly so called, instead of the accused. For punishment among men is properly some disagreeable evil which is inflicted in consideration of the wickedness of the man who has done evil, and is so inflicted with the purpose of reforming either the wrongdoer himself, or else others.[44] And yet the giver of surety has neither done wrong himself, nor by the act of giving surety has he brought upon himself the guilt of wrongdoing. For there is no crime in the desire to have the accused plead his case on a fairer basis, or be under better conditions, until sentence be passed upon him, especially when the magistracy consent thereto; or to promise that he will pay the fine assessed upon the accused, as also the sum at which the magistrate estimates the possible loss of the opportunity to punish the accused because of his taking flight. Nor can the purpose of punishment be attained in the <130> case of such a giver of bail, and, when that purpose is lacking, punishment cannot be rightly exacted from a man. Also that magistrate has not properly understood the nature of punishment and the obligation of his duty in the matter of exacting it, who has, perchance, sometime inflicted punishment upon a giver of surety; except where it appears that the latter has acted in bad faith, so as to frustrate by this means the force of public authority. But if, now, one suffer any loss of property because of having given surety, that is not properly a punishment, nor does the obligation arise directly from the wrongdoing (although this should give occasion for the obligation), but from

44. This definition of punishment, invoking both retaliation and utility, follows the Grotian definition of *JBP,* II.xx.1: "Now punishment in general means an evil of suffering which is inflicted because of an evil of action." But while Grotius ascribes the authority to inflict punishments "to any one of sound judgement who is not subject to vices of the same kind or of equal seriousness" (ibid., §7), Pufendorf follows Hobbes in limiting punishment to "evils inflicted by public authority" (*Leviathan,* chap. 28). See bk. II, Observ. 4, §16: "But the things inflicted by right of war do not properly have the character of punishments, for they do not proceed from a superior as such, nor do they tend directly to the reformation of the one who does the hurt, or of other men."

one's own consent. From all of which it is apparent, that, since the effect
of giving surety properly reaches its end in the goods of the giver of bail,
the obligation passes over also to his heir. Although, when, perchance, the
sum for which he from whom the inheritance descended was obligated, is
greater than the inheritance itself, the heir is not bound for a larger sum
than he received from the inheritance, and so he is not bound to supply
out of his own property what is lacking to the full sum; unless, perhaps, he
has obligated himself anew for the whole sum.

49. Non-perpetual obligations are removed in the most natural fashion
by the fulfilment of that which is due, for if this be done, the obligation
has fully and directly arrived at its effect. Now in those things which can
properly be carried on through the agency of another, it makes no difference
to the person whom the obligation concerns, whether the man who owes
the debt pays it himself, or some one else does it acting for him. Where a
giver of surety has been interposed, if, indeed, the original debtor has paid,
the latter as well as the former is freed; but if the giver of surety has paid,
the original debtor, to be sure, is freed by the creditor, but on the other
hand he begins to be under debt to the giver of surety. An obligation is
removed also by making a present of the debt, when he to whom something
is owed himself frees us from the burden of furnishing it. For that right
which had been transferred to him on the basis of the obligation, is understood to return to us from the second person by his making a present
of the debt, just as also from the outset an obligation is not contracted, if
the second person, to whom something is offered, has refused to accept the
offer. A variety of this was, in the Roman laws, *acceptilation*,[45] or the formal
discharging of a debt, when either there is a fictitious payment, or a receipt
is turned over which has been made out just as though the debt had been
paid in fact; and this was done so that a man could more easily prove that
he owed nothing further, in case, perchance, doubt should arise on that
score. It belongs under this head also, if a man to whose interest it is that
something be furnished, should himself interfere with the act of furnishing
it. For he, likewise, is regarded as having made a present of the debt, and
so it is looked upon as having <131> been paid. I am also freed from an

45. See *The Institutes of Gaius,* in *Inst.* III.169ff.

obligation, if a third person, with the consent of him to whom I owe it, has taken it upon himself as his own. An obligation expires also when a person has changed that status upon which alone the obligation was based; and this holds quite as much of the person in whom the obligation inheres, as of the one in whom the obligation ends. Thus a magistrate who promises to defend his subjects is no longer bound if he give up his office. And thus he who has promised obedience to a magistrate is no longer bound, when he himself has ceased to be a subject, or the latter to be a magistrate. But, in truth, a change of that kind in the subject, which, it may be, perchance, would have interfered with the obligation had it existed at the time when the obligation was being contracted, and at the present moment is out of accord with the subject, and yet for all that does not render the subject utterly unfit to fulfil the obligation, does not have the force of removing an obligation. For my right which has been legitimately acquired over another person, although it may appear to him at a later time to be less advantageous, can by no means perish, unless this contingency had been from the very first expressly inserted in the pact as a condition. Thus, a people subjecting itself absolutely to a king is by no means freed from its obligation towards the king, even if afterwards it has changed its frame of mind, and finds that some other form of government is going to be more advantageous for it. Contrariwise also, by the consent of the contracting parties, mutual obligations can be dissolved, particularly if the situation is still what it was at the beginning, that is, if nothing has been furnished on either side by the force of the agreement. So, if there exist two different pacts with the same person in regard to the same matter, the first pact will be invalid; because it is well enough established from the second pact that the contracting parties have changed their former intention; just as also in positive laws a later law contradictory to an earlier law invalidates the latter. An obligation is lifted also by compensation, when the creditor owes the debtor something on another account, that is, if, for example, he has in his possession some property of mine without any right to it, or if he is owing me either on a contract or on some other promise, or if he has inflicted some loss upon me. For then, on a comparison of the two debts, only that amount by which one exceeds the other will have to be paid. Now it is unsuitable to have obligations removed by the mere passage of time, except in so far as indications of making a present of the debt can be inferred therefrom. So it is that an obligation of the following kind amounts to nothing: "I will owe you 100 pieces of gold for three years, on the terms, however, that neither in the meantime, nor at the expiration of that period, will you be able to demand them of me." For an obligation which does not <132> acquire some effect before it expires is futile. Yet the case is different, if I frame the obligation in this wise: "Unless you demand it within three years, I will no longer owe anything." For that promise which expires on the failure of the condition to appear is truly conditional.

50. Here also should be settled the question, whether a victorious enemy can destroy the rights of the vanquished in such a way that he can remit to a second person the obligation by which the latter was bound to the vanquished. This controversy was at one time carried on with great violence, when the Thebans, after their city had later been re-established, demanded of the Thessalians a debt which Alexander had remitted them when Thebes was destroyed.[46] Those who take the negative use the following arguments: (1) That which has been taken away by force can be demanded back. (2) The right of war is of no avail in the case of those things which are brought before a court; what has been taken away by arms can be retained only by arms. And so where arms prevail there is no judge; where there is a judge, arms do not prevail. (3) Things acquired by war can be held and retained only by war. (4) The victor cannot bestow rights because that only is the victor's which he actually holds and for as long as he holds it. But the right was in tablets, and that right is a thing incorporeal, nor can hands be laid upon it. The condition of the heir is one thing, that of the victor another. To the former passes a right, to the latter pass merely things and persons. (5) The right of a public loan cannot pass to the victor, because what the people has lent is owed to all the citizens, and as long as some one of the citizens survives, he is, and is regarded as, the creditor for the whole sum. Now not all the Thebans were under the power of the victor, Alexander. (6) If the tablets were given over, it does not appear that for this reason what was contained on the tablets was forthwith given over. For a right does not dwell in the tablets, but from the tablets there is sought the proof of

46. According to Quintilian, *The Orator's Education*, V, chap. x; cf. *JNG,* 8, 6, §23.

the existence of the right. But, in truth, these arguments are by no means strong enough to establish beyond doubt what they purpose. For, (1) that which has been taken away by a proper use of force, that is, that which being previously owed upon any perfect obligation whatsoever, has been extorted by force from a debtor who refused to pay it, can by no means be demanded back. And, by the usage of nations, force exercised in any regular war whatsoever is regarded as just, so that there remains to the former owner no claim to those things, after peace has been made. (2) The right of war does have some strength in the case of those matters which are brought before a court. For assuredly, after a war is ended, if a controversy be started against me regarding a possession which I acquired in war, it is enough for me merely to declare the title of acquisition through warfare, unless, per-<133>chance, a special agreement was entered into in making the peace, to the effect that this property was to be restored, or the injustice of the war has been clearly demonstrated. (3) Things acquired in a just war are most decidedly, even in time of peace, held with justice, especially after peace has been established on both sides; for here those things about whose restitution no agreement has been entered into, are understood to remain with the possessor. (4) As regards the acquisition in warfare of things incorporeal, it is to be noted that certain rights so adhere to things, that they immediately pass over to any and every possessor who is legitimate, at least according to the usage of nations. Thus, for example, he who has seized in war a strait, a river, or some road, where, before that time, those who passed were in the habit of paying a tax, has without any doubt acquired at the same time the right to collect that tax, as long as he is in possession of those highways. But, on the other hand, when in war I bring some person into my power [*potestatem*], I do by no means acquire the rights of that person which are properly and directly based upon his very person. For example, by capturing a king I do not immediately acquire the right to rule over his subjects; by capturing a father or a master I do not immediately acquire a right over his children and his slaves. The reason why I do not is because rights of that kind have been acquired by the one captured through the consent of a second person, and that consent had been based upon the person of the one captured, and no other. And so, since that second person is not in the power [*potestate*] of the victor (as I am supposing the case), it depends upon

the free choice of the former, whether he wish to give by his own consent
such a right to a person other than the one captured; and this in addition
to the fact that most of these rights already have those to whom they pass
over, if he who formerly held them has ceased to exist, either in nature or
in his civil status. But, indeed, along with the capture of a man's person I
am able to acquire also those rights which properly and ultimately are based
upon his property, in such wise, however, that the man captured transfers
them to me by his own consent, and I have the faculty of eliciting that
consent by the threat of a more severe evil. Thus, just as I can give a second
person the right to demand what is owed me by my debtor, with the effect
that my debtor is quite as much bound to pay it to him as he was previously
bound to pay it to me; so, if the captured has with his consent transferred
to me the right to what is owed him, the debtor assuredly begins to owe
me what he had owed the captor. And in this fashion Alexander was able
personally to acquire that debt, if, indeed, he had left Thebes as a state after
compelling the Thebans to transfer their right to him; and in very truth it
is understood that he had acquired that right after he had become, without
any question, the master of Thebes. On this score he had the right to demand that debt <134> from the Thessalians, or to make a present of it. Nay,
he might also have compelled the Thebans to remit that debt directly to
the Thessalians, just as I can compel any one in war to renounce some
pretension of his. Hence Alexander, in turning over to the Thessalians the
tablets recording the debt, was not so much denying that the Theban state
which he himself destroyed, could sometime exact the debt, as he was showing that he himself would demand nothing from the Thessalians on that
score. (5) Now this proposition is false, namely, that as long as one of the
citizens survives, he is, and is regarded as being, the creditor for the whole
sum, and so has the same right which the state had to exact the debt. For
those individuals who survive from some state's body after its dissipation
and utter dissolution cannot at all claim for themselves the right of the state,
since they in their persons do by no means any longer constitute the state.
Now it is well established that Alexander utterly destroyed the Theban state,
to such a degree that those who survived the disaster could by no means be
regarded as a people. And those who later established the city of Thebes
were an absolutely new people, and, if the old Thebans had had any special

rights, these later Thebans could by no means claim them for themselves, on the basis merely of their location, unless they had acquired them anew.

51. After having considered in general the nature of obligations, the next step is to add something on the character of pacts. Now *pacts* can be divided into *public* and *private*.[47] Public pacts[48] are those which are ratified by states and their heads and have to do with affairs which regard the condition of the state. They serve either to *confirm peace,* or to *end,* or *suspend,* or otherwise *modify, war.* The former are properly called *treaties,* which in virtue of the object about which an agreement was entered into thereby, are either treaties of *friendship,* by which in general mutual goodwill, or, more than that, the common duties of humanity are promised. They come into existence principally between those who have never known one another before, either in kindness or in injury; although such are not quite properly listed under the head of treaties, as the law of nature long since obligated all to perform such offices. Or else they are treaties of mutual *assistance,* and this only when either party is attacked in war by a third, or even when either party attacks another in war, the former being called ἐπιμαχίαι [defensive alliances], the latter συμμαχίαι [offensive and defensive alliances]. Treaties are also entered into for other matters, as, for example, that one party shall not erect forts on the confines of the other, that it shall not harbour the other's fugitive subjects, shall not let an enemy march through, and the like.

There is also another classification of treaties, by which they are divided into those of *equality* and of *inequality.* They are the former, <135> when, on the strength of the treaty, the contracting parties remain equal on the score of dignity and supreme sovereignty, in such wise that one is not made subordinate to the other as to a superior. But they are the latter, not when parties which are unequal in power make an agreement with one another, but when, on the strength of the pact, a certain superiority is conferred on one party, in such a way that one side is bound to maintain in a courteous way the majesty of the other, and is bound to show it a certain

---

47. According to Ulpian, in *Dig.,* ii.xiv.5.

48. The following division of public pacts is based on Grotius, *JBP,* II.xv, "On Treaties and Sponsions"; cf. *JNG,* 8, 9, §§1–4, 6, 10ff.

non-reciprocal respect. Some of these treaties compromise the force of supreme sovereignty, as *e.g.,* if one may not make war on a third party without the consent of the other; some do not, although they weigh down one state more heavily with burdens than they do the other.

52. There is also another species of public pacts, which they call properly a *guarantee* [*sponsio*]. It differs from a treaty in that the treaty is struck by the highest authority or by its order, but it is a guarantee when those who do not have a mandate for that affair from the highest authority, promise something which touches it specifically. When there is added to those guarantees the condition that they be valid as soon as they are approved by the supreme authority, there is no difficulty about them. Thus, even when some one promises that something will be done by a third person, in such a way that he either be promising merely his own efforts to persuade the third person, or even be promising to take upon himself the obligation, unless he succeed in persuading him, it is perfectly clear to what the guarantor as well as the third person is bound. But, if the guarantees be absolute, the extremely thorny question is commonly raised, whether, namely, these guarantees obligate also the king or the people? Although in thesis, and without special circumstances, this question should be denied, still, in hypothesis, and, indeed, especially in regard to the guarantees at Caudium and at Numantia, which are the examples illustrative of this topic that are everywhere discussed, knotty points of such a kind arise that they make the whole matter extremely dubious.[49]

At the outset it seems that we should clearly determine how far these guarantors were able to make a valid pact on the strength of their command [*imperium*]. It is, accordingly, well established that the consuls in question had been sent out with such authority to wage war that they could of their own free choice move upon the enemy, come to conflict with him, and

---

49. Here Pufendorf refers to the Roman defeat by the Samnites at the Caudine pass in 321 B.C.E. (according to Livy, *Ab urbe condita,* ed. Patrick G. Walsh [Oxford: Clarendon Press, 1999], IX, chap. viiiff) and to a similar event during the war for the Iberian town Numantia in 143–133 B.C.E. (according to Velleius Paterculus, *Compendium of Roman History,* trans. Frederick W. Shipley [Cambridge, Mass.: Harvard University Press, 1967], II.1). In both cases the consuls had to give *sponsiones* [guarantees] unfavorable for Rome, whose subsequent ratification was denied by the senate.

exercise all the acts which appeared to them to contribute at all towards
conducting the war in question according to the usage of nations, without
waiting for mandates from Rome upon that matter. By the force of this
command they had authority to make a truce, at least for no very long time,
or certainly for no longer than they were going to be in command and with
the army; they had the authority, <136> likewise, to lead the army out of
the enemy's confines, and to restore positions already occupied, if, indeed,
the safety of the army should so demand. If the consuls had guaranteed
nothing more than that, assuredly the Roman people could not with any
colour of right have made the pact invalid. But certainly they had no direct
authority to act upon the whole case, as it were, of the Romans against that
people, that is to say, ratify a full peace with them, and a treaty besides. Yet,
in truth, because the consuls had not unreasonably presumed the consent
of the people, since so many thousand citizens could be saved in no other
way, and because the enemy believed that the consuls had legal authority
to make a pact, and on their side had done something for which it seemed
that the promises made by the Roman consuls were not unfairly purchased,
and because this which they had done redounded to the advantage of the
Roman people, assuredly it would have been most fair for the Roman people not to break that pact, especially since the enemy had stipulated for
nothing else in their own interest but the end of an unjust war (such at
least had been that against Numantia, by the very admission of the Romans
themselves), and that they were not to be compelled to be slaves to the
Romans. And so, if we wish to make an honest confession, the sole and
true reason why the Romans were unwilling to stand by that guarantee, was
their unendurable ambition, feeling it to be unworthy for themselves to
experience what they had most unjustly inflicted upon others, that is to say,
to be forced to what they regarded a disgraceful peace. There was, therefore,
nothing but a colour of right and vain insolence in their denying that they
were bound by the pact which had been made without their knowledge,
and in believing that they had been freed from obligation by surrendering
the generals. For, if they were altogether unwilling to keep that pact, they
were bound to restore matters to that status in which they had been before
the guarantees, that is to say, surrender the whole army. But, as it was, by
surrendering their generals only, and keeping their army, they cannot boast

that they acted any more justly than did the Lacedemonians in punishing Phoebidas for having seized the Cadmea, while they still, despite that fact, kept possession of it.[50] Therefore the Samnites and Numantians altogether had the right, not merely to avenge the violation of a pact upon the generals themselves and the army, but also upon the whole Roman people. And yet, since, I know not for what reason, the majority of learned men admire the Romans as models of justice, the poor Samnites and Numantians, whom fortune also had ere that deserted, lose their case before judges prejudiced by their emotions.

53. Pacts which are customary in war either *end a state of war,* or <137> else *leave* the same. Since pacts of the former kind commonly have no special designation, they are wont to be listed under the name of peace or pacification. In this sometimes consent is founded upon some event, as, for example, when victory, whose effects have been already determined, is assigned the one whom either fortune has favoured, or on whose side the fortunes of battle between two or more persons, or between whole armies, has stood, or the one in whose behalf chosen arbitrators have pronounced.

The pacts which leave a state of war are truces, whereby warlike and hostile acts are suspended for a definite time. Here belong pacts about giving free transit to definite persons, about ransoming prisoners, and whatever others there are. What law of nature there is in regard to them, is readily gathered from what we have to say elsewhere; let the other points about them be sought from those who in their writings have thrown light upon the manners and customs of nations.

54. *Private* pacts are those which are entered into by private persons as such, or have to do with private affairs, and they are commonly listed under

50. The Spartan Phoibidas had been charged with leading troops to Chalcidice in 382 B.C. (to be employed against Olynthus, the capital of the Chalcidean league). By request of Theban oligarchs and (probably) in a secret Spartan mission, he occupied the Cadmea, the castle of Thebes which was the exponent of the anti-Spartan movement in Greece. The action caused a widespread indignation, and Phoibidas lost his command and was fined. Nonetheless, the occupation that had been approved by the Spartan king Agesilaos was not removed. See Victor Ehrenberg, "Phoibidas," in *Paulys Real-Encyclopädie der classischen Altertumswissenschaften,* edited by Georg Wissowa (Stuttgart: Metzler, 1893), XX, 1, pp. 347–48.

the designation of contracts.[51] These can be divided into *beneficial* and *burdensome.*[52] Beneficial contracts are so called because he who furnishes something to a second person on the basis of these, does not stipulate for an equivalent value for himself, and so they are burdensome upon one side only, although the other side is not altogether free from obligation. The principal contracts of this sort are *commodate, mutuum, mandate,* and *deposit.* It is a commodate when a thing of ours is gratuitously granted to be used for a definite length of time without any transfer of ownership, so that the same thing and not another thing of the same kind is to be returned. Here natural equity demands that the most painstaking diligence be employed to guard the thing lent, so that another's kindness may not be a loss to him. And so, if it suffers some damage in excess of that which necessarily followed from the use conceded by its owner, the person accommodated is bound to pay for it, or to return the thing in like kind or else in value, if it has been utterly lost or rendered useless, unless it would have altogether perished even in the possession of its owner. For the commodator is understood to be stipulating this much at least, namely, that he be not deprived of his property through his doing a service.

But it is called a mutuum when a thing consisting of a definite number, weight, and measure is given to a second person, with the understanding that, after a time has elapsed, the same amount and the same kind is to be received, of the same quality and excellence. But if, now, the lender, or the one who gives on loan, should stipulate for himself a definite reward for the use of the thing, the granting of an accommodation or a loan of that kind changes into burdensome contracts. <138>

It is called a mandate when one entrusts to a second person, with the latter's consent, the conduct or the performance of some licit business, but

---

51. This definition of contract as a private pact follows Grotius's interpretation of *Dig.* II.xiv.5, in *JBP,* II.xv.1. In *JNG,* 5, 2, §4, in contrast, Pufendorf makes the distinction according to the object, saying that contracts "have to do with things and actions which are used in commerce and presuppose dominions and prices of things, and the general name of pacts to all agreements entered into regarding other matters [*de praestanda opera non mercenaria*]."

52. On the typology of private pacts in §§54–59, which largely derives from Roman law, see *JNG,* 5, 2–5, 8 with references.

the other undertakes it gratis. Among the Romans there were great scruples about observing this kind of contract, because they considered that in its sacred observance there rested a strong support of civil life.[53] Now it is to be noted here, that sometimes the conduct of a business is entrusted to one with precisely circumscribed limits of action; sometimes the matter is left to the fidelity and prudence of the one who accepts the mandate. If, in a mandate given in the former fashion, one had exceeded the limits of the mandate, the Roman laws did not grant action on the mandate against the giver. And yet, in general, it is fair, not merely to make it good, if anything has been spent to the order of the mandate (for the receiver of the mandate promised merely his efforts, not expenses); but even if, perchance, something has been done beyond the terms of the mandate, which accrues to the advantage of the giver of the same, so that the former's zeal in our behalf may not be his own undoing. And so he who had conducted the affairs of another in his absence without an express agreement, had, according to the Roman laws, action to recover the amount expended.

Guardianships have a resemblance to a mandate. In them, as a ward can demand of his guardian an account of his stewardship, so, on the other hand, a guardian can demand the repayment of that which he spends upon the property of his ward, and deliverance from the obligations contracted for the ward's sake. The following also is readily apparent, namely, that the mandate expires at the death of its recipient, and the obligation to complete it does not pass over to the heir. Because, since it was gratuitous, and so there was nothing added thereby to the goods of the recipient from the other, assuredly there adheres therefrom to the goods no obligation which is passed on to another possessor also.

A species of mandate is the deposit. This is when a mobile piece of prop-

---

53. Cf. *JNG*, 5, 4, §2, with reference to Cicero, *Pro Sexto Roscio Amerino*, "In private affairs if any one had managed a business entrusted to him, I will not say maliciously for the sake of his own gain, but even carelessly, our ancestors thought that he had incurred the greatest disgrace. Therefore, legal proceedings for betrayal of a mandate are established, involving penalties no less disgraceful than those for theft. I suppose because, in cases where we ourselves cannot be present, the vicarious faith of friends is substituted; and he who impairs that confidence, attacks the common bulwark of all men, and as far as depends on him, disturbs the bonds of society."

erty over which ownership is retained is given to some one gratis, to be guarded, on the understanding that it is to be restored to the depositor whenever it so please him. Here, although the Roman laws bid that the recipient make good only dishonesty, but not also fault and neglect, and this because he who has entrusted his property to a negligent man ought to impute the loss to himself;[54] nevertheless, since the depositor is understood from the very nature of the transaction to have stipulated from the recipient at least an ordinary degree of diligence, it is fair that the recipient also make good a fault which he has committed, and that at least a general and slight one, if not the very slightest.

Trusts [*fideicommissa*][55] have some relationship to <139> a deposit, when a man so makes some one an heir to his goods that he is to restore them, or a part of them, to yet another person. Since certain positive laws of the Romans caused these bequests to be devised, their nature is to be learned from those who treat of that law.

55. *Burdensome* contracts are those in which that which is furnished by one party must be offset by the other with some equivalent. These are conveniently reduced to the three following classes: "I give, so that you will give"; "I do, so that you will do"; "I give, so that you will do," or, what amounts to the same thing, "I do, so that you will give"; for the law of nature knows nothing of a distinction between contracts which bear names and contracts which do not. From the nature and purpose of these contracts it is readily understood that in them a simple equality is sought, by way of price, between the things which are mutually exchanged, or are the subject of contract. For the contracts are entered into with the purpose of my receiving for my own article another equivalent article, which, for definite reasons, I prefer to have rather than the other. And so, no one ought to exact more for his property or for his service than it is worth. Nor does the nature of a contract allow, that, what a second person gives beyond a fair equivalent (supposing this to be due to the guile of the one who sets the price) ought to be reckoned as a gift; and so the man who defrauds a second person in a contract, cannot legitimize, as it were, his unjust gain by calling it a pre-

54. Cf. *JNG*, 5, 4, §7, with reference to *Dig.*, XLIV.vii.1, §5.
55. See bk. I, Def. 5, §19, note 30.

sumed donation, but, on the basis of the law of nature, is altogether bound to make good the loss which the other suffers thereby, unless it be well established that the other knew the thing had a less value, and of his own accord gave more for definite reasons, let us suppose, that is, for the sake of magnificence. This is not unusual among magnates, who frequently regard it as due their dignity to pay more for some one's service than in fact it is otherwise worth, tempering a contract with liberality. Just as, on the contrary, a man may, if it so please him, set a low valuation upon a service which was, perchance, worth much, and do it in such a way that the man who hires his service is not bound to make up the difference. Nay more, even if, without the fault of the parties to the contract, an inequality be discovered, suppose, for example, that some defect was not noticed, or an error made in the price, this also should be made good, and the amount should be taken from the one who has more and given to the one who has less; because the contract was undertaken with the purpose that each should have the same amount. Although, in order to avoid multitudes of suits and uncertain prices for things, especially among those who have no common judge, it has been recognized by the customary usage of nations that inequality of things to which <140> an agreement was made, is regarded as equality, where neither falsehood was in evidence, nor reticence regarding what should have been said about the substance or the qualities of the thing in exterior actions. But the Roman laws do not grant an action for these reasons, unless one has been injured to an amount greater than one-half of the right price.

Now it is by no means simply to be admitted, what some take for granted as indubitable (to show that simple equality in the justice of exchange which governs these contracts is not necessary), namely, the position that the purchaser, who wanted and asked for the sale, is done no wrong, if we sell him our property for as much as we can. For this is true only in so far as the purchaser was aware, not only of the qualities of the thing, but also of its common price, in which, if it should allow some latitude of variation, there can be no doubt but the vendor may strive to secure the highest price in that class. But that to a purchaser ignorant of the common price a thing can rightly be offered at a rate far above that same price about which he is understood to be making inquiries, or, that the purchaser can otherwise be impelled to pay any price whatsoever by cunningly taking away the other's chance to buy, or by abusing some present necessity which he is under, no one will approve, except one who regards everything as of less account than gain. But if, now, the contracting parties agree upon the price of some thing, the quantity of which, not being well known to the contracting parties, depends upon chance or natural causes, supposing, for example, that one should purchase for a large price the right to fish in some great river, or the expected crop from gardens, a vineyard, &c., the sum upon which they agreed will be held as a fair one, although the catch or crop afterwards be greater or less than that price. Because, since those things have about them a notable latitude of variation, men generally consider in their case what is ordinarily wont to obtain; surplus and deficiency are ascribed to chance, and a contract does not lose any of its force therefrom.

Furthermore, that this equality be rightly recognized and determined, the contracting parties ought to indicate to one another, not merely the valuable qualities of the thing about which they are treating, but also its lack of the same, or, in other words, its faults. For these are of the utmost effect in either increasing or diminishing the prices of things. And yet this must be understood of the characteristics which properly affect the thing which is entering into the contract. For certain other extrinsic characteristics may attend the thing and contribute to its value, and yet the nature of the transaction does not require that they be pointed out, although, perchance, on some other score, as, for example, the law of beneficence or humanity, they were to be pointed out. From all this it is understood what judgement <141> should be passed in that case upon the Rhodian merchant, who, at a time when food was scarce, brought a quantity of grain to Rhodes and sold it at a high price, at the same time concealing the fact that a number of ships would soon arrive.[56] For that act of dissimulation, of course, does not make the contract become invalid even on the basis of the law of nature, because, as a matter of fact, at that particular moment at which the grain was sold, it was worth that amount. But that the price would soon fall, he was, perchance, bound by the law of beneficence to say; nevertheless, that has nothing to do with the validity of the contract. The

---

56. According to Cicero, *On Duties,* III.xii; cf. *JNG,* 5, 3, §4.

same judgement must be passed regarding the merchant who sells a bit of merchandise whose use he knows will soon be forbidden, or who pays some one coin whose value will soon after diminish. But, in truth, he who knew the faults of a thing before the contract, and nevertheless made an agreement for it, cannot at all rescind the contract afterwards for such reasons, or complain that wrong has been done him.

56. The more common species of contracts of that kind are *exchange in kind,* by which almost alone in ancient times, and where there was no use of money as yet, business transactions were carried on; *agio* (*collybus*) or money-changing (*cambium*), by means of which moneys are most conveniently transported from one locality to another; *purchase and sale,* whereby a thing is acquired by, or exchanged for, money of an equal value. In regard to this last, it is to be noted that full right to the thing passes over to the purchaser, and the obligation in the vendor to turn over the same thing begins just as soon as an agreement has been reached about the price and the method of paying it, and so the contract is fully concluded, whether earnest-money has been given or not; although the custom of the state, or the free choice of the contracting parties, is in the habit of defining in different ways the existence of a perfect contract. Where a contract is made with Greek faith, the contract becomes valid with the payment of the money; when the parties are pleased to have consent expressed in writing, after the completion and approval of the written document. Yet if the force of the contract be not expressly dependent on handing over the thing, but the contract was simple, and right to the thing has been given to the purchaser, as soon as an agreement has been reached about the price and the method of payment, the risk which the thing runs falls upon the purchaser, unless there has been dishonesty on the part of the vendor. For, since the vendor in this case ought to have brought about immediately the transfer of the thing to the purchaser, let the purchaser charge it against himself, if, while he interposes some delay, what is now his own property has suffered any damage. And it makes no difference that otherwise the thing is said to be lost to its proper owner; but that here the ownership does <142> not yet appear to have passed to the purchaser from the vendor of the thing sold, since the thing itself has not been handed over. For he, within the confines of whose property a thing still stays, not by some right, but merely at the

free choice of the purchaser, and who is bound to give it up as soon as the purchaser has called for it, and who has in the meantime been left no faculty to dispose of it, can no longer be regarded as its owner; unless, perchance, when the contract was entered into, a definite time-limit had been set for paying the price and for accepting the thing, and before that time it was not to be handed over. For, within that time-limit, the risk which the thing runs falls upon the vendor, and after the time-limit has elapsed it falls upon the purchaser, if, indeed, it has been agreed that the contract does not become void because of such delays.

In *leasing and renting,* whereby the use of some piece of property is granted for a definite fee, accidents which interfere with the use of the property involve a loss to the renter, unless it has been otherwise provided for by laws or by an agreement. But if, however, the lessor, when the first renter was prevented from using the property, has let it out to another before the expiration of the lease, whatever he shall have gained thereby he shall repay to the first renter, or else shall sign a receipt for the rental, so as not to make profit out of the second person's loss. But if, however, the property is lost through no fault of the renter, the loss falls upon the lessor, unless the renter has specially obligated himself to make good the property.

Now since one and the same service may be useful to a number at the same time, although it is not repugnant to the nature of a contract to let out to each individual that service at its true value, and so to bargain with each individual for the fee which one would exact from a single person, because the service rendered each individual amounts to as much as the fee does, and is worth no less to each one, because it is doing some good to a number at the same time, and so the circumstance that this service may be useful to a number also is extrinsic to the contract which was agreed to with the first party; nevertheless, a contract of this kind may scarcely be consistent with the law of humanity. Because, when one person pays me just as much as my service is worth in itself, and in respect of others, to whom the same service is also doing some good, it is no more toilsome than if it were being performed for one person alone, my service is valued as a thing of innocent utility, which neither bothers me nor requires any more labour on my part, but does serve a second person; unless, perchance, the art in question be of such a character, that, when it has been communicated to a number, it loses its value to a certain extent in me. For then I can charge against others only that amount which my skill has lost in value, because they also know it. Because, further-<143>more, this also appears hard, namely, that one person pay the full price, while others who enjoy the same advantage therefrom go scot-free, it is fairest to have the payment of the fee divided among those to whom the service is rendered.

57. Most frequent also is that contract, whereby for a loan a fee is given which men are afraid to call *usury*, because, by the divine law, profit seeking under that designation is forbidden.[57] And so they[58] would rather make this contract to be different from usury, for example, a contract to make amends for the loss which he who lends money suffers; and similarly, of the gain which comes from the loan, or, in other words, the amount which it is worth to him; or to meet the expenses of the man who lends money to many people, and keeps it on hand for that purpose. Now, of a truth, in this contract, under whatever name it be listed, unless a man stipulate for an unreasonably large sum for the use of his money, especially from the poor, there is nothing repugnant to natural equity. For there is no reason why I should lend out my money gratis to a second person who seeks therewith his own gain and advantage, when I myself in the meantime might either have made the same gain, or else certainly was undergoing the risk of losing my principal by the misfortune or dishonesty of the second person, in such wise that I would either have to lose it altogether, or would have to extort it, not without inconvenience, by a suit at law. And, in fact, money is not a sterile thing, since, forsooth, by means of money other things from which an immediate gain may be secured, can be most easily acquired; nay, rather, by the ingenuity of man it has been brought about that even when it is not spent for objects of merchandise, it can multiply itself.

As for the words of Sacred Scripture which are adduced against usury,[59]

---

57. On the Old Testament's prohibition of usury and on the same matter according to natural law, cf. *JNG,* 5, 7, §§8ff, which mainly draws on John Selden, *De jure naturali et gentium, iuxta disciplinam Ebraeoram* (London, 1640), VI.ix; Grotius, *JBP,* II.xii.20–21; and Luke 6:35 (Grotius, *Opera omnia theologica* [Amsterdam, 1679; repr. Stuttgart–Bad-Cannstatt: Frommann-Holzboog, 1972], II.1).

58. Allusion to Grotius, *JBP,* II.xii.21.

59. For example, Exodus 22:24, Leviticus 25:37.

if, indeed, this is something different from that kind of contract by which what it is worth is paid for the use of money, those words have no bearing here. But if, by that precept, it is altogether forbidden to receive a fee for the loan of money, we shall say that the purpose of those words is that no one should demand from his fellow-citizen, especially one of the humbler sort, anything for the use of money which he requires to meet his needs, but should rather furnish him the use of it gratis. For the divine law allowed one to take that same usury from a stranger.[60]

58. There is, finally, a special kind of contract which is called a *partnership,* wherein two or more share their services or their property, so that each secures a proportionate part in the profits. In this some contribute their services alone, some money alone, some both, and at the same time in amounts either equal or unequal to the property or the services of the second person. The distribution of the profits here is to be so adjusted with regard to respective equality, that the <144> assigned shares in the profits should stand in the same relation to one another as do the money or the services of one partner to the money or the services of the other. Now, as for the contention which Servius Sulpicius long ago maintained against Scaevola, namely, that a partnership is valid, if, for example, Titius and Seius have agreed that two-thirds of the profits come to Titius, and one-third of the loss, but to Seius two-thirds of the loss, and one-third of the profits; his contention is valid, not as though for the reason that there could be a partnership not repugnant to nature in which those who contribute equal amounts should not get equal returns; but only this much is meant, namely, that it is not always necessary for each individual partner to contribute an equal sum of money, or for each individual to share in the profit and the loss exactly in proportion to the money and the merchandise contributed; but that it is not uncommon for one who contributed less money, to gain a larger share than the other in the profits, because he has contributed services which are more valuable than the money. Here what might appear unequal on the score of money is in the highest degree made equal in consideration of the services. Nevertheless, it is contrary to the nature

60. Deuteronomy 23:21.

of partnerships for one to experience loss without any gain, for, of course, the purpose of these partnerships is a community of advantages.

The following also has been shrewdly remarked by others, namely, that a comparison of services with money takes place in two ways: to wit, that the services be compared either with the mere use of the money, or with the actual ownership of the money, in other words, the capital. In the former case the owner parts with the capital and it is safely invested, while the services of the partner are compared merely with the profits which otherwise might with probability be expected from that money, or with the risk of losing the capital, in such a way that the relation in which the services of the second partner stand to the usury or the interest on the money, is the same as that in which his share of the profits stands to that of the first partner. But in the second case, the value of the service is added, as it were, to the capital, and he who furnishes the services has a share in the capital itself proportionate to their worth, in such a way, that the capital and the worth of the services seem to have coalesced, as it were, into one sum. And so, if the services of the one are going to be worth as much as the money of the other, they will not merely share equally in the profits, but even one-half of the capital is regarded as belonging to the one who furnishes the services. If the services are going to amount to merely one-half of the money, the one who contributed the money will get two-thirds of the profits, the one who contributed the services, one-third; and this latter will have a right to one-third of the capital invested, and so on. <145>

59. Finally, something is to be added on the subject of those pacts in which there is an agreement and, as it were, a compromise between the contracting parties regarding some uncertain chance, by the turn of which they promise one another that they will abide. Such pacts are common in public and in private relations. In public relations they are quite as much in evidence during war as during peace. In peace, indeed, the use of the deciding lot is recognized among a large number of peoples, as, for example, in selecting judges, in assigning provinces, in distributing offices, when the competitors are equal, as much in regard to right, as in regard to the qualities necessary for administering the office. For otherwise, if men of unequal right or unequal arts vie with those whose right and arts are superior, the interests of the state are badly cared for. The purpose of these lots is not to

seek by an unusual method to learn the will of God, but to get rid of cases of strife and discord, and to enable the one who in any event was able to make disposal by virtue of his authority to avoid the ill will of either side, and to prevent the possibility of quarrels being started about an unfair decision. Also in private business there is a very extensive use of the lot in conferring the shares of an inheritance, as also if a certain indivisible good thing or burden is to be assigned a certain individual among a number of persons who have the same right or obligation. Such pacts are no less frequently employed in war, not merely when the end of the entire war is made to rest upon the outcome of a battle between whole armies, or between two or more chosen men on each side, but also when some perilous post is to be assigned to one of the commanders. Nay more, practically all regular wars, at least those which have been entered into after rejection on both sides of a pacific agreement, seem to presuppose an understanding of that kind, to wit, that he to whose side the fortune of war inclines, may impose upon the vanquished whatever so pleases him. This is, properly speaking, the reason why by the usage of nations in regular warfare the belligerents on both sides, when they come to make peace, are regarded as being on an equality as far as the cause of the war is concerned, and no decision is made as to which of the two had a just cause for fighting. For he who has decided to enter upon a war with a second person, when he might settle the controversy by a pacific transaction, is understood to have committed the decision of his cause to the dice of Mars, and so cannot complain at all of whatever condition thenceforward the doubtful vicissitudes of war may bring upon him.

A similar agreement is entered into by those who entrust the decision of their private controversies to the outcome of duels. The result of the agreement is that the slayer is not bound to make good <146> to the other's wife or children the loss which has been experienced by his death (which otherwise rests upon the one who slays another without such agreement), unless this has been especially enjoined upon him in the way of punishment by the magistracy; and this is because the other person of his own accord entered a dangerous struggle. Nevertheless, these duels, because they are directly opposed to the purpose of established states are properly forbidden by the magistracy under very heavy penalties.

To this class of pacts are referred also those which are commonly designated *wagers,* when one of two affirms, and the other denies, the existence
of some event which is not yet generally known, and on both sides a definite
pledge has been deposited, which goes to the one with whose assertion the
event is found to agree; likewise, any and all kinds of games in which a price
is paid for contesting. Under the heading of wagers you might also put that
which they call a lottery, when a number of persons, after buying something
with the money which they have contributed, decide by lot to what individual alone the whole of it ought to go; as also the jar of fortune, as it is
styled, when, after casting into an urn a definite number of tallies or tickets,
some blank and others inscribed, the chance to make a drawing of the same
is sold for a sum of money, on the terms that the one who draws shall receive
that which the inscription on the tallies or tickets calls for. All these contain
nothing wrong in themselves. For men descend to them by mutual consent,
each one exposes his own property to an equal risk, and they have to do
with things the disposal of which is in our hands, namely, each one's own
goods. But, in truth, because it is to the interests of the Commonwealth
that no one make a bad use of his property, and, indeed, through agreements and games of that kind one can easily be deprived of one's goods,
or be led on to other evils, it is in the hands of the magistracy either to
allow or to forbid such pacts, and so either to leave or to take away their
validity, or else at least to set definite limits to the value of the things deposited therein. <147>

A law is a decree by which a superior binds one subject to him to direct his actions according to the command of the superior.

 1. A law differs from a word of counsel.
 2. From a pact.
 3. From a right.
 4. He who is about to pass a law for some one ought to have authority over him.
 5. The object of laws.
 6. Whether civil laws may be opposed to natural laws.
 7. Something can be permitted by civil law which has been prohibited by natural law.
 8. Are the precepts of the Decalogue natural laws?
 9. A law is a notional norm.
10. The legislator and the law itself ought to be known.
11. Precisely who are obligated by a law?
12. Precisely what coercive force is there in a law?
13. The division of a law.
14. Disputes concerning the source, as it were, of the law of nature.
15. Things not comprehended by the law of nature are left to positive enactment.
16. The laws of nature are principles or conclusions, absolute or hypothetical.
17. The necessity of civil laws.
18. Their origin and force.
19. Their object.
20. Precisely what laws render acts committed in their despite invalid?
21. What are legal permissions?
22. Equity.
23. Dispensation.
24. The law of nations.
25. The laws of war.
26. Of embassies.
27. Affirmative and negative law.

1. At the outset, a law is to be accurately distinguished from those things which seem to be related to it in a certain way, and so are confused by some persons with it, I mean, a word of *counsel,* a *pact,* and a *right.*[1] Now a law differs from a word of counsel, indeed, in the fact that through the latter, by means of reasons drawn from the facts of the case, a person endeavours to induce some one over whom he has no authority, at least as far as the present affair is concerned, to undertake or to give up some thing, without bringing any obligation to bear upon him, and in such a way that it is left to his own free choice whether he wish to heed the counsel, or not. But even though a law ought not to be without its own reasons, nevertheless, these are not properly the cause of bestowing obligation upon the law, but rather the authority of the one who gives the precept, who, in signifying his will, lays upon the subject the obligation of acting altogether according to his prescript, although, perchance, the reasons for the same may not be so clearly apparent to the latter.

2. Nor, in truth, are those sufficiently accurate who speak of laws as certain common agreements, or in other words, κοινὰς συνθήκας,[2] since thereby they confuse a law with a pact. For assuredly, neither the <148> positive divine laws nor the laws of nature can be said to have arisen from the agreement or consent of men. Nor are civil laws, properly speaking, pacts, even though they have their origin in a pact. For even if some multitude not bound to one another by supreme sovereignty should entirely agree with one another upon certain formulae for living together, still this would be in vain, if a supreme sovereignty had not yet been set up, through whose force the disobedient could be restrained by punishments. For this agreement would have no other force than that which, on the basis of the law of nature, inheres in pacts. But, in truth, the end of civil laws is to have men held to the performance of something by a tighter bond than natural obligation, to wit, by the addition of a penalty to be inflicted upon us in

1. The following distinction of *law* from *counsel, pact,* and *right* (§§1–3) follows Hobbes, *De cive,* chap. 14, §§1–3; cf. *JNG,* 1, 6, §§1–3.

2. In question are authors who had the legislation of Greek city-states in view; cf. *JNG,* 1, 6, §2 with references to Isocrates, *Against Callimachus;* Aristotle, *"Rhetorica ad Alexandrum,"* chaps. i–iii; and Dionysius of Halicarnassus, *The Roman Antiquities,* 1. bk. X.

a human court of law by men having, as it were, authority over us. What of the fact that it appears altogether impossible to enter upon an agreement of this kind without establishing a supreme sovereignty? For, when no one is given the right of forcing me to perform an agreement, if I should be unwilling to do so of my own accord, then nothing has been performed between us. But if to the rest as a whole authority has been given to use coercive force upon the recalcitrant, and to reduce them to order, the equivalent of a democracy arises. Nevertheless, a pact gives the civil laws their origin, because by it there is established a supreme sovereignty, in whose hands is the authority to enact laws in a gathering subject to it. Nor does it make any difference that in democracies, at least, the majority of the citizens ought to agree in enacting a law. For that agreement is a means whereby there is displayed the force of that supreme sovereignty which, on the basis of the pact, has been bestowed upon the gathering of one and all, so that, namely, one and all might be able, in the exercise of authority, to enjoin upon individuals what the majority had approved of. Add also, that, since pacts, as far as their origin goes, depend upon our free choice what is to be done in them should be determined before we obligate ourselves to the performance of it; but, in a law which presupposes another's authority over us, we are obligated beforehand to do something, while what is to be done is determined afterwards.

3. Now as the word *jus* (law) often means the same as *lex* (law), especially where it is used for a complex of laws, so we should be on our guard not to take it in the sense of law, when it denotes the authority to do something; for example, we are not to fancy, when it is said we have a right (*jus*) to this or that by the divine law (*lex*), that this has also been ordered by the divine law, and so we can rightly do it, even if it be forbidden by human laws. For, since a man has the authority or right to do all those things which can proceed from his natural powers, except such as are prohibited by law, there arises therefrom the common form of expression, namely, that those things which are permitted <149> by some law or are not prohibited, we are said to have the right to do on the basis of that law. But this is something utterly different from what is ordered by the laws, as will soon appear.

4. Now in the one who is going to enact a law for another, it is first of all required that he should have such authority over him upon whom the law is to be enjoined, that he can force him to the observance of that law,

by proposing a penalty; for it is vain to order one to do that which can be neglected with impunity. And so no one is obligated by the laws of a person or a group which has no authority over him. And the faculty of enjoining something by way of a law or an order, implies superiority, just as the obligation of obedience convicts us of being inferior to the one who can give an order to us, at least where his command [*imperium*] extends. For the same cause no one can be irrevocably obligated by his own decisions directly. For the fact that in pacts or promises, by my own agreement, I am so obligated that I am either altogether unable to be freed from my agreement, or else only with the consent of the one to whom the agreement was directed, is due to the law which keeps me from going back on that agreement by which some right has once been given a second person. Where such a law fails to exist (a natural as well as a civil law), nothing keeps me from being able to change, according to free choice, the determination of my will once made by myself. Now this point also ought to be observed, namely, that it makes no difference, just who it was that drew up the formulae of the laws in their enactment, provided only that he who properly has the legislative faculty, recognizes and promulgates them as his own. Thus, in a monarchy, whatever is enacted by the authority [*autoritate*] of the prince is valid as a law, whoever he be in the last resort who formulated the wording of the law. Thus, in a democracy, it may be that the people enjoin upon one or upon several the duty of drafting laws, yet their force comes not from those who write them, but from the people, and so the legislative authority does not inhere in them, but in the people.

5. The matter or the object of laws in genus is whatever may be done by those people for whom the laws are passed, at least at the time at which the laws are passed. For, if afterwards a man should lose by his own fault the faculty to fulfil the law, its force does by no means altogether expire, but there is left to the legislator the authority to punish him, because he can no longer obey his laws. But, otherwise, to lay upon some one a law which he cannot fulfil, and yet it is not his fault that he is unable to do so, is not only futile, but is connected with the utmost injustice.[3] But in species natural laws have to do with those matters which so harmonize with the social

3. Only actions that can be imputed to an agent may be the object of law; see bk. II, Axiom 1, especially §6.

nature of rational man, that, unless they are observed, violence is done in a certain fashion to nature herself, and an ordered and tranquil society cannot be preserved <150> among men.[4] Those things which are not determined by the laws of nature it is permissible to adjust by means of positive laws.

6. Furthermore, since God is quite as much the author of natural laws as of his own positive laws, and it were impious to think that he ordains things contradictory to one another, it is assuredly apparent that the divine positive laws cannot at all be opposed to natural laws. But there are some who deny the possibility that even civil laws can be opposed to natural laws (unless, perchance, they be passed in contumely towards God), and this position they base on the argument that those who unite to form a state, bind themselves by a pact to the effect that they are willing to obey the mandates of him who has supreme sovereignty, that is to say, the civil laws; and the law of nature bids them to keep this pact. But, since that pact, and so the obligation to preserve the civil laws, is anterior to the actual promulgation of the laws, by the force of the same natural law about not violating a pact we are bidden to observe all civil laws. For, where we are obligated to obedience before we know what bidding will be given, there we are obligated to obey universally and in all things. Furthermore, although by a law of nature, as it were, theft, homicide, adultery, &c., are forbidden, nevertheless, it is in the province of civil laws to define what is another's, what is one's own, what force it may be permissible to employ against a man, and just what kind of sexual connexion constitutes adultery.[5] And so, although boys among the Lacedemonians secretly stole the property of other persons, nevertheless they did not commit theft, because the civil law had defined that a thing taken in that fashion was not another's.

---

4. Pufendorf takes the idea that natural law is based on the rational and social nature of humanity from Grotius (*JBP,* Prolegomena) and thus indirectly from Stoic moral philosophy (Seneca, *On Benefits,* trans. Aubrey Stewart [London, 1905], IV, c. xviii), but, to be sure, without accepting that the matter of that law is "acts . . . in themselves, either obligatory or not permissible" (*JBP,* I.i.10). For Pufendorf the obligatory force of natural law does not arise from rational nature as such, but from divine command. See especially *Eris,* "Specimen controversiarum . . . ," chap. v, §30, p. 186.

5. Allusion to Hobbes, *De cive,* chap. 14, §§9–10.

Or, when the same people allowed an impotent old man to substitute some vigorous young man in order to get his wife with child, that was not adultery, because the civil laws did not include under the head of adultery such sexual connexion with another man's wife at the instigation of the husband himself.[6]

Now, in truth, because all these contentions flow from an hypothesis about the natural state of man, the weak points of which we shall show in the proper place, they cannot be allowed in any such crude form. For, at the outset, among us who venerate Sacred Scripture, it is possible from the very laws which were divinely promulgated for the Jews, and from the extraordinary revelations by which God made known his will unto men, to ascertain in the case of a large number, surely, of crimes prohibited by the law of nature, just how God, the author of nature, wishes them to be defined; and so, no matter if a state has in fact excepted certain actions from the brand of that charge, these actions are none the less opposed to the divine law, especially since a sufficient reason cannot be shown, why God should have assigned to those things, in the laws given to the Jewish people, definitions such as ought not to obtain equally among the rest of the <151> nations. Thus, since it appears from the divine laws, that, by the law concerning adultery, any sexual intercourse at all with a woman actually still united in marriage to another is forbidden, it must assuredly be said that those vicarious services exercised among the Spartans are contrary to the law of nature. But, if any should herein make some exception against the declaration of the Sacred Scripture, they will still be forced to grant that the definitions of acts forbidden by the law of nature are so to be formed by the civil law, that the intent and purpose of the law of nature shall not come to naught, and this intent and purpose is that an upright and peaceful society be preserved among men. If, therefore, some definition of a civil law be opposed to this end, it must altogether be admitted that the same is repugnant to the law of nature. Nor is there reason for believing that enough is being done in this way for peace, because definitions of that kind are universal, so that even if, perchance, sometimes they inconvenience some one person, on another occasion again they may help him; and that

6. Cf. *JNG,* 6, 1, §15, referring to Plutarch, "Lycurgus," XV.6ff.

the equality of right which laws of that kind set up among citizens removes the cause of complaints. For there are some things which, although, perchance, we might be eager to be solely permitted to do them, nevertheless, if others also were going to be permitted to do them to us, we should not even desire to be permitted to do ourselves; and if such things be established by civil laws, it is impossible that peace and the proper order intended by nature be not disturbed. Why, if that equality of which they speak were sufficiently valid to introduce a right, it would be permissible in the same manner to destroy all laws, for thereby the utmost equality would be introduced; and yet no one would undertake to assert that. Thus some author or other[7] reports of the Tartars that it was a custom among them for one who had taken something away from a second person, merely to give as an excuse to the judge that he needed it, and the judge would render this decision: "Because you had need, keep it; and so you of the other party, if you shall likewise need anything, you will be allowed to take it from another person in the same way." Therefore, by Tartar definition, it will be theft when something is taken from its owner, against his will, which was not needed by the one who took it. Yet one can scarcely doubt that the narrowness of this definition all but utterly overturns that law of nature about theft. And surely no one, in my judgement, would wish for such a law, since it might very frequently happen that he himself would be robbed of that which was the last thing in the world that he would be willing to part with, and whose like he could not find in the possession of another, or else, because its owner watched over it, would be prevented from carrying off.

7. Whatever this may amount to, however, the whole matter can be settled clearly, if it be carefully observed that permission is one <152> thing, precept another; or, in other words, that it is one thing to have a precept given by civil laws, another to have something permitted, or not prohibited by the same. For these two conditions are not mutually at variance, namely, that a thing is forbidden by the law of nature, and permitted by civil laws. For the permission of the civil law does not prevent a certain act from being

7. Sigismund Freiherr von Herberstein, *Rerum moscoviticarum commentarii* (Basel, 1571); Haythonus, *De Tartaris liber,* in *Novus Orbis regionum ac insularum veteribus incognitarum,* ed. Simon Grynaeus (Basel, 1532), chap. 48; cf. *JNG,* 8, 1, §3.

contrary to the law of nature, or allow one to commit it without sinning against God; but it merely declares that, by civil authority, the one who desires to commit the act is neither prevented from doing so, nor punished, and that in a human court of law those acts are granted the effects which otherwise attend also upon acts that are licit and legitimate on the basis of the law of nature. Thus, among the Tartars, a man was not bidden to take another's goods from him, but if he did so, he was not punished, nor was he compelled by the magistracy to make restitution, and so, in that court of law, taking things away in such fashion was regarded as a legitimate mode of acquisition. The same is to be judged of the thefts committed by boys among the Laconians and of the vicarious procreation of offspring, where, to be sure, no legal precept compelled either an aged husband or a young man qualified for breeding purposes, to this act, but, if they agreed, the laws did not prevent it, and in their own court they allowed such sexual intercourse to have the same effect as, otherwise, marital cohabitation has, namely, that children so engendered were regarded as legitimate. But whether the magistracy may rightly permit such things, is a different question, and one which depends on the answer to the following: Whether, namely, a civil magistracy be bound to punish all wrongs whatsoever that have been committed against the law of nature? This I should not dare to affirm in general, though, certainly, it is necessary that one man punish another for violating the law of nature or the divine law, not because the legislator's authority [*auctoritas*], damaged by the misdeed, must necessarily be asserted among men, since the legislator has his special tribunal for that; but in so far as, without punishment of this kind, a decent society and peace cannot be maintained among men. If, now, the highest civil authority has decided that the society of which I have spoken can be well enough preserved, even if the force of a civil law be not assigned to some precept of the law of nature, it scarcely seems that this civil authority is bound to exact punishment from violators of that law of nature, at all events, where because of the peculiar disposition of the citizens, or for other reasons, greater disadvantages would come from the civil prohibition of the matter than from permitting the same. If, however, the state, by way of a precept, and with the threat of punishment, enjoins upon its subjects either to do something which the law <153> of nature forbids, or to give up doing what it orders, we emphatically deny that obedience is due the state herein. From which it is evident that the pact, whereby a man obligates himself to obey the supreme sovereignty, is not so absolute but it involves at least the limitation, "as far as what is ordered be not opposed to the laws of God and nature."

8. From what has been said this question also is to be decided, whether, namely, the laws of the Decalogue about honouring parents, about theft, adultery, homicide, and false witness,[8] be natural laws, as men commonly judge, or, in truth, civil laws, as some think. This much, indeed, is certain: in so far as they are viewed as laws promulgated by God through the instrumentality of Moses for the Jews, they are in fact civil; because God himself in that commonwealth performed also the function of a civil legislator, and those precepts had there in every way the force of civil laws, punishment, which it was in the hands of the magistracy to exact, being provided against transgressors. But when those laws are considered with reference to their substance, as they necessarily harmonize with the condition of human society, and so obligate all men, even apart from their promulgation by Moses, they are in fact laws of nature. And it makes no difference, that they seem to presuppose certain pacts, for example, marriage, ownership of goods, constitution of the state, and courts of justice, which are established among men by pacts. For the very law of nature requires that men enter into such pacts, since, without them, human society could not be preserved at all. And those laws also which presuppose some human deed can altogether be called laws of nature, even if the performance of that deed, at least here and now, does rest in the free choice of man.[9] But, if one should suppose that the state of nature was the war of all against all, and should call those laws natural which obligate one in that state alone, then, of course, we should confess it to follow, on the hypothesis just mentioned, that those laws are not natural. However, we shall set forth below what should be thought of this hypothesis.[10]

---

8. Exodus 20:2–17; Deuteronomy 5:6–21.

9. Cf. Grotius, *JBP,* I.i.10: "It is necessary to understand, further, that the law of nature deals not only with things which are outside the domain of the human will, but with many things also which result from an act of the human will."

10. See bk. II, Observ. 3, §6.

9. Now the nature of law consists principally in this, namely, that it is a notional norm for actions, showing how far they should be conformed to the will of some superior. I use the expression "a notional norm," because it touches actions only through the intellect, in envisaging to the intellect the will of a superior relative to doing or avoiding something. For, when this is made known, immediately there arises in the subject the obligation to act in accordance with that law, and this because he understands that he who enjoins that law upon him has the authority to compel him by the imposition of some evil, if he refuse to obey,[11] and that he will exercise this authority is well established from the fact that no one is presumed to wish his action to have no effect. <154>

10. The consequence of this is, that, in order for a law to exert its force, knowledge both of the legislator, and of the law as well, is required on the part of the one for whom the law is passed. For how can a man render obedience if he knows neither whom he ought to obey, nor to what he is bound? Nevertheless, it is sufficient here for him to have known that once. For, if a man should forget what he has known once, he is not on that account released from obligation, because he could very well have remembered it, if he had had the desire to obey, which he ought to have had. Also the knowledge of the legislator, indeed, cannot easily escape one. For no one who knows how to use his reason, will fail to recognize that He who is the author of the whole of nature, is the author of nature's laws. Much less is the maker of civil laws obscure to a citizen, since, forsooth, he is appointed either by the express consent of the citizens, or their tacit consent, while they are subjecting themselves in every way to his sovereignty. Furthermore, we shall set forth below how it comes about that the law of nature is recognized from the contemplation of the condition of mankind.

Now civil laws became known through promulgation. In this two points ought to be clearly established: one is that the laws are actually proceeding

---

11. Apart from the fear of sanctions, obligation requires above all an inner bond "arising from a consideration of the causes, which should be sufficient, even without the fear, to lead one to receive the command on grounds of good judgement alone" (*JNG,* 1, 6, §9), as Pufendorf emphasizes (*JNG,* 1, 6, §10) when criticizing Hobbes, *De cive,* chap. 15, §5: "God in his *natural kingdom* hath a right to rule, and to punish those who break his laws, from his sole *irresistible power.*"

from the one who has supreme sovereignty, the other is their meaning. The former is known when the very person who enjoys the supreme sovereignty promulgates the law, either with his own voice, or through the instrumentality of those who have been delegated by him. There is no reason for doubting that these delegates of his are bringing forward laws by the authority [*autoritate*] of the supreme sovereignty, if it be clearly established that they are commonly employed by the sovereign for the purpose of setting forth his will; if they observe the method recognized by custom; if the laws in question be accepted for use in trials before a court of law; and if they contain nothing derogatory to the supreme authority of the sovereign. And it is not credible that a minister is going to traffic with something alleged to be the will of the prince, when in fact it is not, or is going to usurp a function of that kind without the prince's bidding; since one who attempts things of that sort has no hope of avoiding discovery or of escaping punishment for attempting such effrontery. Now in order to have the meaning of the law rightly understood, it is incumbent upon the promulgators to use the utmost possible perspicuity. If anything appear to be obscure in the laws, its interpretation is to be sought from the legislator, or from those who have been publicly appointed to administer justice in accordance with them. For it is their special function to apply the laws to individual instances by interpretation, or, in other words, to make clear, when particular acts have been proposed, just what provision the legislators have made regarding them.

11. Moreover, the subjects whom the legislator desired to obligate, <155> are easily ascertained from the words in which the laws have been expressed. For in all laws the subjects to be obligated are designated either through an express definition, which is made either by an indication of universal applicability, or by restriction to men of a definite status, or to definite individuals; or else through some condition and characteristic which each subject of the legislator recognizes in himself, and at the same time perceives that he is obligated by that law. In general, therefore, a law obligates all the subjects of a legislator whatsoever, with whose condition the character of the law squares, and to whom the subject-matter of the same can be applied. For, since a legislator is believed to have desired to introduce or to preserve by means of his law a certain harmony among those to whom it has been

given; and since, in truth, there would be introduced the utmost disso-
nance, as it were, among them, if certain subjects, whom the character of
the law fits, should not be bound by it, no one is regarded as having been
exempted from the law except the one who has especially made known his
privileges.

12. Now just as it is required, in order to enjoin efficaciously an obligation
upon a second person, that it be made clear to him what is to be done, and
the fact that he will not go unpunished if he has not performed what is
enjoined (for there is no use giving a command to one who, through natural
faculties, may go in the opposite direction, unless he is to expect more evil
from neglecting the command than from fulfilling it); so the same conditions are found to obtain also in a law, in that they define what must necessarily be done, or let alone (whence also one infers what is licit), what is
ours, what another's, what we may demand from another, what not, and
the like; and at the same time they indicate that evil threatens the one who
neglects a precept or does a forbidden thing. This latter feature, however,
the laws of nature leave a little more obscure, in that they do not so clearly
define the kind of penalty which the Deity is going to exact for their violation. But civil laws always indicate this clearly, in that they either expressly
determine the punishment, or else, without defining it, hint at it, leaving
to the free choice of the legislator the kind and degree of punishment which
he wishes to exact. And from this is understood also the sense in which
there are ascribed to laws the force of obligating, the force of directing, and
the force of coercing or vindicating, of course, only in a notional way, that
is to say, in so far as they indicate the will and the decree of the legislator,
and display the punishments which he is about to impose upon the violators
of the laws. For in the legislator himself there resides properly the authority
to exact from his subjects the conformity of their actions to the norm which
he has <156> prescribed, and to threaten them with penalties as well as
actually to inflict the same. Now legislators as such are said to be using
compulsion, not in that they so bind a man by the exercise of some natural
violence, that he is utterly unable to do the contrary, but in that they make
it difficult for any one to wish to act contrary to the law, by imposing punishment upon transgressors, because the punishment makes it preferable to
obey the law rather than to violate it. Nevertheless, the laws always leave

that natural liberty to the will, so that if, indeed, it be pleased to subject itself to the risk of punishment, it can in fact act contrary to the laws.

13. In respect to their authors laws can be divided into *divine* and *human,* the divine being again divisible, on the score of promulgation, into *natural,* or general, and *positive,* or special.[12] Every human law is *civil.* Now as to the subject-matter, some things manifestly harmonize with the very conditions of human nature as such, and flow from it; and some arise from the free choice alone of the legislator, as harmonizing especially with a definite status of men. Of these two classes the former are called natural, the latter positive.

14. As to what the law of nature properly is, what is its fountain-head, as it were, and by what indication a matter is recognized as pertaining to the law of nature, there is no complete agreement among the learned. The Roman jurisconsults commonly define the law of nature as that which nature has taught all living beings.[13] Those depart very little from this position who call the law of nature that order implanted in all things by the Creator, whereby each thing does what is in accord with its nature and moves towards its destined end.[14] But, in truth, we are seeking such a law of nature as will direct the actions of the rational man, and, although light can be thrown upon it from the contemplation of other creatures, and by their customary mode of action, nevertheless, since we see them for the most part engaged in doing things which suit their nature, indeed, but are alien to the nature of man; and we do not find any one animal in which all the duties of man appear, but different things are done by different animals,

12. Cf. *JNG,* 1, 6, §18, and Grotius, *JBP,* I.i.10 and 13. Of course, Grotius does not make the distinction on the score of promulgation: "In this characteristic the law of nature differs not only from human law, but also from volitional divine law; for volitional divine law does not enjoin or forbid those things which in themselves and by their own nature are obligatory or not permissible, but by forbidding things it makes them unlawful, and by commanding things it makes them obligatory."

13. *Dig.,* I.i.1, §3.

14. Allusion to the Thomist doctrine of eternal law, the rule and measure of divine providence directing all things to their due ends (Thomas Aquinas, *The "Summa theologica" of St. Thomas Aquinas,* trans. Fathers of the English Dominican Province [London: Burns, Oates & Washburne, 1915], vol. 8, I–II q.93a.1co). According to that doctrine, natural law is the participation of that rule and measure by rational beings (*Summa theologica,* I–II q.91a.2co).

while other animals avoid these things; that law is to be derived from the proper nature of man alone, and it is not to be drawn from brutes or inanimate objects.[15]

In no less obscurity have they left the essence of the law of nature who are satisfied with the statement that it is the law which is universal in time, in place, and among men. Most of these have been pleased to seek its idea and, as it were, prototype in God himself. These divide, nevertheless, into two parties. For some derive it from the divine will, and, since that is free, they conclude therefrom that God can change the law of nature, nay more, can ordain the opposite of it, as is <157> commonly the case in positive laws.[16] But others assert that it is founded upon the essential holiness and justice of God, and since that is immutable, they conclude that the law of nature also is immutable.[17] Now, in truth, although it has always seemed to us to be profane for a mortal to peer more curiously into things divine than by the path along which God leads him, nevertheless, it seems well to observe with regard to the former opinion, that most assuredly it lay in the free choice of God to give man a nature such that the law would necessarily correspond with it. For there appears to be no necessity which compelled God either to create man at all, or to create him with an obligation towards the law of nature different from that of brutes. But, in truth, since God has so formed the nature of man, that, for the maintenance of His glory, as it were, the natural law was altogether to be observed, we have no right at all to believe that He is willing to destroy or to change it, as long, indeed, as He introduces no change in human nature, and so, assuming the constancy of human nature, even though human nature has been formed in such a fashion by the divine free choice, the law of nature admits of no change, being different therein from those laws which depend upon the

15. On the idea of natural law as law peculiar to man, cf. *JNG*, 2, 3, §2, with references to Grotius, *JBP*, Prolegomena, and Selden, *De jure naturali et gentium,* I.v.

16. See, for example, the *Controversiarum illustrium aliarumque usu frequentium libri tres,* I, c. 27, n. 11, by Fernando Vázquez, whom Pufendorf cites in *JNG,* 2, 3, §4.

17. See, for example, Aquinas, *Summa theologica,* vol. 8, I–II q.100a.8ad2: "As the Apostle says (2 Timothy 2:13), 'God continueth faithful, He cannot deny Himself.' But He would deny Himself if He were to do away with the very order of His own justice, since He is justice itself."

divine will in such a way that they do not seem to be necessarily required by the condition of man. As for the latter opinion, although no one is going to be so absurd as to dare assert that this law of nature contains in itself anything repugnant to the divine holiness and justice, nevertheless it will be extremely difficult to prove that the law of nature has been so made to correspond to the divine holiness and justice as to a prototype, that, just as God acts towards creatures, and especially towards men, in the same way men ought to conduct themselves towards one another, on the basis of the law of nature. For the quotations which can be made from Sacred Scripture to the effect that man was made in the image of God,[18] do not apply here, since even those who admit that this image has been lost, recognize that a sense of the law of nature has remained in man's reason. Among men we commonly call him holy who refrains from the grosser vices and is observant of his duty. To conceive of the holiness of God in this manner would be utterly ill advised. Among men justice is wellnigh contained in the principles, "Injure no man," and, "Give to each his due." But, in truth, that God, even without respect to antecedent deserts, may inflict some painful thing upon a creature, nay more, may utterly destroy it, cannot be doubted. Nor, in truth, can God owe anything to any man, so that if it be denied He can be said to have done him an injustice. The rules which the punitive justice of God is in the habit of observing are beyond our ken. This much, at least, is well established, that it does not always follow in the footsteps of a human court of law. Finally, those who say that the law of nature is the dictate of right reason, which <158> points out that there is a moral turpitude or a moral necessity about some act, derived from its agreement or disagreement with rational nature itself, and, consequently, that such an act is forbidden or enjoined by God as the author of this law,[19] are correct enough on every point except that they do not define just what is the foundation of the congruence or the incongruence of those acts with rational nature. But this we conclude to be the fact, namely, that man was made by the Creator a social animal. For that this is properly the reason why that which is said to pertain to the law of nature so harmonizes with the nature

18. Genesis 1:27.
19. Grotius, *JBP,* I.i.10.

of man, that, if the contrary should take place, it would seem as though violence, as it were, had been done to his nature, all this we shall set forth at greater length in Book II.

15. Here, furthermore, the point on which we touched above is to be carefully noted, namely, that in common parlance natural law includes not merely what is ordered by that law, but also what is not forbidden, or what is merely permitted. He who does not make this discrimination accurately must necessarily involve himself in numerous errors and difficulties. But if we should desire to speak correctly, that which is not forbidden by the law of nature lies outside that law, and, unless it has been prohibited by a positive law, pertains to the object of human liberty, whereby we are understood to have the authority of doing all those things which are not forbidden by any law, although, perchance, the state of nature inclines to one of the alternatives rather than to the other. Moreover, these same matters, if, indeed, they be ordered or prohibited by some legislator, we say belong to positive right; to wit, such matters as do not necessarily proceed from the state of social nature, or such as whose establishment in a general way, indeed, nature urges, but leaves their particular determination to the free choice of men. Now that which is alien to natural equity, is by no means a positive right. For a positive right may be in perfect harmony with natural equity, especially if it be referred to the status of definite societies, notwithstanding the fact that originally it derives its force from the will of those who establish them. So also, he who wishes to call all civil laws whatsoever positive laws too, will be misusing the word, because they have the character of civil laws only by the free choice and imposition of the state. Now the force of positive laws, which fill human and divine right, depends upon the free choice of the legislator not only in origin but also in duration, in such wise, that, as long as he wishes them to be valid, they are necessarily to be obeyed by his subjects, and when he abrogates them, even though no change in a man's condition takes place, his acts become once more free and indifferent. And so in positive laws the free choice alone of the legislator is to be regarded, even though, perchance, a reason for the law may not <159> be forthcoming. But, on the other hand, natural laws can be called mutable only in a partial sense, that is, to the extent that it lay in the Creator's free choice so to form the nature of man that these laws should

necessarily harmonize with it, and this harmony lasts as long as human nature undergoes no change. Nevertheless, because that immutability of the laws of nature is derived merely from the supposition that man's estate will persist in the same tenor, it does not seem absurd to say that God can control them, in such wise, however, that under these conditions, there has been enjoined upon men merely the simple performance of that act by the special mandate of God; but that other men may not at all imitate this, or take it as a general mode of action towards one another.

16. The laws of nature are commonly divided into *principles,* which below we shall call the fundamental laws of nature, whose truth and necessity arise directly from the very character of human nature; and *conclusions,* which are deduced from these principles by necessary consequence or subsumption. These latter can be deduced from the principles sometimes more clearly, sometimes less so; some also are closer to the same, others more remote. In the next place, among the precepts of the law of nature, some are *absolute,* namely, those which obligate all men whatsoever in any state whatsoever; others *hypothetical,* namely, those which presuppose a certain definite status or act depending upon the free choice of men, or which have to do with those matters which follow upon the will of man. For there are many things which are matters of free choice as far as the performance of the act is concerned, or where it rests with men's free choice whether they care to undertake some act or not; yet, when that act has been undertaken, from some precept of the law of nature moral necessity or obligation follows upon the act, or the method and the circumstances are determined on the basis of the same precept. Thus, for example, although the law of nature does not instruct me to buy something from a second person; assuming, nevertheless, that I do buy freely, the same law bids me not to seek my gain in the other person's loss, nor to defraud him in a contract. It does not follow from this, however, that all positive laws also belong to the law of nature, because we subject ourselves to the supreme sovereignty of a second person by our own consent, and the law of nature bids us to obey his orders.[20] This much, indeed, is certain: Through the medium of the said precept, the law of nature obligates all persons whatsoever to obey the posi-

20. This is aimed against Hobbes; see *De cive,* chap. 14, §10.

tive laws of their superiors, and therefore, those who neglect these laws are sinning against the very law of nature. But what prevents those positive laws from being called natural is that, in the case of the hypothetical precepts of the law of nature, the reason is sought in the universal condition of men; and this cannot be the case in positive laws, but the reason for obeying <160> them is to be sought solely in the authority and will of the legislator. And so positive laws are not the hypothetical precepts of the law of nature, but from a hypothetical precept borrow their obligating force before the divine judgement-seat.

17. Now, just as the law of nature has the efficacy of an obligation from the most exalted lawgiver, God, in such wise that he who has violated it should be thought to have contravened God's own will, so there is no doubt but it rests with Him to punish the violation of the law of nature as such. Of a truth, because few have such goodness of character that they are willing to do, solely out of reverence for God, what nature bids; since, forsooth, the divine vengeance unfolds itself for the most part in hidden ways, and most men scorn it because they are unable to find it everywhere; therefore, the law of nature by itself did not suffice for the maintenance of peace and society among men, but, above and beyond that, it was necessary for these to be established through a pact of men, by the very men who were to administer the execution of the law in a human court. For, since the law of nature does not expressly determine just which one is to rule the other, or which ought to obey, and also does not mark the measure of punishment to be inflicted among men; assuredly, when they have formed a pact with one another, men ought to have determined who were to have sovereignty over the rest, by the force of which they could prescribe for others rules of action, and exact punishment from those who broke these same rules, precisely as they judged it to be for the public good so to do.

18. Whatever laws, therefore, are enjoined by the supreme civil sovereignty for their subjects to observe, under the threat of inflicting punishment in a human court of law upon the violators of the same, are called *civil* laws. These, whether taken from the body of the law of nature, or from the body of positive law, or proceeding from the mere free choice of the sovereigns, obtain the whole effect which they exert in a civil court from the force of supreme authority [*potestatis*] lending its authority [*autorita-*

tem] to them. And, indeed, in all commonwealths, most features of the law of nature, at all events such as those without which peace in the society itself cannot stand, have the force of civil law, or have been included in the body of civil laws. But if, now, some law of nature, due to some actions of the civil sovereignty, has not taken on the force of civil law, it obligates men, indeed, but in such a way that no action is brought because of its violation, nor punishment there inflicted, but the prosecution is left solely to the divine judgement-seat and to one's own consciousness of having violated that law. Thus, for example, even if every one whatsoever be bound by the law of nature to the duty of gratitude, in such wise that he is in fact sinning who has <161> not exhibited, as far as in him lay, gratitude towards his benefactors; nevertheless, where nothing upon that subject has been embodied in the civil laws, a second person cannot be compelled to return thanks by the force of a civil court of law. It is here properly that there should be referred that saying of Seneca: "How slight a thing it is to be a good man according to the law! How much more broadly does the rule of duties extend than the rule of law! How many things do piety, humanity, justice, fidelity demand! And yet they are all outside public records."[21] Now the reason why legislators have not assigned to all the precepts of the law of nature the force of civil law, is because they had primarily to attend to those matters without which the internal tranquillity of the commonwealth could not exist at all. It seemed best to let the rest pass, partly because to follow them up would produce a boundless harvest of suits before tribunals; and partly because they wished to leave good men a large share of their praise, as it were, unimpaired, the praise, namely, for having done right solely out of reverence for the Deity, without fear of a punishment which was to be imposed by men. And this praise disappears where it is impossible to discern whether one has done right out of fear of punishment, or solely from love of right. From the foregoing it is perceived at a glance that the application of the trite saying, "No one is under compulsion to help the other person, but merely forbidden to hinder him," is to be restricted merely to civil laws. Yet in all states natural laws supplement the civil law, so that when the latter has failed on some occurrence which altogether de-

---

21. Seneca, *De ira libri tres,* l. II, c. 27.

mands a decision in a human court of law, there is recourse to the laws of nature and to the analogy resulting from their comparison, whereby, however, that which is borrowed, as it were, from the law of nature takes on the force of civil law. Positive divine law among men obtains the same force as a law of nature, namely, that, through the sanction of the supreme sovereignty, it gains the effect of a civil law, which otherwise would be obligatory only before the divine judgement-seat; although, among the Jews, by the divine promulgation, divine laws received directly the force of civil laws, because God was in a special way also the civil lawgiver for that commonwealth. From what has been said, however, it by no means follows that human laws can derogate from the divine law in any respect, or that it depends upon human authority to decide, how far it may be necessary for the divine laws to be observed. For men cannot be freed by any human law at all from the obligation to fulfil the divine precepts, and the divine judgement-seat does not experience any loss of authority in dealing with transgressors, even if the civil court of law, the circuit, as it were, of whose jurisdiction is circumscribed by the utility to the commonwealth, has excused them from <162> punishment. And so it is a true saying that utility is the mother of law, that is to say, the civil law as such (but not of natural law), or, in other words, that utility gave the reason for establishing law. For nothing but utility or public good decided to which natural laws, in this or that commonwealth, the effect of a civil law is to be assigned, and to which not, what regulations are to be superadded to natural law, how punishments are to be directed against one, and how they are to be remitted, for practically the whole of the civil law is contained under these headings. Nor can any reason be advanced beside this one, why, in different commonwealths, or at different times, the laws vary, and the same punishment is not everywhere imposed for the same misdeeds. That fact, however, is not at all derogatory to the sanctity of natural law, nor do we regard the magistracy as sinning, if, indeed, it has failed to ratify by a civil penalty some precept of the law of nature, because it foresaw that a greater inconvenience would result from so doing than if every one whatsoever be left to his own conscience in that matter—a topic on which we have made an observation just above.

19. The object of civil laws is, in general, all that which can be effectively enjoined by a supreme human authority. The inner acts of the mind, in

regard to which laws are enacted in vain, are excluded therefrom, because, forsooth, it is beyond the power of other men to know whether obedience has been rendered the laws or not, so long as external acts do not reveal it. Nor is there any reason why the civil authority should be disturbed on account of things from which, as long as they remain such, there is no danger to the public tranquillity; although, when they have broken out into external actions, the internal action of the mind is most carefully regarded in aggravating or mitigating the crime, as is patent from what we shall say below on the quantity of actions.[22] Nor is it within the prerogatives of the civil sovereignty to give precepts contrary to the divine laws, for the reason that the more powerful obligation deriving from the divine law leaves no place to the obligation deriving from human law, and tending in the opposite direction. As for the rest, since, under the direction of the civil magistracy, there fall, in addition to the other things which look to the natural end of man, merely the external aspects of divine worship, it is apparent also that the magistracy can pass laws quite as well about the former as about the latter, the former being called by the general word civil, or secular, the latter *sacred* or *ecclesiastical*. These latter, whether they derive directly from the civil authority, or are framed by those who have been especially set aside for the exercise of divine worship, borrow all their authority [*autoritatem*] in the commonwealth from the supreme civil sovereignty. For the contrary involves the contradictory propositions, <163> namely, that the magistracy possesses supreme sovereignty, and yet that another man in the same state may pass a law on any matter whatsoever, which will be valid even against the will of the supreme sovereignty. But, in truth, in those things which have been defined already affirmatively or negatively by the law of nature or the divine positive law, authority belongs just so far to the supreme civil sovereignty, that it can assign, or not assign, to both, the force of civil laws, just as it may seem best for the commonwealth; and, in the case of affirmative laws, if, indeed, they have not been determined by the nature of the matter or the free choice of God himself, assign definite circumstances to the performance of the same, for example, time, place, manner, and persons.

22. See bk. I, Def. 18.

20. This observation also should be made about civil laws, namely, that in most of them certain acts are prohibited in such wise, that they are even rescinded, when they have been performed contrary to the laws. But, in the case of certain laws, the prohibition, indeed, is against something taking place, but when it has taken place, the act is not rescinded, but merely a fine or some punishment is assessed against the man who has acted contrary to the law, and when this has been met, the act has the same validity as if it were legitimate. Such laws can be called imperfect.[23] Among laws of this kind, if we desire to make observations with especial care, some are equivalent to a tribute, in such a way that the licence to do something is sold for a fixed price, and it is expressly left to the free choice of the subjects, whether they prefer to leave the act undone, or to pay a fine which they may even sometimes deposit in advance, the act to be exercised afterwards without impediment. This has no place at all in perfect penal laws, where the penalty assessed upon delinquents is by no means a complete equivalent for the fulfilment of the law, but has rather the purpose that neither the lawbreaker himself, nor others, shall violate the law again. Now certain laws do not rescind the act, indeed, although they impose a penalty properly so called upon those who undertake it. This is because a greater unseemliness appears in the act than in the effects, and frequently the inconveniences which follow rescinding are greater than the inconveniences of the act itself, when, after having once been undertaken, it remains valid. And this happens primarily in regard to those acts by which an obligation has been contracted towards some person or other, which is valid merely on the basis of the natural law, not the civil, an obligation to which satisfaction cannot be accorded, unless an act once undertaken remain effective. But, in truth, that is no law at all, which merely prohibits something from taking place, but still does not rescind it after it has taken place, and does not set a penalty upon the transgressor. Some put in this class the Cincian law, which forbade giving more than a definite amount to an advocate, but <164> did not rescind the gift.[24] And yet, in truth, since no one is presumed to have desired

23. See Ulpian, *Liber singularis regularum,* I.i.

24. See Rudolf Leonhard, "Donatio," *Paulys Real-Encyclopädie der classischen Altertumswissenschaften,* V. 2, pp. 1533–40, especially 1535.

that his action have no effect, wherever such a law appears which does not expressly mention the penalty, it is understood that the penalty is arbitrary, or, in other words, is to be modified according to the free choice of the judge, as it shall seem fair to him.

21. It is also customary for those declarations of the supreme sovereignty, whereby they merely signify what may legally be allowed in a civil court of law under a definite kind of act, to be comprehended in the body of the civil laws, and, in common parlance, to be listed under the name of laws. These are, properly speaking, not laws, but permissions, and their effect is not so much that one can legally undertake those acts, since, forsooth, any one whatsoever has the authority to do anything whatsoever which has not been forbidden, at least, by the laws; but, because men had either been forbidden to do certain things previously, or else doubts might have arisen about the legality of the same, so that certainty could be secured regarding the validity of the obligations which can arise therefrom. But if, in this way, something contrary to divine laws be permitted, the effect is not that this may be undertaken without sin, but only that the act obtains impunity in a civil court of law, and there enjoys the same effects which other licit acts habitually enjoy.

22. In regard to the correct application of the meaning of the law to particular cases, wherein lies the duty of the judge, diligent attention is to be paid to what is commonly called *equity*. This consists in prudently making clear that a certain case, clothed in special circumstances, had not been comprehended by the legislator under the general law. For it happens frequently that an absurdity follows from applying to special cases the letter of the law, because the legislators have not been able to see and make exception for these special cases, owing to the variety and number of them. But, since no one is presumed to have established absurdities by a law, it is thoroughly understood that the legislator had not intended to include such cases, and so, the judge who restricts through equity the universality of the letter, is not setting himself in opposition to the legislator, but rather is prudently gathering his intent by inference from the analogy and sense of other laws. There is also another significance of equity, as of that whereby disputes are settled on the basis of what is fair and good, disputes, that is, which are not expressly defined by civil laws, but are left to the judge or the arbitrator to be decided by comparing the law of nature and other civil

laws. Finally private persons as such are said to show equity to one another, when, out of the law of humanity or beneficence, they make a present of what they could exact by the force of civil laws, or else give up something of their right.

23. Now it is a *dispensation* when, in a definite case, individuals <165> who otherwise were bound are freed by the supreme authority from the obligation of a civil law as such. It is in the hands of the legislator to exercise this, who, since he may utterly abrogate his own laws, can undoubtedly suspend their effect in the case of a definite person. Now a dispensation differs from equity in that the judge is altogether bound to employ equity, to such a degree, that, if he had followed the bare letter of the law in a case where there was room for equity, he would be judged to have acted contrary to the intention of the legislator. But a dispensation, in truth, depends upon the mere grace of the legislator, and failure to grant it furnishes no cause for complaint. Equity makes clear that a certain case had not been included by the legislator under a general law; but dispensation sets a person free from his obligation, who was bound by that law. In granting a dispensation, however, the legislator will use prudence, lest, in granting it promiscuously, he either be enervating the force of the law, or else, without very serious grounds, he be giving others who are in the same condition cause for envy and indignation, because, though equal in condition, they have not been held worthy of an equal favour.

24. Something must be added now also on the subject of the *Law of Nations,* which, in the eyes of some men, is nothing other than the law of nature, in so far as different nations, not united with another by a supreme sovereignty, observe it, who must render one another the same duties in their fashion, as are prescribed for individuals by the law of nature. On this point there is no reason for our conducting any special discussion here, since what we recount on the subject of the law of nature and of the duties of individuals, can be readily applied to whole states and nations which have also coalesced into one moral person. Aside from this law, we are of the opinion that there is no law of nations, at least none which can properly be designated by such a name.[25] For most of those matters which the Ro-

---

25. Cf. *JNG,* 2, 3, §23. Pufendorf follows the Hobbesian equation of natural law and law of nations (*De cive,* chap. 14, §§4–5) and denies—against Grotius, *JBP,* I.i.14—that

man jurisconsults and others refer to the law of nations, for example, matters having to do with modes of acquisition, contracts, and other things,
pertain either to the law of nature, or to the civil law of individual nations,
which, in matters of that kind, coincides with the civil laws of most peoples.
These, however, do not rightly constitute a special species of law, since,
forsooth, the nations have those rights in common with one another, not
from some agreement or mutual obligation, but they have been established
by the special order of the individual legislators in the individual states, and
so can be changed by one people without consulting others, and are frequently found to have been so changed.

25. Finally, there are wont to be listed under the name of the law of
nations among most nations (at least those which claim the reputation of
being more civilized and humane), those customs which, by a certain tacit
consent, are habitually employed, especially in regard <166> to war. For,
after these more civilized nations came to regard it as their greatest honour
to seek glory in war (that is to say, to exhibit their superiority over others
in this, namely, that one was bold enough to kill many men, and skilful
enough to do it dexterously), and so unnecessary or unjust wars were entered into; under these conditions, in order to avoid exposing their ambition to excessive ill will, if they exercised the full licence of a just war, most
nations have seen fit to temper the harshness of war by some humanity and
a certain show of magnanimity. Hence came customs regarding the ex-
emption of definite things and persons from the violence of war, a fixed
way of injuring foes, a fixed way of treating prisoners, and the like. And,
if any one in legitimate warfare disregard these exemptions, in cases, of
course, where the law of nature allows such an act, he cannot be said to
have contravened a valid obligation; he is merely, as a general thing, blamed
for his rudeness, because he has not conformed to the customs of those
who regard war as one of the liberal arts, precisely as, among gladiators, he
who has wounded his opponent contrary to the rule of the art, is accused
of being maladroit. If, therefore, a man wage just wars, he can conduct
them by the law of nature alone, and he is not bound by any law to these
customs just mentioned, unless of his own accord he so wish, in order to

---

the voluntary law of nations constitutes a distinct branch of law (separate from natural
and civil law).

obtain some advantage of his own. But he who ravens in unjust wars ought to observe those laws, so that he inflict his injuries with at least some kind of moderation. But they are assuredly wasting their efforts who collect what the nations in common with one another habitually practise, especially in war, and conclude these matters to be legitimate on the basis of the law of nations; as if, in truth, there were less injustice, cruelty, and avarice in what is found to have been done often by those whose crimes have gone unpunished among men, because they had no one over them, and so they have not been vehemently castigated, since the rest of men do not shrink from perpetrating the same crimes. And, assuredly, if some special law ought to be set up on the basis of the common usage of nations, the very first heading in it will treat of the legitimate waging of wars for mere ambition, or with the prospect of making gain, than which nothing is more frequent among most nations.

26. But, as regards legates, who commonly constitute one of the principal headings of the law of nations, even those who have been sent to the enemy, if, indeed, they have the appearance of legates, and not of spies, as long as they are in the presence of him to whom they have been sent, and contrive no hostile acts against him, for example, in exciting treachery, sedition, and the like (although, perchance, in any ordinary manner they seek by negotiations the advantage of their own lord rather than that of the other), they are inviolable <167> by the very law of nature. For, since persons of that kind are necessary, in order to win or to preserve peace, which the very law of nature bids us embrace in all honourable ways, it is well understood that the same law has also provided for the safety of those persons without whom the end which it orders cannot be obtained. But, in truth, the other privileges which are commonly granted to legates, especially those legates who are located in some particular place, rather to spy out the secrets of the other commonwealth, than to establish or preserve peace, I mean such privileges as that their goods may not be attached to secure their debts, and the like, these depend upon the mere grace and indulgence of the one to whom they are sent, and, if it seem to his advantage to do so, he can deny them without violating any right, except in so far as some attention be paid to the consideration that his own legates be treated in a similar way, at the court of another.

27. Now, in general, in regard to laws, it is to be noted that some are

affirmative, and some *negative.* The former, when they require an occasion which is not always and everywhere present, are understood to obligate to the exercise of an action, namely, when it can take place, that is to say, when the object and other requisites for action are at hand. And so, he who from failing to have an occasion does not perform an action otherwise ordered by the laws, does by no means deserve reprehension; nor ought the man who, while striving to the utmost limit of his powers, has been over-whelmed by the mass of the matter, or has failed of success through no fault of his own, have his effort to obey criticised. But the obligation of negative precepts is always uniform, as it were, forasmuch as it demands the giving up of voluntary evil actions, that is to say, things which are not entities, and so do not require an object, a place, and a time.

From the same source, also, as we may add in passing, can be derived this trite principle: "There is naturally no proof of the denial of a fact," that is to say, direct proof. This is because he who denies that something was done, says that what the doer intended became a non-entity, which has neither cause nor circumstances. Now every proof is made up of causes, circumstances, and indications. If, however, it be denied that a thing was done in a definite time and place, this can be proved indirectly, to wit, if it be shown that he who is accused of the deed, at the time when something is said to have been done, was in another place. <168>

Authority is an active moral power by which some person legitimately and with a direct moral effect can perform an action.[1]

    1. Natural power and moral power.
    2. The authority to act in those matters which
       belong to a man.
    3. How he whose authority to act depends upon
       another ought to presume upon that other's will.
    4. Rules about authority.

1. In man the power to act is twofold. One is the *natural* power to act, through which he is able by his natural strength to perform an action, or to neglect it, without considering whether it be right or not. Thus men are able in fact to do things forbidden by laws, and to neglect their precepts. But *moral* power in man is that whereby he is able to perform a voluntary action legitimately and with a moral effect, that is to say, so that this action shall harmonize with the laws, or at least be not repugnant to them, and be able to produce moral effects in others. Now a man is judged to have authority to do all that which can be done by him through the exercise of

---

1. There is only a slight difference from Def. 7: "Authority is an active moral power by which some person legitimately and with a moral effect is able to perform a voluntary action." But the scholion to Def. 7 predominantly deals with "authority over the persons of others" as a presupposition for the subsequently introduced concepts of obligation and law which, according to Pufendorf, are constituted by prescription from an authority. The scholion to Def. 14, on the other hand, deals with authority as a right to act under the law ("to do all that which can be done by him through the exercise of his natural power, whatever, namely, is not forbidden by the laws") and that cannot conveniently be discussed until law has been introduced.

his natural power, whatever, namely, is not forbidden by the laws, or is also enjoined by the same, or else left indifferent. Nay, frequently authority is ampler than the measure of natural force. But, in truth, there has been taken away authority to do those things which were legitimately forbidden him, either by some universal legislator, or by some other to whom in a special way belongs command [*imperium*] over his actions.

2. But commonly, in truth, when a man performs an action enjoined by the laws, the question is not apt to be raised whether he had the authority to undertake it, since, forsooth, in the case of all for whom some law which has not been made invalid by a higher law, is passed, it is understood, from the very nature of the transaction, that they have been given at the same time authority to act in accordance with that law. And, in short, when it has been well established that what a man is doing is not repugnant to laws, no one any longer doubts that he may do it legitimately. But, truly, the most careful scrutiny is made about the agent's authority, in regard to those actions by which some moral effect is to be produced upon others, that is to say, by which an obligation or a faculty to do something ought to be conferred upon another. For an act is treated as invalid and null, when the authority to act was lacking. Here, however, the observation must be made, a matter which we have noted above, namely, that just as imperfect laws demand a penalty, indeed, for the commission of an act <169> contrary to them, but do not rescind the act; so the authority to act, which is utterly taken away by perfect negative laws, seems to be not so much extinguished by those imperfect laws, as granted together with an accompanying burden of punishment or fine. Furthermore, not merely are those things which have not been forbidden either by divine or human law, said to be permissible, but also those which, although opposed, indeed, to the divine law, either natural or positive, are permitted by the civil law, that is to say, are neither forbidden nor punished in a human court of law. The authority corresponding to things of the former kind is called *internal,* to things of the latter kind *external.* Its effect is impunity in a human court of law, and other things which follow licit acts, although that authority cannot at all be adduced before the divine judgement-seat.

3. Now he whose authority to do something must be sought from the will of a second person, should see to it that where an express indication

of the same is wanting, he conjectures and presumes it with skill. This can be the case if he observe the following rules: (1) He who receives the authority to act from the will of another person, where the contrary has not been signified by an expression of his will, can rightly do what is useful to the other, in such a way that it does not appear likely that a greater inconvenience will result therefrom. For, in the absence of express signs indicating something else, it is presumed that every one wishes to have his interests advanced, because this is to the highest degree in accord with nature, and presumptions are commonly apt to follow nature. (2) It is not right to do the opposite of what has been signified expressly. For a man's will is indicated with just this purpose, namely, that no one, on the basis of a presumed will, should do something different from that which had been prescribed by him; unless, by means of a general clause, the second person has been bidden to follow the advantage or the necessity of the circumstance, to the extent of his skill. On this principle a soldier, or a commanding officer of lower rank, who has been expressly forbidden to join combat in any way with the foe, does not do right in entering a combat without the knowledge of the commander-in-chief, although it may appear to him that it is possible to achieve a success. (3) He who acts with the knowledge of the second party, and when the same is able to indicate without any trouble his dissent, rightly presumes his will from his silence. And so it follows that the vows of a wife, or a daughter under her father's authority, and of a slave, were valid by the divine law, if the husband, father, or master, on hearing them, had kept silence.[2] (4) He who has entrusted some action to a second person is regarded as having assented to that which the latter does under the compulsion of extreme necessity, unless either the laws have forbidden it, or he has been forbidden expressly to avoid a necessity in that way, or what <170> necessity was going to bring about would be a less evil than the one which is accepted in order to avoid it.

4. Finally, in regard to authority two rules are to be observed. One is, *"He who has the authority to do the greater has also authority to do the less,"* as the latter, of course, is contained in the former; or, in other words, "He who can do more, can also do less." On the basis of this rule Justinian

2. Numbers 30.

emended that paragraph of the Aelian-Sentian law, by which a master under twenty years of age was forbidden to liberate a slave, except by a manumission staff before a court in a legitimate case;[3] since, however, such a young man had at that time the authority to make a testament, that is to say, to dispose of all his goods, why, therefore, should he not be able to give freedom to his slave by his testament? And yet it might happen, that, when authority depends upon the mere will of him who grants it, there is granted one the faculty of doing the greater, when the less, which otherwise in due order appeared to be included under the greater, had been denied. The second rule is, *"He who gives authority for an end, is regarded also, as far as he is concerned, as having given authority for all those things without which the end cannot be obtained."* For otherwise it would be a case of his willing that at the same time something take place, or else not take place, and that is absurd. This almost coincides with the trite saying, *"The necessity of the end produces right or authority in things moral."* <171>

3. *Inst.,* I.vi.7.

The affections of a voluntary action are the modes through which it is denominated or defined in a certain manner.

1. Precisely what are the affections of actions?
2. What is a necessary action, and what a licit one?

1. AFFECTIONS are directly regarded in the actions themselves, just as the effects are regarded directly either in the objects, or in the agent himself. Now those affections are either *denominative,* or else *determinative,* or, in other words, *estimative.* The former are the qualities by which actions are called *necessary* or *unnecessary, licit* or *illicit, good* or *bad, just* or *unjust.* You might express them by the single word *competency,* which is regarded, either from the point of view of the subject, from whom the action proceeds, and so the same are necessary, licit, and good; or else from the point of view of the object in which they terminate, and so they are just. The latter are the *quantities and estimates of actions,* and have no special designation. We shall here add a few observations on the necessary and the licit; the others we shall take up separately.

2. That is a *necessary* action which one to whom a law or a command of a superior has been given is altogether bound to do by that law or command. The opposite of this is not so much a *forbidden* action, which is prohibited by laws from taking place, but even a *licit* action, which the laws neither order nor forbid, but the undertaking or neglect of which has been left to the agent's free choice alone. Here it is to be observed, as we have already noted above, that certain actions which have been prohibited neither by

divine nor by civil law can be called *perfectly licit;* certain others, which, though forbidden by divine laws, the civil law permits, to the extent that it imposes no penalty upon them in a human court of law, can be called *imperfectly licit.* From this it is easy to gather by inference what an illicit action is. <172>

∞ DEFINITION XVI ∞

A good action is one which agrees with law; a bad action is one which disagrees with the same.

1. The formal basis of goodness and badness.
2. An action is good which has all the requisites; bad, in which even one is lacking.
3. Whether an action in an individual case may be indifferent.
4. The cause of badness is by no means to be sought in God.

1. The formal character of goodness and badness consists in a bearing, or in other words, a determinative relation to a directive norm which we call a law (by this we always understand here a law which necessitates, not permits, and, if it be a human law, one which is not repugnant to divine right). For, in so far as an action of free choice proceeds from the prescript of the norm, and is instituted in accordance therewith, in such wise that it agrees exactly with the norm, it is called good; in so far as it is undertaken contrary to the prescript of the norm, or disagrees with the norm, it is called bad, and, in a single word, designated a misdeed. Moreover, as each and every directive norm, for example the compass, is called the cause of itinerary correctness, and of arriving at the port, not so much in that the ship cuts that course which coincides with its pointing, as that the skipper directs his course according to its prescript;[1] so a law is said to be the cause of correctness in an action, not so much because an action, undertaken from any

---

1. Cf. Weigel, *Analysis Aristotelica,* sect. II, chap. XII, §24: "in the same manner as a house comes from the possessor, namely from an agent or moral cause who has legitimately ordered (i.e., caused) the house to be built, . . . arrival in port stems from the nautical compass, namely from an agent or notional cause that has directed the mind of the skipper by the objective arrangement of its parts (i.e., as by a cause)."

cause at all, squares with the law, but primarily because the action proceeds
from the dictate of the law, and from dependence upon the law, that is,
with the intention of rendering obedience to the same. And so, if a man,
led by chance, or by some reason other than to show himself obedient to
the law, does that which the law bids, he can be said to have done rightly
indeed (in a sense rather negative than affirmative, that is, not wrongly),
yet not well in a moral sense; precisely as he who has brought down a bird
by the accidental discharge of an escopette cannot be said to have shot
expertly and skilfully.

2. Now, since the law determines either the quality or disposition of the
agent, or the object, or the end, or, finally, the definite circumstances of an
action; it follows thence that a certain action is morally good or bad, either
because the agent has been so disposed as the law <173> requires, or otherwise disposed; or because the action is directed to the object with the same
purpose and circumstances as those with which the object is disposed by
law, and the contrary. Here, however, it is to be noted, that, in order for
some action to be good it is necessary for it both to agree with the law
according to all quasi-material requisites, and also, as far as its formal character is concerned, to have been performed not from ignorance or from
some other cause, but in order to render an owed obedience to the law. And
so an action otherwise materially, as it were, good, is charged against the
agent as a bad action, because of a bad intention. Thus he who, while intending to do harm, actually does good, deserves no reward. Thus he who
uses his legitimate authority with a bad purpose (for example, a judge using
his authority to exact punishment from the guilty, so as to glut a private
passion), does wrong. And yet an action otherwise materially, as it were,
bad, does by no means become good because of the good intention of the
agent. Thence it follows that no one can use his own transgressions in the
way of means, as it were, to attain a good end, and things bad are not to
be done so that things good may result. For, to have an action made bad,
it is sufficient that there be failure on the part of a single material or formal
requisite to harmonize with the law. Hence an action becomes bad immediately, if either the quality of the agent, or the object, or the end, or
some one of the circumstances, or the intention, be in disagreement with
the law. And not merely is a complete misdeed, and one which has reached

its end, regarded as a crime, but even the misdeed which has been only planned and begun,[2] upon which even civil laws sometimes inflict the same punishment as they do upon the consummated misdeed, or a punishment not much lighter, according as they judge it to be expedient for some crime to be crushed, even in the first attempts.

3. From what has been said one gathers also the answer to the question, whether some moral action in an individual case, or, in other words, considered here and now, be indifferent. Here the question is properly not about licit actions, or such as have been neither ordained nor forbidden by laws, for that they are indifferent, or, in other words, are neither good nor bad in a moral sense, is beyond doubt; but about those which the laws ordain or forbid. It is no more possible for these to be indifferent in an individual case, than it is possible for something to exist intermediate between agreement and disagreement with the law. And it is a vain statement of some, that an action, as far as the substance of the deed is concerned can be good, even if a legitimate end be not intended by the agent.[3] For the end is of the utmost pertinence in determining the essence of an action, forasmuch as it coheres with the intention, which is the principle that most of all distinguishes the quality of an action. And so it is not merely a misdeed, to refer <174> actions to a bad end, but also to refer them to an end different from that prescribed by the laws.

4. Moreover, as this goodness and badness of an action consists in a formal way in what I have called accord and disaccord with the moral norm, so, in an efficient way, it depends exclusively upon the one by whom that action, prescribed or forbidden by the law, is performed, forasmuch as the determination of this point so constitutes an action in the class of moral entities, that it can be charged to him alone and not to another. And so

2. Cf. *JNG*, 1, 7, §4, with reference to Seneca, *De constantia sapientis* [*On the Steadfastness of the Wise Man*], chap. 7: "All crimes, as far as concerns their criminality, are completed before the actual deed is accomplished."

3. Grotius, *JBP*, II.xxiii.2: "First of all we must hold to the principle that, even if something is in itself just, when it is done by one who, taking everything into consideration, considers it unjust, the act is vicious. This in fact is what the Apostle Paul meant by saying, 'Whatsoever is not of faith, is sin,' where 'faith' signifies the judgement of the mind on the matter."

they have been tormented by a vain fear who, in order to avoid the appearance of making God, the creator of all things, the author also of sin, have placed the formal basis of sin in a lack of congruence with law.[4] For, in truth, although the establishment of any form whatsoever necessarily implies the lack or absence of the contrary form, nevertheless, the man who has sought the essence of the matter in that lack is utterly mistaken. Nor has he made much progress who recognizes that straightness is the lack of curvature, and curvature the lack of straightness. But that was a vain fear which drove them to such recourses. For, without doubt, God is the creator of all physical entities, but it would be utterly absurd for one to wish to make Him the creator of all moral and notional entities as well. Those, however, who, as a notable specimen of their subtlety, declare that they have intertwined God in any way whatsoever among the causes of sin, are suffering from an utterly profane itching of the intellect. For he who has any perception of moral entities, will judge nothing more absurd than the inquiry, whether he who forbids an action by law, and punishes it when committed against his interdict, be the cause of the action. But God's concurrence in the physical aspect of the action can no more be called the cause of the misdeed, than, for example, he who furnishes the cloth for an article of clothing, can be called the cause of a deformity in the same, when it has been made up unskilfully by a tailor. Now to force the word "cause" here into an improper meaning, and one alien to the common understanding of it, is to make oneself to appear in no slight degree irreverent towards the Divine Spirit. <175>

---

4. An allusion to Augustine's privative theory of sin. See, for example, Augustine, *The City of God Against the Pagans,* vol. 3, trans. David S. Wiesen, Loeb Classical Library (Cambridge, Mass.: Harvard University Press, 1968), XII.9: "For evil has in itself no substance, rather the loss of what is good had received the name evil"; and idem, *The City of God Against the Pagans,* vol. 4, trans. Philip Levine, Loeb Classical Library (Cambridge, Mass.: Harvard University Press, 1966), XII.7: "So too our mind glimpses objects of thought by thinking them; but where they are deficient in something, the mind is instructed through unknowing. For 'who can discern lapses?'"

A just action is one which of free moral choice is rightly directed to that person to whom it is owed.

1. Universal and particular justice.
2. Distributive.
3. Commutative.
4. Vindicative.
5. Injustice.

6. What a wrong properly is.
7. A wrong comes from free moral choice; where also the subject of fault is treated.
8. He who consents suffers no wrong.

1. JUSTICE can be considered in a twofold aspect, as it denotes either the person, or the action. On the basis of the former kind of justice, he alone deserves the designation just, who has maintained a constant and perpetual will to give each man what is due him;[1] on the basis of the latter kind of justice, even a single and solitary action, rightly applied to the object, is called just. We shall be concerned here much more with the latter significance than with the former. When, therefore, of our free moral choice we give a second person what is due him, but particularly when we rightly apply an action to a person to whom it is due, this is called a just action.[2] Now something is due a person either on the basis of an imperfect right, which, as we have said above, is also called an aptitude, or else on the basis of a perfect right. The right application of actions, both those which are pure,

1. See *Inst.*, I.1, and *Dig.*, I.i.10 preamble: "Justice is the constant and perpetual desire to give to every one that to which he is entitled."
2. Cf. *JNG*, 1, 7, §7: "Now justice of actions differs from goodness of actions mainly in this, that goodness denotes simply an agreement with law, while justice includes further a relation to those towards whom the action is performed. Consequently, in our opinion, an action is called just which is applied from previous choice to the person to whom it is owed, and therefore, on this definition, justice will be the right application of actions to a person."

as well as those which are united with the transfer of some property to persons who had merely an imperfect right to its possession; as also the application of actions not coming, under the relations of exchange, to persons who have a right to them, we shall call *universal justice,* as when one helps with counsel, effort, or property, a man's action, and displays the due offices of piety, reverence, and gratitude towards those to whom he is bound to display them. This justice looks merely towards rendering to the other person what is due him on any score whatsoever, without considering whether that which is furnished equal the cause for which it is due, or be less. Thus, a man satisfies the duty of gratitude, if, as much be returned as his means allow, even if the benefaction, perchance, has far surpassed that. But the right application of actions which enter into exchange, or by which some property to which one had a right is transferred to another, will be called *particular justice.*[3]

2. Furthermore, this right arises either for individuals, on the basis of a pact, tacit or express, entered into with some society, having <176> as its end that they become members of the same; or else for a society, on the basis of the same pact with individuals, so as to add them to itself as members; or else, finally, in regard to other matters or actions entering into exchange. The right application of those things which are due on the basis of the pact of a society with a member, or of a member with a society, to the end already mentioned, is called *distributive justice.* For whenever one is received into a society, such a pact is either expressly or tacitly entered into between the society and the member to be received, namely, that the society, indeed, is willing to give the member his fair share of the goods which properly belong to the society as such; and the member, on his side, is willing to bear his fair share of the burdens which make for the preservation of the society as such. Now the determination of the fair share of the goods to be assigned the fellow-member is made according to an esti-

---

3. Pufendorf's distinction between universal and particular justice and the latter's distinction into distributive and commutative justice follow *Nicomachean Ethics* V (cf. *JNG,* 1, 7, §12). The Aristotelian distinction is between universal justice as "exercise of complete virtue in relation to others" and particular justice as exercise of a "part of virtue." Pufendorf interprets this as a distinction between imperfect duties of humanity and perfect legal duties (*JNG,* 1, 7, §8).

mate of the effort or expenses incurred in preserving the society as such, when these are considered in proportion to the effort or expenses incurred by other members of that society. As, on the contrary, the determination of the fair share of the burdens to be imposed upon the member, is made according to an estimate of the advantages, which that member receives from the society, considered in proportion to the advantages received by other members from the society. And so, since for the most part one member contributes more towards the preservation of the society than another, and one person also derives more advantage than a second from the same, it is readily apparent why, in distributive justice, a comparative equality is to be observed. Such comparative equality consists in this, namely, that in the proportion in which a man's dignity or merit stands in relation to the dignity or merit of a second person, so his reward should stand in relation to the reward of that second person. Thus, for example, if six things are to be divided between Gaius, Seius, and Titius, assuming that the merits of Titius surpass the merits of Gaius threefold, and those of Seius surpass them twofold, Gaius will have to be given one, Seius two, and Titius three. Nor is it required, for this equality, that the reward simply equal the merit of the person; but it is sufficient that the proportion which the dignity of the one maintains to the dignity of the other should be kept also in the proportion which the share of the one, in the common property, maintains to the share of the other. The same principle must be observed also in imposing burdens. But, in truth, the assertion made by some, for the purpose of overthrowing the respective equality which is observed in this species of justice, to the effect, namely, that, "Out of what is my own I can distribute less to the one who deserves more, and give more to the one who deserves less, provided only I give what I have agreed to give," at the same time quoting from the Gospel the <177> pronouncement of the Saviour, has assuredly nothing to do with the case.[4] For, in the example adduced, it is shown that he who, out of liberality, has given some a reward greater than their desert, provided only he does not deny to the rest the just reward which

4. The reference is to the parable of the workers in the vineyard (Matthew 20) and its interpretation by Hobbes, *De cive,* chap. 3, §6, who tries to reduce all justice to the keeping of faith and carrying out of agreements, thus doing away with the distinction into distributive and commutative (cf. *JNG,* 1, 7, §§9, 13).

they had bargained for, is not sinning against the commutative justice which governs that contract of letting and hiring. But what has this to do with our distributive justice, in which a fair share is to be assigned of a thing to which several have, as it were, a right unequal in point of degree? Now the word "distribute," occurring in that example, by no means indicates a pertinence to distributive justice, but that there were several hired men, to each of whom his own reward was to be given.

3. But, in truth, the right application of those things which are owed on the basis of a pact, concerning things and actions entering into exchange, is called *commutative justice.* Since those pacts look to this, namely, that, in return for my property or action entering into exchange, I should receive from a second person a piece of property or an action of equivalent value, it is readily apparent why this form of justice demands simple equality, whereby the price of a second thing or action ought to correspond, exactly as its moral evaluation goes, with the price of the thing or action coming into exchange.

4. Now, in truth, what is called *vindicative justice,* which has to do with imposing punishments, does not square exactly with either species of distributive justice. But, in a misdeed, there are to be kept accurately distinguished the essential badness of the action in itself, and the damage done the second person thereby, punishment corresponding properly to the former, and restitution of the damage, to the latter. In making amends for the damage, the procedure is, that, what one loses by the other's misdeed, whether it be still in the possession of the wrongdoer or has perished, that, or the same amount, should be taken from the wrongdoer and given to the one who has suffered the loss; and that this be done in such a way, that, simply out of the goods of the wrongdoer, amends are made for what loss the other has incurred, due to his fault. But in the matter of imposing a punishment, this, indeed, is certain, namely, that it cannot be inflicted, except in view of some misdeed, but when it is to be inflicted, and to what degree, or of what kind it shall be, is to be decided, not so much from the very nature of the misdeed, as from the advantage redounding therefrom, either to the wrongdoer himself, or to society. For it is repugnant to reason to have one man impose some evil upon another man for any cause whatsoever, when, in so doing, he considers nothing but the pain of the sufferer.

Therefore, just as, for the sake of preserving society among men, the principal laws of nature in practically all states had to be given the force of civil laws, so that those, for whom otherwise reverence for the Deity would prove to be too ineffective a stimulus to doing their <178> duty, could be compelled to observe these laws also from fear of human violence; so also every punishment in a human court of law ought to aim at that same mark. And so, since nature defines neither the quantity nor the quality of punishment, and altogether does not allow one man to exact punishment from another, except in the respect just mentioned, he who has tempered punishments well to that end will rightly administer vindicative justice. And hence punishment is properly owed, not to the wrongdoer, as something which cannot rightly be denied him (unless, perchance, in so far as he is to be reformed thereby), but to society; and if, in that case in which it ought to have been inflicted, it be neglected, a wrong is not done to the delinquent, but to society, which is disturbed by that kind of impunity or bad dispensation of punishment. And, in the quantity of punishment, to which the public utility sets the measure[5] (just as the character of the evil-doer sets the measure to his castigations or corrections), a wrong is not done the delinquent, if he undergo the degree of punishment which he knew had been set for the degree of his misdeed (if, indeed, he had not been impelled to the wrong by the very one who exacts the penalty), even if, perchance, the punishment, absolutely considered, may seem more severe than the wrong done. For a man has no right to demand that another should take cognizance of that danger which he voluntarily brought upon himself, although he might easily have avoided it. And so we feel that vindicative justice is by no means violated by the general who inflicts a previously announced and promulgated penalty of death, even for the theft of a hen, if, indeed, he has decided that it is for the public good to have the security of the defenceless provided for by such a severe punishment. But, where that end which I have mentioned is not regarded, or can be obtained more conveniently in some other

---

5. For Pufendorf vindictive justice is a part of the sovereign's prudence. It is the sovereign's task to interpret the public utility according to his own discretion and subject only to natural law. Such activity does not fall under any species of particular justice but belongs to universal justice, as he points out in a phrase added to *JNG,* 8, 3, §5, in the second edition of 1684.

way, in our judgement the punishment not only can be omitted with pro-
priety, but even ought to be omitted.

5. From what has been said, it is easily understood what an unjust action
is, that is to say, one which, on the basis of free moral choice, is in an evil
way applied to a person, to whom a different action was due, or, when what
was due a person is denied him. For we act unjustly, when we inflict upon
a second person some evil we did not have the authority to inflict (now
good things are of such a nature that they may be given any one whatsoever,
even without cause, if this be without harm to a third person), or deny, or
take away, some good which was due him (for, if his act does not involve
damage to others, we cannot inflict upon a man the evils which he has
deserved, without doing him a wrong). And so, an unjust action either
inflicts what it ought not to inflict, or takes away what it ought not to take
away, or denies what it ought to give. (For, also in a moral sense, the denial,
or the neglect of an action due, is regarded as an action.)[6] <179>

6. Now an unjust action, if, indeed, it be inflicted upon a second person
by free moral choice, together with a breach of right which properly belongs
to the second person is very commonly called by the single word *injury.* In
order to understand this accurately, it should be known that a man can be
injured in a threefold manner, either by being denied what he ought to have,
or in having taken from him what he now has, or in having some evil done
to him, which one had no authority to inflict upon another. In regard to
the former method, it is to be observed that something is due somebody,
either on the basis of the mere law of nature, in such a way, however, that
he does not have a perfect right to it, such being the duties of humanity,
beneficence, and gratitude; or else, on the basis of a pact, and this either a
special pact, or else contained in our obligation to the civil laws, by which
we bind ourselves to supply that which the civil laws bid us furnish to a
second person. If the latter be denied some one, it is properly called injury;
but not, if the former be denied him, even if there be a sin against the law
of nature. Nor, by the very law of nature, is it permissible to compel a
second person by force to furnish those things, at least where one does not
properly have command [*imperium*] over him, unless, perchance, necessity

6. See bk. I, Def. 1, §2.

urge; since, forsooth, the genius of those duties requires that they be rendered voluntarily, and without fear of punishment. In this sense it is true that injury is not done except to him with whom one has a pact.[7] But, in truth, when, with malice aforethought, an evil be brought upon a man in his despite, whether by stealing some good thing which he possessed until then, or by inflicting in a positive way some evil upon him, an injury is always done, whether a pact had intervened or not. For the law of nature grants to every man whatsoever, that no evil shall be brought upon him by another man, without some antecedent desert on his part; and a man has not the authority to injure a second person, when he himself has not been hurt, except in so far as the necessity of exercising command [*imperii*] has required that of him.

7. Also, in order to be an injury properly so called, it is required that it proceed from the exercise of a free moral choice. And so it is not customary to list under the head of injury hurts of such a kind as come about by some chance happening at the hand of a man who did not know what he was doing, and did not intend to do it; for example, if a soldier, while exercising with javelins in his usual place, runs one through a passer-by, or if a tree-cutter, while chopping wood in the midst of his farm, has unexpectedly wounded a stranger who had no right to be in that place (for such things are counted among those evils which are sent upon us out of mere chance, where a complaint cannot be lodged against any man, or a restitution of the damage demanded); or hurts that come about from negligence, which might have been <180> avoided, if, indeed, one had observed due diligence, for example, if a person working beside a public road has hurt a passer-by, without having first given a signal, so that the latter might look out for himself. The same holds true if a man has undertaken some work beyond his powers, by performing which poorly, damage is done to a second person; since no one ought to attempt that in which he knows, or might know, that his weakness or lack of skill will involve the danger of others. A hurt of that kind the jurisconsults commonly call a *fault,* which is either *extremely light,* when, by lack of circumspection and deliberation, there is a deviation from that diligence which unusually careful men are wont to show; or *light,*

7. Hobbes, *De cive,* chap. 3, §4.

when the sagacity of careful men of that profession is not exhibited; or else *broad,* when common carefulness is not manifested. The broad fault and the light fault agree in this with wrong, namely, that they create the obligation of making good the loss suffered by them, an obligation which the extremely light fault does not produce, unless one has expressly bargained for the most exact and special diligence. But those hurts also are commonly excepted from the class of injuries, where the intention is only partial, for example, when one is driven to hurt a second person either from a necessary affection, as hunger, thirst, &c., or from a natural affection, as love, pain, fear, &c.; although, properly, that diminution of the intention does not take away the whole character of the wrong, but merely tempers the guilt.[8]

8. But that which is to be called a wrong must also be done to a person against his will. For it is a trite saying even in common speech, that he who consents suffers no wrong. This is because the good thing which I take away from a second person with his consent, or the debt which I do not pay with his consent, he is regarded as having presented me with. But who will say that I have done a wrong, if I have received what is given? Nor can what a person is willing to have inflicted upon him be looked upon as an evil, since, forsooth, an evil necessarily involves an abhorrence of the will. Some even conclude therefrom that certain ancient barbarians who were accustomed to kill and feast upon men worn out with old age, did not do a wrong, because death was inflicted as a regular custom to which they had given their common consent. And yet no one will deny that the old violated the law of nature, in that, from merely being wearied with the troubles of old age, they were willing to anticipate their fate; not to mention how utterly the savagery of that custom is abhorrent to the common feeling of mankind [*à communi sensu*]. <181>

---

8. This discussion of preceding choice as a necessary element in injury and also the distinction of involuntary harm into misfortunes and errors according to the degree of ignorance derive from Aristotle, *Nicomachean Ethics,* V, 1134a17–1136a9. Cf. *JNG,* 1, 7, §16, which also cites Michael of Ephesus's commentary on that passage (*Michaelis Ephesii in librum quintum Ethicorum Nicomacheorum commentarium,* modern edition, Michael Hayduck, ed., in *Commentaria in Aristotelem Graeca* 22.3 [Berlin: Reimer, 1901]). On the degrees of fault according to the Roman jurists, see *Dig.,* XIII.vi.18 preamble and L.xvi.213.2.

The quantity of moral actions is the estimative measure by which they are said to be of a certain degree.

1. What is the nature of an absolute estimate of moral actions?
2. Determination of the moral sphere.
3. Defect of actions as regards their execution.
4. The divisible or indivisible objects of actions.
5. Defect of actions as regards their intention.
6. The grade of intention.
7. Just what is a perfectly good action?
8. Just what is the greatest sin?
9. Sins of lower degree.
10. A computation of the quantity of sin.
11. What the nature is of men's knowledge regarding the quantity of sins.
12. The relative estimate of actions drawn from their object.
13. From the status of the agents.
14. From the condition of the action.
15. From the effect and the circumstances.
16. Whether repetition intensifies an action.
17. Just what duties yield to a second duty, when both cannot be performed at the same time?

1. Moral actions are estimated either *absolutely* and in themselves, or *relatively* and in comparison with one another. In an absolute estimate of a moral action, and especially of a good one, speaking precisely and quasi-geometrically, there is no degree; but goodness itself consists, as it were, in a point and is a kind of coincidence, as it were, and congruence with the law, and as such has no measure. And so, also, considered formally and precisely, one good action is not better than another, since, forsooth, nothing can be more right than the right, although, considered materially and on the score of its object, one action is superior to and nobler than another. But, since an evil action declines from the law, it assuredly is at a certain

247

distance from the law, greater or less, from which a sin obtains the character
of greater or less degree, as one deviation from a straight line is greater than
a second. Now this divergence from the law is like neither length, breadth,
nor depth, which can be measured by a straight line; but it resembles a
rectilinear angle, whose magnitude is measured by the arc of a circle described from the point of intersection of the two sides as a centre, and
intercepted by the aforesaid sides. For, as a rule of law, which, like a straight
line, marks out by its course precisely what is to be done, has the character
of the first side; so the determination of our will, which is always joined
by our conscience to the rule of the law in what resembles the point of an
angle, is the other side, which, if the action swerve aside from the law, has
a certain angular distance, as it were, from the first side, and by this the
degree of bad actions is estimated. <182> But, as around any point in space
in which two or more lines unite, when treated as the centre of a sphere,
an infinite number of tracts are conceived to be gathered, to which straight
lines can run, diverging in different modes from one another; so the number
of ways is infinite by which bad actions will be able to take their course, in
diverging from a rule of the law. And so we shall not incongruously picture
to ourselves the field of moral actions in the shape of a sphere, in whose
centre gather the sides of the moral angle, like the radii of a circle; but
on whose surface there are marked the points of the tracts to which the
radii tend. Now as a sphere is marked by three cardinal circles, as they
might be called, whose common circumferences, planes, and diameters
strike each other at right angles, such as are the horizon, the meridian,
and the prime vertical, in the mundane sphere, the first of which embraces
the sphere's tract of latitude and longitude, and the second its thickness,
while the last divides the first two into two parts, and the whole sphere
into a polar and an antipolar hemisphere; so, likewise, in the moral sphere,
there are marked three cardinal circles, as they may be called, the first of
which, like the horizon, represents the limits and object with which the
moral action has to do, and represents the exercise itself; the second, like
the meridian, suggests the elevation, as it were, and the intention of the
mind of the agent; the third, like the prime vertical, divides the former
two into two parts, and delimits the whole sphere into a polar and an
antipolar hemisphere.

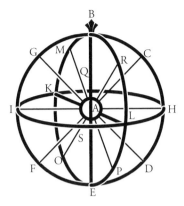

2. To understand this better, in the accompanying diagram, which represents a right sphere, let the circle BHEI be the right horizon; the circle BKEL be the meridian, here seen obliquely, and declining <183> to an elliptical line; as also the circle HSIQ, the prime vertical, coinciding in a right sphere with the equator. Let B, the point of common contact of the horizon and the meridian, be the arctic pole, which we shall call the polar region; and let the other common point of these same circles, but opposite to this, namely E, be the antarctic pole, which will be called by us here the antipolar region. Let God, the searcher out of hearts and the most clear-sighted judge of human actions, be conceived of as seated at the centre of the moral sphere, A, as though in our heart, from which proceeds, and, be it noted, from the side of God, the radius of the law AB, the finger, as it were, of God, pointing out precisely to us the polar region, B, as though it were the cynosure of our actions, with the positive ordinance, indeed, that this be so; but let Him be conceived as leaving behind Him, as though He had turned his face away from it, the antipolar district E, opposite to this, and solemnly warning us by a negative ordinance, that is to say, a prohibition, that this shall not be done. Furthermore, from the same mid-point of the heart, as though from the centre of the moral sphere, let there be conceived to proceed, on the part of man, radii of moral actions, and, indeed, (1) by way of foundation, the radius of conscience, as a radius the offprint of the law, which, if it is straight, coincides throughout with the radius the archetype of the law, and, as a certain scintilla of the divine image, shares in the direction of the same towards the polar region. But, if it be less straight,

supposing, for example, either because of the hardness and opacity of the heart it is turned back (this is erroneous conscience), or else, because of the surrounding atmosphere, it is refracted (this is probable conscience), or else has a fluctuating scintillation (this is a doubtful and anxious conscience), it turns thither to the opposite regions, and hither towards the polar region, indeed, but by certain roundabout ways, as it were, and not in such a direct manner; here around the polar region it wavers on this side and on that. (2) The formal radii of moral actions, which, in a physical sense, indeed, that is, as far as regards their natural principle, are coterminous in a central point, A, with the radius of the law, that is to say, dependent at the same time upon God, as the universal cause moving in nature; but morally, that is to say, as far as concerns the determination of mobility and course, are left free to men, and so are capable of being drawn freely from the heart, as though from the point of an angle, around towards all the regions of the moral sphere, so that if a man will, the radius of his moral action can coincide with the right radius of the law, or can decline to a greater or less degree towards either side, or else turn about to the diametrically opposite. Now, although actions may have an infinite number of radii, nevertheless, there are two quasi-cardinal radii, from whose location the moral quantity principally depends. One of them is the <184> horizontal radius, as it were, which can be called the *radius of execution;* the other, as though running down in the meridian, the *radius of intention.* The other radii which fall outside both of these circles are quasi-collateral, and have the character of possible, rather than necessary, radii.

3. All this being so determined, if, as regards the first, the radius of execution strike at the very polar region on the horizon, it will have no horizontal declination from the rule of the law, and, in so far, will not be a sin. But, if it decline from that region, on the score of execution it will be a sin, and, indeed, if the radius of action should turn to the opposite point, E, that is, if man does not merely omit to do what the law bids, but also at the same time commits its contrary, which the law, by facing in the opposite direction, is understood to be prohibiting, we shall call this an action's maximum horizontal declination from the law. But, if the radius of human action run out to the point H, or I, where it is perpendicular to the line of the syzygies of conjunction and opposition with the

law, BE, and does not lean any more towards the positive quarter, B, than towards the negative quarter, E, that is to say, if a man merely omits what the law orders done, we shall call this a median horizontal declination from the law, and a sin of omission. But, if the radius of action be between B and H, or between B and I, for example, in the point C, or G, where it comes closer to B than to E, we shall say that there is done, indeed, what the law bids, but imperfectly, in that the action does not express everything which is ordered in that law, but omits something large or small. This sin is to be judged less than the crime of omission, to the degree that the action omits less. But, if the radius of the action be placed between H and E, for example, in the point D or F, where it comes closer to E than to B, that is, when, what the law bids, is not merely omitted, but even a certain element of those things which the law at the same time prohibits (although this element be not quite diametrically opposed to the law), is expressed in action, it is now a sin of commission, and the closer the radius of action comes to the opposite of the law, the greater is the degree of the sin.

4. Now here it should be noted that the objects of laws, which are located on the horizon, as it were, have a twofold difference. For some are *indivisible,* some *divisible;* that is, some are so constituted that it is necessary for them to be either totally expressed in action, or wholly omitted, or the absolute opposite take place; but in some others only a certain part can be expressed, and the rest can be omitted, or merely some part of the opposite can take place. And in these again there is an element of discrimination. For some divisible objects of laws include those things into which they can be divided, *as species.* Thus, the affirmative law of the fifth commandment is, "Meet the <185> needs of your neighbour's body." This comprehends under it, like species, as it were, the preservation of life, limbs, and health, warding off of pains, supplying food in time of famine, &c. But the opposite law, which prohibits us from hurting our neighbour's body, comprehends under it homicide, mutilation, wounding, beating, &c. Thus, the affirmative law of the sixth commandment, which orders chastity, contains under it purity of thought, modesty of speech and gesture, purity of the body, &c. The opposite law prohibiting sexual immodesty, includes adultery, whoremongering, shameless gestures and movements, obscene words,

&c.[1] Here, for instance, properly speaking, shameless words do not occupy a grade equal to adultery, nor purity of mind one equal to purity of bodies. But, because legislators, in order to be brief, wished to comprehend under one general act many special acts, it results that the radius of execution will fall upon the point B, if a man preserve purity of language, quite as much as it will, if he preserve purity of body, and, on the contrary, the same radius will fall equally on the point E, if a man has wrongly inflicted a blow of his fist upon his neighbour, quite as much as if he has killed him. And so the indivisible part of these actions, as also of those which have an object, cannot be a horizontal declination, except through a quadrant or a semi-circle, that is, when that is not done which is ordered by the law, or the thing is to be omitted, or the contrary is to be done.

But, in truth, certain objects of laws are so divisible that they contain *in the manner of integral parts* those things into which they can be divided. Here the radius of execution does not immediately decline through the entire quadrants, but it can strike intermediate grades, and as many of these can be constituted as is the number of the more notable parts into which one cares to divide the object. Thus, for example, when I owe a workman for his labour 24 units, if I deny his pay absolutely, the radius of execution will strike the prime vertical; if I give him merely a part, and subtract the balance, the less I take from the sum due, the closer will the radius verge towards the polar point. But such grades appear to exist merely in the polar hemisphere. For when the radius of execution has struck the other hemisphere, that is, if, in addition to denying his pay, I take away something wrongly from the workman, it becomes an action of an utterly different kind, which has nothing to do with the former action, but is prohibited by a special law.

5. As for what concerns the other [*radius*], if the radius of intention has struck the polar point itself, the action will have no meridian declination from the law, that is, it will have no elevation or depression of the pole, and so no obliquity of intention. But if the radius of intention should

1. The distinction of the particular commandments into affirmative and negative precepts is probably modeled upon Martin Luther's interpretation of the Decalogue with a list of their respective fulfillments and transgressions ("Eine kurze Erklärung der zehn Gebote" (1518), in *W.A.,* first department, vol. 1, pp. 247ff).

remain in the polar semicircle of the meridian, to be sure, and so verge towards the pole, indeed, a line of estimation <186> being drawn through the vertical point and through the region of the intention (as they habitually estimate, who are outside the sphere, and refer everything to the horizon as the limit of vision), but yet not strike exactly on the polar point B, the intention, indeed, will be said to be swinging to that which the law bids, but with a relaxation which is greater, the closer the radius of intention comes to the prime vertical. For, in that case, since the constituted radius AK, AL, is perpendicular to the line of syzygies BE, and inclines no more to B than to E, a man will have neither the intention of that which the law bids nor the intention of the opposite. And when that happens, it is understood to have taken place from ignorance of what the law disposes, or as a result of coercion. But if the radius of an action has been between the points of the meridian KB, or LB, the intention, indeed, will be swinging towards that which the law prescribes, but with a greater or less relaxation, as, starting from the negation of the same, the radius has, according to different grades, come more or less close to the full intention.

6. Furthermore, the more notable grades of intention in both hemispheres can be not inaptly fixed at twelve in number, which, in the diagram, the belt of the meridian represents, although we would by no means bring suit against the man who wanted to make a larger or a smaller number. When, therefore, the radius of human intention begins to move from the point L towards B, it must necessarily strike some one of these grades which seem to follow in this order. (1) The idea of a good action admitted to the mind. (2) The simple approbation of the same as being honourable. (3) Deliberation whether it should be done here and now. (4) Inclination to action aroused by some extrinsic violence. (5) Inclination to action aroused by fear of loss. (6) Inclination to action aroused unexpectedly by the convenience of a favourable opportunity. (7) Inclination to action as something useful, that is to say, for a gain. (8) Intention partial, languid, and easily responding, with a legitimate end, that is, to render obedience to the law. (9) Intention partial, united with an impulse. (10) Intention complete, easily responding, that is, which can easily be changed by setting before it a different object. (11) Intention full, not easily responding. (12) Intention full, and most firm, which strikes precisely upon the point B.

Now when the movement is from the point L towards the point E the same number of grades seem to appear. (1) The idea of sin admitted into the mind. (2) The simple approbation of sin as useful or pleasant. (3) Deliberation whether it ought to be done. (4) Inclination to sin aroused by extrinsic violence. (5) Inclination to sin for fear of loss. (6) Inclination to sin by the seduction of others, due to lack of consideration. (7) Inclination to sin for some apparent <187> utility. (8) Intention partial, languid, and easily responding, due to lack of obedience. (9) Intention partial, conjoined with impulse or emotion. (10) Intention complete, easily responding. (11) Intention full, not easily responding. (12) Intention full and most firm which strikes on the very point E.

We admit, nevertheless, that the first three grades on both sides are certain acts, preliminary, as it were, to eliciting inclination or intention, rather than grades of intention properly so called. Therefore, if the radius of intention advancing along the same meridian strike its antipolar semicircle, KEL, which, with the point E, embraces the opposite of that which the law prescribes, the intention is understood to be swinging towards the opposite; and, indeed, if the radius strike precisely on the point E, the whole opposite will be perpetrated with the utmost intent. But if, on the same semicircle of the meridian, the radius of action fall on intermediate points, whose notable differences are marked by grades, the action will be said to have been done with a less or greater relaxation of intention, in proportion to the closeness to or remoteness from the point E of the grade upon which the radius falls.

7. From what has been said thus far it is apparent: I. That for an action to be perfectly good, it is required that each radius, namely, that of execution as well as that of intention, fall precisely upon the point B, that is, that not only everything be done which the law prescribes, but also with such an intention and such a mind as the law requires. Now, indeed, those men who enact civil laws in the commonwealth of men, are completely satisfied if the acts prescribed by the laws are done, whatever in the last analysis the intention of the agents may be, since, forsooth, with their laws they regard the advantage of the commonwealth, which, for the most part, results sufficiently from the external performance of the act, even though, perchance, the agent may not directly intend this advantage; although, on

the other hand, in actions contrary to laws, human courts of law are extremely solicitous to determine the intention of the agent, so that they rarely impose a penalty, where it is proved that there was no guile. But God who has greatly desired to bind in obedience to Him the minds of men by means of His law, does not so much regard the external act, as the intention of the agent, whereby he binds himself to obey the law. And so, in that compendium of the divine law we are bidden to love God with all our heart, with all our mind, and with all our strength, and our neighbour as ourselves.[2]

8. II. If each radius, that of execution as well as that of intention, swings precisely to the opposite point E, it is the greatest sin in that category, since not only is it the direct opposite of that which the law orders, but it is also done with that firmness of intention which the <188> law otherwise was wont to require for the performance of a good action.

9. III. But if either of these two radii, or both, have declined from the point B, yet in such wise that each still remains in the polar hemisphere, in itself, indeed, the action will not be good, nevertheless, among men, in one way or another, it will be reckoned as good. For men are also in the habit of calling an action in which each radius is closer to the point B, better than an action of the same kind in which the radii are farther away from the said point; although the former should properly be called less bad than the latter. But, when each radius strikes in the antipolar hemisphere, not even in a human court of law will it be judged that there is any goodness in such an action. But it also happens that the radius of execution strikes in the polar hemisphere, the radius of intention in the antipolar, and vice versa. The former comes about when an action, good on the score of the object, is undertaken with an evil end, as if some one with the intention of wounding another, cuts with his sword an otherwise incurable abscess, and by that cut the other person is restored to health. The latter occurs, when, with an erroneous understanding, but with a good intention, a good action is undertaken, which, although in itself bad, the agent thought to be good.

10. Now the quantity of a bad action is determined by the quantity of the angle which the two radii of execution and of intention make with the

2. Matthew 22:37–40.

radius of the law; the greater this angle is, the greater becomes the sin and vice versa. And so attention must be paid not merely to the amount of the bidden action which a man has omitted, or to that of the forbidden action which he has performed, but also to the intention with which he has done the same. And, indeed, the quantities of both angles are to be added together. Thus, let us suppose the semicircle of the horizon to include 24 grades, and the quadrant of the meridian 12. In this way, if both radii strike E, it will be understood that the sin is of grade 36. But, if the radius of execution strike, for example, on grade 15, and that of intention on 9, the sin will be of grade 24, and so on. But, since the quantity of the sin, absolutely considered, increases or decreases primarily because of the intention, therefore this latter will also have to be most particularly regarded in determining that quantity.

11. From what has been said there flow also the following consequences: (1) God, situated in the centre of the sphere, notes with the utmost accuracy even the most minute aberration, and is not content merely with a tendency, but requires coincidence of action in every way with the rule of the law, quite as much touching the radius of execution as that of intention. When this has been duly weighed, there will be none who will undertake to boast of his uprightness in the presence of God. (2) Since human judges are placed outside the centre <189> of the sphere, that is to say, since they cannot penetrate into the heart of the agent, they cannot judge so accurately of the degree of actions. This is primarily because they cannot know the intention of the agent (which is, however, the consideration of utmost consequence here) except from signs which strike the senses, and these signs never produce an absolutely infallible knowledge of the things which were meditated within. Hence these judges estimate the degree of actions only by sense perception, that is, as best the state of human sagacity allows; just as in astronomy the parallax which goes beyond tens of seconds is regarded as imperceptible, and the position seen is supposed to coincide with the true position, although an indefinite number of lesser arcs may lie between the two, because, of course, our eye does not consist of a point, but is surrounded by thick humours and several lenses which refract the rays, so that it is unable to perceive such extreme minuteness. Thus, in a human court of law, that part of the intention which eludes the acumen of our

judge, nay, even the declination of the execution, are not attended to, in the spirit of the trite principle: "The Praetor does not concern himself with trifles." Nay more, there you hear, that, in regard to evil actions, the intention is scarcely divided into more grades than two, to wit, full and half-full. (3) Considered formally and in itself, there is absolutely no merit in a good action; but in a bad action, the demerit is greater, the farther each radius retires from the point B. And this formal defect of an action, unless it be condoned, will have to be compensated for by a satisfactory equivalent. Also what we have said hitherto can and ought to be applied to individual moral actions.

12. Actions contrasted and compared with one another are estimated, according as one is said to be superior, or worse, or more harmful than another, and, as regards good actions, according as one ought to yield to the other, when both cannot be performed at the same time. Now this relative degree of actions is determined: I. *By their object.* For, according as this object is noble and precious, so also will one action be reckoned eminent and noble in comparison with a second whose object is less so; and, on the contrary, the more eminent the good which has been violated, the more serious and the worse an action is thought to be. Now, among those objects, just as God, the Best and Greatest, infinitely excels in nobility, so that action is deservedly to be detested far beyond others, which tends directly to His contumely. And just as His worship, existing primarily in the mind, ought to temper the action of the whole life, so, through His will, those actions by which the external aspects of His worship are displayed, yield precedence to these which bring some notable advantage to men. The grade next to these is held by those actions which touch the universal society of men, and after them, those which <190> touch the public society of the state. Then follow individuals. In regard to them, those of us who have professed the Christian faith reckon the greatest good to be the eternal salvation of the soul, and the greatest evil its ruin. This is followed by life, which is the foundation of all temporal goods. Almost side by side with life come modesty, civil respectability or reputation, and whatever is so necessary to life, that, without it, life either cannot be preserved at all, or can be dragged out only in the most miserable estate. Here belong bodily members not vital, but which are esteemed by virtue of the nobility of their use.

Among the other goods which merely render life more ornate and pleasant, and such as one can in any event do without, the goods of fortune yield precedence to the goods of the body, and these in turn to those of the mind. Now, in truth, most good or evil things admit of various intensifications and relaxations, according to the disparity of the subjects on which they are exhibited or inflicted, this disparity being of status, good or ill fortune, age, seasons or necessities, a special affection by which they are inclined to some particular good, or shrink away from some definite species of evil, &c., all of which are accurately observed in determining the merit of actions which are not owed, and, in part, also, in imposing punishments.

13. II. *From the status and condition of the agent.* Here applies the trite saying: "Every fault of the mind has about it a more conspicuous blame, the higher the person of the delinquent is held." Thus it is notorious that the same kind of sin committed by a priest is reckoned as graver than that committed by another. Thus a kindness shown by an enemy is judged to be greater than that shown by a friend, and, on the contrary, the wrong done by a friend hurts more severely than that inflicted by a foe. And it is a more serious thing to be mocked by some sordid fellow, than by an equal or superior, by your own children and your own servants, than by strangers. And it makes a great deal of difference whether something be done by a wife, or a woman, by a husband, or a youth and a boy, an old man, or a young man, a magistrate, or a private citizen, a famous, or an obscure man, a barbarian, or a citizen of some civilized nation. For the natural strength of the spirit intensifies the badness of an action, just as the weakness of the same sheds a lustre upon the goodness of actions. And splendour of status lends an element of baseness to misdeeds, while obscurity of status bestows admiration upon things brilliantly done.

14. III. *From the condition of the action,* according as it could be performed with ease or difficulty. A good action, other things being equal, is more beautiful, the more difficult it is; a bad action, on the contrary, the easier it is to avoid, the worse it is reckoned to be, in comparison with another action of the same kind which was not of the same character. Here also the consideration whether the <191> mind of the agent was free from an emotion, or disturbed by the same, has some bearing. For, where emotions tend toward the object of an action, they make it easy; if they tend

in the opposite direction, they make it difficult. Of these emotions the ones aroused by the idea of evil generally apply sharper spurs, and certainly command more favour or pity than those which the idea of good excites. And so, there is a great deal of difference, in the baseness of the act, between perjury committed through fear of death, and that whereby one refuses to return a deposit for the sake of gain. Also the thief who steals what is another's because of hunger or need, is regarded as less base than he who pillages others because of an insatiable lust for gold. And the consideration whether you have done something under a fresh emotion, or under one long cherished, has no small bearing; since, forsooth, fresh impulses sweep more violently, and it is so much more difficult not to be carried away by them, but the delay produced by lapse of time renders them more amenable to the sway of reason. Thus, also, he who is the first to commit a certain crime in some state and teaches it, as it were, sins more grievously than he whom the surrounding multitude of wrongdoers has robbed of the sense of shame.

15. IV. *From the effect and consequences of an action,* these being either good or bad. If good, the more excellent and greater they are, the more excellent is the action; if bad, the more numerous and grave they are, so much the worse is an action reckoned than another of the same kind not attended by these circumstances. V. *From the circumstances of place and time,* which contribute greatly towards making an action more grave or less serious. Thus the same crime committed in a public place and in the presence of witnesses is more serious than that in which an effort is made to have it concealed, and this partly because what is hidden does less harm by example, at least, and partly because his wickedness is judged to be very intense who makes an open display of his crime and seeks to win glory therefrom. Thus, since some reverence is due to matters which look to the worship of God, it is more base to practise debauchery in a temple than in a tavern. Thus it is a graver thing to be beaten at a sitting of judges, than within one's private walls. Thus he who gets drunk on an ordinary day, other things being equal, commits a lesser sin than he who wantons on a day peculiarly set aside for prayers or penitence, &c.

16. Now the more or less frequent repetition of an action of the same kind does not in itself render the action better or worse, except in so far as

it is an indication that the action proceeds from habit. And, as a habit, in the case of moral actions, is most carefully considered (since, forsooth, actions habitually undertaken are understood to be done <192> for the most part with full intention), it is clear enough why a good action which one has frequently done before, is commonly regarded as superior to that which is now being done for the first time, or vice versa; because, of course, the latter is judged to have been undertaken not with such full intention as the former; likewise, why an evil action very frequently repeated is judged to be more grave than that which has been committed only once or twice by the same person, and this notwithstanding the fact that a good habit facilitates a good action, while a bad habit, on the contrary, makes it hard to refrain from a bad action. For the effort spent in acquiring a good habit causes the action which is done easily, and with pleasure, by the good man, to be of no less value; and the odium of the evil man is so much the greater, because, by acting badly, he has brought it about that he can scarcely act otherwise than ill. And this consideration is observed in the demand for punishment which men make. For the delinquent on his first offence (unless, perchance, it be a monstrous crime) is more easily accorded pardon, or else punished more lightly, than the man who over and over again strikes upon the same stone, and this is because of the intensity of the free moral choice by which, as is evident, such a misdeed has been undertaken. Also, when pardon for former misdeeds depends conditionally upon reformation in the future, and that fails to take place, the punishment for all past crimes is exacted at the same time as the penalty for repeating that particular one. From this it becomes apparent in what sense there is truth in the common saying: "The estimation of a past misdeed is never increased by any subsequent act."[3]

17. As far as concerns the special comparison of good actions and of duties, it will be easy to decide the question of just which one ought to yield precedence to the other, when it is impossible for both to be performed at the same time, if the following points be kept in mind.[4] (1) An affirmative

---

3. *Dig.,* L.xvii.138, §1.
4. See bk. I, Def. 12, §37, "How do concurrent obligations yield to one another?"

precept always yields to a negative, that is, no one can rightly do anything ordered by the law of nature, with the result that he must necessarily do at the same time something forbidden by the same. The reason for this is to be sought in the nature of affirmative precepts and of negative precepts, because the obligation of the latter is perpetually uniform and equally efficacious, whereas the obligation of the former presupposes for them an occasion which is not understood to exist, when something cannot be done without a violation of law. And so such things are judged to be morally impossible. Hence, no one can do a wrong to a second person, or break faith with him, so as either to advance his own personal advantage or that of his intimates, or to obtain the means for gratitude and benefac-<193>tions. (2) An imperfectly mutual obligation yields to a perfectly mutual obligation which concerns both parties. Thus what is owed on a contract is rather to be paid than what is owed on a gratuitous promise or on the law of gratitude, if it be impossible for both to be satisfied at the same time. (3) Other things being equal, the law of beneficence yields to the law of gratitude. Because gratitude to that object has a kind of prior right, as it were, and one that has more to be said in its favour than has beneficence, since, forsooth, the former requires you to pay back, the latter to be the first to give; and so, in such a case, it is understood that the object of beneficence is wanting because of the competing necessity of gratitude. And this holds so far that beneficence even towards our kinfolk, unless, perchance, it be connected with some closer debt, ought to be rendered after gratitude. (4) Among those to whom we owe something on the basis of an affirmative precept, with the force merely of a natural, and not a civil law, the propinquity of the persons is the deciding consideration, and this is commonly regarded so, that, after caring for one's own person, come children, parents, kinsmen, and finally all men whatsoever, and, among these, in the degree to which they are either suffering from indigence, or appear likely to become helpful to others in their turn, if they be helped by us. Here, in the same kind of need or help, late-comers are understood to be excluded by predecessors, although a greater need of beneficence in the late-comers makes even the predecessors yield place to them, especially when it is possible to satisfy the latter more conveniently at another time.

Appendix to Definition XVIII in Which
the Moral Sphere Is Explained

For the sake of more copious instruction and illustration, by means of exterior orbs there can be represented in the diagram, in addition to the grades
of intention and execution, also the objects of moral action divided into
definite classes. This can be done in quite the most convenient fashion, it
appears, if, according to the guidance of the Decalogue, the orbs, as it were,
of human actions be constituted, and each orb be divided into two hemispheres, to wit, a polar hemisphere which includes actions enjoined, and
an antipolar hemisphere, in which are located actions opposed to the in-
junctions. And, indeed, according to the analogy of the Copernican system,
the sun can be placed in the very centre of the universe, inasmuch as it will
represent to us God, Best and Greatest, whose nature one will otherwise
scarcely illustrate by means of a more convenient simile than that derived
from the centre and the periphery of the circle. For, aside from the fact
that, as the periphery is produced from the centre, so are <194> all other
things produced by God, there is also a very great appropriateness, in that,
with respect to the centre, nothing in the periphery ascends, and nothing
descends, nothing is added, and nothing passes away, nothing is closer, and
nothing more remote, nothing is on the right hand, and nothing on the
left, nothing is set above, and nothing placed below, but all are present at
the very centre in the same way, however much the circle move around and
around in continuous motion; so, in respect to God, there is nothing past,
nothing future, nothing more close, nothing more remote, although, in the
continuous succession of duration, created things move round about, as it
were, ascend, and descend, come into being, and perish. Consult Erhard
Weigel's *Disputation on Duration,* Leipzig, 1652, thesis no. 40.[5] It was this
among other things which the Pythagoreans, men without doubt far wiser
than they are commonly thought by some to be, had in mind, when they
defined God as a sphere, with its centre everywhere, and its periphery no-

---

5. Erhard Weigel, *Dissertatio metaphysica posterior de modo existentiae qui dicitur duratio* (Jena, 1652).

where. And, in a special way, God can be called the centre of moral actions, as has been said above already, while, established in the heart of man as in a centre, not only does He flow into the physical being of actions, and with His finger point out the pole, that is, the rectitude of an action, but also while all human actions run back to Him, as to the centre from the periphery. Now we apprehend that the finger of God first of all points out Himself, and so constitutes God Himself as the prime object of moral actions. And as in the sun we see three things principally, substance, warmth, and light, so our actions towards God fall into three classes principally, (1) as we recognize in Him a Being supreme, one, best, and greatest, which, for its Majesty, is to be loved by us, cherished and honoured above all things. (2) As He is a benevolent being, by whose heat we are, as it were, warmed and animated, in consideration of which His name is to be invoked alone by us and treated with reverence. (3) As He is a most glorious being, which wishes the splendour of His praise and glory to be seen and celebrated by men. These matters are contained in the first three commandments of the Decalogue, and occupy the first three orbs of our system. Mother Earth follows the sun, and by her we designate the persons of men from whom we depend, for example, our superiors as such, who are made of the same earth as we are, and whose majesty is constrained within the limits of earth. Such are parents, and they who are equal to parents, namely guardians, magistrates, rulers, lords, to whom we are bound to show due honour, and whose legitimate commands we are bound to execute; and these are ordained in the fourth commandment. In the fifth place follows the sphere of Mars, which indicates the actions of man concerning both his life and his body, which is violated and destroyed by martial activities. These matters are contained in the fifth commandment. <195> After Mars follows Venus, and thereby we suggest that the actions deriving their designation from her, are so to be regulated, that we preserve our body and our mind pure from every illicit lust, and do not molest the limits of another's bed. Warning is given against this in the sixth commandment. Mercury holds the seventh Sphere, among astrologers the indicator both of those who make wealth by commerce, and of those for whom things not utterly lost are found. And thus disposition is here made concerning those actions which arise from commutative justice, and in regard to which every one is forbidden to have it appear that he desires to derive his lineage from Mercury by emulating the pitch-covered hands of Autolycus.[6] This is the substance of the seventh commandment. By the eighth, or Jupiter, is indicated he, who, by the decree of horoscopes, when well disposed, promises good repute, when injured or weakened, accuses man of having a virulent tongue, and being a backbiter, bearing a serene countenance, but after he has mollified the credulous by flattering them to their face, delighting to cast infamy upon their backs when they are absent. So a bridle is here set upon the tongue, that it dare not attack wickedly the good name of others or riot in falsehoods, but that it cover their blemishes rather with honourable excuses, and give each his due praise. Those matters are promulgated in the eighth commandment. We assign the ninth orb to Saturn, the tenth to the moon; of which the former, in the understanding of the astrologers, is the index of a domicile, the latter, of marriage and children. On the former of these disposition is made in the ninth commandment, on the latter, in the tenth, that is to say, that we do not set our mind on them with the intention of defrauding our true Lord thereby. But if, according to the opinion of many theologians,[7] we decide that, by the ninth commandment, actual concupiscence is forbidden, by the tenth, original concupiscence, the planets just mentioned will possess their orbs by a different title. For not inappropriately can that cold and sluggish and gloomy Saturn denote those appetites in man which make him cold and languid towards doing every good thing, and arouse sadness among the upright, who grieve that they cannot here be utterly freed from this low estate. But the moon, the mistress of fruitfulness and humours, indicates that fatal poison deeply infused in our nature and ever fruitful in a countless offspring of sins. And this poison, furthermore, causes our reason to have some brightness and penetration only in the darkness of things terrestrial, but to be utterly blind in the spir-

---

6. Autolycus, son of Hermes and Chione, father of Anticleia, the mother of Odysseus, was delegated the task of theft and of swearing by Hermes (Homer, *Odyssey*, trans. Stanley Lombardo, intro. Sheila Murnaghan [Indianapolis: Hackett, 2000], XIX.395).

7. See, for example, Johann Gerhard (1582–1637), professor of theology in Jena, in his *Loci theologici*, ed. Eduard Preuss (repr. Berlin, 1865), vol. 3, loc. 12 "De lege dei," pp. 20ff).

itual light; just as the moon dares to put forth her pallid countenance at night, indeed, but through the day fades away to the appearance of an obscure cloudlet. But all this, ὡς ἐν παρέργῳ [as a side issue], is merely for the sake of instruction, and to render the quantity of moral actions so much the clearer. <196>

By the effect of a moral action is meant that
which is produced by it.

1. The formal effect of actions.
2. The material effect.

1. We are here considering primarily the effect of good and bad actions as such, and this is either *formal* or *material;* and again, the former is either *internal* or *external.* The internal effect of a good action is the approbation of conscience which follows, and gives itself sweet joy in the recollection of that act. The internal effect of a bad action is the condemnation of conscience which follows, and the perturbation of the mind, anxiously held fast in contemplation of the evil deed, and shamefacedly turning away from those who know of it. The external effect of a good action is the approbation of it on the part of good men, and principally on the part of him who commanded that action; likewise, the good esteem and honour. The external effect of a bad action is the disapproval on the part of him who forbade it, and of other good men; likewise, the evil repute and ignominy.

2. The material effect of a good action, profitable and not owed, is *merit;* of an evil, *demerit.* Of these the former is recompensed by a *reward* and a *premium;* the latter is followed by *punishment.* <197>

Merit is an estimative moral quality resulting to a man from an action which he is not bound to perform, in accordance with which there is owed him an equivalent good on the part of the one in whose favour that action was undertaken.

     1. No merit results from an action which was owed.
     2. But merely from one which was not owed.
     3. What is a reward, and what a premium?

1. The foundation and, as it were, the fountain head of merit, is the performance of a work not owed, or, in other words, to receiving which at our hands the other person, for whose sake the deed was done, had no just claim. For, if I furnish the other person merely that which I am thoroughly bound to furnish, so that he has the authority to demand the same from me, it is perfectly patent, that, by the very act of furnishing the thing in question, I am merely meeting a debt and my obligation, and in the action itself there is nothing superabounding, as it were, wherefrom merit can arise for me. Hence it is well established that a mortal cannot have any merit at all towards God, even if we should grant that he can fulfil perfectly the divine law, and so God cannot in any way be man's debtor, except on the faithfulness of a gratuitous promise, which, however, itself confers no right upon man. Thus, also, other actions which are enjoined upon us by men in virtue of their command [*imperio*], cannot directly produce for us merit towards the one who made the injunction, although God as well as men who are able to obligate one completely, are apt very frequently to provide definite good things and to confer them upon those who have fulfilled their

commands, so as to excite promptitude in obedience. But they are not bound to furnish these because of merit on the part of the agent, or as though on the basis of a contract, but by the force of a generous promise. And so these good things are listed under the designation, not of a reward or premium, but of a gift or gratuitous premium.

2. For the acquisition of merit towards men there remain, therefore, those actions which were not owed them, whether it be that there was absolutely no binding obligation to furnish these, or nature, indeed, commanded or urged that those same actions be undertaken, the application, however, to individual cases having been left to our free choice; or else they were not commanded by a civil law, at least. The reason for this is that what I owe completely to a second person, he himself now has a right over, so that if I render it, properly speaking <198> nothing is lost to me from that to which I myself have a right at the present moment, since, forsooth, if I am going to keep back or deny the same, I shall be doing an injury to the other party. This makes it clear enough that the thing is now his and no longer mine at all, and so there is left to me no place for merit in giving it over to him. But, in truth, when I perform something for another beyond a complete obligation, assuredly that matter, since it is lost to me, and accrues to him, leaves with me a perfect or an imperfect right to have from the second person, upon whom it was bestowed, that which will equal it in worth. And this very thing is merit.

3. When we expressly stipulate for the satisfaction of merit, it is properly called *reward.* But when the satisfaction of merit in all that concerns manner, time, and amount, is left to the free choice and equity of the second person, it is called *premium.* Now this is either a corporeal thing, as money, land, house, &c., and incorporeal, as the concession of immunities, privileges, and definite rights; or moral, as honour, praise, &c.; or else notional, as statues, inscriptions, crowns, and the like. <199>

Demerit is an estimative moral quality resulting to a man from a bad action through which he is under obligation to make amends for the injury done to a second person thereby.

1. He who has damaged a second person is bound to restitution of the damage and to bond.
2. What bond is required on the basis of the law of nature?
3. In states a bond is furnished by means of punishment.
4. The purposes of punishments.
5. How many kinds of punishments are there?
6. No one is bound to a punishment.
7. No one can be punished for another.
8. To what measure are punishments to be imposed?
9. Is the divine law the measure of punishments among men?
10. What is to be judged of talion?
11. What equality is to be observed in punishment?
12. Just what sort of an obligation to inflict punishment rests upon the magistrate?

1. In any misdeeds whatsoever, at all events those which terminate in another person, there are found two things, the defect itself, or the divergence from the norm of law according to execution or intention, and the damage done, directly or indirectly, to a second person thereby. It is our task here to investigate what is wont and ought to be observed upon both of these points in a human court of law, for, as it is not ours to set forth the edicts of the Divine Tribunal, so we are averse to having them introduced there. It is certain, therefore, on the basis of the law of nature about not bringing upon a second person that whereby peace and human society would be disturbed, that every man whatsoever is bound to make amends to the other party for damage done him in any way at all by his own fault, and, if that

damage has proceeded from malice, he is bound to give bond not to offend in the future.

2. Furthermore, among those who, being bound by no civil law, use merely the law of nature among one another, if, indeed, a person induced by repentance, of his own free will, and not compelled by force, presents himself in order to make amends for the damage, this same law of nature appears to obligate him to furnish no other bond than to pledge his good faith with a simple asseveration, or even with an oath, that he will avoid offences for the future, and this because that repentance is a sufficient indication of a change of mind and of a firm determination to refrain from injuries henceforward.[1] And so, if the one who had received some damage should be unwilling to be content with that, but out of unjust lack of confidence or some asperity <200> of temper should wish to ex-tort a bond by the use of superior force, although by the law of nature the other be not bound thereto, the blame for violating the peace will attach to the first party himself, and the other can rightly resist by force the man who, out of a desire for vengeance, or excess of fear, is unwilling to be content with a fair satisfaction. In this case it results that he who did the injury is waging a just war, he who suffered it an unjust one. But, when one has to be driven by force to make satisfaction, since this very same circumstance renders quite clear his obstinacy in badness, and satisfaction cannot be obtained unless the injured forcibly overpowers the injurer, it rests with the victor to determine just what kind of bond will best provide for his own security. Here he may not merely proceed to taking away arms, demolishing or occupying fortified places, to hostages, perpetual imprisonment, and the like, but even to death itself, if, indeed, it be well enough established that the one restored to liberty will plot our destruc-tion, and no more convenient remedy be found for avoiding that. For the rest, it cannot properly be said that one is bound to furnish a bond of this kind; because a bond presupposes and involves in him from whom it is taken some fault of the mind, and a sin against the law of nature, to wit, the denial of a spontaneous satisfaction and the defence by force of his misdeed.

1. See bk. II, Observ. 4, §19.

3. Now, in truth, as states have been instituted for fastening with stronger bonds society among men, so the laws which they enact tend not merely to prescribe to citizens what is to be given to each man, and how each is to be recompensed for the damage done him by the fault or malice of a second person, but also to have all men whatsoever, as far as that is possible, protected, as it were, in advance against receiving injuries and losses, namely, by establishing *punishments* against delinquents; and this is done primarily because persons are very rarely found who without force or fear descend to making amends for the injury they have caused, and damage and injury are done not without disturbance, even if the same be afterwards made good in the most full measure. Therefore, the greatest and most convenient bond for security, which, indeed, the condition of human society allows, is this, namely, that, because of the punishment, it be more damaging to have injured a second person than not to have injured him. To that end all punishments which men exact from other men ought to tend. For that men should regard nothing but the pain in the one who is punished, is not only repugnant to the gentleness of human nature, but also quite useless, and it is characteristic only of children or weak women to get some solace for their own grief out of the suffering of their injurer. And so it appears to harmonize very poorly with reason, that among some states, for example, in homicide, it rests with the kinsmen of the murdered man to condone or to leave the punish-<201>ment for homicide, as if it be proper for a man to be slain, not as an example, but to assuage the grief of the murdered man's kinsmen.

4. In a state, therefore, aside from the fact that he who has done wrong is compelled by the supreme authority to make good, as far as nature admits, the damage done to a second party, precautions are taken for the future security of all men by inflicting punishment, the severity of which is to deter everybody from crime. In imposing these punishments there is regarded both the advantage of him whose interest it was that the misdeed did not take place, as well as the advantage of all other men in general, namely, that for the future neither he nor they suffer anything of the sort from the same person or from others.[2] The former end can be attained if

2. Pufendorf follows the Grotian definition of punishment as both retaliatory and utilitarian according to reason (see bk. I, Def. 12, note 44). Blind satisfaction of anger,

either the delinquent be destroyed, or his powers of doing harm be taken away, or by the evil which he suffers he be taught to give up his wrongdoing. That injuries be not done by others is brought about through open and conspicuous punishment, which by its example inspires terror in them. But those inflictions of pain upon others which regard nothing but the reformation of him who has done wrong, can scarcely be listed under the name of punishments, although most punishments which stop short of inflicting death, produce at the same time that effect also.

5. Now a threefold division can be made of punishments, to wit, into *real* punishments, which are paid in person or money, to which class also belong instances of removal from a lucrative office as such; *moral,* as reproof, relegation, ignominy, infamy, loss of civil status, &c.; and *notional,* as affixing a man's name and effigy to the gallows, demolishing statues, erasing a man's name from the records of some society or from some works which he has himself set up, adding to the same an ignominious designation, and the like. All these are applied with the purpose of bringing some suffering to the one upon whom they are inflicted. Hence, although laborious tasks are commonly imposed upon some persons in place of punishment; nevertheless, in so far as they are annoying to the agent, the same purposes are in mind, and so they are here regarded as suffering.

6. From all this one gathers just why it cannot be said properly that some one is bound to punishment, or punishment is owed by some one; because, namely, punishment signifies something which is to be imposed upon a man against his will, and it involves an abhorrence of the will from it[3] (for otherwise it would not be adapted to its end, namely, by the sight of it to

---

on the other hand, results from an instinct man has in common with beasts (Grotius, *JBP,* II.xx.5). The real end of punishments and the sole measure of its degree is as a precaution against injury, and this is secured by reforming the offender, protecting the victim and society against further injuries, and deterring others, thus strengthening the authority of the state and its laws (*JNG,* 8, 3, §§9, 11–12; *JBP,* II.xx.6).

3. Cf. *JNG,* 8, 3, §§1 and 4. §1 discusses whether the right to exact punishment—a harm inflicted upon someone against his will—may arise from a voluntary transfer in a pact. Following Hobbes, *De cive* (chap. 2, §18; chap. 5, §§7ff), Pufendorf explains it as the result of the individual's obligation in the pact of submission not only to refrain from defending others against the sovereign but to put his strength at the latter's disposal to coerce others.

frighten men away from their evil deeds). But, in truth, the things to which we are properly bound are understood to be such that we ought to be moved of our own accord and gladly to furnish them. From this the reason is apparent why, for example, when, in constructing the same rampart, some countryman <202> at the order of his master, and a criminal condemned thereto, do the same task, to the latter the work is a punishment, but not to the former; because, namely, the former is understood to be doing it on the basis of an obligation, and so willingly, but it is imposed upon the latter as something abhorrent to his will. Thus he also does not suffer a punishment who is compelled to pay a fine while giving surety for a second person. For, on the occasion, indeed, of the second person's misdeed he sustains a loss, but in such a way that the second person's misdeed is not the proximate cause of his suffering the loss, but his own will is, by which he bound himself through the giving of surety. From all this, likewise, it results that, just as a person when he has made good a damage done by him of the kind, indeed, which could be made good, is by no means bound to report upon himself, so that the punishment assigned by the law may be measured out to him; so, for the same reason, he can rightly avoid punishment by hiding or through flight. Finally, since that which I inflict upon myself cannot happen to one who is unwilling to bear it, it is patent also that no one can exact penalty from himself; and since the unwilling cannot be compelled to submit to punishment except by a superior, neither can he who does not have a superior in some state be subjected to human punishment.

7. Now as every punishment presupposes a misdeed or demerit, in such wise that it is contrary to nature for one to be punished because of some deed which cannot be imputed against him; so that pain or loss which in due consequence comes from the punishment of one person upon other persons who have done no wrong, cannot be designated by the name of punishment. For, just as other persons are by the punishment to be deterred from wrongdoing, so also the punishment ought to be imposed directly in view of the misdeed, and the pain or loss, which, in the case of a second person, is to have the character of punishment, ought to regard his own misdeed as the cause. And so that pain which one feels at the punishment of a kinsman or friend of his, is not a punishment, unless, perchance, he himself has concurred in that misdeed. Thus, properly speaking, children

are not punished when their father because of some misdeed is fined in money or by the loss of his feudal holding; especially since on that score damage is not done directly to the children by taking away that to which they had their own right, but the loss comes to them merely as a consequence, namely, in that they do not have what they otherwise would have had, to wit, by the expiration of that condition without which they had no right, this condition being that the goods in question should have been kept by their parents until their death. Thus, when, on the parents having been reduced to servitude because of some misdeed, the children born thereafter to them become slaves also, in the case of the latter slavery does not at all have the character of punishment, but <203> merely of a misfortune; especially since no one, before he is born, can have a right to be born in such and such a condition and no other. Precisely as an infant existing in its mother's womb, if, indeed, it also lose life or liberty while its mother is being punished, cannot properly be said to have been punished; although the laws of many states rightly forbid that a pregnant woman suffer the death penalty before her child has been born. Also the Roman laws ordain that, if a free-woman conceive, and become thereafter a slave because of a misdeed, and give birth in this status, the child which is born of her is free.[4] But those are improper expressions, whereby, for example, one extremely poor or sickly is said to be born of his parents to punishment.

8. Moreover, as it is in the highest degree conformable to nature for any one whatsoever to entrust to some honest third person the decision of his controversies with a second; so how each is to be safeguarded in his own security, or what the measure of punishment ought to be, is most conveniently fixed by a third person, because the sensitiveness of self-love, when irritated by a hurt, commonly forces us to punish the injurer more harshly than in the judgement of reason might otherwise suffice us. Since in states both of these matters are in the hands of those who enjoy the supreme sovereignty therein, it has also been placed in their free choice to determine what punishments they desire to inflict upon what crimes, and how severe these punishments shall be. Now in determining the degree of punishments, although the defect of the formal action is altogether to be consid-

4. *Dig.*, I.v.5, §2.

ered, above all, as regards the intention, in such wise that the delinquent out of weakness, and the delinquent out of malice, be treated differently, as also the one who is carried away through emotions immediately followed by penitence, and the one who approaches the crime with his mind deliberately made up; nevertheless, it is not necessary that there always be the same proportion between punishments that there is between the objects violated through the misdeed; since, forsooth, the reason for not committing some misdeed does not properly result from the nobility or ignobility of the object, but from the authority and decree of the legislator, whose will he who commits a misdeed about a smaller object opposes quite as much as he who does the same about a larger one; although here legislators do not so follow their mere free choice, or ought not so to follow it, but intensify or remit punishments as it is of great or small concern to the commonwealth, or at the immediate moment, for some misdeed not to be committed. Thus he can be visited with the utmost punishment who is caught in the lowest grade of that crime by which the greatest injuries can be inflicted. From this is apparent also the reason for that trite saying: "Punishments are to be made more severe, as misdeeds increase or grow more frequent." Just as, on the contrary, when some fault has passed into a custom, with the <204> result that, because of the multitude of delinquents, there is no room to exact punishment, unless you wish utterly to exhaust or overturn the state by inflicting penalties, the necessity of the commonwealth orders that the punishments be remitted. This could not take place if we imagine vindicative justice among men to be of such a sort as to order that the punishment, appropriate in itself to the crime, should always be inflicted promiscuously upon any one at all, and not rather such as to adapt itself to the seasons and the advantage of the commonwealth, especially since in no other respect is it necessary for one man to exact a punishment from another for any crime at all, except to insure the preservation of human society. Thus, when a war is on, if other suitable men are wanting, who would doubt that a vigorous general ought deservedly to have the punishment of exile or death remitted, simply because the commonwealth cannot well do without his services at that time?

9. Now we are not of the opinion that it is always in all commonwealths necessary for that penalty which is expressed by the divine law to be imposed

upon misdeeds; and this because that was the civil law of the Jews, in which the punishments attached were determined by the positive direction of God according to the genius of that people and commonwealth. Nay, since the character of different peoples is different, it is also proper that punishments be adjusted to the same. But, in truth, it can very well be doubted whether this principle ought to be applied also to the capital punishment for homicide expressed in the divine writings, since this punishment seems to have been enacted into law, not for the one nation of the Jews, but for the whole race of men. The reason for that is assuredly clear; because he whose wickedness is so great that he does not fear of set resolution to shed human blood, cannot be adequately guarded against by other men unless he be deprived of life. And so, as they who have committed murder with some incomplete intention only, which was soon followed by penitence, may be punished more mildly than they deserve; so the malicious murderer, as one who sets out to subvert the foundation of human society, is not to be spared, unless, perchance, the utmost necessity of the commonwealth require it. Nevertheless, even in this we by no means feel that that divine law is violated, partly because the determined quantity of every punishment is a matter of positive law, which it is no more than right should be adjusted to the needs of the commonwealth (and an exception is properly presumed to have been made of this circumstance in that divine law);[5] and partly because no matter if sometimes a murderer of that sort has escaped the punishment of men, nevertheless, the divine vengeance is generally so accustomed to pursue him, that he perishes in a bloody death by an act of violence, either in some fashion by the sword of another man, or <205> punished for some different crime. And assuredly it appears that this punishment of homicide is not so much a constitution given to men by means of the civil law, as it is a declaration of the vengeance to be exercised by God himself through the instrumentality of men, or through other tragic chances upon murderers, no matter if they have escaped the severity of a human court of law.

5. Cf. *JNG,* 8, 3, §26, where Pufendorf refers to Grotius's commentary on Matthew 5:40 and Genesis 9:6 (*Opera omnia theologica,* vols. I and II).

10. Nor is it to be thought necessary that a man should suffer the same thing which he has inflicted on another, or in other words that misdeeds always be punished by talion. For there are a great many crimes with which that kind of punishment does not at all square. For how would you conveniently punish adultery, lewdness, vile forms of copulation, crimes of lese-majesty, and the like by talion? Now in most crimes that punishment would be lighter than is just, and it would not adequately attain the end of punishments, which is to safeguard the security of each of us. For on that score the status of insolence would be better than that of innocence, if, indeed, the former should fear nothing more from the laws than the latter from the malice of evildoers, while in addition there was the dominating hope of avoiding punishment either by deceit, or by flight, or in some other way.

11. Nevertheless, in this point, as far as is possible, an equality is to be observed in punishments, namely, that those who are equally guilty should suffer equally, and the misdeed which in the case of one is punished, should not in the case of the other be condoned, without a very weighty cause;[6] since, forsooth, an inequality of that kind frequently furnishes matter for dangerous disturbances to commonwealths; and punishment which seems to be meted out, not for the public welfare, but for private satisfaction, lacks its proper effect. For the rest, that equality is to be understood of the same misdeed, not of different ones. For frequently in a human court of law, due to the necessity of the commonwealth or the free choice of legislators, a rather severe penalty has been assigned a misdeed which in itself appears somewhat light, and vice versa, but the accused cannot by any means allege this inequality, as though he were being unfairly dealt with, for, of course, he knew it beforehand, and, in having subjected himself to the magistracy, he is regarded as having himself approved of it. Thus, for example, although the crime of theft be in itself far lighter than homicide, nevertheless the thief has no cause for complaint if he himself, who has not committed

6. Cf. *JNG,* 8, 3, §23. The sovereign's liberty in defining the measure of punishment according to public utility does not refer to individual cases, but to the threat of punishment contained in the laws; as a rule these should be applied equally to equal cases. See also ibid., §§4 and 7: "not every evil, inflicted because of an antecedent sin, is a punishment, but such as has been announced in advance, and was imposed after cognizance was taken of the crime."

things equally guilty with the murderer, should nevertheless suffer equal punishment with the same, namely, capital punishment. The reason for this is that punishment is imposed separately, as it were, for the individual misdeeds, in that quantity which the advantage of the commonwealth seems to demand, and it ought not necessarily to be attempered to the punishment of other misdeeds of a different kind, in such wise, that, as the gravity of one <206> misdeed stands in relation to the gravity of the other, so the punishments for the same ought to correspond with one another. This is because, of course, the measure of punishments in a human court of law is not alone the gravity of the misdeeds in themselves, but it is that conjoined with respect to the advantage of the commonwealth. Thus, also, there are many misdeeds, of which one, although worse than another, is yet equally punished with death, because a more grievous punishment than death cannot be found, except that sometimes, when the misdeed has been very atrocious, tortures precede death. As for the rest, that equal punishment be rightly imposed upon those who commit the same misdeed, regard must assuredly be taken of the condition of the persons, for this has the utmost force in intensifying or diminishing the punishment. Thus the ignominy which to some very common man is a slight misfortune, affects most severely the eminent man, and the fine which is light for a man of means, will turn the humble man out of all his fortunes. All these points are to be carefully observed by him who has set his heart upon properly attempering punishments of that kind.

12. From all this it is easily understood how far there is incumbent upon the magistrate the obligation to inflict punishment, so that, namely, quite as much in the very exercise of the punishment, as in its determination relative to quantity, the good of the state may be advanced; and when this good urges the contrary, it is not to be believed that he is altogether bound to inflict punishment. And so, if one who has suffered injury calls upon the magistrate in regard to it, if, indeed, he obtains the restitution of the damage, but because of the condition of the commonwealth it should not appear wise to the magistrate to inflict an additional punishment upon the injurer, the magistrate does by no means derive the guilt of the misdeed upon himself, nor does the injured party have reason to complain of justice denied himself, because he could not satisfy his grief or his vengeance.

Thus, when a man on committing a crime in one state has fled to another, the magistrate of the latter state is bound, indeed, to see to it that he give satisfaction for the damage done; but that he should give him over to corporal punishment, or himself punish him, is not necessary, unless definite considerations tending towards the advantage of the commonwealth persuade him; especially since the former state has still the faculty of proceeding against him with moral and notional punishments. This much with regard to human actions in *genus*. The consideration of the same in *species* is excluded by the narrow limits of this work. <207, 208>

THE ELEMENTS OF
UNIVERSAL JURISPRUDENCE

BY

SAMUEL PUFENDORF

BOOK II

Any action whatsoever that may be directed according to a moral norm, which is within a man's power to do or not to do, may be imputed to him. And, on the contrary: *That which neither in itself nor in its cause was within a man's power may not be imputed to him*

(that is, as a matter of desert, yet it is well if that be done as an act of grace on the part of the one who makes the imputation, in case some good has come to pass).

1. Now that we have thrown light, in our first book, according to the scheme of our plan, upon the definitions of matters contained in Universal Jurisprudence, the next step is, in this book, to look into the principles to which in juridical demonstrations one ultimately ascends. Therefore, in addition to the common axioms[1] which, derived from prime philosophy, occur here

---

1. According to Aristotle, the common axioms which are universally valid in any discipline—in contradistinction to those peculiar to individual disciplines—are the principles of contradiction and of the excluded third. Aristotle, *Posterior Analytics* I.11, 77a10,22 in *Analytica priora et posteriora; Metaphysics,* IV.3.

and there throughout that work, there are found to be here two kinds of
principles proper to this discipline, the *rational,* namely, and the *experimental.* The truth of the former, their certainty and necessity, flows from
reason itself, without the perception of particulars, or without undertaking
an examination, merely from the bare intuition of the mind. But the certainty of the latter is perceived from the comparison and perception of
particulars uniformly corresponding to one another. These latter we shall
call *Observations,* as we shall call the former *Axioms.*[2] Now, since man is in
this world more for the sake of action than for the sake of contemplation,
and so it is more necessary for him to act rightly than subtly to contemplate
matters which he may approach only with the mind's vision; it has come
about, not without the special providence of the Creator, that the certainty
of theoretical verities would have to be extracted from first principles for
the most part laboriously, and, as it were, through a prolonged series of
consequences; but the certainty of practical matters rests very easily upon
an extremely small number of principles, and those most perspicuous, from
which, for the most part, these practical matters can be deduced by a simple
operation. And this, of course, was so that no one who has even slight
intellectual <210> ability, could advance as an excuse for his sins, that, because of the obscurity of the case, it was not vouchsafed him to understand
what was to be done. And so it does not appear to us that there should be
set up more than two rational principles for this discipline; to wit, *A man
must render an account of those actions which are within his power to do or
not to do,* and *The obligation to act can be enjoined upon us by the authority
of a second person.* If any one add to these the principles which are most
manifest through common sense and experience, namely, that upon man,
to whom it has been given by nature *to understand matters, and from an
intrinsic movement of the will to bestir himself to action, it has been enjoined
by God, to whose sovereignty he is absolutely subject, to lead a social life, and
to observe that which, on the basis of the dictates of right reason, makes for the
preservation of the same,* it will then be easy for any one whatsoever to rec-

---

2. The distinction between rational and experimental principles is taken from Weigel's *Analysis Aristotelica.* See preface, note 7, and *Analysis Aristotelica,* sect. II, chap. ix,
§1.

ognize what he ought to do or to leave undone, especially after civil sovereignties *which the necessity of social life required should be established* have ratified most of them with civil laws.

2. Imputation, therefore, is when the moral effects of an action proceeding from some one directly or indirectly, or exercised upon him by a second person, are declared by him whom that action regards, to inhere and exert their force actively in the person of the former. Now men commonly make imputation twofold, namely, *as a matter of grace* and *as a matter of desert*. It is the former when a man out of benevolence derives upon a second person the effects of the action of some third person, which otherwise that second person could not rightfully claim for himself. Such imputation has place only in matters which are favourable, and not likewise in those which are odious. For just as the nature of good things is such that they can rightly and without a cause be presented to anybody, but evils cannot be inflicted without antecedent demerit; so, if any one should be unwilling to confer some good upon a second person under the name of a pure benefaction, it will be permissible to do it under the designation of some imputed action, which otherwise the second person could not claim for himself. But it is not at all permissible to impute some evil to a second person, unless the second person by his own deed has been made a participant in the guilt. Thus, for example, a prince can rightly impute to a son, not himself conspicuous because of any merits, his father's benefactions, and in view of them confer upon him honours otherwise not his due. But an innocent son should by no means in the same fashion pay for his father's misdeeds. Since the case in which children are compelled to lose their feudal holdings on the occasion of felony committed by their parents, does not properly possess the character of a punishment, for they do not have a right to those things except after they have been turned over intact to them by their parents. But our <211> discussion here is principally about the latter kind of imputation, where the cause of imputation inheres in the person to whom something is imputed.

3. Imputation can also be divided into *bare* imputation, or imputation of simple approval and disapproval, and *effective* imputation. It is the former whereby we but barely approve or disapprove of some action, in such wise that no effect redounds therefrom to the agent. This imputation can

be made by any persons whatsoever, whether they have an interest in the action or not. It is the latter through which the effects of an action put forth their force in the agent, and it is with this that we shall have to deal here.

4. Now *actual imputation* and *imputability,* if I may use such an expression, or in other words, for a thing to be imputed in act, and that it be possible for it to be rightly imputed, are very different things. For not all actions which can be imputed are also always actually imputed to the agent, or are they necessarily to be imputed; but that the imputation be actual, and that effective, rests with him to whose interest it was that the action take place or not. Now when he has either not imputed from the outset some imputable action, or afterwards has ceased to impute it, all the moral effects which otherwise were about to redound to the agent from that action expire. Nevertheless, it is to be noted here that, when it is to the interest of several that some action either takes place or does not take place, if one of them has not imputed that action to the agent, nothing is thereby lost to the right of the rest, which remains, indeed, after that waiver, as it were, of the imputation. Thus, as far as I am concerned, I can forgive the man who has done me a wrong; nevertheless, the right of the magistrate and the right of God against the delinquent, which has come to them as a result of that action, is by no means done away with on that account. Thus, even if God has by the act of remission forgiven some one his imputation, nevertheless the right of men is by no means done away with on that account. For, as an example, an accuser can prosecute before a court and a magistrate can put to death a murderer for whom God has already forgiven his misdeed. But that which all who are concerned fail to impute is regarded as not having been done, as far as its moral effects are concerned, since, forsooth, moral effects do not follow except upon the free choice of those who are concerned. Now that a certain action takes place or does not take place, concerns those who are either the object of the action or the directors, that is, those against whom some action is undertaken, or for whose good or evil it is, and who properly possess the authority to direct the action. Thus, if I have done an injury to a second person, and he to whom it was done, and the magistrate, have forgiven me, no other man has further the right to make trouble for me on that score. <212>

5. A distinction, however, is to be observed regarding the imputation of

good and of evil actions. Evil actions can always be imputed to the agent by those concerned, when they wish; because both he who prevents them has the right not to be compelled to allow them to take place with impunity, and any second person whatsoever has the right not to be bound to allow the same without some antecedent deed on his own part. But good actions are either deserved or undeserved. The former are followed merely by that imputation which we have just called bare imputation, on the part of those who are concerned. For he who has furnished only what he owed has, indeed, done well, yet he deserves nothing further. But actions hitherto undeserved can be effectively imputed, for, of course, they are adapted to produce moral effects as much in the agent as in him for whose sake and advantage they are performed. In the former, so that he may receive the right to demand compensation for his effort; in the latter, so that he may contract the obligation to pay the second person. In order, however, that this obligation arise in actuality, it is necessary not merely that there be in the agent the intention of doing some good to the second person, but also that the action be one undertaken upon the express or presumed will of the second person to whose use it tends. Otherwise, I am able rightly to repel, as it were, the imputation of a service which is thrust upon the unwilling. But if, by the consent of those whom it concerns, it be determined at how much something is to be imputed, there arises a pact, in which the imputation reaches its limit and has nothing further toward which it may tend in that matter. And so, when a man has accepted the estimate of his action expressed in a pact, there is nothing further left him which can be imputed.

6. Furthermore, the foundation of imputability, or, in other words, the condition in which an action can be imputed to an agent, is that the occurrence or non-occurrence of that action rested with the agent.[3] For, after it came to pass that man was no longer to live in such wise that it was permissible for him to do whatever struck his fancy without taking any one into consideration, the next thing was that some account could be de-

---

3. The idea that imputability rests on rational free choice and likewise the reasons for exclusion or diminution of imputability (in §§6–7) derive in general from Aristotle, *Nicomachean Ethics* III.1–5 and V.7–8 (1134b20–1136a9); see Pufendorf's references in *JNG*, 1, 5, §§7ff.

manded from him concerning those actions which he himself had the faculty of doing or of neglecting. From this it is patent that the following
cannot be imputed to a man: (1) Those things which are contingent upon
a physical necessity, or those things which are contingent upon natural
causes; except in so far, perchance, as a man for producing that effect has
applied things active to passive, or in some way started the cause which
directs those things to determining that effect, as if some one, for example,
should obtain by prayers from God that it should rain during a drought.
(2) Actions of the vegetative faculties in themselves; except in so far as one
has suggested the object to them. Thus, from the fact that one <213> has
been endowed by nature with a body robust, vigorous, tall, &c., no one
can demand that something be directly imputed to him. And, on the other
hand, it cannot rightly be regarded as a fault for any one to have a body
weak, frail, and tiny, if, indeed, no fault of his own has intervened therein.
Here come in also the other things which we have from nature without any
effort on our part; suppose, for example, that one rejoices in a genius somewhat active, or somewhat slow, in senses somewhat keen, or somewhat dull,
&c. (3) Compulsory actions, that is, those by which a man is compelled to
accommodate or to apply his members by the inescapable force of a
stronger than himself, and he himself was not to blame for the possibility
of its being applied to him. For just as no one can obligate a second person
by his bidding or authority, or in any other way, to do something of that
second person's own accord contrary to the laws; so, if, by the exercise of
force, the first person has applied the other's members to some act otherwise
illicit, the first person cannot cause this to be imputed rightly against the
second. And so no one can be compelled by another person to commit a
misdeed, provided he himself does not wish to commit it. Thus, for example, even if a virgin be compelled by force to accommodate her members
to the lust of a stronger action, the violence of which she could not ward
off from herself; nevertheless, against her herself nothing can be imputed
for that reason, unless, perchance, her own fault brought her to that place
where she had foreseen that force would probably be brought to bear upon
her. (4) Things which can neither be prohibited by our powers, nor advanced or accomplished, if, indeed, that impotence has not been contracted
by our fault. This is the source of that common saying: "There is no ob-

ligation to do the impossible," or, in other words, "No one is bound to the impossible." And just as the fact that a man has not performed things which were impossible to him (if, indeed, he was not to blame that they were such), or the fact that he does not understand what is beyond his ability, cannot be imputed to him, and, in consequence, for that reason there is no room for punishment in his case (from which fact that other principle also results, namely, that the objective of the laws must be possible for those for whom the laws are enacted); so no sane person is reckoned as having charged the impossible upon any one. And so, in human laws, in testaments, and in contracts, one departs from the exact meaning of the letter, if it involves something impossible. Thus, also, sheer misfortunes are not imputed, unless one has specially obligated oneself to meet them. (5) The actions of those who do not enjoy the constant use of their reason, unless they have ruined it by their own fault. Such are the mad, whose actions are regarded morally as null; likewise infants, before their reason begins to exert itself in a very clear fashion. (6) What has been committed out of concomitant or effective ignorance insuperable in itself and in its cause. <214>

7. But, on the other hand, there can be imputed not merely deeds which are done of previous knowledge and of full and deliberate intention, but also those done of imperfect intention; suppose, for example, when the mind has been shaken by some very violent emotion. For by the right use of his reason a man might have reduced that emotion to order, and he does not properly make it an involuntary action, unless, perchance, the object by which he is excited brings upon him a terror too great for human steadfastness. And so an excuse on the part of a thief that the thing so greatly pleased him that he could not keep away from it, would be ridiculous. Just as those things, also, that proceed from a habit which has so firmly set the mind in one direction that a man can scarcely act otherwise, and often does not know when he is acting badly, are not excluded from imputation. For it rested with the man himself not to contract such a habit. There can also be imputed not merely those things in which it is in our power [*potestate*] at the present moment either to do them or not to do them, but also those, the faculty of performing which was formerly in our power, but has been lost by our own fault; or those which, in the present status, indeed, are impossible for a man, in the circumstance, however, that his inability to

perform them now is due to his own fault. Thus the man who by his own fault has brought himself to that point (supposing, for example, this to be due to petulance or idle curiosity, where, if he had employed due diligence, he might have foreseen that force would be brought to bear upon him), can have imputed to him those bad actions to which he was forced while in that state. For he who has voluntarily admitted some act is reckoned as having also consented to all those things which he might have foreseen would follow from that act; and so he who is bound on the score of the act is also bound on the score of that which has followed by the force of the act; even if, when once that act has been committed, the effects depending thereon could no longer be prevented or stopped. Nay more, even though a man be effectively ignorant that there will emerge from the illicit act, which he knowingly commits, what does emerge thereafter, he will, nevertheless, not be free from all imputation of those consequences. And yet those things which have followed an act in an extraordinary fashion and contrary to the common course of affairs, which also would certainly have happened, even if that act had not preceded, cannot be imputed. From this source arise those common sayings: "A man is reckoned to have been willing to have brought upon himself that from which he knowingly did not turn aside, when he might have done so conveniently"; nor does it seem that what a man has cast himself into, or from which he can extract himself, is in a moral judgement to be regarded as a peril. Likewise, "He who has always acted guilefully so as not to have is to be treated as if he had; and he who has dissipated his <215> resources through luxury or ambition, alleges with no effect an inability to make payment to his creditors."

Finally, those things also can be imputed which were contracted by voluntary or consequent ignorance, of one's own accord, or by supine negligence, or which were committed out of ignorance of the law or of universal principles; especially those things which proceed from ignorance of the common precepts of the law of nature, of such, namely, as a man who enjoys the use of reason cannot be invincibly ignorant, although, when ignorance has crept upon a man through inadvertence, he is in so far excused because of the absence of evil intent.

8. Now not merely are those actions imputable to us which proceed directly from us, but also those which are undertaken by others in such a way

that we also concur in the same. For otherwise the moral effects of bad actions do not pass over from person to person without fault or culpable omission on the part of the second person. Thus, therefore, things can be imputed to us for which we give the order, for which we give advice, to which we furnish the requisite consent, when we supply a place of refuge for a crime, or knowingly help it on, give permission without which the other could not act, do not hinder when we can and ought, by our example incite a second person to the deed which otherwise he would have left undone, &c. And this imputation can be for the whole, if that deed otherwise would altogether not have taken place except for us or another who would have furnished the same service; or else, in proportion to the degree of our influence upon the action. Thence come these trite sayings: "A man is himself reckoned to be the author of that which he does through the instrumentality of another"; "We make our own that to which we impart our authority [*autoritatem*]"; "What has been done by a second person at our bidding along with others, regarding matters which concern us, binds us ourselves." Likewise, "Whatsoever action put into execution by a second person, which he would not have undertaken at all without us, and would not have been able to undertake, is reckoned as our own, as far as its moral effects are concerned."

9. Now it is to be observed that the deeds of some can be imputed to others, then, and then only, if there exist a certain mutual community among them in regard to the same. This comes about in a twofold way; either if they concur in a special way regarding the production of some definite deed, although in a different way of acting, for example, that the one concurs physically, the other morally, which is the case in most of the examples already enumerated; or else if they constitute one body, so united to one another by a pact, that whatever the whole body as such wishes, each and all also of the same body are understood to wish, because, in the case of those things which concern the whole body, they have each made their own will to depend entirely upon the will of the body, or of those who rule it. For, as is shown elsewhere at greater length,[4] those who unite to form a society having the <216> likeness of a single moral person, each and all

4. See bk. II, Observ. 5, §2.

obligate themselves to be willing to hold valid whatever that person or council upon which authority to transact the public business of the society has been conferred, has done regarding the affairs of the society, and so, to recognize its acts as their own. And these are no more mere legal fictions than that all men united in a society can be obligated by orders of a single person. And so it comes about that the individual members are held for a debt contracted in the name of the society. So, what a syndic has done in the name of the people is imputed to the whole people by whom he was appointed. Thus, when a prince or a commonwealth makes war upon a second prince or commonwealth, the separate individuals living under that commonwealth are all regarded as enemies. Thus, when a magistracy, by not rendering justice, has made the debts of private individuals its own, pledges can be taken from any person belonging to that state, and reprisals inflicted upon him. Thus, in the case of David, for whose deed the people were stricken with a pestilence,[5] it is not necessary to take refuge in the absolute law of God, who, since He always finds a cause for death in man, can impose it when it so pleases Him; but, because that act, namely, the ascertaining of the strength of the people, pertains to the acts of a prince as such, according to the constitution of states the people also are understood to have consented to that act. And the perjury of Zedekiah was for the same reason imputed to the whole people; and for that reason, when the king makes war on some one, the whole people are regarded as enemies.[6] But, as regards the deed of Alexander, who utterly destroyed the race of the Branchidae because their ancestors had betrayed Miletus,[7] it is not sufficient to have said that those separate instances of guilt which are derived upon the state from persons individually, expire upon the death of the same,

5. 2 Samuel 24.

6. 2 Kings 25; 2 Chronicles 36:13ff.

7. The Branchidae were a Milesian priesthood who administered Apollo's oracle at Didyma near Panormus. Although their friendly attitude toward the Persian conquerors did not prevent the final destruction of their temple and oracle during the sacking of Miletus in 494 B.C.E. and the deportation of the priesthood to Persia, Alexander the Great is said nevertheless to have seized the descendants during his Persian campaign and to have punished them for the high treason of their ancestors. (Friedrich Cauer, "Branchidai," *Paulys Real-Encyclopädie der classischen Altertumswissenschaften,* III.1, pp. 809ff)

because the same can be continued as long as the deed in question is defended by the state, or satisfaction is not accorded a second person who
demands it; but this consideration is rather to be looked into carefully,
namely, whether down to that time the Greeks had had any intercourse
with that people, from which it could appear that the former had forgiven
the latter the misdeed and the debt which came therefrom. For, if the imputation of these things is once remitted, it can never be demanded later
on. But if, from the time of the misdeed onward, there had never been
peaceful intercourse between the two parties, even though the authors of
the crime have long since passed away, satisfaction for the damage done
could be demanded; and if those who, in the same moral body, had succeeded to their rights and goods, should refuse it, then by the right of war
the same punishments could be inflicted upon them which the authors of
the crime had deserved.

10. It is also to be noted here that the imputation of some future <217>
deed cannot tend backwards, as it were, unless, perchance, that future deed
depend, as the effect from a necessary cause, upon a present or past act of
ours, in such wise that he to whom the cause can be imputed, can have
imputed to himself also the necessary effect. Indeed, it is by no means absurd for some future act of oneself or of a second person to exert in advance
its effects in some one, by imputation, as an act of grace; because, since it
is permissible to give any one whatsoever a benefaction gratis, it rests with
the benefactor to decide whether that is to be imputed to him upon some
ground. But, since evil actions can be imputed only upon desert, it is entirely unsuitable for them to be imputed backwards upon others who had
no knowledge of the future act in question, no obligation to avoid it, and,
finally, no community of actions with him who committed that deed.

11. Now from the circumstance that a nonentity has no positive affections, it is readily apparent that bare avoidance of moral actions which are
bad and forbidden by the laws, cannot be effectively imputed. Hence I do
not owe anybody something because he has not injured me. Avoidances,
however, of actions licit by civil laws, can be imputed, although they have
been prohibited by the mere law of nature, if, indeed, they are especially
avoided for some one person's sake. For he is altogether in my debt for
whose sake I do not use my authority, even though it be imperfect. And

nothing is better known than that avoidances of actions due and prescribed by the laws, are imputed, although one has done no further evil. The reason for this is that those avoidances which we have mentioned, with the exception of the first, are reckoned as positive moral entities, and so are suitable to produce also positive effects. <218>

Any person whatsoever can effectively, or with the obligation to perform them, enjoin on someone subject to himself those things to which his authority over the other extends itself.

1. The authority of a second person makes a man's actions necessary.
2. Whence comes effectual authority?
3. Whence legitimate authority arises.
4. That authority to which consent has never been given expressly or presumably, is null.

1. That a man can conform his actions to a definite norm is due to the fact that he has received as his lot from nature such a mind as does not necessarily act always in one way, but may be turned to either side of a contradiction. But, that he is also bound to it, comes from the circumstance that, aside from the general dominion of God, the condition of human nature ordered also the establishment of sovereign powers of men over one another, which can bring upon those whom they embrace, the necessity of determining their actions in a definite fashion. Now a certain action becomes necessary for a man in consequence of the authority of a superior, who, when he has declared what he wants done or not done by the other person, has such strength that he can compel him by the fear of some evil, if perhaps he shrinks from doing those things or can certainly inflict some evil upon him if he violates the orders. For otherwise no obligation can dispose a man to this, namely, that he be altogether unwilling or unable to do something, that is to say, that he no longer enjoy the natural liberty of contrariety or

contradiction; but this liberty at least is always left him, namely, that he can elect either obedience, or else the risk of undergoing punishment.

2. Now, as a matter of fact, the authority from which obligations are fit to be generated resolves its efficacy ultimately into nothing but the force or faculty of inflicting punishment. For all other things bind the will with a bond too weak to be able to temper it to a stable harmony of its actions. A man's own decisions hold him no longer than it suits him. The hope of future good moves most men too languidly for them to be willing to undertake present labours or neglect present advantages. And you find very few who, when nothing but praise for obedience attends upon the man who acts, and no evil but the reputation for disobedience attends upon the man who neglects, would be willing to act always in a uniform manner, and, indeed, for the most part, contrary to the inclination of the will, merely so as to be said to have <219> obeyed a second person steadfastly. Finally, the force of all commands [*imperiorum*] is precarious, unless the commander [*imperans*] be possessed of strength of such a kind that he can bring upon the other, when disobedient, a more grievous evil than the inconvenience of necessarily undertaking to do his bidding is judged to be.

3. And, of a truth, so that a man may not be able to complain that wrong has been done him when he is compelled to adapt himself to the free choice of a second person, it is necessary that the authority in question also be legitimate, that is to say, that it be derived and constituted from the expressed or with probability presumed will of him over whom command is exercised. For, on account of the natural equality of men among one another, about which we shall later have more to say,[1] authority over a second person cannot come to one except by the consent of that second person, which consent is expressly signified either in a pact, as in civil subjection, or is presumed from a tacit pact, as it were, as comes about in servitude following a state of war, and in filial subjection.[2] But, in truth, when once the authority of a second person has been established by our consent, although afterwards the same begins to displease us, it can no longer be re-

1. See bk. II, Observ. 4, §22.
2. See bk. II, Observ. 5, §§2ff.

fused, because the other has now acquired a right which the law of nature has by no means allowed to be taken from him against his will.

4. Now for the rest, no one can effectually enjoin anything by way of a precept upon a second person over whom he has no measure of legitimate authority. For, however one may by force alone, without any consent on his part, hold him bound for a season, nevertheless, whenever a favourable occasion smiles upon him, he will be able rightfully to throw off the yoke and assert his freedom; a thing which is not at all permissible to those who have consented to their own subjection. For the rest, from the axiom stated above flow the following consequences, which extend over the whole subject-matter of law: *Whatever the law bids is to be done. Whatever the law forbids is to be left undone. Any one whatsoever is bound to do the bidding of him who has authority over him, as far as that authority extends.* <220>

∞ OBSERVATION I ∞

A man can judge properly of things apprehended by the power of his intellect.

1. The representative faculty of the intellect is not free.
2. How far may civil sovereignties enjoin a religion upon one?
3. The judgement of the intellect.
4. What rules are to be followed in deliberation regarding things useful as such?
5. How many kinds of conscience are there?
6. Right conscience and probable conscience.
7. Erroneous conscience.
8. Doubtful conscience.
9. How many kinds of ignorance are there?

1. In man there are, as it were, two faculties of the intellect, which it exerts in the case of voluntary actions, the *representative* faculty, and the *judicative.* By the former the object is placed before the will as in a mirror, and there is displayed the character of the good which is in it. Since this faculty is regarded as belonging to the class of those which men commonly call natural, in contradistinction from free, and so it is not in man's power to apprehend things otherwise than as their images present themselves to the intellect, it is readily apparent that neither is there left any room for the laws to make a disposition about this faculty, nor can anyone's inability either to apprehend some matter at all, or else to apprehend it in another way, be imputed to him. And so it is most utterly unfair to desire, by establishing a punishment, to compel some one to believe that some thing is other than he knows it to be; since, forsooth, assent or faith cannot help but respond to the image apprehended by the intellect. That position, however, is to be restricted in this wise: Unless some one's supine negligence enters into the case, in that he, who, otherwise, if he had applied due zeal,

298

would have secured the true image of the matter, attends to it but drowsily. And so, in regard to the question of a man forming a right conception of some matter in his mind, there is room for laws and obligation only in so far that he receive information regarding the same, and attend carefully to meditation. But it may happen, and it is apt to do so frequently, that, although a man may with impunity cherish in his mind his own particular view about any matter at all, nevertheless, a penalty is ordained against the one who has openly set it forth, or laboured to spread it among the common mass.

2. In view of all this the decision must be made as to how far it is appropriate for the magistracy to exert force in the matter of enjoining religion upon men. Since, of course, persuasion in regard to things divine is formed on the basis of the intellect's apprehension, the <221> manner of which is by no means subject to man's free choice, it is readily apparent that a man cannot be compelled to give his assent to some matter otherwise than as it presents itself to his intellect. For this end, accordingly, only gentle means of persuasion are in place, tortures and violence are in vain, by which, perchance, a simulated confession will be extorted, but it will not be possible to extort a true assent, although by penalties a man can be compelled to receive information and use the means which, otherwise, assent to the matters in question is generally in the habit of following. Now where these are of no avail, civil sovereignty is applied in vain; especially since it is required that, for a man to give his assent to the Christian religion, a special grace be divinely granted. But, in truth, because the formulas in which religion is publicly presented are of no small concern to the commonwealth, and it contributes very greatly to the tranquillity of the state if all citizens openly profess the same view regarding religion, whose power in exciting or calming emotions is great; the magistracy can rightly, even by threatening to exact a penalty in a human court of law, forbid all who are subject to its jurisdiction to set forth, either in public or in private teaching, anything opposed to that formula which the magistracy has promulgated, as being congruent with the foundation of faith, to be followed by the citizens. To this end it is the accepted custom in some regions, for persons who are to be advanced to public offices to be bound by an oath to a definite confession about religion, whereby they are obligated, as long as

they remain members of that commonwealth, to teach or propound nothing in public which is opposed to that confession.

3. Through its judicative faculty the intellect discerns and dictates what, when, and how, action is to be taken, and takes counsel regarding the means best adapted to this end. That faculty is otherwise called the practical reason and the practical judgement (for it is not ours now to inquire into what the force of the intellect is in the bare contemplation of things). Since this faculty is, as it were, the torch of human actions, and when it is not lighted in the proper manner a man must fall; and since, in truth, it can be shaped into rectitude by diligent culture and meditation, so that the cause of delinquency may not arise in it; certainly man ought earnestly to strive, in order so to form the judgement in question, that it correspond exactly to the feeling and intention of him to whom he is bound to render his actions acceptable.

4. Now, although it is our purpose to deal here especially with the good and the evil, the just and the unjust, leaving to another body of doctrine the investigation of the profitable and the unprofitable,[1] still it will not be amiss also to touch briefly upon what rules the intellect ought to observe in its deliberation about a profitable judgement. <222> Because, forsooth, there is frequently enjoined upon some one the obligation to act in the manner which he himself judges to be most expedient; and here, indeed, he who through lack of prudence has undertaken what was less profitable, has done badly. In the deliberations, accordingly, which are customarily instituted regarding matters to which we are not bound by some necessity or a definite obligation (necessity, of course, excludes deliberation, and a definite obligation leaves the agent nothing but the execution), it is presupposed as a foundation, that nothing be undertaken wherefrom the same amount, in moral estimation, of evil and of good, or also a greater amount of evil than of good, seems likely to come. The reason for this is obvious.

---

1. Cf. *JNG,* 1, 3, §7. "Another body of doctrine" refers to *prudence* (phronesis), which concerns "the successful management of one's own actions and those of others, with an eye to the security and welfare," in contradistinction to moral *science,* which "concerns the rectitude of human actions in their order according to laws" (see preface, note 5). The following rules of "deliberation about a profitable judgement" rest on Grotius, *JBP,* 2, 24, §5, "Rules dictated by prudence regarding the choice between things that are good."

For so much is lost from the goodness of each matter as it has of evil united with it, and so it puts off the character of good, if the evil be equal. Moreover, things of the kind about which we are now speaking are undertaken in order that we may acquire therefrom some emolument for ourselves. From this, furthermore, the following consequences flow: (1) If the matter under deliberation seems to have in moral estimation an equal efficacy for good and for evil, it is then, and only then, to be chosen, if the good have somewhat more of good about it than the evil have of evil. (2) If it should appear that the good and the evil which may proceed from the matter in question are equal, then, and only then, will the thing have to be chosen, if its efficacy for good be greater than its efficacy for evil. (3) If it should appear that both the good and the evil are unequal, and the efficacy of the matters no less unequal, the thing is then, and only then, to be chosen, if the efficacy for good be greater in comparison with the efficacy for evil, than is the evil itself compared with the good, or if the good be greater in comparison with the evil, than the efficacy for evil in comparison with the good. (4) If the good no less than the evil of each matter, as well as the efficacy for each, be uncertain, there should be abstention from both, if that be possible. (5) Even such things as may apparently be added by accident to our intent, are to be borne in mind, unless the good towards which our action tends be much greater than the evil which is feared; or, in equal good and evil, there be much greater hope of good than fear of evil.

5. Now, in a special way, the judgement of the intellect about actions morally necessary, in so far as the intellect is imbued with a knowledge of laws, is called *conscience;* although by this name is designated also the reflexive judgement, as it were, about acts, approving things done well, and condemning things done ill, followed as a companion by peace or anxiety of mind, according as conscience bears witness to each matter. For the sake of differentiation we can call the latter <223> *consequent conscience,* because it follows the deeds of men, and subjects the same to scrutiny; but the former we can call *antecedent conscience,* which is antecedent to the deeds, declaring what is good, and what evil, and so what is to be done or avoided.

6. Now conscience is either in a good state or in one less good. That which is in a good state, either knows with certainty that it is such, or merely opines it. The former is called *right conscience,* the latter *probable conscience.*

Right conscience is one that dictates the performance or omission of what is altogether to be done or left undone, or, in other words, one which knows certainly and indubitably that it is in agreement with divine and human law. Probable conscience rests upon an opinion based on reasons which are not thought to be obviously infallible, but only probable, in such wise that it is not regarded as impossible for the opposite side perhaps to be true, although, on the basis of the present reasons, that is not apparent. About right conscience it must be known that every spontaneous action which is done contrary to it, and every omission of an action which it declares necessary, is a sin; since, forsooth, right conscience and the sense of the law intended by the legislator, correspond to one another, and so, what is done contrary to the former, is discordant also with the latter. The same is to be judged of probable conscience, which coincides with right conscience as far as rectitude is concerned, and differs only in regard to the obvious and unshaken knowledge of its own rectitude. For the purpose of moulding this conscience it is well to note the following: (1) In probable conscience, regarding matters which have to be deduced by a somewhat obscure logical consequence, primarily from the laws of nature, when two opinions have been proposed, and, although neither is opposed to the law, nevertheless one rests upon firmer reasons, while the other appears to be safer, whichever one you please may be undertaken. (2) When two opinions have been proposed, of which the one rests upon less firm reasons, the other seems more safe, the safer is properly preferred before the other. (3) In probable conscience a learned man can follow that opinion which seems to him most probable, although to others, perchance, it may not seem to be such. (4) An unlearned man follows most safely the opinion of the more prudent. (5) A man subject to the command [*imperio*] of another can rightfully do at the bidding of superiors what he does not certainly know to be illicit, although it may not appear to him to be so very commendable. (6) In matters of small moment, if there be probable arguments on both sides, whichever one you please may be chosen. (7) In matters of great moment, if probable arguments present themselves on both sides, the safer side is to be preferred. Hence, in <224> the case of uncertain proof of crime, it is better to absolve than to condemn, if the verdict *non liquet* be insufficient.

7. That *conscience* which is in a less good state is called *erroneous*, dis-
agreeing, that is to say, with divine or human law through an error conceived from an apparent shadow of good, or judging that something is to
be done or left undone, which was not to be done or left undone. Now the
error in which conscience is circumstanced is either *invincible*, which a man
has not been able to drive away with the exercise of all morally possible
diligence; or else *vincible*, which a man ought and could drive away with
the exercise of morally possible diligence. Regarding this conscience it is to
be noted: (1) If conscience is circumstanced in a vincible error regarding
an evil thing, he who acts according to it is sinning. The reason is because
the action, as a matter of fact, is discordant with the law, and he was bound
to know the true sense of the law. (2) If conscience is circumstanced in a
vincible error regarding an evil thing, he who voluntarily acts counter to
the same is sinning. For, although here, that should materially, as it were,
come to pass which in itself was to have been done; nevertheless, because
the intention of the agent is repugnant to the law with which he thinks his
conscience is in harmony, the action in question will be imputed to him as
a sin; since, forsooth, the evil intention of the agent makes an action which,
materially, as it were, is not contrary to the laws, to appear to be evil in the
eyes of the agent. From this it is apparent also that right actions cannot
proceed from the erroneous judgement of the intellect, and in the eyes of
him who has been persuaded falsely that something is unjust, it is regarded
as illicit, as long as he has not corrected that persuasion. Thus he sins who
violates a false religion which he himself holds to be true. Thus, as far as
in him lay, a husband to whom his own wife has subjected herself in place
of another woman with whom he had intended to have intercourse, has
committed adultery, and vice versa.[2] Thus he lacks very little of the ap-
pellation of thief who, with all secrecy, in an attempt to steal the property
of a second person, has unwittingly strayed over into his own property. (3)
He whose conscience is bound by an invincible error regarding a matter in
itself indifferent, that is, if he persuades himself that some matter is for-

---

2. Allusion to Seneca, *De constantia sapientis,* chap. 7: "If a man lies with his wife as
if she were a stranger, he will commit adultery, but his wife will not"; cf. *JNG,* 1, 3, §16.

bidden, which is, nevertheless, licit, sins if he acts contrary to that conscience, not if he acts in accordance with the same; or, in other words, he sins if he undertakes it, not if he lets it pass.

8. But if, in truth, the judgement of the intellect hang in the balance, and be unable to discern to which side of the contradiction it ought to give its assent, this is called a case of *doubtful* conscience. Of this you may know that action is to be taken neither in accord with it, nor contrary to it, because an error is committed in either direction. For in neither case does a man's own intention agree with the sense of the <225> law, yet this is required for a good action. For he decides to act even if that which he does be contrary to the laws, and so, as far as in him lies, he is violating the laws. There is a relationship between this kind of conscience and that which they call a *scrupulous* conscience, when an anxious timidity attends upon the judgement of the intellect, lest, perchance, that very thing which one has thought good, be bad, and vice versa. Moreover, when a scruple of that kind rests upon probable reason, action will have to be deferred until the scruple be removed; but the scruple which arises from some weak superstition is to be neglected and cast out of the mind.

9. Absence of cognition in the intellect is called *ignorance,* which, as far as our purposes are concerned, is divided either on the *score of influx into action,* or on the *score of origin.* In the former case it is twofold, one being the cause of what is done in ignorance, the other not. The first of these you may call *effective,* the second *concomitant.* The first denies in the intellect that knowledge by which, had it been present, the action would have been impeded; as if Abimelech had married Sarah, whom he would never have wished to marry had he known that she was married.[3] The second denies the cognition which would not have impeded the deed, in such wise that a man would have performed the deed none the less, even if he had known what he did not know: as if one has unexpectedly killed his enemy, whom he would none the less have wished to kill, even if he had known that he was in that place where he is hurling the missile by chance. Such a deed is properly said to be committed *by the ignorant,* as

3. Genesis 20.

that which arises from effectual ignorance is said to be committed simply *out of ignorance.*[4]

But, on the score of origin, ignorance is divided into *voluntary* and *involuntary;* the former being called by some consequent and vincible, the latter antecedent and invincible. It is the former (whether it be directly willed and striven for, or contracted out of lethargy) when a man does not know what he could and ought to know; it is the latter when one does not know those things which he neither could know, in this matter or in that, nor was bound to know. By others the former is styled ignorance of the law or of universals, as the latter is styled ignorance of the fact or of particulars. Moreover, insuperable ignorance is such either *in itself, but not in its cause;* or else *in itself, and at the same time in its cause.* It is the former when a man in the very action, indeed, is unable to overcome the ignorance from which that action proceeds; nevertheless, he is at fault because he fell into such ignorance. Thus, frequently, he who sins through drunkenness, clearly does not know what he is doing; nevertheless, he is at fault, because he does not know it.[5] It is the latter, when one is not merely ignorant of those things which he could not know before the action, but also was not to blame for remaining in that ignorance, or falling into the same. <226>

---

4. This discussion of ignorance, the distinction between deeds committed by the ignorant and those committed out of ignorance, likewise the distinction between (inexcusable) ignorance of universals and (excusable) ignorance of particulars, rests on Aristotle, *Nicomachean Ethics* III, 1110b19–1111a21; cf. *JNG,* 1, 3, §10.

5. Cf. *Nicomachean Ethics* III, 1113b30ff.

From an internal principle a man can move himself to undertake or to leave undone a certain action.

1. An act of the will.
2. A spontaneous action.
3. An allowed action.
4. Compulsion.
5. Free choice of will.
6. The will commands man's faculties.
7. The will cannot be compelled.
8. The will can conform itself to the norm.
9. Whence it comes that it is capable of obligation.
10. Where obligation is wanting the will is free.

1. Since man was to be made by the Creator an animal to be governed by laws, he had to have a will as an internal moderator of his actions, to wit, in order that, when objects had been placed before him and recognized, he might move himself towards them from an intrinsic principle, without some physical necessity, and might be able to choose that which seemed most suitable to himself. This will is conceived as exerting itself through two faculties, as it were, through one of which it acts *spontaneously,* through the other, *freely.* To spontaneity are commonly attributed definite acts or movements, of which there are certain interior ones called *elicited,* certain exterior ones called *commanded.* Elicited acts are those which are directly produced by the will and received in the same. Some of them are occupied with the end, as volition, intention, fruition; others with the means, as consent, election, and utilization. *Volition* is applied to an act of the will whereby the will itself simply moves to an end, without regard to whether that be present or absent, or, in other words, simply where an end approves itself to the will. *Intention,* or moral choice, is an effectual desire to obtain the end, or, in other words, it is an act of the will by which it effectually

moves to an absent end and strives to attain it.[1] Although there are several grades of this, nevertheless, it is commonly divided into complete and incomplete. Men call a complete intention that whereby the will, after having weighed a matter sufficiently, and without being swept away by the vehemence of emotions, moves to something. They call an intention incomplete when it was accompanied by no sufficient deliberation, or reason was shattered by a whirlwind of emotions. *Fruition* is the rest or the delight of the will in the end already obtained and present. Now *consent* is applied to a simple approval of means, as far as they are judged useful to the end; and these means, when in our power, *election* destines to the obtaining of the end, and *utilization* employs. <227> They call those acts commanded acts which are entrusted by others to the faculties of the mind for execution.

2. Now to spontaneous actions, which, of course, are undertaken from an internal movement of the will together with previous cognition, are to be referred also those which men commonly call mixed, when a minor nonmoral evil, useless or unpleasant, is undertaken for the purpose of escaping a greater evil, which could not be avoided in any other way. For, whatever reduction can be made in a greater evil, otherwise inevitable, is to be reckoned as a gain; and so, in this case, a less evil is in very fact rendered desirable, and one to which the will in its present state spontaneously moves, seeing that for it the avoidance of the whole evil, or merely a part, is the equivalent of a good. This is the source of that trite saying: "Of two evils (non-moral) the less is to be chosen, if it be necessary to undergo one or the other." Thus, although, for example, the casting of merchandise into the sea is not in itself something desirable, nevertheless, under definite circumstances, it is, as a matter of fact, eagerly done, supposing, for example, if I am unable to save my life in any other way when a storm has arisen.

---

1. Pufendorf's distinction between *volition* that simply approves an end and *intention or . . . choice* that is the "effectual desire to obtain an end" follows Aristotle's distinction of *wish* (βούλησις), which might relate to impossibles (*Nicomachean Ethics* III, 1111b20ff), from choice (προαίρησις) as the "deliberate desire of things in our own power"; cf. *JNG*, 1, 4, §1. *Choice* in particular qualifies an action as "voluntary . . . of which the moving principle is in the agent himself" (*Nicomachean Ethics* III, 1111a20ff). It also forms the background to Pufendorf's discussion of liberty as a faculty of the will (see below §5, p. 309, and *JNG*, 1, 4, §2) that in the first place is understood as the faculty of choosing.

For it is better to make a loss of the merchandise than to lose my life along with it.[2] Now judgement is to be passed upon actions, not so much upon the basis of the object, considered alone, but also upon the basis of the end and the circumstances which are here and now present; forasmuch as many of them enter into the very essence of the action, and a single one of them frequently determines the whole nature of the same.

3. For the rest, spontaneous actions depend upon the will, either *directly*, and these are properly called *willed* actions, which the will has produced by some positive influx; or *indirectly*, and these are properly called *allowed* actions, to wit, those which, although they are undertaken by others, we not directly willing or ordering them, are, nevertheless, reckoned to be our own, in so far as, although we might have done so, we neglected to stop them in the way in which we ought. Now the other actions which are called permissions, involve no morality, since, forsooth, they are pure negations of moral actions. As when God is said to permit the sins which He is not bound to prohibit in such a way that they cannot take place at all. Or when in jest we are said to permit what takes place of necessity, absolute or physical. Thus permission of an action undertaken by a second person which it is beyond our power to prohibit, amounts to nothing (if, indeed, the inability to prohibit has not been contracted by our own fault); as, also, permission of an action taken up without our knowledge; or permission of a good action which in fact I was able, indeed, to prohibit, but ought not to have prohibited. But, in truth, when I permit or grant, for example, a starving person to use my food, this is an <228> action directly willed. Now the permission of legislators was discussed in the preceding book.

4. Moreover, just as the spontaneous involves two things, namely, the intrinsic movement of the will, and a previous cognition; so its opposite, the *unwilling*, indicates quite as much that which from an extrinsic principle is forcibly required from our locomotor faculty, with reluctance on the part of the will, as what proceeds from a defect of cognition. The latter has been discussed above, and the former is commonly called by the special

2. For mixed action and the illustration of casting merchandise into the sea, as well as for the involuntary action (§4), the source is *Nicomachean Ethics* III, 1110a4ff; cf. *JNG*, I, 4, §9.

term *compulsion.* Under this name we do not properly treat those actions which are undertaken so as to avoid a greater evil, although nothing but the present necessity makes them desirable; but only those to which a man is forced by an extrinsic stronger principle to adapt his members, and does so in such wise that he shows his aversion and dissent by signs, or principally by actual resistance. Such resistance is presumed in a civil court of law to have been present in regard to any actions or passive states whatsoever, which are commonly not thought of as being allowed spontaneously, where all signs of actual consent are lacking; and this is called by some *interpretative resistance.* As when, in the divine law, a virgin with whom one has lain in a field, away from the presence of onlookers, is judged to have suffered force against her will.[3] Now something is compelled either *in itself but not in its cause,* when a man is circumstanced for the present in such a status that he is unable to repel the force brought to bear upon him, and yet was to blame for coming to that state; or *in itself and in its cause at the same time,* when a man was not also at fault for having come to such a status as that in which something could be forced upon him by violence.

5. *Liberty* is a faculty of the will, which, assuming all things requisite for action, is able, among several objects set before it, to choose one or several, and reject the rest; or, when one thing is set before it, to admit or not admit it, do or not do it. Now, in a special way, they call the faculty of choosing one or several out of a number of objects, the liberty of specification or contrariety, and the faculty of having to do with the choice of rejection of one object only, the liberty of contradiction or of exercise. Liberty, therefore, superadds to spontaneity, partly the indifference of its own acts as far as regards their exercise, in such wise that the will does not necessarily elicit the second of its acts, namely, the act of willing and of being unwilling, but, in regard to the particular object proposed, it is able to choose either one it pleases, although, perchance, it has more propensity towards this one than towards that; and partly, free determination, in such wise that the will, from an intrinsic impulse, elicits here and now either one of its two acts, namely, the act of willing or the act of being unwilling. <229>

3. Deuteronomy 22:25–27.

6. Now it is well established that the will maintains command [*imperium*], as it were, among the faculties of man which, indeed, are capable of that direction. For there are those which altogether reject that free regimen of the will; such as the forces of the vegetative soul, preserving a natural mode of acting which it is not given man to change, or, granted all things requisite for acting, to suspend the exercise of their actions. Merely the application to oneself of the object has been left the will, and when that happens through the medium of the locomotor faculty, it is in the power of the will to turn this faculty speedily or slowly to the service of these forces; in such wise, nevertheless, that the times when nature desires the application of the object, do not depend upon the free choice of the will. Thus hunger and thirst press upon us, not when it pleases a man, but when his more solid or more liquid sustenance has been consumed. But a man may also furnish these forces with an object more or less congruous from which they may take substance for increase or decrease; in such wise, however, that when once the object has been applied, there is no longer room for the regimen of the will. Thus it rests with a man's free choice to supply food of good or inferior quality to his stomach; but the stomach, when once the sustenance has been placed within it, treats it in the way naturally implanted within itself, and not according to the free choice of man. Internal and external senses, when the organ is rightly disposed, cannot but perceive an object applied to them, and judge of it, just as it appears to them, although, by the intervention of the locomotor faculty, the will is able to apply objects to these senses or to take them away. It will be permissible to apply the same principles to the intellect. For, in truth, the will exercises absolute command [*imperium*] over the locomotor faculty, not only when that has been left to itself, but also when it is impelled by a desire of the senses. For the will has command also over the desire in question, although not so peaceful a command, nay, from time to time the emotions within a man rise up in tumults which require a great effort to suppress. However, victory is never to be despaired of for the will, when it has applied its forces rightly, even when the emotions, through lapse of time, or by habit, have become strong. But, in the case of those whose mind has been disturbed through disease, there is no longer room for reason, nor are the actions of such persons regarded as the actions of human beings.

7. But the following also is obvious, namely, that neither by an extrinsic principle, nor by an intrinsic one, can the will be so compelled to avoid something harmonious with itself, or to desire something inharmonious with itself, that absolutely no liberty, at least of exercise, is left it. For external force does not properly bring it to pass that we move towards that from which our will is abhorrent, but it either makes the lesser evil desirable, and so harmonious to the will, by <230> proposing a greater evil, just as it is profitable to be freed from the whole debt on payment merely of a part; or else force persuades us to measure the desire for something and the aversion from it by external indications. All other matters which set out to weaken the will by soft enticements or to terrify it by harsh things, cannot bring to bear any necessity for obedience. The will, indeed, in general always seeks a good, and avoids an evil. Yet there is no particular good, even one commended by the judgement of the intellect, but the will may still neglect it.[4] Just as the will is able to seek even that which the reason has judged to be a moral evil, when the appearance of good, which is united to that evil, commended by the judgement of the senses, prevails. Thus, whatever obligation the mind be clothed with, produces only this effect, namely, that reason judges you should act in accordance therewith, not that you are altogether unable in fact to tend in an opposite direction.

8. From all this it readily appears also that man is allowed to direct, in accordance with a notional norm, actions immediately dependent upon the will, or subject to its command [*imperio*]. For, since the will is a free faculty whose acts are bound by a natural necessity, neither with regard to the spec-

---

4. Cf. *JNG*, 1, 4, §4: "From what has been said it is clear that it belongs to the nature of the will always to seek what is generally good, and to avoid what is generally evil. For it implies a clear contradiction that you should not incline to what you see is agreeable to you, and should incline to what you feel is not agreeable. And so this general inclination of the will can admit no indifference, as though the will might seek good and evil by an appetite of simple approbation. But the will of individuals exerts the force of its indifference on particular goods and evils, as men incline to different things at particular times. . . . Hence, in almost any thing or action, aspects of good and evil, both real and apparent, present themselves and draw the mind this way and that way until finally the will by some intrinsic power determines on one side or the other. An action undertaken in this way is called spontaneous, according to Aristotle, *Nicomachean Ethics,* Bk. III, chap. xiii [III.iii]: 'An action would appear to be voluntary, if the agent originates it with a knowledge of particular circumstances.'"

ification nor the exercise; and the will is not limited to one way of action
always resembling itself, but by some intrinsic impulse, as it were, bestirs
itself to action, and itself designates the manner of its own action; it is
assuredly manifest that, if some rule pointing out a definite manner of
acting should become known (for an antecedent cognition of the intellect
is always required, and it cannot be that a man should conform his actions
to a norm of which he is ignorant), the will itself can elicit its own acts and
direct the other faculties subordinate to it in accordance with the prescription of that rule, if it shall have so desired. About this rule, however, it is
presupposed that it should not conflict with the universal inclination of
the will, that is to say, it should not order the will to seek after something
which is opposed to its own nature, or to turn aside from that to which it
naturally goes; or, in other words, that it should not bid the will to turn
aside from the good as such, or to seek after the evil as such. For that the
first be done cannot in any manner be demanded from the will, even if
external acts be able to pretend that which is contrary to the inclination of
the will.

9. The consequence of this is that the will of man is fit to receive an
obligation from an extrinsic principle, so that it may determine, according
to its prescript, the specification and execution of its own acts, and its mode
of action. For, assuredly, an obligation presupposes a natural faculty of
action and non-action, which, if a man so determine by some physical necessity, that, after the fashion of natural causes, he be utterly unable to strive
towards the diverse, he would <231> destroy all the morality of his own
actions, just as also he who should restrain men with nothing but physical
bonds, would reduce them to the condition of brutes. But, when moral
bonds are placed upon the will, that is, when what is to be done unless a
man should be willing to expose himself to the danger of undergoing some
evil, is indicated by him who has the authority to inflict that evil; then,
assuredly, although the natural faculty of tending towards the contrary remains, nevertheless, his liberty is bounded by a moral necessity, so that from
the judgement of right reason he will always feel that what has been prescribed, rather than the contrary, ought to be done.

10. But, in truth, where an obligation is lacking, the will is understood
to be free, and to have the authority of doing all those things which can be

performed by it through the instrumentality of its natural powers. Nay, also, when it has once settled itself upon something, unless some law stands in the way, its own decree has by no means such force that it cannot rightly change or do away with it, whenever it so pleases. This change is reckoned as having intervened, not only when a man has expressly signified it, but even when he has done something which cannot comport with the decree of his former will. But, if there be a definite conflict between the instruments of the conventions regarding the same thing, that agreement which was later reached between the parties to the contract will derogate from the agreements previously reached; because no one is able at the same time to have willed to do contrary things, and such is the nature of acts which depend upon the will, that it is possible to depart from them by a new act of the will, either all together, as in contracts, and in pacts which can be dissolved by the consent of both parties, unless they have been made irrevocable by the law of a superior, or else $\mu o\nu o\mu\epsilon\rho\hat{\omega}s$, that is to say, from one side only, as in testaments and in positive human laws. Here, however, it is to be observed that the decree, which cannot be established except in some definite present status or condition, after these have been removed, cannot be rescinded by the founder, when once it has been duly established. So the law which a prince has passed, he cannot do away with when he has given up sovereignty. Nor does it make any difference, if, in the preceding decree, it was stated that the one to be established later would be invalid. For he was right who said, "It is absurd to wish to invalidate some future statute by an antecedent statute." For absolute authority cannot constrain itself, nor can that which is by nature revocable be fixed.[5] No more so than if a man has declared in his will that, if he should make a new will, it would be invalid. For, although a clause of that kind might, possibly, cause the assumption to arise that, in the later testament, his true will had not been expressed; nevertheless, if that clause be revoked here, the previous testament will be altogether vain. Thus the express addition <232> to certain constitutions (a thing which is not infrequent among princes), that, even if by a special rescript they issue some order contrary to them, magistrates or judges are, nevertheless, not to obey that rescript, has no such effect as

5. See bk. II, Observ. 5, §18.

though they were unable to abrogate those constitutions again; but the princes signify rather thereby that their later rescripts are not serious, or have escaped from them imprudently; and by this shrewd device they rid themselves of the impudence of forward petitioners, whom they could not bring themselves to deny openly.[6] Nevertheless, it should be well observed that the decree of one's own will can then, and only then, be revoked, when thereby some right has not been conferred upon some second person, of which he ought not to be robbed against his will. And from this it is apparent why, for example, in renunciations, when a man has yielded up his right in a second person's favour,[7] the following words are customarily employed: "Contrary to this instrument no attempt ought to be made by me or my heirs, and if, perchance, one should be made, it is to be held invalid and null." For by this act I abdicate my right and confer it upon another. Hence, indeed, if anything contrary to that renunciation be decided upon in time to come, it will be null; because, of course, I have no further right to that thing, and it is without effect that I attempt to dispose of another's property. <233>

6. See bk. II, Observ. 5, §19.
7. See, for example, *Dig.,* XLI.ii.12, §1.

A man is destined by nature to lead a social life with men.

1. Every man whatsoever loves himself most.
2. Nature has implanted in the same the necessity and desire of cultivating society.

3, 4, 5. Answer is made to the arguments of those who deny that by nature man is a social animal.
6. The non-social life is the life of beasts.

1. Man has this in common with all living things to whom it has been given to realize their own existence, that he loves himself most, is zealous to protect himself in every way, and strives to acquire the things which seem good to him, and to repel the evil. And commonly, indeed, this love of each man whatsoever towards himself is so great that any and every inclination towards any and every other man yields to it. At times some seem, indeed, to embrace others with a more tender affection than themselves, and to rejoice more in the blessings of others than in those which are especially theirs, and to grieve more over the ills of others than over their own. Thus frequently parents would prefer to have transferred to themselves the pain which they see their children suffering. Thus it is well established that many have met death with equanimity, in order to save others united to them by a special bond. But, in truth, this was done either because, as the result of an intimate relationship, they regarded the good or evil of others as their own, or else because, by that display of affection or fidelity, they were on the way to acquire some special good for themselves. Thus some parents rejoice more effusively in the blessings of their children than in their own blessings, because the blessing which affects equally both themselves and their offspring is in their judgement doubled. Thus we would often be will-

ing to redeem the suffering of one of our loved ones by our own suffering, because the weapon, as it were, which seeks us would be inflicting a more severe wound by passing through so dear a body. And he who does not refuse to die for another, either hopes for so much glory from that act that he judges he can well afford to pay for it with his life, or else he fears that on the other's death such evil would come upon himself that life would no longer be worth living for him.

2. Now, in truth, man would have been very little different from beasts, nor would he be living a life much more civilized or comfortable than they, were it not that he had some other inclination also implanted in him by nature, namely, that he enjoys living in the society of his <234> kind. This is so clear that it does not need to be set forth at length. Nothing is more gloomy for a man than perpetual solitude. To him alone among animate beings has it been given to set forth to others in articulate sound the feelings of his mind, than which there is no instrument better adapted to form or to preserve society. In no genus of living beings can the advantages of one be so much promoted by others, as in that of men among one another. Such is the state of need of human life, that, were not a number to unite upon a mutual task, life could be preserved only with the utmost difficulty. The weakness of human beings just born is greater than that of any other animal, and while in the case of others but a few days or months are sufficient to enable them to look out for their own food, in the case of men a number of years is hardly sufficient. Add, also, that the earth has everywhere placed their food before beasts, but what suits man requires generally industry and cultivation. And yet the ability to gather food for the stomach is but a very small part in one's deserving the dignity of the name man. Nay, we should not simply be the prey of beasts, but should also rage against one another mutually, in the manner of wild monsters, were it not that nature had altogether bidden us to unite to form a peaceful society.[1]

3. However, so that the reasons of those who undertake to deny matters as clear as the foregoing, may not, perchance, move one, it should be known: (1) These two inclinations, by which man loves himself and seeks

---

1. On the Stoic origin of the double foundation of natural sociability in the natural weakness [*imbecillitas*] of man and the *telos* of his reasonable nature, see *JNG*, 2, 3, §§14–15, with numerous references to Cicero, Seneca, and Marcus Aurelius.

after society, ought, by the intention of nature, so to be tempered that nothing be lost to the latter through the instrumentality of the former. That is to say, nature commended to man self-love, in such a way that he should, nevertheless, commit nothing because of it, which would conflict with his inclination to society, or injure the very nature of society. And when, through the exorbitance of his emotions, he neglects that, and seeks his own advantage together with some hurt to others, there arises whatever disturbance there be in which men conflict with one another. (2) That definite individuals unite to form a definite kind of society comes about either in consequence of a special congruence of dispositions or of other qualities, or else because they imagine that they can obtain some special end better with these persons than with those. Now it is by no means necessary for all men to coalesce into one society in which all are equal to one another; but it is sufficient if the same persons get together in several and distinct groups, which are, nevertheless, by no means altogether mutually unsociable, but refrain from unjust injuries towards one another, and, as far as they are permitted by closer obligations, share with one another their advantages and blessings.

4. All this being posited, answer can be made without difficulty to the following position which some maintain: "It is, indeed, true that <235> for man in the course of nature, or as far as he is man, that is, immediately after birth, to have a state of perpetual solitude fall upon him, is irksome; infants need the help of others in order to live, adults their help in order to live well; and by the compulsion of nature men seek to gather together. And yet, in truth, civil societies are not mere gatherings, but they are treaties, for entering into which good faith and pacts are necessary. The force of these is unknown to infants and the uninstructed, their usefulness is unknown to those who are without experience of the losses which come from the absence of society. And so it comes about that the former, because they do not understand what society is, cannot enter into it, and the latter, because they do not know what it is good for, show no interest in it. Therefore, all men, since they are born as infants, are born unfit for society, and a very great many remain so all their life long; but, by discipline, and not by nature, man becomes fit for society."[2] But it is readily apparent that the

2. See Hobbes, *De cive,* chap. 1, §2, no. 1.

colour of objection rises pretty much from a quibble about the Greek word πέφυκε, which Latin translators commonly turn *aptus natus est* [has been born fit for], and by this is properly signified a natural inclination towards something, together with a natural potency of receiving an actual fitness for exercising that thing; even if that actual fitness should not be in him immediately by birth, but have to be introduced by industry, and it alone. And so the sense of that trite saying, "Man is by nature a social animal," is this: Man is destined by nature to society with his like, and this is most suitable and useful to him; and man has been endowed with such a disposition that, by cultivation, he can receive a fitness for acting well in that society; nay more, this is perhaps the principal fruit produced by societies, namely, that the recently born, in whom no actual understanding of those things has been implanted by nature, may, within societies, be fashioned into suitable members of the same. Nor does this fitness exist merely within the limits of marriages or families, but it extends also to the establishment of states, where several families come together for the sake of security and a richer life, and manage their affairs by the common counsel of the society under definite laws about commanding and obeying. Such societies nature has altogether wished to have among men, although it has been left within the free choice of men, and so is to be determined by pacts, just what individuals are to be united to what society, or who is to be set at their head for governing them. Nor does the state cease to be in itself congruent with nature, because many struggle to its helm by unjust force and crimes. But, as there are a number of special forms of states, so the diverse dispositions of men better agree with diverse forms. But if, in truth, some one's disposition out of pride disdains to accept the equality of conditions, without which society cannot coalesce or stand, this is by no means an <236> indication that man is not a social animal; but that the individual in question is either less fit to live in some special kind of society, suppose, for example, one in which all enjoy an equal right; or else in a faulty way indulges more than is right in self-love, which, however, nature bade agree peacefully with the inclination towards society. But the objection which is advanced, namely, that the advantages of life can be furthered better by mastery than by mutual effort, is of no moment. For there is no stable mastery at all without society, and it is altogether impossible for all men to have dominion over other men.

5. Now as for the further objection: "If man loved man in the course of nature, that is, as man, no reason could be given why each single individual should not love each other single individual, as being equally a man, or why he should the rather frequent those in whose society honour and advantage are accorded him beyond others."[3] To meet this it should be known that all men, indeed, have been brought together by the similarity of their nature towards one another, so that in actual fact that general friendship resulting from a common nature ought also to be common to all, unless some one, perchance, has by his crimes made himself unworthy of it. Now, in truth, a number of circumstances are added to that common nature which are responsible for one loving this one more than that one; suppose, for example, that there was between them a greater congruence of dispositions in regard to special inclinations, or else that their birthplaces were not far apart. But then and only then could no reason be given, if all men had grown up out of the earth together like fungi, without any relationship to one another,[4] or if they had among one another a similarity of dispositions at every point. But as such a state of men has never existed, so no conclusion can be drawn from supposing it, contrary to what the actual facts show.

As for the rest, a man more gladly frequents those in whose society honour and advantage are accorded him, rather than to a second person, because each man loves his own advantages. And this is by no means repugnant to nature, provided only the harmony of society be not disturbed by that love. For nature has not bidden us to cultivate societies with the purpose of neglecting the care of ourselves; since, forsooth, societies bring about in the very highest degree the condition that, through the mutual sharing of aid and of blessings with a number, we can the more conveniently look out for our own blessings. And even though a man, in uniting himself to some society, should be accustomed to regard primarily his own advantage, and secondarily that of his associates, nevertheless, nothing prevents him from owing so to foster his own private advantage that the advantage of the society be not hurt, or injury brought upon individual members; or from sometimes neglecting his own advantage to care for the advantage of the <237> society. And the argument which is advanced,

3. Ibid.; cf. *JNG,* 7, 1, §2.
4. Allusion to *De cive,* chap. 8, §1; cf. *JNG,* 2, 2, §7.

namely, that the origin of great and long-enduring societies, that is, of
states, did not come from the mutual benevolence of men, but from their
mutual fear (using this word for any prevision and precaution whatsoever
taken against a future evil),[5] has nothing to do with the case. For it was in
the highest degree congruent with human nature that, since one by one, or
a few at a time, they had been exposed to injuries, a number united with
one another should fortify themselves against ills; nor is the sole end and
use of states the avoidance of evil. Nor is it required, in order for some
society to be called congruent with nature, that it have arisen out of mutual
benevolence alone, although neither is that entirely absent in establishing
states; since, forsooth, at least those who lay the first foundations, as it were,
of states, are most of them united to one another in mutual benevolence,
although, perchance, others afterwards may be induced to join them out
of fear.

6. Now it is worth while to have considered in just what condition men
would be living if they should be deprived by nature of every obligation
to cultivate society among themselves, or if they were not social animals.
Here it is assuredly apparent that, since no right had obtained mutually
among them, the result would have been that each individual whatsoever
would have had equal rights with others to any thing whatsoever; and, without any injury, any one whatsoever, as far as each one's strength had admitted of so doing, could have inflicted upon any one whatsoever what he
thought would make for his own preservation; and from that would have
resulted the war of all against all, which is the very life of beasts.[6] For, just
as, because of the fact that man has no community of right with the brutes,
any man whatsoever (when you remove the respect in which particular men
have already acquired for themselves above others rights over brutes) may
properly, as far as his strength allows him, whenever he so pleases, either
kill any animal whatsoever, or compel it to perform a service, without
thereby doing an injury to the brute; thus, if I had no obligation towards
any man, assuming that I had the natural faculty to hurt or even to kill a
second person, I might properly defend my life and limbs as far as I could,

5. *De cive,* chap. 1, §2 (at the end).
6. *De cive,* chap. 1, §§3ff; *Leviathan,* chap. 13.

and employ all the means serving thereto, and it would rest with me alone to judge of their aptness to that end; and so I might not merely appropriate to myself all those things which I judged to be conducive to my interest, but I might even kill any man whatsoever, or weaken or constrain him in some fashion, if, indeed, that should seem to be expedient for my security, especially since, in such a state, I could take no precautions for my security except by violence, as no mutual obligation existed. And, since any one whatsoever would have had the same licence regarding any one else whatsoever, what else would men have been but wild beasts, rapacious against their own <238> kind? But, in truth, since men have never existed in such a state, and by the intention of the Creator ought never to exist in it, it is utterly incongruous and almost self-contradictory to call this the state of nature. And so the inconveniences also directly resulting from such a state ought not to be substituted as the foundations of the law of nature (although, in actual fact, that no such state exists among men is due to the law of nature); but rather this, namely, that God has directly destined man to cultivate a social life.[7] For had this not been the direct intention of God, it would not have been more necessary for men to enter into pacts with one

7. Pufendorf does not yet see the methodological function of Hobbes's natural state of war of everyone against everyone and its right to everything. It serves as a counterfactual supposition in contrast to the civil state, showing the necessity of the latter by a deduction ad absurdum of the former. See Thomas Hobbes, *The Elements of Law Natural and Politic,* ed. Ferdinand Tönnies, intro. M. M. Goldsmith (London: Cass, 1969), chap. 14, §§10ff: "But that right of all men to all things, is in effect no better than if no man had right to any thing. For there is little use and benefit of the right a man hath, when another as strong, or stronger than himself, hath right to the same. . . . The estate of hostility and war being such, as thereby nature itself is destroyed . . . he therefore that desireth to live in such an estate, as is the estate of liberty and right of all to all, contradicteth himself. For every man by natural necessity desireth his own good, to which this estate is contrary." That methodological procedure is later adopted by Pufendorf himself in his mature work, the *JNG, Eris,* and the *Dissertatio de statu hominum naturali,* when he contrasts the fictitious "state of single individuals left alone by themselves" (*in se*) with the "state of culture," and the (pure) "natural state of individuals in relation to one another" (*ad alios*) with the "civil state" in order to prove the necessity of the latter states for the survival and appropriate development of mankind. See *JNG,* 2, 2, §2 and 3, §15; *Dissertatio de statu hominum naturali,* in *Dissertationes academicae selectiores* (Uppsala, 1677), §§4 and 7; *Eris,* "Specimen controversiarum," chap. iii "De statu hominum naturali," §3 (pp. 134–35).

another because of the disadvantages resulting from a non-social life, than for other animals to enter into a pact with bears, wolves, or lions to avoid the disadvantages of the non-social life which they lead. Nor is there ground for retorting that they do not have reason by which they may understand the force of pacts. For neither would God have given men reason, had He not wished to destine them to cultivate society. <239>

Right reason dictates that a man should care for himself in such a way that human society be not thrown into disorder.

1. The law of nature comes to be known through the dictate of reason.
2. How that dictate is to be limited; do not do to a second person what you do not want done to yourself.
3. Whence the obligation of the law of nature arises.
4. The fundamental laws of nature.
5. Whether the laws of nature are to be derived from self-love alone.
6. What may one lawfully do to the life of a second person in one's own necessity?
7. Or to his property?
8. The laws of nature regarding one's own preservation.
9. Whether a law of nature and an instinct can have to do with the same object.
10. What may a man lawfully do to his own life?
11. War becomes licit on the score of care for one's own safety.
12. When is one's own defence in place?
13. How far is it possible to proceed?
14. The force of war is an extraordinary means for men to deal with one another.

15. War is not properly undertaken on merely any grounds whatsoever.
16. What may be permissible towards an enemy?
17. Whether it be permissible to corrupt enemy subjects.
18. Restrictions of the licence of war.
19. War is to be ended as soon as possible.
20. What kind of guarantee is to be demanded about giving no offence for the future?
21. The law of nature regarding the cultivation of peace and the exercise of humanity.
22. On what score are men equal to one another?
23. The general law of nature about not doing hurt to the right of the other person.
24. Laws about not violating the body of the other person.
25. About not violating chastity.
26. About not defaming.
27. About not committing adultery.
28. About not hurting the goods of the other person.

1. Although, when man comes into the light of day, his mind is found to be imbued with no knowledge of affairs, nevertheless, his intellect thus disposed God has so shaped that, after his powers have begun to exert themselves simultaneously with advancing years, from the inspection of natural matters he conceives certain notions serviceable to a richer knowledge to be erected upon them later; and, from the contemplation of himself, he recognizes what actions, as being in accord with his own nature, the Creator has wished him to perform, <240> and what to avoid, as being repugnant to the same. To be occupied with the former is the part of others; it is for us here to look with a little more care into the latter class. By experience, therefore, it is well established that, when, out of a state of infantile ignorance, the light of reason in man reveals itself with a little greater clarity, and turns itself to the contemplation of its own nature, his reason which has not been corrupted by emotions or vicious habits, dictates to him that it is right, indeed, for him to care for and save himself as far as he can; nevertheless, because he has observed that he has been destined by the Creator to cultivate society with other men, it is necessary so to modify his care for himself as not to become himself unsociable with others, or not to have society among men disturbed. It is this very thing which we call the law of nature. This law, as has been said, comes to be known, without any supernatural aid, from a consideration of nature and the condition of man. Nor does this nature cease to be known because many have not that strength of natural capacity which would enable them to investigate the same by their own processes of reasoning, or because knowledge of it is acquired by most men through information derived from others. For it is sufficient that the perspicacity of but mediocre intelligence can deduce it, and the rest of men, when, under the instruction of others, they have compared their acquired knowledge of it with the condition of their own nature, are able to observe that this law is necessarily in accord with them. And, as human society

coalesces and is preserved by the law of nature, so this is by no means the least fruit of societies already established, that, in them, through instruction from others and by its very exercise, even the duller may learn the law of nature.

2. But the method of reaching easily a knowledge of most of the laws of nature, which is strongly recommended, namely, that, when a man is on the point of doing something to a second person he should think of himself as being put in the place of the other with whom something is to be done, and the other in turn set in his place, is so to be restricted that, in such a case, there should be considered not only what would be pleasing or displeasing to have brought upon us, but also what obligation or necessity rests upon us of conferring something upon the other person. And so that trite saying, *"Do not do to the other person what you would not wish to be done to you,"* is valid only thus far; just as you do not wish it to happen to you that the other person brings upon you something unpleasant, to which he is not forced by some obligation or necessity; or, in other words, what amounts to the same thing, as you do not wish done to you by the other person what is unjust or inhuman, so do you not bring anything of that sort upon the other person. On this score the judge, assuredly, is not hindered by that dictum from inflicting punishment upon the guilty, although he <241> himself, put in the place of the guilty, would desire to escape punishment quite as much as they. Thus, in regard to what was enunciated by the Saviour himself, "Whatever ye wish that others should do unto you, do ye also unto them,"[1] there must likewise be borne in mind not merely what would be pleasant to have done to us by the other person, but also what the other can conveniently do. Hence it is by no means proper for me to clean my servant's shoes for him, because I want him to clean mine for me. And there is enjoined by that precept before all things the exercise of justice and humanity. Now this humanity, assuredly, does not require me to do something for the other person which I myself cannot be deprived of without great inconvenience to myself, or supply him with things which either I cannot myself supply conveniently, or which are not so very necessary to the other that they must be supplied by me.

1. Matthew 7:12, Luke 6:31.

3. Now that dictate of reason or law of nature has force to obligate men on the authority [*autoritate*] of the Creator, as of one exercising supreme sovereignty over them. And, since He has so formed the nature of man as to make it apparent enough that man has been destined to cultivate society, and, for that reason, has made his mind capable of those notions, it is understood, assuredly, that He also wished man to attemper himself to the end prescribed by Himself. And so, since that end is obtained by the law of nature, He has obligated man also to preserve it, as a means not discovered by the free choice of man, and subject to change in accordance with their humour, but expressly established by God Himself for attaining this end. For he, who, by virtue of his command [*imperio*], enjoins upon a second person an end, is reckoned also to have obligated him to employ those things which are necessary to obtain that end. And the laws of nature would have had a perfect force to obligate man, even if God had never set them forth also in His revealed word, nor are they any less laws because they appear to be merely certain conclusions, perceived by the reason, touching things to be done and to be avoided, and not the discourses of Him who rightfully commands something to be done or not to be done. For man was bound to obey his Creator, even if, by a special revelation, He had not manifested to him His own authority [*autoritatem*]; since, forsooth, he might otherwise perceive that he was subject to the authority of the Supreme Arbiter of things, even without a revelation of that kind; and law is the decree of a superior, in what fashion soever it may finally become known to the subject, whether it be promulgated by means of notional signs, or a discourse expressed by the voice, or in writing, or whether from the condition of nature, or that of the transaction which must be done, it has to be inferred or presumed by the process of reasoning. And no one will deny that those also to whom the Sacred Scriptures have never become known, have sinned against the law of nature; which could <242> not be said, if, indeed, it borrowed the force of a law from promulgation through the Scriptures.[2]

---

2. Cf. *JNG*, 2, 3, §19: "if these dictates of reason are to have the force of laws, it is necessary to presuppose the existence of God and His providence, whereby all things are governed, and primarily mankind." Pufendorf follows the Hobbesian voluntarist

4. Now the fundamental laws of nature and those from which all the rest flow are two: (1) *That any one whatsoever should protect his own life and limbs, as far as he can, and save himself and what is his own.* (2) *That he should not disturb human society,* or, in other words, *that he should not do anything whereby society among men may be less tranquil.* These laws ought so to conspire, and, as it were, be intertwined with one another, as to co-alesce, as it were, into one law, namely, *That each should be zealous so to preserve himself, that society among men be not disturbed.*

5. Now, indeed, there are those who, with considerable subtlety, deduce all other laws from the first alone. To wit, since, if all society among men were abolished, any man whatsoever would have an equal right to any thing whatsoever, and from that the war of all against all would have arisen, yet this status would be utterly repugnant to the conservation and security of men, and would bring with it infinite troubles and miseries: Therefore, peace is to be sought, as far as some hope of having it shine upon us, and where it cannot be had, the aid of war is to be sought:[3] And so a right to everything is not to be retained, but with pacts, by which one must alto-gether stand, society must be established for the sake of mutual aid, and so on. But, in truth, since it has been shown above that nature has directly destined man for a social life, in such wise, that, although he may have bound himself by a special bond to some particular society, nevertheless, with all men, even those who live outside of that society, he should cultivate universal peace as far as they may allow him to, and he should exhibit the services of humanity which he can conveniently; the preservation of the social life is also deservedly laid down as the basis for the laws of nature, but is not assumed in a secondary way as something which men have been compelled by accident to take up. Hence, also, it is incongruous to wish to

---

conception of law as command of a superior and turns against the Grotian dictum, that natural law "would have a degree of validity even if we should concede that which cannot be conceded without the utmost wickedness, that there is no God, or that the affairs of men are of no concern to Him" (*JBP,* Prolegomena, p. 13). But he criticizes the Hobbes-ian qualification that those dictates of reason are *laws* "only as they are delivered by God in Holy Scriptures," because for Pufendorf the promulgation by means of notional signs does not belong to the essence of the law (*JNG,* 2, 3, §20, with reference to *De cive,* chap. 3).

3. Hobbes, *De cive,* chap. 1, §15.

derive from the dictate of reason, cutting off the supposition of the social life, some primeval right of nature; since, forsooth, everything which is inferred in that way is necessarily to be attempered to the nature of social life. And let us assume that a certain people which cherishes internal peace among its citizens, has such strength that it may be feared by all the rest, and so is by no means kept from hurting others by the fear lest, perchance, its own example be applied to it: If such a people should, to its own pleasure, raven against the persons or property of other weaker peoples, drive off, carry away, kill, or drag others into slavery, just as it might judge to be expedient to itself, who would not recognize that the law of nature was directly violated by them? Or who would say that they differed from a pack of wolves? And yet (as we are supposing) that people might <243> preserve itself, even if, perchance, it should employ no right in its dealings with others.[4] Nay, beyond all other things, the persuasion that a man is sufficient unto himself, that he has made abundant provision for his own safety, and that there is no reason why he should be zealous to deserve the services of the rest, induces him to violate the law of nature. Nor from any other fountain head has flowed the custom, formerly accepted among many peoples, of disturbing strangers with brigandage and practising piracy; because men felt that they were bound only to their fellow citizens, and were obligated to strangers by no bond of right; and so, that there was peace only with their fellow citizens, and war with all others. It stands, therefore, that, as the life of men without society is destined to be like the life of beasts, so the law of nature is principally founded upon the principle that social life among men is to be preserved. And the condition of our nature is so far from conflicting with our assertion, that it rather supports it firmly. Now this condition, even if we were bound by no law of nature to cultivate society, would urge us to establish it of our own accord, because of the

---

4. Pufendorf refers to *De cive,* chap. 1, §3. Here Hobbes grounds natural law on self-preservation alone because he assumes that individuals in the state of nature are equally vulnerable and consequently all subject to mutual fear. Pufendorf tries to show that the assumption of equal vulnerability does not hold under certain circumstances (as in some international relations). See also *JNG,* 3, 2, §2, where he accuses Hobbes of the methodological error opposing equality of physical vulnerability to inequality introduced by civil law.

advantages flowing therefrom, and so as to avoid the disadvantages which accompany the non-social life.

6. But we must here consider whether that law about preserving oneself without disturbance to society or hurt to the other person, be not restricted through the case of necessity; or, in other words, whether it may not be permissible to hurt the body or the property of a second person, if, indeed, I cannot otherwise save myself and what is my own. On this point we here lay down the principle that, on the basis of the law of humanity, any one whatsoever is bound, when not under an equal necessity, to the extent of his power to come to the aid of a second person placed in an extreme necessity, and necessity gives the authority to claim this aid in very much the same manner as we claim the things to which we have a right; while there remains the obligation to make restoration, at least by way of gratitude, when the present necessity has been removed. For to necessity is deservedly ascribed such force, that it prevails over those reasons by which, otherwise, we are bidden not to claim by force what is due us by the law of humanity.

But the principal controversy is as to whether necessity gives one a legal right to the life of a second person. Here in different cases the judgement must be different. And, in the first place, indeed, if, for example, a prince, or one who otherwise has in any way at all for the present the power to dispose of my life, should bid me kill a second person, of whose innocence I was convinced, if I did not wish to be killed myself; and of course, if he have enjoined upon me merely the execution, hardly any one will doubt that I may rightly turn my hands to that service for the sake of saving my own life. For there is <244> no reason why I should throw my life away, when the second person is going to be put to death by others just the same, especially since he who brings that necessity upon me, takes full responsibility for the deed himself, and does not appear to be deriving upon me any part of the guilt. Although I very properly deprecate such a service, where it is permissible to avoid it without great peril, even when only the execution is entrusted to me. But, in truth, the case is different, if a prince, under threat of death, should give orders to condemn as guilty a man who, in the judge's own opinion, is innocent. For in this wise the judge lends the violation of his office to furnishing a specious occasion of wreaking vengeance upon an innocent man as though he were guilty, and so the judge

derives a large part of the guilt upon himself. A good man should account
it a glorious thing to escape the turpitude of such a deed even at the risk
of his life. There are other cases, besides, in which, in order to save my life,
the life of another can be exposed to probable peril of death, not, indeed,
in direct intention, but indirectly, and as a consequence. Thus, for example,
when two of us are in present peril of our life, so that both will have to die
together, or only one can be saved, it is permissible to bring his fate upon
the other person, who would otherwise perish anyway, so that I be not
myself compelled to perish with him. Thus, in a shipwreck, when I have
seized a plank not large enough for two; if some one should swim up and
wish to throw himself likewise upon it, and so destroy me together with
himself, nothing prevents me from driving him away from me by any kind
of violence.[5] Thus, when the enemy, intending death, follows hard upon
two who are fleeing, in the present peril to his life one can abandon the
other by breaking down a bridge behind him, or by closing a gate, if it be
impossible for both to be saved at the same time.[6] In like manner, if some
stronger man should pursue me with threats of death, and if some one who
was otherwise in no danger from him should meet me by chance in the
road by which I had to flee, if, indeed, when admonished, he did not get
out of the way, or the shortness of time or the narrowness of the way did
not allow him to do so, it will assuredly be permissible to strike him down,
and to betake myself to flight over his prostrate body; even if, in all probability, as a result of that assault, it should appear that his body would have
to be struck down violently; unless, perchance, the person in my way be of
such a sort that I ought rather to run a probable risk of my own life than
that he should be severely hurt on my account. But, in truth, if any one
has impudently or inhumanely stood in my way, and has refused to grant
me a way of escape, I can kill him as an enemy and with direct intent, if,
indeed, he cannot be removed from the way by any less severe means. If,
however, in shipwreck, for example, more persons should leap into a boat
than it can carry, in such wise, that, if the <245> rest wish to be saved, one

5. The example is from Carneades (Cicero, *De re publica*, ed. Konrat Ziegler [Leipzig:
Teubner, 1969], 3, 20).
   6. Cf. *JNG*, 2, 6, §4, referring to Virgil, *Aeneid*, IX [722ff] and XI [883ff].

or more must necessarily be thrown out; assuming that all enjoy an equal right here, those who are thrown out will have to be chosen by lot, and if any one refuses to have the lot cast, he can be thrown overboard without further delay, as one who is seeking the ruin of all.[7]

He who has carefully weighed these cases, and others similar to them, if such occur, will not fear at all, lest therefrom follow the possibility of also doing harm to the life of a second person, in order to save some limb; and lest the matter come finally to such a pass that we feel any inconveniences of ours whatsoever can rightly be warded off to the damage of a second person. For the favour accorded the saving of one's own life does not attend other blessings in equal measure, and no law of humanity bids me to avert, with equal or greater inconvenience to myself, inconveniences of that kind from a second person; and so force cannot be employed here by a second person with any colour of right.

7. But, when the necessity has merely to do with the property of the other, or when our life can be saved only by the property of the other, there is scarcely any doubt but that, when no other means are available, this property can be appropriated by force, and against the will of the owner, who is not under pressure of the same necessity. And this is not on the basis of some exception, added or understood in the pact establishing private ownership in the first instance, namely, that, in a case of necessity, community of goods was to return,[8] but on the basis of the reason just given. And hence, if, by the exercise of violence, one man prevents another, when oppressed by such a necessity, from the use of the first man's property, it is not said properly of the first that he has done the second an injury, but merely that he has sinned against the law of charitable affection; nevertheless, the former would necessarily have to be said, if, indeed, private ownership ceasing to exist in this case, need should grant a right to property equal to the right of the possessor of it. Nor yet is a wrong done the owner, when a service, otherwise to be furnished by him as a voluntary agent, is, because of necessity, extorted from him as an unwilling person, especially when resti-

7. Cf. *JNG*, 2, 6, §3, referring to Jonah 1:7ff.
8. Allusion to Grotius, *JBP*, II.ii.6, according to which in cases of dire necessity things revert to original common ownership; cf. *JNG*, 2, 6, §6.

tution, at least by way of gratitude, is to be made in due time. But, in truth, just as in the case of need, which stood on the same footing with this, each man is naturally his own best friend; so also, a second person cannot take away from me by violence my property which I need quite as much as he does. Hence, we are of the opinion that the following is even less congruent with the truth: "The debtor left in extreme necessity is not now bound, the present moment having been fixed for payment, to restore the property to the creditor who is labouring under an equal necessity." For it is certain that the creditor in this case can rightly take away by force from the debtor the property owed <246> him. And yet it appears absurd for one properly to have the right of taking away any property from a second person by violence, if, indeed, in that second person there be no obligation to give him that property. For, that necessity makes things common, we have already denied, and the assertion that the legal position of the possessor is better, is valid only when the right of the claimant has not yet been clearly demonstrated. But the following case has very little doubt about it, whether, namely, when a conflagration has broken out, it may be permissible to tear down my neighbour's house, so as to save my own. For by that tearing down my neighbour suffers properly no loss at my hand, since his house was otherwise going to burn down; nor has he ground of complaint because his house succumbed to the hands of men rather than to the flame, so that in this way damage might be averted from his neighbours.

8. Now from the former fundamental law this general law flows: *Every one whatsoever ought to leave undone that which either weakens the use of the reason, or brings harm or ruin to the body.* The exercise of this law, although it terminates directly in each man's own person, does, nevertheless, altogether involve some regard for the preservation of society, and redounds consequently to its own advantage, in that it orders the very members who constitute society to preserve themselves, or so to attemper themselves that they may not be a burden both to themselves and to society. Nay more, it appears that there was scarcely any need for this law, and nature might have left each man to his own instinct regarding care for himself, had she not wished to destine man to the cultivation of a social life. Furthermore, from that law there flow the precepts of the law of nature *about composing the*

emotions and bringing them under the command [imperium] *of reason,*[9] for-asmuch as they hinder us in forming a right judgement about things, and frequently carry us off to those things which are harmful for ourselves and others; also the precept *about avoiding drunkenness,* since, in addition to the harm done the body, drunkenness very commonly casts down the mind from its station. And so drunkenness makes us tend in a direction opposite to the law of nature which altogether demands the use of reason for its observance. Now it makes no difference whether a man be acting directly contrary to his duty, or be voluntarily undertaking that by which he is rendered unfit for the performance of his duty. From that law comes likewise the precept *about avoiding irregular sex relations,* or those vile comminglings with one's own sex or with different species, which throw a foul stain upon body and mind, the dignity of human nature being violated by such shameful acts; aside from the fact that they tend directly to overturn the foundation of human society, which cannot endure without the propagation of the species. And finally the precept *about not mutilating one's members* (except, perchance, <247> for the safety of the whole body), *and not throwing one's life away, nature and obligation not demanding it.* But that a member already irreparably injured by some disease or accident can be separated from the body, so as not to infect and destroy the whole body with its contagion, is beyond doubt.

9. But there are those who start a controversy here, as though these matters were not enjoined by the law of nature, for the reason that instinct and sense appetite moved long since to such things with adequate force, and it was not necessary for man to be obligated to them by the law of nature. Now they understand here not merely one's own preservation, but also the appetite for society and matrimony, and the care and bringing up of offspring, which to some of the ancients were the first dictates of nature, in regard to which reason had place only in so far as to prevent a second person from being unjustly hurt by them. But, in truth, it is so far from following that the law of nature does not prescribe these matters, because natural

9. On the Stoic background to Pufendorf's doctrine of *cultura animi* [cultivation of the mind], see bk. I, Def. 11, note 2.

instinct long since moved toward them with sufficient keenness, that rather it clearly appears nature wanted them to be most carefully observed, as preserving the seed plot of the human race, in that, being doubtful of reason's dictate alone, she bade so strong a natural instinct support it, that man can with the utmost difficulty strive in the opposite direction. For, if there could be carefully weighed the troubles which necessarily attend human life, far exceeding that trifling and cheap amount of pleasures (and for how many life is prolonged so that they furnish fortune material on which to vent her fury!), how few there are who would not at the very first opportunity break off this life, if reason alone urged its preservation, and a natural instinct did not so carefully commend the love of it. Exactly as every day we see great numbers of men sin against those laws of nature which reason alone dictates. Thus how few there are who would take pains with their children, who often give occasion for grief, or at least furnish the most certain cause for cares and labours, were it not that, in addition to reason, natural inclination also propelled us in that direction. Especially as all this is attended by an act so little decorous and by intercourse with women, which would be both trivial and tedious to the wise man except for their allurements. We know, indeed, that the natural instinct and the dictate of reason, or law of nature, are utterly distinct things. In most matters also these two tend in the opposite direction, in such wise that instinct leads us away from that honourable course which reason urges. As man ought to overcome instinct when resisting reason, so the ability to overcome it belongs to the mind not degenerate. But to dull the point of that instinct which conspires with the dictate of reason, is the part of a madman. And so it is not the act of overcoming every natural instinct, which is connected with <248> praise, but only that instinct which strives against the dictate of reason. And, although instinct alone never obligates a person to do anything, nevertheless, it happens that we are obligated to something, to which we are inclined also by instinct, because the dictate of reason also prescribes the same. Just as also brutes for that reason cannot at all be said to be capable of legal right, even though, by instinct alone, they move to those things which tend to preserve the individual or the species. Nor, in truth, for that reason is a mother who kills her offspring in order to avoid disgrace, excused from a sin against the law of nature, although she be overcoming her instinct towards her offspring by another instinct, namely that of shrinking from disgrace. For the infant's life had been protected not by the mother's instinct alone, but also by the law, and the mother ought to have known that her disgrace is of less consequence than the death of that which came into being by that act to which she had herself previously consented. Hence, if her good name meant more to her than the pleasure of copulation or the love of her offspring, before copulation was performed she ought to have thought about that; but, afterwards, the offspring by no means deserves to die so that the parent's sin shall not become known. Now that it is not absurd or superfluous to ratify such matters by civil laws also, is shown clearly enough by laws of the Spartans and the Romans, among whom, to be sure, citizens were compelled to enter upon matrimony by rewards or through the fear of ignominy. As far as the law of nature is concerned, however, assuredly it enjoins matrimony upon all who are naturally capable of it, unless with the greatest probability they have foreseen that they will contribute more good to the human race by passing their life in chaste celibacy, than if they procreate their kind. However, since that is an affirmative precept, it will not obligate unless a convenient occasion has been given, and this is not to be measured merely by marriageable age, and the material means appropriate for that condition, but it is also to be borne in mind whether considerations for the status which one ought to maintain in the state, allow it.[10] Now when matrimony has been contracted, as the stimulation merely of the genital field is in our power, but the germination depends upon natural causes by no means subordinate to our free choice; so, for the same reason, he who has begotten but two children only, if, indeed, nature denies him more abundant progeny, satisfies the law of nature as well as he who has been made a parent by a wife fertile with numerous offspring.

10. Furthermore, it is not superfluous to have here considered the question how far that precept of the law of nature about preserving oneself extends, and whether one in spurning the sweetness of life, or for the purpose of avoiding great miseries, may hasten one's own fate. <249> Here, although it be extremely invidious to depart from the common persuasion, we shall see what can be said with probability only. We presuppose, there-

10. On matrimony see bk. II, Observ. 5, §4.

fore, what was demonstrated above, namely, that just as no one can properly be obligated to himself, so also he who has inflicted violence upon himself is doing himself no wrong. Now the reason that a man is obligated by the law of nature to preserve himself, seems to be that he has been destined by the Creator to cultivate human society, which he cannot at all abandon at will after the fashion of a deserter or a soldier who fails to appear. Now, since, on removing that consideration looking toward the social life, non-social man would have been without any obligation, like a brute, it appears that instinct alone would have commended to man the custody of his own life and body, and, since this instinct alone does not have the force of a law, he would also not have sinned, who had done something contrary to it. Because, therefore, our life, for the good of human society, has been fortified, as it were, by a law of nature, it follows that a man can, on the basis of an obligation enjoined upon him by his sovereign, or one which he himself in the exercise of reason undertakes in behalf of the safety of a number, undergo with deliberate purpose a peril of the kind from which he can with probability foresee that he will not escape with his life, except, perhaps, on some unexpected chance. And this is approved not merely by the consent and usage of all nations, but also the very histories subscribed with the divine authority [*autoritate*] glorify and praise those who for the king or their fellow citizens have entered upon danger threatening present death, although sometimes it has happened that, by their own valour, or some unexpected chance, they have escaped; and yet upon the hope of escaping death it was not permissible to undertake an act otherwise in itself illicit. Hence this much, at least, is well established, that by the law of nature a man may for the safety of a number undertake an act of a kind in which he foresees that his life will probably be lost. On this score even those ship captains can be excused who, when the enemy captures the ship, throw a lighted fuse into the powder and destroy themselves along with the enemy. Although the heads of the state ought carefully to consider whether it be to the public good for lower officers to be bound by such a necessity. And the same question is to be raised by a lower officer, if, indeed, he should undertake a thing of that kind upon merely the presumed will of his superiors.

However, what may be permissible beyond this case is a matter for deeper delving. Any one, indeed, would justly excuse from the crime of suicide those who, from a disease disturbing the use of the reason, lay hands upon themselves. For their acts, since they cannot be directed by reason, are not reckoned as moral acts; unless, perchance, in so far as they themselves were at fault for having lost the use <250> of the same. Nor does the question whether a person falls by his own hand, or in any way whatsoever forces others to put him to death, seem to have any bearing in the case. For he who did not owe it to die here and now, is not excused if he has used the hands of another in bringing about death, since, forsooth, he is reckoned as having done himself that which he does through the instrumentality of another; although he who has committed his hands to this ministration, can also contract guilt. In general, therefore, there come to be weighed the causes whereby a man has been moved to anything of the sort. For, if the cause be of the kind whereby he is going to preserve the safety of a number through his death, it appears that he can use the same excuses which are open to those who devote their lives for the public safety. But favour is merited, or at least pity, rather than a harsh judgement, is due also in the case of those who lay hands upon themselves, because, with a morally in-fallible certainty, they foresee that death with torture will soon thereafter be inflicted upon them by the enemy, and it does no good to the state for them to die at the free choice of a second person; or because they see di-rected against them by others something on the commission of which they will thenceforth be objects of disdain to the rest of men. Such persons are those who, when they see death at the hands of a truculent foe or tyrant hanging over their heads, have preferred to hasten their fate so as to escape tortures; likewise women who have avoided the violation of their chastity in this manner. With plausibility, indeed, can they put forward in excusing themselves, that, from so great a necessity brought to bear upon them they had gathered that their dismissal had already been given; also, that it is a small matter to anticipate death by so slight an interval of time, so as not to feel the torments and the insults which might, perchance, drive them to a grievous sin; and that nature does not appear to have wished to enjoin upon noble minds the necessity of altogether putting their life at the plea-sure of a second person, after first having been abused with contumely. But, truly, he who has voluntarily broken off his life out of sheer boredom at the annoyances common to life, or indignation at its evils, which were not going to render him useless in human society, or through fear of torture, by having endured which bravely he might have benefited others by his example—for him assuredly no excuse avails to prevent him from being regarded as having sinned against the law of nature.

11. As for the rest, just as the latter fundamental law obligates all men whatsoever to render one another in a free and friendly fashion what they owe, and, as a result of carefully observing that law, there results peace, which is the status best suited to human nature, and for the establishment and preservation of which the law of nature has <251> primarily been implanted in man: so, by the former law, war is licit and sometimes necessary, that is to say, when a second person has violated the latter law of nature in my case, and refuses to make good the damage incurred thereby. For here the former law about preserving myself gives me the authority to defend the welfare of myself or mine in any way at all (of course, where there is no chance to avail myself of a judge) against him who violates the same unjustly, notwithstanding the latter law which otherwise prohibits the doing of a hurt to the body and property of a second person. For, since the law of nature obligates all men equally to exercise towards one another the duties due on the score of the law of nature, it is assuredly patent, that, as long as another does for me that which the law of nature prescribes, I ought to do the same for him. But, in truth, when a second person violates right in his relations towards me, then assuredly it will be most impudent for the same man to demand from me that I continue to show him the offices of right, unless he has repented and binds himself to take them up again. Otherwise, also, all the goods which nature or industry has given us would have been granted in vain, if it were not permissible to oppose force to a second person unjustly violating them; and force, the proper means of acting in war, as it were, nature has allowed us to employ, where my welfare cannot be obtained by peaceful means. The exception, however, made by the obligation of subjects towards those who have supreme authority, is elsewhere explained.

12. Furthermore, there is need of force for a twofold purpose, either to defend myself and my property against him who is attempting to harm them; or else to compel another person to restore the damages already done

by him to me and to give a guarantee that he will not offend in the future; and from all this arises the distinction between defensive wars and offensive (just) wars. Now regarding defence, it is to be observed that the right of war or of exercising violence begins when the second person attempts to injure me, whether he do that of set purpose and of malice, or out of ignorance; suppose, for example, that he was mistaken in my person, or was affected by insanity. For by what cause soever the aggressor be impelled there is no obligation upon me to throw my life away as a favour to him. But the beginning of doing hurt is not merely defined by the performance of the actual hurt, but is also reckoned as existing already at the moment when a peril is clearly threatened, and it is apparent that the other is already manifestly preparing to attack me. Here it is assuredly stupid to offer yourself to the first blow; but force is rather to be brought to bear promptly, and he who is already preparing to hurt me must be forestalled. But an uncertain suspicion of peril, although it can persuade you to surround yourself with defences, nevertheless does <252> not give you the right to use force first,[11] not even to the end that the other furnish what they call a real guarantee not to give offence, that is to say, hostages, sureties, pledges, &c. For, as long as one man has not hurt the other, and is not caught in the very act of doing hurt, he surely has the presumption of being prepared to do his duty for the future also; especially if he confirm that presumption with words and by giving a pledge. From such a person one cannot rightly extort a guarantee by force; for this would make the latter to be in a condition inferior to that of the person himself, since the latter would be demanding to be believed without a guarantee, a thing which he refuses to do for the other without a guarantee. Therefore, either each should guarantee the other, which in such a case is useless and also absurd, unless both consent to that voluntarily from the beginning, or should be content with receiving and giving an assurance of good faith.

---

11. This is aimed against Hobbes, according to whom the mutual diffidence in the state of nature gives everyone the right to "master the persons of all men he can" in order to anticipate being mastered by them (*Leviathan,* chap. 13). For Pufendorf, as for Grotius, *JBP,* II.i.5, only an immediate and imminent danger justifies a defensive war (*JNG,* 8, 6, §5).

13. Now as to the intensity and mode of defence, the law of nature does not merely permit me to employ such as will preserve me and mine for the present, but, more than that, allows me to take measures to obtain a guarantee for the future, and while the other allows himself to be driven to this guarantee by force, he shows that he has still the mind to commit an offence against me in the future, and so, when I cannot obtain a more convenient guarantee, I can legally put him to death, even if the harm first directed against me by him has not touched my life. For, from him who has in me violated the law of nature in one matter, I can expect nothing of a friendly sort, unless of his own accord he come to his senses and satisfy me on the score of the damage, or give me a guarantee for the future. Nor does he receive wrong from me in that he suffers an evil greater than he was trying to inflict; because, while unjustly hurting me, he has left himself no right which will be of avail, at all events towards me, to prevent me from inflicting upon him any amount of violence whatsoever. But when a man unjustly hurts a second person, unless he hurt me indirectly at the same time, or unless I myself am under obligation to defend that other person against unjust violence, there does not come to me the right of bringing force to bear upon the first person, as long, indeed, as he shows no evidences of a hostile mind towards me. For a wrong done to a third person does not supply me with a morally firm certainty that he will also be doing wrong to me; since special causes which are not found in me may incite him against a third person. And yet I ought quite properly to be carefully on my guard against such a man. But, truly, in states where security is protected by the common forces of individuals, to undertake the defence of oneself and of one's own property by one's own private strength is allowed any one only when time does not permit us to call in public aid; and, indeed, only to the extent of putting outside of present peril my life, or property not admitting <253> of restitution; since, forsooth, the authority of the magistracy and the punishment to be inflicted upon the one doing hurt, furnish a guarantee adequate for the future. And so, he who in a state wishes to exercise in some case the control of blameless guardianship, ought to examine not merely the law of nature but also the positive civil laws.

14. Now it is to be observed further about war, that it is an unnatural status of men, permitted, nevertheless, by nature to man in a definite case,

to wit, when the wrongs done by a second person do not allow me to enjoy peace. For then nature allows me to employ all means of securing my safety against those who criminally attack it; for, along with care for himself, she implanted in man's mind a bitter sense of wrongs, so that he is unwilling to let himself be ruined through the wrongs done by others, and she armed his body with nimbleness and strength of hands so as not to be compelled to endure the same with impunity. But nature allows war only in such a way that he who wages it ought to set before himself peace as his end, or in other words, that both belligerents be allowed to exercise towards one another the offices of the law of nature, as well as to come into possession of their right and enjoy it without impediment. Otherwise, it is certain that those who wage war for war's sake only, trampling under foot the law of nature, lead the veriest life of brute beasts, who are at war with one another and with men, without any intention of securing peace.

15. Besides that, although he who has hurt me, immediately gives me the authority, as far as he is concerned, to wage war against him; nevertheless, one ought to take heed to see how much good or evil is going to redound therefrom to me or to others who have not hurt me. For the wrongs which do not utterly destroy my welfare I ought not to avenge in warfare, if either the disadvantages which are going to come upon me and mine therefrom outweigh the advantages; or if, on the occasion of my making war, there will come to others with whom I still cultivate peace, losses of a kind which, on the basis of the law of humanity, I ought to avert by tolerating un-avenged a wrong of the sort which has been inflicted upon me. Hence, rightly and laudably, any one whatsoever avoids avenging with warfare the injury done him, from the punishing of which it is judged that an evil greater than the good arises.

16. Now, since the performance of duties due on the basis of the law of nature ought to be mutual, in such wise that he who was the first to break them should absolve also the other person, as far as in him lies, from the obligation to observe the same towards him; it is readily apparent that he who has unjustly hurt me has on his side remitted to me whatever he otherwise could have demanded from me by the law of nature, and has destroyed all the intercourse of right <254> between us: And so he has given me the faculty of waging war against him, that is, of exercising force against

him without stint or limit.[12] And this not merely if he attacks my life, but even if he should knowingly and willingly direct some lesser evil against me. Because he has no more right to inflict upon me unjustly a buffet, than he has to kill me.[13] For the objection which some men raise here, namely, that retribution ought to be proportionate, has place only in tribunals where penalties are inflicted by superiors. But the things inflicted by right of war do not properly have the character of punishments, for they do not proceed from a superior as such, nor do they tend directly to the reformation of the one who does the hurt, or of other men; but to the defence and vindication of my welfare and my rights, which have been unjustly violated by the other. Here, since the one who does the damage has by his injury broken off the intercourse of right between us, it will be permissible for me to employ against him any force at all, openly or treacherously, until, induced by penitence, he has pledged his good faith once more to observe towards me for the future the offices of the law of nature. And all this is in place between those who do not recognize a common judge among men, whether they be individual moral persons, or composite, in other words, societies. For among members of the same society it is forbidden to exercise such a right of war. Here every one whatsoever is bound to commit to the magistracy the prosecution of his wrongs, except where the present crisis does not leave him time to call upon its aid.

17. But whether it be permissible to use promiscuously the service of any persons whatsoever in war, does not appear to some sufficiently clear. For a few make a distinction between traitors and deserters from their own mas-

---

12. Cf. Hobbes's "first and fundamental law of nature" (*Leviathan,* chap. 14): "every man, ought to endeavour peace, as far as he has hope in obtaining it; and when he cannot obtain it, that he may seek, and use, all helps, and advantages of war." For Hobbes the first part of that law (and the resignation of the right to everything that it implies) obliges "in effect then only when there is security" (that is, in the civil state). For Pufendorf, on the contrary, a peaceful law-bound state grounded in the reciprocal exercise of offices constitutes the natural state, properly speaking, while war, characterized by a "faculty . . . of exercising force . . . without . . . limit," forms an exceptional state even when civil authority is missing (see bk. I, Def. 3, §§5–6).

13. This refers to Grotius, *JBP,* II.i.10: "For although death and a blow are not on the same level, yet the man who makes ready to injure me by the very act confers on me a right, a sort of actual and unlimited moral right against him, in so far as otherwise I cannot ward off the injury from myself."

ters who offer themselves voluntarily, and those whose fidelity is corrupted by promises or through rewards, to wit, that the services of the former can properly be utilized even by the customs of nations, not so those of the latter.[14] Of this distinction, however, the mere right of war seems to be ignorant. For those two things which are striven for in seducing the subjects of my enemy, namely, to strip him of aids and defenders, and besides to inflict damage upon him, both of them, assuming a just cause for war, I have the right to do. And no sufficient reason appears why I should not be permitted to attain that end even by corrupting through hope of rewards the minds of his citizens. For, since even those individuals who come over to me are in the number of the enemy against whom war gave the licence to vent my rage with violence, and I can exercise or remit that violence as the consideration of my interests demands; it will assuredly be permissible for me to acquit them, as it were, from all the fury of war, and, more than that, heap certain blessings upon them, and this either wholly *gratis,* or under the condition that they <255> perform for me a certain useful deed, to wit, that without trouble on my part, they separate themselves from my enemy, or do something additional which is of value to me. And although, perchance, they cannot do this without committing a crime themselves; nevertheless, no blame seems to redound to me from this, because there appears no obligation for me to avoid that which looks like the most convenient way to get my right, so as not to give an occasion for wickedness to those who, by their doing me wrong, have suspended the intercourse of right with me. Especially, since whatever solicitations be brought to bear upon them in any case, it is left in their own free choice whether they want to have me for an enemy, or to buy back my friendship on terms laid down by myself. But the reason why, in peace, I may not, for example, tempt a second person's servant to desert his master and come over to me, is twofold: partly because I have no proper authority to defraud him of his property; and partly because I could not rightly inflict any evil upon the servant himself, if by that very act of fleeing over to my side he should not conciliate me to himself; but both of these conditions appear in our case. And hence, the objection otherwise made to this view, namely, that it is impossible for

14. Ibid., III.i.21–22.

one person to incite another to that in doing which the other is sinning, or, in other words, he who gives a second person cause for sinning is himself sinning, seems to be valid only between non-enemies. For an enemy, in respect to me, is in such a status, that, while I am prosecuting against him my right, I do not have to care whether he find therein an occasion for sinning or not. But if, however, a man should prefer to say that, although on such a score no right either of him who is tempted or of the principal enemy suffers damage, nevertheless, such a way of harming enemies ought to be avoided, because the law of nature wishes the licence of war, as far as possible, to be tempered to the mode in which vindicative justice is commonly exercised in peace, he would not find us strongly resisting him.

18. But, in truth, that latitude of licence in war has been greatly restricted, partly by the usage of nations, which has declared certain methods of destroying the enemy to be illicit or indecorous, and in favour of warlike fortitude has established a certain intercourse, as it were, of arms, so that the victor should not interpret unfortunate valour as a crime; or because it was also to the interest of the innocent that the injuries done by those who set on foot unjust wars should be more endurable; but especially by the law of nature. For, as the latter has granted men war only as a sort of extraordinary means of establishing peace; so it has also desired that the just warrior, in regard to the foe, should restrict as far as it might be his to do so, the violence which the latter had no right to keep from ravening without stint or limit, to the customary method of exacting punishment and making restitu-<256>tion for damage in time of peace. Hence, there are very many things that the enemy can suffer without wrong, which, however, the humane victor rightly avoids inflicting. Thus, in a public and just war, even if all who are within the enemy's lines, even those who have been caught there by fate, even women and children, be regarded as enemies; nevertheless, the leader observant of humanity ought not to kill any one, except as a just penalty, or in so far as without doing so he cannot protect his own life and property and those of his men, and only for great causes and such as will bring about the welfare of many may he try anything of a kind that may threaten to bring ruin upon the innocent. From this it is well established that boys ought not to be killed, or women, unless they have done something calling for special punishment, or take upon themselves the of-

fices of men. Nor are males to be killed whose mode of life is alien to arms, such as are those who attend to things sacred, husbandmen, merchants, workmen, and artisans making a living from peace, likewise those who give themselves up, suppliants, &c., unless they have especially committed a deed worthy of death. It is humane also to remit something from an extreme right on account of the multitude of those who have deserved death. On this score, also, are prohibited all those acts which are of no use for attaining our right or for finishing the war, but have as their object the mere demonstration of strength. Similarly, although the injury done by the enemy allows me an unlimited licence in regard to his property, nevertheless, the law of humanity demands that I destroy none of the enemy's property except because of necessity, or in compensation of a debt and of the expense incurred in securing it, or in place of a fine, as it were, equal to the wrong done by the enemy. Now no fruitful thing is by any means to be destroyed, which one holds in such wise that it cannot be profitable to the enemy, nor, although it be in doubtful possession, is a field to be laid waste if there be a great hope of speedy victory, whose reward will be both the field and the fruit, or if the enemy have any other source from which he can sustain himself. Nor is property to be destroyed which is of no consequence either for making war or for carrying it on. Nor may hands be rashly laid upon things sacred or religious, nor is one to descend lightly to the violent plundering or demolition of cities. Thus, since ravishing matrons and virgins contributes nothing to the attainment of our right or to the establishment of peace, the humane enemy will consider rather what he can reputably inflict upon the other party, than what he can inflict with impunity. Thus, although the injury which the enemy has done, creates for us the licence, as far as he is concerned, to reduce to servitude all who have been captured in war, and to exercise an unlimited authority over slaves; nevertheless, it will be the part of humanity (where this kind of servitude has not been abrogated <257> by custom) not to go ravening about in the infliction of servitude, except in so far as the amount of the original debt, or of that which arises later, allows, or unless, perchance, in the case of some persons there be a special misdeed, which deserves to be punished with loss of liberty. Upon those caught in such a position the right of life and death is to be exercised with the same religious scruples as by a public judge; as regards lesser punishments clemency is to be shown, services are to be demanded in a moderate measure, and attention is to be paid in a humane fashion to the health of slaves. Likewise, if they have saved something by denying themselves, it is to be left to them, and is not to be taken away from them except upon the demand of necessity; and after long or highly useful ministrations, liberty is to be granted. Thus, in the matter of reprisals, a man will be acting humanely, if to those who are free from the guilt of injury he leaves their property, which he can more readily do without than they, especially if it be apparent that they will not recover from their own state what they have lost in such a way. Nor is this right to be rashly exercised upon the goods of innocent subjects, as long as there is hope that we can obtain our own with sufficient ease from the original debtors, or those who have made the debt their own by not according us our right. Most things of that kind, however, regarding the licence of war, which we have called restricted by the law of humanity, are commonly said to be licit on the basis of the Law of Nations; not because they have their origin properly in an agreement of the nations (for not to have employed them deserves the very greatest praise among the more civilized nations); but because, by a certain common custom among the more civilized nations, he who has employed these means for his own advantage or through the violence of his passions, and for the purpose of striking terror into others, is not regarded as a barbarian.

19. But, in truth, because nature has granted us the faculty of waging war merely for the purpose of having our security established against those who disturb our peace, but, as for the rest, in every war bids a secure peace to be regarded as the end, and to be preserved, where it can be had conveniently; hence, the law of nature ordains for the ending of wars, *that one party, after taking a guarantee for the future, grant the other pardon for the past, when he asks for it and repents:*[15] that is, one is to make peace with the one who gave cause for the war by doing the harm, after he has repented of the injury, made restitution for the damage done, and asked for peace.

---

15. The Latin text (*ut alter alteri, sumta cautione futuri temporis, praeteriti veniam, petenti & poenitenti concedat*) almost literally agrees with Hobbes's fifth precept of natural law (*De cive,* chap. 3, §10: *oportere alterum alteri, sumtâ cautione futuri temporis, praeteriti veniam petenti & poenitenti, concedere*).

For when the other has offered peace, I have no longer left a just cause for fighting against him. Now to concede peace to one not asking for it, that is to say, still retaining a hostile spirit, and not furnishing a guarantee for the future, that is <258> to say, looking for an opportunity to do more grievous hurt, is to betray one's own safety through craven fear. It is, however, commonly received among the nations, for reasons adduced elsewhere, and because those who did the harm would, from the fear of disgrace, bring themselves only with the utmost difficulty to peace by confessing that they had done wrong, that, in making peace, the parties are treated as equals in regard to the justice of the war, especially when they enter upon the peace with the forces on both sides equal.

With this precept is related the one that *security and safety is to be accorded the mediators of peace,* since, forsooth, they are labouring upon a thing ordained by nature, which they cannot do, unless adequate provision has been made for their security.

20. From the same foundation principle proceeds also the following, namely, that *in imposing punishment upon men precaution against future evil is alone to be regarded* (for the payment of damages is not properly punishment), that is to say, that either he who did the wrong should be reformed, or others warned by his punishment should be afraid to do wrong, and so the severity of a punishment is to be tempered as such action seems to be required for attaining that end.[16] For, in exacting a punishment, to look merely at the past misdeed and to punish with the end merely of making it hard for the wrongdoer, is the part of a man who rejects peace, where it can be had, and of one who thinks of war instead of the end of war. For the man whom I so hold under my authority that I can inflict punishments upon him, I must certainly so hold bound that I can obtain from him also a guarantee not to offend in the future. Beyond that end there appears no reason why a man should wish or rightly be able to bring evil for any deed whatsoever upon one who shares the same nature.

21. We have mentioned another fundamental law of nature: *The social life is to be preserved by men towards one another, nor is anything to be done that will result in disturbing it.* That social life is contained in pretty much

16. See bk. I, Def. 12, note 44.

these general offices, namely, that a hurt be done no man in person or in property without some antecedent deed of his by which there is brought to us the licence or necessity of hurting him; and that any one whatsoever should furnish a second person of his own accord and without the application of external coercion, quite as much that which is owed him on the basis of obligations especially entered into, as that which common kinship demands. Such are generally held to be things in which we can help another without inconvenience to ourselves, for example, to indicate the way to a man who is lost, or who asks it of us; to allow the use of flowing water for purposes of watering, where our ground is not made worse thereby; to grant innocent passage, and that which does not tend to any one's injury, through our lands on a public way, especially where adequate precautions are taken, <259> and there is no danger from contagion; not to spoil that which neither hurts nor helps me, but can be useful to another; to grant shipwrecked men the use of the shore, and the like. But the following also is required by the force of that precept, namely, that each person whatsoever freely unite himself to those special societies which necessity, or a marked advantage of life, has recommended be established.

22. Now since that obligation to cultivate the social life attends upon human nature as such, it is clear that the same binds all men equally and all men are equal in so far that, no matter how great be the blessings of mind and body in which some one surpasses the rest of men, he has no more right than the rest to inflict wrongs upon other men; just as also, on the contrary, the insufficient liberality of nature in itself, or an humble estate by itself condemns no one to be worse circumstanced in regard to the enjoyment of a common right among men than others.[17] He who disdains this equality can show himself to be no more helpful a member of human society than he who desires to live in some particular society, and yet is not zealous to adjust himself to its laws. And this equality has the force of a mutual agreement, by which a second person is no longer bound, if the first falls away from it, and besides he receives the right of compelling

17. See *Statu*, §13: "Indeed, the equality we principally mean here consists not only of the fact that no one is entirely exempted from or more loosely bound than another by men's equal obligation to observe the law of nature toward one another." The idea of the universality of law presupposes the axiom of equality.

the first person by force to make good his agreements. For he also who has not treated others according to the terms of a common obligation, cannot refuse to have his own examples practised on himself, and besides that be forcibly brought to order by the rest. This equality, however, is to be understood without any antecedent human deed, whereby it is restricted either on consent, or on account of misdeed, as far as concerns the action which comes to the injured party against the injurer. For, although whoever has not treated another according to the prescript of the same law, has equally violated the law of nature; nevertheless, on account of the necessity of supreme sovereignties, it was expedient for the human race that those men upon whom sovereignty has been bestowed, should herein be of a slightly better condition, in so far that others may not have the faculty of bringing them to order, even if, perchance, in some matters they may have violated the law of nature. And this, not because they themselves do not in that matter sin equally with others, but because in their case the force of supreme sovereignty renders those subject to them unfit to coerce them; since, otherwise, all the efficacy of sovereignties would be overturned, if, between subjects and sovereigns you should wish to devise some reciprocal authority to exact punishment because of a violation of a law of nature. The odium of this prerogative, however, if there be any, is made milder partly because it is brought about by the prerogative in question that the rest enjoy an equal right in a more secure manner among themselves; and partly because others consent to it, and this either of <260> set purpose and directly, or else indirectly, by the infliction of a wrong upon the other person, and while the latter sets out to repress it by force, he acquires at the same time sovereignty over him from whom the injury proceeded.

From equality, so as to add this also here in passing, one may otherwise readily infer on what score things ought to be divided among several,[18] to wit, so that, other things being equal, if the right of individuals be equal, things may be divided into equal shares. But what cannot be divided is to be used in common, if that may be done, and to the amount that any one wishes, if the quantity of the thing permits. If, however, the quantity does not permit, then it is to be utilized with a fixed limit and in proportion to

18. See bk. I, Def. 5, §§15ff.

the number of users. But, if a thing can neither be divided nor possessed in common, its use should either be alternate, or be assigned to one man only by lot, for a more convenient means cannot here be devised. Such lot is either arbitrary, that is, cast with the consent of the contestants and directed by mere chance; or natural, like first occupancy and primogeniture. Concerning these kinds of lot this procedure is commonly observed, namely, that the arbitrary lot is employed where several compete for something to which they have acquired for themselves a right by some antecedent act; but the natural lot, when no one has acquired for himself the right to the thing in question by some antecedent act. Hence, things which are regarded as derelict go to the one who first takes them up, and the hereditary indivisible dignity of the father goes to the first-born, unless disposition shall have been made otherwise by an express statute.

23. From the preceding fundamental law flows this general one: *Let no one so bear himself towards a second person that the latter can properly complain that this equality of right has been violated in his case.* (Now that is especially true if one's own right be violated by a second person.) This right has to do with those things which by nature or from the institution of men have been so specially assigned some man, that, if they should not be vouchsafed, be taken away, or be injured by a second person against his will, he is offended. This law breaks up into a number of special laws.

24. I. *Let no one do harm to the body of a second person.* By this law are prohibited not merely those things which directly hurt the body, but also those which do so as a consequence, for example, terror, and the like, which excite the more gloomy emotions, whereby not merely the mind, but also the body is grievously afflicted. Chastisements, however, inflicting a moderate pain to the body, whereby children especially, or servile dispositions are admonished to do the right, or to abstain from evil, are not included here. But, by the institution of men, this kind of chastisement is not granted to any one whatsoever to exercise upon any one else whatsoever, but has been assigned to <261> definite persons enjoying a special kind of authority over others, and this for the sake of avoiding disturbances which might arise, if the one chastised were not convinced of the good intent of the chastiser, and if he should interpret what is in itself an office of hu-

manity[19] as a wrong coming from an unfriendly mind. Hence, if, for example, a man who had not been authorized to do so by the parent should chastise the son of a second person, unless, perchance, he be doing so on the presumed desire of the parent, he is doing an injury to the parent as well as to his son. To the latter, because either by law or by custom he was not bound to endure chastisement by a stranger; to the former, because, against the will and without the knowledge of the master, he is usurping another's authority. From this law are also excepted corporal punishments justly imposed by magistrates because of antecedent misdeeds. For these furnish no cause for complaint, since he who unites himself to a state subjects himself also to its laws, and he knew that these punishments had been constituted for those who violate them, especially since the rest of his fellow citizens enjoy also the same condition.

25. II. *Let no one violate the chastity of a woman against her will.* For women are esteemed primarily by its preservation. But that those who mutually consent ought not to indulge a roving passion, that is, when they do it merely for the satisfaction of lust, follows because they are thereby assailing the foundations of human society, which by those enticements wished to promote the propagation of the species. But if they intend to secure offspring, they are disturbing civil society, whose harmony is to the highest degree involved in scrupulous observance of marriage. But virgins who have the hope of marriage sin in a special manner when they consent to the defloration of their chastity. For thenceforward they offer damaged goods instead of sound to purchasers.

26. III. *Let no one detract from the good name of a second person, or lessen the esteem in which he is held.* For the soundness of this esteem in communal life builds, as it were, a road to most advantages from which those who are aspersed with infamy are excluded. Also every person is regarded by those to whom he is not very intimately known, as being the sort of man that

---

19. This view of castigation as an "office of humanity" is derived from Luther's conception of the secular office as a service toward your neighbor and an act of charity. See *W.A.*, 1. dept., vol. 21, p. 307: "Und ist solch Straff ampt ein Werck der goettlichen und Christlichen Liebe, Denn solchs hat Gott auch Vater und Mutter stand auffgelegt, da doch die höheste Liebe gegen jre Kinder von Gott in die Natur gepflantzet ist."

common report makes him out to be. Besides, to be despised by others and treated with contumely affects the minds of men with a most bitter feeling and is the very greatest stimulus to wars; and, in general, the more high spirited a man is, the more incensed he is at being insultingly rated lower by a second person than he esteems himself.

27. IV. *Let no one pollute in adultery the wife of a second person.* For, by the nuptial pacts, the husband acquired the right that his wife should not be available for the sensual pleasures of any second person whatsoever, to wit, that he may not be compelled to nurture another's <262> offspring as his own. By this precept males, both unmarried and married, are prohibited from abusing the bridal bed of a second person. And wives are obligated, on the basis of the law about observing pacts, to lend their bodies to no one but their husbands, a thing which also the end of matrimony altogether requires. Any such behaviour with the consent of the husband (although otherwise it is permissible for him to grant the use of his property to a second person) is prohibited by divine laws and among most nations also by civil laws, which have circumscribed the propagation of so noble a being with great religious scrupulousness, as it were.[20] On the strength of the same pact, also, the husband, whether monogamy or polygamy have been introduced by positive laws, ought not to bestow himself upon other women except his wives; although the misdeeds of husbands under this head, when, perchance, they have happened to find some loose woman, do by no means so directly conflict with the end of matrimony as does faithlessness on the part of wives.

28. V. *Let no one usurp, corrupt, or purloin the property of a second person against his will.* For, since the tranquillity of social life does not allow those things which a man needs for self-preservation to be possessed in common and used promiscuously by any one whatsoever,[21] on the basis of a mutual agreement each one has such a right to what he has properly acquired that there is left to others no authority to dispose of it, much less to corrupt it or take it away. And this principle is valid as much in regard to things incorporeal as corporeal. For he who prevents some one from using his au-

20. See bk. I, Def. 13, §6.
21. See bk. I, Def. 5, §15.

thority or sovereignty is just as guilty in regard to this law as he who furtively or by open violence takes away his money.[22]

29. VI. *Let every man whatsoever furnish what he owes on a pact or on his pledged word.* For, since there are a very great many things which can be furnished by a man for the use of a second person above and beyond those offices comprehended in the general law of humanity, in order for a man to be able to demand these things by right and to erect his calculations, as it were, upon them, it was necessary to the preservation of society among men, that, when a second person has, as it were, accepted my consent expressed in signs in regard to furnishing some matter, there should arise in me, indeed, an obligation or internal necessity to furnish the thing agreed upon, and for the other the right of exacting it. And these agreements are called pacts, by the scrupulous observance of which societies among men are held together as by a very firm bond, and, when they have been violated, the most just causes for complaint arise. For if, indeed, I have furnished something on the basis of the pact, while the other betrays my confidence in him, my property or effort has perished in vain; but if I have as yet furnished nothing, it is none the less annoying to have my calculations <263> upset, and it is contrary to my deserts for me, when accepting the other's good faith, to be made a laughing stock. Now why one should accept the other's good faith, even when no further guarantee has been given, or why it should be judged that there is some force in the giving of good faith, comes from this, namely, that, since there is no more convenient bond than this for preserving the social life of men to which nature has destined them, any one whatsoever is presumed to be ready to attemper himself to this end, as long, indeed, as his acts have not manifested the contrary.

30. VII. *Let a man make good the damage he has done to a second person by his own fault.* For I should be in an inferior status, if the malice or folly of a second person could bring it about that I should be compelled against my will to go without my own property gratis. Now we are properly said to be suffering damage in regard to those things to which we duly have a

---

22. For the broad sense of *damnum* [damage] as including any "injury which concerns a man's body, reputation and virtue" (*JNG,* 3, 1, §3), likewise for the different kinds of damages listed in §30 and their corresponding obligations of restitution, the main source is Grotius, JBP, II.xvii; cf. *JNG,* 3, 1.

perfect right, to wit, where what we now possess is either hurt, destroyed, or taken away, or else where what is due on the basis of a pact or a civil law, is not given us. For if those things be denied us to which the law of nature has given us merely an imperfect right or aptitude, it is not properly judged to be damage; and so we do not duly have therefrom the faculty of bringing one to restitution. But that a person be bound, as far as in him lies, to see to it that the property of the second person which has come into his own hands in a blameless manner should return to the real owner, that is to say, to indicate or to confess that such property is in his possession, and to restore it when its return is asked for, is based upon the universal law of humanity about caring for every one's advantage and warding off damage, as far as that can be done without inconvenience or damage to oneself. For man's obligation to the social life demands that he ought not to acquire something for himself, or treat as a legitimate matter of gain, that which is connected with the damage of a second person not deserving the same; nor to count it as damage if he goes without an undeserved profit, which he knows he cannot keep without the damage of a second person not deserving the same. However, because I am obliged to do this by a general bond, the other party cannot, assuredly, demand that, in saving his property, I should suffer damage to my own property; and so he will be bound to refund to me at least the expense to which I was put in saving his property, unless, perchance, some special arrangement has been made upon this point by positive laws. Now, as damage can be done to a second person directly or indirectly in a very great many ways, so the law about making good the damage, divides into a very great many particular laws, some of which we shall subjoin here in a haphazard manner, as it were. <264>

(1) The man who has defrauded a second person in the matter of a contract is bound to make good the amount which the other has accepted less than was just, and, if an interval of time has elapsed, with the difference which that makes. Under this law are included those who defraud workmen of their due reward or a part of it; those who do not pay their stipends to men who have let them any kind of service; those who bargain for a higher reward than their services are worth; merchants who force purchasers to pay an unfair price; those who use an unfair measure or weight; those who substitute counterfeit for genuine money, to whom, however, it will be pos-

sible to return that same counterfeit money upon another occasion at the same rate at which they gave it out, although by no means to a third person, forasmuch as the wrong received from a second person gives me no privileges over a third, &c. (2) The borrower is bound to make it good if anything in the matter borrowed has been spoiled, or if it has utterly perished, unless it would altogether have perished even with its owner. (3) The one who receives a mandate is bound to make it good to the giver of the mandate, if any damage has been done by his fault or his bad faith in regard to the matter entrusted to him. (4) The one who gives surety ought not to lose what he has spent for the sake of the one for whom surety was given. (5) The loss or destruction of a pledge brought about by the creditor's fault is imputed to him towards the payment. (6) He who being bound to do something gratis *ex officio,* was unwilling to do it without receiving pay, ought to restore the same. (7) The magistrate who has not employed those remedies which can and ought to be used to prevent highway robbery and piracy, is bound to make good the damage done to travellers by land and sea. (8) The debtor who was to blame for the creditor's being compelled to incur expense in order to obtain his right is bound to pay back that expense, and he who rashly engages in a lawsuit is condemned to pay the costs of the trial. (9) The advocate who raises obstructions with calumnies and quibbles so that the other person may not be able to obtain his right is bound to pay the amount of damage which the other person has received from that delay. (10) The true debtor, even if he has been absolved before a court by an unfair sentence, remains a debtor, nevertheless, in nature; although a subject, because of the efficacy of civil sovereignty over him, cannot prosecute his right, even against an unjust sentence. (11) In a certain people, those who, by not paying what they owed, or by not rendering justice, have given cause for taking pledges, are bound to make good the damages to others who have unfairly lost something on that account. (12) He who orders, gives counsel, helps, supplies a place of refuge, does not forbid by a command, or does not give aid to the one on whom a loss is inflicted, when he can and ought to on the basis of a perfect obligation; who does not <265> dissuade when he ought to; or keeps silence about a deed which he was bound to make known on the basis of a perfect obligation, is bound to restore as much as he contributed to the damage, and, if restitution cannot be obtained from the one who did the original hurt, to restore the whole amount. (13) He who has promised something in view of a certain thing which he has neglected to look into, or if on purpose he has not expressed his meaning correctly, is bound to make good the amount of damage which the other has suffered therefrom. (14) He who by guile has caused a man to fall into an error in view of which he was induced to promise, is bound to make good whatever damage the promisor has incurred from that error. (15) If he to whom a promise is made, or with whom a contract is entered into, has brought to bear unjust fear, as a consequence of which the promise or the contract resulted, he is bound to absolve the promisor, if, indeed, the latter so wish. (16) He who has promised another person's deed is bound to what it amounts to, if he has failed on his side to do what he could perform with the purpose of getting the thing done. (17) Those who exercise monopolies, when, by an agreement, they bring about the sale of commodities at a price above that which is at present the highest in ordinary traffic; or when, by force or fraud, they prevent a larger supply from being imported; or buy up wares so as to sell them at a price which is unfair at the time of sale, are bound to make good that which others lose on this account. (18) An unjust homicide (that is, one who has killed a man who had a right not to be killed by him; a right which is not in the man, who, on a challenge, enters upon a fight with a second person or attacks a second person unjustly, because these men are regarded as having renounced that right; although this circumstance does not interfere with the possibility of their being punished by a magistrate, as far as the deed concerns him) is bound to pay the outlay, if any has been made, upon physicians; and to give as much to those whom the slain man was in duty bound to support as their expectation of sustenance, considering the age of the slain person, amounts to. (19) He who has mutilated some one is bound to make good the expense incurred in curing the wound, and the estimate of that which the person mutilated has now lost in his capacity to make gain. (20) Adulterers ought not merely to free the husband from the expense of supporting the offspring of adultery, but also to make it good to the legitimate children, if they suffer any damage from competition in regard to the inheritance on the part of offspring thus brought into the world. (21) He who has deflowered a virgin by force or fraud, is bound to pay her back the value of the loss to her hopes of marriage. (22) The thief by stealth and the thief by open violence are <266> bound to restore the thing taken, together with its natural increment, and together with the subsequent damage and the loss of profit, as also, if the thing is lost, at least a moderate estimate of its value. The same is owed by those who have done damage by an unjust judgement, an accusation directed by calumny, or false testimony. (23) Those who take part in an unjust war are obligated to make good the expenses and damages which by their efforts they have caused him who is waging a just war. (24) In an unjust war whoever has done damage is bound to make it good. Generals are bound on the score of what has been done under their leadership; all the soldiers who have joined in some common act, as, for example, the burning of a city, are bound for the whole; in divisible acts, each one is bound for the damage of which he was the sole cause or among the causes. (25) The leader who has not paid his soldiers the wages due is obligated not merely to the soldiers, but is also bound to make good to his subjects or neighbours the damages which his soldiers have been compelled by want to inflict upon them. (26) A subject who defrauds the magistracy of a part of its revenues or taxes, either by concealing some of his goods or resources, or in any other way, is bound to restore that which has been kept from the magistracy in that fashion, by whatever title the same holds sovereignty, provided only that the citizens have expressly or tacitly subjected themselves to it, notwithstanding the fact that the portion which the subject keeps out, seems to him to have been imposed above what was a fair measure, unless the magistracy itself remit such to its subjects, or renounce the claim in question. This renunciation, however, does not cause the subject's previous act to have been no misdeed. (27) Whoever himself takes by unjust violence and keeps another's property is bound to restore it together also with what the act amounts to, even though the person despoiled shall have himself renounced it "for the sake of buying off trouble," as men commonly say; and this, whether he seek to get it back or not. For renunciation of that kind, since it has been extorted by unjust force, does not prevent one from being in duty bound to restore the whole on the basis of the law of nature. But when one has offered again to its owner a thing which was stolen, and he has refused to receive it, then, and only then, does the former begin to possess it on the title of donation, as it were.

From all these laws it is patent that the most harmful person is most heavily in debt; and each is understood to be owing to a second person the exact amount of damage which he has done him by guile or through neglect.

31. VIII. *Let no one in his own controversy lay down the law for himself, but let him debate it in the presence of arbitrators.* It is of most frequent occurrence among men, even those men who are zealous to <267> observe the laws of nature, that controversies arise regarding the proper application of the laws to special facts, to wit, whether what has been done be contrary to the laws, or not (which controversies are called questions of law). Here, assuredly, before anything can be demanded from a second person by law, it ought to be well established which person's intention corresponds with the law. Neither party of the litigants can rightly claim for himself the faculty to define that matter. For, let us assume that either one wishes to look seriously into his own case and return a candid judgement, the other is, nevertheless, not bound to stand by that judgement; because, as among equals, no reason can be given why the latter ought rather to follow the opinion of the former, than the former that of the latter (for if both agree there remains no further controversy). Also any one will always be judged to favour himself more than the other person. It is necessary, therefore, for both parties to a dispute about some matter to agree upon some third person, whose opinion they obligate themselves by a mutual pact to follow.[23] Now there should by no means be any flying to arms immediately, for arms can rightly be drawn only upon him who is caught in the act of doing wrong, although, perchance, out of stubbornness he himself deny it. For, to attack some one in warfare on account of a case not yet ascertained, amounts to pronouncing in one's own case, a thing which nature allows only for manifest injury.

32. IX. *Let the arbitrator show himself fair to both sides.* For those who engage in controversy with one another come before the arbitrator as being themselves worthy of an equal right. And when he, beyond what is just, favours one side more than the other, there arise immediately causes for complaints, and matter for wars is ready at hand. From this it follows, that,

---

23. The discussion of arbitration in the natural state in §§31ff largely paraphrases Hobbes, *De cive,* chap. 3, §§20, 23–24.

between the arbitrator and the two sides there ought to intervene no pact or promise by the force of which the former is bound to pronounce in favour of either side. But a pact cannot intervene also between the same parties, by the force of which the arbitrator is obligated to pronounce what is fair or what he thought was fair. The reason for that is not so much because, otherwise, by the law of nature, the arbitrator would be bound to pronounce what seems just, to the obligation of which law nothing can be added on the basis of a pact, and so, such a pact would be superfluous; as, that in this wise the purpose of having taken an arbitrator would be rendered vain, and the process would go on infinitely. For a pact of that kind is so to be conceived as that the two sides promise to place themselves under the judgement of the arbitrator, if, indeed, he have rendered a fair decision. But if, accordingly, his decision afterwards appear unfair to either of the two sides, or be in fact unfair, a controversy would again arise regarding the fairness of the decision. Since the settlement of that question could not properly belong either to the arbitrator or to the <268> parties in dispute, there would have to be recourse necessarily to another arbitrator; and if again doubt should arise about this one's decision, once more another arbitrator will have to be appointed, and so on infinitely. But, where questions of fact are to be decided by an arbitrator, to wit, when the question is raised whether a thing was really done which is said by one side to have been done, the judge ought likewise to show himself fair to both sides, and, in fairness to both, believe neither, because at the same time they are asserting contradictory statements to be true. But, when signs do not bring us to the knowledge of the truth, the decision will have to be rendered according to the statement of witnesses, who ought not to be so bound to either side that they can scarcely be fair to the other.

33. X. *Do not allow the one who, trusting to your humanity, has been the first to do you a benefaction, to be any the worse off on that account;* or, in other words, *Let the one who was the first to receive a benefaction, see to it that the other does not repent of having done it.*[24] This is what happens when he

---

24. The Latin text (*Ne eum, qui fiducia humanitatis tuae prior tibi benefecerit, eam ob rem deterioris esse conditionis patiare:* seu; *Ut qui prior beneficium accepit, operam det, ne alterum dati poeniteat*) agrees almost verbatim with Hobbes's third precept of natural

who has received a benefaction gives no sign to the one who did it, that it was gratefully received, and neglects an opportunity to do the like; or, what is wont frequently to follow thereafter, repays with hatred instead of gratitude. In this, although there be done no wrong properly so called, since, forsooth, some right acquired by pacts is not violated, and that which is furnished upon a pact is not customarily called a benefaction; nevertheless, ingratitude is reckoned an odious and detestable thing, both because it destroys all beneficence among men and the first steps in winning goodwill, and because to be unwilling to show that the second person is by no means deceived in his creditable opinion of you, is the part of an extremely ignoble mind. In returning benefactions, however, it is not necessary for us to return exactly the same as that which was given us amounted to, but merely as much as we can conveniently. Hence to keep the reputation of being grateful is possible even for him who has by no means such faculties as would enable him to make a like return to his benefactors.

34. XI. *Let no one deceive a second person by signs devised to express the feelings of the mind.* For, since it was of the utmost concern to human society that men might be able to know among one another the feelings of the mind, and this cannot be achieved except through definite signs, it was altogether necessary for a definite force to be ascribed by tacit agreement to those signs, by the intervention of which it was permissible to judge of the feeling of a second person, and to communicate thoughts with one another. Now, although these signs do not produce an infallible, but only a probable certainty regarding the mind of the other person, men being ready to simulate and dissimulate anything; nevertheless, it was in one way or another sufficient for the preservation of society, that, especially in regard to acts < 269 > by which some obligation is to be contracted, the same signs should be valid in that sense which common usage and the present business showed. Now those signs are sounds of the voice or articulate words, either formed by the tongue, or later expressed in writing; an instrument which is so much more convenient for nurturing the social life, as men enjoy a

---

law (*De cive,* chap. 3, §8: *Ne eum qui fiduciâ tui tibi prior benefecerit, eam ob rem, deteriore conditione esse patiaris, sive ne accipiat quisquam beneficium, nisi animo nitendi ne dantem dati meritò poeniteat*).

more voluble tongue and more nimble hands than the rest of living creatures.[25] Now the power to signify this or that definitely does not inhere in
the words by nature or by some intrinsic necessity, but by the choice of
men. It is no presumption to the contrary that Adam is said to have imposed
upon things, with the very best reason, names derived from their proper
nature; and that in any languages whatsoever there are some primitive
words from which the rest are derived more by reason than by free choice.
For, although we concede that to animals and certain other things, names
were given denoting their nature or principal affection; nevertheless, those
primitive words themselves from which these have been derived, come from
mere free choice. Now, afterwards, although cognate words were for the
most part given in turn to cognate things, preserving in most of them the
conformity of inflexion which men call analogy; still analogy is not everywhere present, since a number of words follow a course peculiar to themselves, and analogy itself, also, consisting of a definite flexion and combi-
nation of words, has likewise been determined by free choice. Now,
although there are also other signs by which the feelings of the mind can
be expressed in one fashion or another; nevertheless, in regard to none besides this has there been a tacit agreement of that kind, and this universal
agreement has been entered into, namely, that, in conformity with the common usage of life, it is necessary to use this sign, unless, perchance, some
special agreement has intervened. Accordingly, since no one ought to hurt
a second person with whom the relations of the law of nature are still mutually exercised, except, perchance, on the occasion of a disservice; but, on
the contrary, every one whatsoever is bound to promote, according to his
ability, the advantages of a second person, and to furnish without fail what
he owes him on the basis of a pact; it is assuredly patent that any one whatsoever, in his relations towards a second person, who, either on the basis of
a pact, or on the basis of the mere law of nature, has the right to know the
feeling of his mind, should so use signs that the other person be not led by
them to his hurt. And that is the very foundation of moral verity, or veracity,

25. Cf. *JNG*, 4, 1, §1. For the connection of language and sociability, Pufendorf refers
to Aristotle, *Politics* I.2; Pliny the Elder, *Natural History,* XI, chap. 51; and Quintilian,
The Orator's Education, II, chap. 16.

which consist in this, namely, that the signs should conveniently represent the concepts of our mind to the other person who has the right to know them, and to whom we are under a perfect or an imperfect obligation to disclose them.[26]

35. From all this it is not difficult to gather what *falsehood* is,[27] <270> when, namely, signs present the sense of our mind as different from what it truly was, although he to whom the signs are directed has the right to know and to judge that sense. Here, in general, it is well established that, then, and only then, I am bound to make the signs conform to the sense of my mind, when there rests upon me the perfect or imperfect obligation to indicate it to the other person, and this, either in order that he may understand it directly himself, or, in order that, if I have expressed to him a different sense I may not trouble him with damage beyond his desert; and the other person likewise has the perfect or imperfect right to understand that sense, a right which, indeed, has not been taken away by the opposition of a stronger obligation or right. When such an obligation or right does not exist, a man will be by no means telling a falsehood if he put forth signs discrepant from the sense of his own mind, or dissimulate it altogether by keeping silent. Thus, since between enemies the obligation to indicate the feelings of the mind does not obtain, a man may, without being guilty of falsehood, tell what is false to the foe, or terrify him by fictitious rumours, or inflict any detriment upon him, just as he judges it to be to his own advantage, provided no unjust damage to a third person result therefrom.[28] If some reprehend this way of doing harm to enemies, that is not because thereby some right is violated; but because among more elevated minds

26. The moral veracity implying a right (respectively an obligation) to information has to be distinguished from "logical" truth: "And so to logical truth, which is a conformity of words with facts, ethical truth, which we are now discussing, adds the intention and obligation of the speaker" (*JNG,* 4, 1, §8); cf. Grotius, *JBP,* III.i.11.

27. The following discussion of different kinds of licit falsehoods is largely based on Grotius, *JBP,* III.i: "General rules from the law of nature regarding what is permissible in war; with a consideration of ruses and falsehood" (§§11 ff; cf. *JNG,* 4, 1, §§8–19).

28. For Pufendorf the lack of any legal relation between enemies also implies a lack of any obligation to veracity. For Grotius, on the contrary, this holds true only when applied to falsehood in assertions but not to promises which confer a new and particular right even upon the enemy (*JBP,* III.i.18).

only those things done to a foe are regarded as glory, which indicate some vigour of mind or body, not those which are done without any trouble by the unwarlike and the timid also; to which latter class of deeds belongs also the scattering of tales for the purpose of deceiving the enemy. This principle, however, is not at all to be extended to any pacts entered into with the enemy for the sake of ending or of suspending war. For, since the law of nature bids peace to be preserved as far as it can be done conveniently, or, when broken, to be mended, it is also understood to bid that those means be used without which that end cannot be obtained, to wit, that enemies may be able to judge of the feeling in each other's minds. For otherwise it is impossible for them to unite in making peace, were not the necessity of suspecting one another removed by the obligation to employ the truth in regard to the agreements of peace. And so the instant that a pact begins to be entered into with the enemy, there arises on both sides the right to understand the sense of the other, at least in regard to the present business, and he who has not rightly expressed it, is to be reckoned as having told a falsehood, and having done a wrong. Thus there are a great many things which I am not bound to signify to a second person, things, of course, which are known to my detriment by a second person who has no right to know them from me; and to one who asks me about them it is best, indeed, to refuse an answer altogether. Just as also it has been introduced by the tacit agreement <271> of the nations, that letters protected by a seal should be opened by him alone to whom they were written, and if any one else unseals them, unless he has done so on the presumed or express will of the one just mentioned, he is doing wrong to him, and is reckoned to have violated the common agreement of nations; a right, however, which like the rest, expires between enemies. But, when I cannot conveniently get rid of the importunate curiosity of a second person by keeping silent or dissimulating, then, assuredly, it will be permissible for me either to mock him with a fabricated tale, or to use ambiguous language, although it may be apparent that the other is understanding it in a sense different from our meaning. Here, however, precautions are to be taken, lest, in addition to the mockery which his curiosity deserves, something further by way of damage be inflicted upon him. This is valid also in case some third person, who has no right to hear my speech, be deceived, as he overhears my conversation with the second person with whom I have exchanged remarks purposely falsified. Thus, in human courts of law, since no one, when he has made restitution for damage done by his own fault, or is prepared to do so, is bound to offer himself voluntarily to punishment, or to report himself for a crime, a man will also not at all be bound to confess voluntarily to a crime, but he may either deny it or avoid it by false arguments. And yet where a matter is to be asserted on oath, out of reverence for the Divine Spirit he ought not to tell anything other than what is the fact. But, in truth, where some one is interrogated by a magistrate about the crime done by a second person, even a man who has not been sworn ought to tell the truth, on the strength of the obligation by which he is bound to promote the public good, which is presumed to be regarded in the punishment of any misdeed at all about which the magistrate judges that an inquiry should be held. But a falsehood is also [not] told,[29] when, for example, a judge, in order to elicit some fact from the accused, makes up something, for example, that he has already learned the fact from another, or that he will do this or that if the accused persists in dissimulating, and the like. For, assuredly, the judge has the right to extract the truth in any way whatsoever, even if the accused be not obliged to disclose the truth in any way whatsoever; and so, if the judge elicit the truth in some shrewd way, while exercising his right, he is not doing a wrong. Thus he also deserves praise in addition, who, with a fictitious statement, protects a second person's innocence, or placates an angry man, consoles a sad one, or does some good to somebody, which could not be secured by an open confession of the fact. For, because he was bound by the law of humanity, or by some closer obligation, to exhibit those offices to a second person, it is well established, assuredly, that he was not obligated to apply signs in that way in which they were not <272> destined to attain their end, namely, the other's advantage. Here belong also the figments of physicians by which they strive to persuade a morose sick man of the sweetness or the mildness of their medicine.

29. Here all other editions of Pufendorf's *Elementa* (Den Haag, 1660; Zwickau, 1668; Jena, 1669 and 1680) deviate from the Cambridge edition by containing an additional "non." From the sense of the paragraph it is clear that the affirmative version must be mistaken, because Pufendorf has above defined "mendacium" as a false statement directed to someone who has the right to know the truth.

Likewise, when an infant or an insane person is soothed by untruths, or if in battle one arouse the languishing spirits of one's own men by a false message. Now we contract the reproach of falsehood much less when we ourselves say beforehand that we are going to tell what is false, as is the case when stories are told or written, or when we employ jesting or humour, since that is either being done for the other person's advantage, or else we assume that this discrepancy between the words and the sense of the mind, or the figurative language, will not at all inconvenience the other person.

36. For the rest, it is not out of place here to subjoin something about the interpretation of signs[30] without which the employment of them is utterly vain. Here the following general rule is to be observed: Signs or words are valid in the sense which the common usage among men of the same language conveys. For the right and norm of speech rests with this sense, and words would be deprived of their proper end if any one whatsoever could, to please himself, assign to them such sense as he wished, diverse from common usage. But the words peculiar to the arts are valid in that sense which is used by men skilled in that art, if, indeed, it be well established that these words have been invented for those engaged in it. But, if artisans disagree about the definition of a word in question, or there be otherwise some obscurity about it, it will be best to express in common words what you wish properly to be understood by such an expression. But where there is obscurity or ambiguity in the words, then the true sense will have to be drawn either from the subject-matter itself, or from the effect, or the reason which led one to use them. Thus, also, where some word has several meanings, one more strict, another more loose, if the ambiguity cannot be removed, the stricter meaning properly obtains in odious matters, the looser in favourable ones; in such wise, however, as not to relieve one party by personal favour, while the other one, on the contrary, is too much oppressed. And this, either because any one whatsoever is presumed to have preferred to have an advantage rather than a burden come upon a number of others; or else because the error is slighter if favour be extended

---

30. The following rules of interpretation have been compiled from Grotius, *JBP,* II.xvi, "On Interpretation"; cf. the corresponding chapter in *JNG,* 5, 12.

further than odium. Thus, since no one is reckoned to have desired absurdities, or that his action have no effect, that sense of words is rightly rejected which either involves something absurd, or makes an action amount to nothing, or which is contrary to the reason in view of which the words in dispute were uttered. <273>

The law of nature alone is not directly sufficient to preserve the social life of man, but it is necessary that sovereignties be established in particular societies.

1. Although all the precepts of the law of nature which flow from the second fundamental law tend to the cultivation of a peaceful society among men, without the infliction of injuries upon one another; nevertheless, many causes are found for those precepts not being directly sufficient to produce this end. For, although conscience sufficiently indicates to each man what is to be done or left undone; nevertheless, few have such modesty of disposition that they are willing to follow this constantly where no present punishment, and one which strikes terror to the senses, has been set before the violator; especially where, through growing accustomed to them, the sweetness of vices has entered his heart, and, shame being cast forth, the mind addicted to the passions has grown deaf to the admonitions of the reason. Since, therefore, where each man should be left to his own conscience in regard to observing the law of nature, there would come to be a most abundant crop of wrongs to the rest of men, and all others also would have to seek the protection of their own safety in nothing but violence; the result of all this would be everything resounding with <274> warfare between those who repel and those who inflict wrong. To this is added further the fact that, although the law of nature orders that controversies be taken before arbitrators; nevertheless, since these arbitrators as such have no competent jurisdiction over the litigants whereby the latter can be altogether forced to follow their decisions, this remedy for preserving the peace will prove to be vain, if, indeed, the second person rejects that judgement of the arbitrator which displeases him. And what would result if no one should recognize the sovereignty of any man over him, when to-day among so few absolved from human sovereignty over them, so many wars are waged, in an almost unbroken series, now that the numbers of the human race and the infinite multitude of transactions have not allowed men to unite into one body, forasmuch as that one body, in such huge dimensions, would be threatened through internal disturbances by the same inconveniences as those which exercise the human race, and almost greater ones, divided, as the race is, into a large number of smaller sovereignties.

2. It was, therefore, altogether necessary for the preservation of peace and security among men, to have something established whereby it might commonly be rendered more preferable for men to perform to one another their due offices, than by injuries to contract for mutual hurt, as it were.

But here no more convenient means could be found, to which the intention of nature also moves, than that men should band together for the sake of bearing mutual aid to one another; and, indeed, not merely some few, but those who from their number have such strength that the ones who are on the point of attacking to do them wrong, would gain no adequate advantage, from the accession of but a few, in their purpose to overwhelm them.[1]

Here, however, this much is certain, namely, that however large the number be of those who have come together for mutual defence, if they should not agree among themselves about the best means by which that ought to be brought about, but each should use his strength according to his own best judgement, the end proposed will never be attained. For either discrepant opinions in regard to the method of defence will enervate their divided forces, or rivalry will involve in domestic warfare those who refuse to yield to one another; unless they be held together by some common bond by which each and all are bound to follow one decision in regard to the common defence and safety, so that they cannot separate and go off after anything else; although this decision may have displeased certain few, or appear to be very unprofitable to their own private interests. But that cannot be obtained by any more convenient means than for each individual so to subject his own will to the will of some one man or council, that <275> whatever this man or council shall decide upon in regard to the public welfare shall have the force of the will of all, and that this same man or council may be able to use the strength and faculties of the individuals for the common[2] welfare. For this end two pacts are necessary, one, whereby individuals bind themselves with individuals to subject themselves all together to the sovereignty of some one person; the other, whereby each and all bind themselves to that one person, to the effect that they are willing to furnish for the public good the use of their resources and their strength, according to his free choice, and not to resist his bidding.[3] By this same pact individuals

---

1. Cf. Hobbes, *De cive,* chap. 5, §3.
2. Ibid., §6.
3. On the contractual formation of the state, see bk. I, Def. 12, §27, and *JNG,* 7, 2, §§7–8, where a decree concerning the form of government is added as a third element. In contrast to the Hobbesian solution, which leaves the sovereign contractually unbound so that his continuing right to everything absorbs all right of the citizens, Pufendorf's

give up also that right to attack in hostile fashion, on their own judgement, the man who does them harm, making up their minds to look to the decision of the sovereign for the prosecution of their wrongs, unless, perchance, a present necessity does not permit them to call upon him for aid. From this it results that, because to him has been transferred the right to use the force and faculties of all for that which he himself has judged to be expedient for the common interests, he is endowed with that same force, by which he can bring all men into harmony and internal peace, even if some, in view of a special advantage, should be in the highest degree desirous of seeking diverse ends; and he can also vigorously repel the injuries done by outsiders. Those men, therefore, between whom such pacts exist, have coalesced into one moral person or society, which has its very own will, property and rights distinct from the property and rights of individuals as such, and these neither a few of the members, nor even all of them together, if he in whom the sovereignty inheres be excepted, can appropriate to themselves.

3. For the rest, such pacts productive of societies exist either on the occasion of birth, or of a war in which one side has succumbed, or else in view of more ample security. By the first two methods *families* are established, through which that end which we have just spoken of cannot be so fully obtained; by the last method the *state* is established, which attains perfectly the end mentioned above, in so far as the condition of human affairs permits. Now a nuptial society, or matrimony, although it is the fountain-head and seed-plot, as it were, of all societies, is not properly contracted with that end in view. For it both exists among a number of persons too small to be able to furnish mutual security by their united strength, since, forsooth, one single man can get but a slight defence from the union with one single woman or particular women; nor does matrimony have as its end the security of the human race, but the propagation of the same; nor is any sovereignty established by matrimony in itself. In truth, not only from the superiority of the sex, but even from the very nature of the mat-

---

construction with its continuing contractual relation between sovereign and citizens preserves the latter's legal capacity in the civil state and emphasizes that sovereign authority is limited by the end of civil society.

rimonial pact, the husband properly has a right to his wife's body only in so far as is sufficient to enable him to be certain with a degree of <276> probability that his wife's offspring have been procreated by him. Hence, since each man is presumed to use his own right, any one whatsoever is regarded as the son of that man to whom his mother was married at the time of his birth. And not without all reason is some stain of ignominy commonly cast upon husbands as a result of their wives' unchastity, because from imprudence or from abjectness of mind the husbands have not used their authority aright; although there be those who derive the cause of that circumstance from the fact that it is looked upon as an opprobrium for one to be without those gifts which can deserve love or maintain a stipulation. And so the fact that, in matters concerning matrimony, the wife is bound to follow the will of her husband, and not he her will, comes properly and directly from the force of the matrimonial pact, not from some sovereignty; just as a wage-earner is bound to apply his services according to the free choice of the one who hires him, although the latter does not properly have any sovereignty over him. Hence, also, if the contractor has not furnished what he ought, the hirer has properly an action against him, not as against a refractory subject, but merely as against the violator of a pact. Thus, as the following obligations, indeed, flow from the matrimonial pact, namely, that the wife is bound to cohabit with her husband, and that she cannot go abroad or lie all by herself against his will; so, whether direction over other actions of a wife which do not touch the essence of matrimony, as also full authority over her goods, belong properly to the husband, depends upon the special agreement of the husband and wife, or on civil laws. For a stand is by all means to be taken on these, if, indeed, they have defined whether women are to be given in marriage with a dowry, or there ought to be a complete union of goods between the husband and wife, or the husband should have full or restricted authority over the goods of the dowry, and the like. Where civil laws make no disposition on this point, in regard to such matters it will be permissible for husband and wife to make such agreement with one another as they see fit.

4. Now as far as the law of nature is concerned, whoever are fit by the condition of body or age can contract matrimony. And, since by that same law we are bound to cultivate the social life whose foundation, as it were,

is matrimony, it is patent that mankind are also obligated to enter upon it, in the way, however, of an affirmative indeterminate precept, that is to say, when an occasion offers itself to them, and when they do not foresee with a high degree of probability, that, in a life of celibacy for which they find themselves fit by the requisite continence, they can do more good for the human race or for their own state, than as married persons. Hence, they are not at all to be thought of as sinning who put off matrimony, so as more conveniently to cultivate the mind in freedom, and to prepare themselves <277> for performing notable ministrations to human society, something which married men, because of the customs of the state or the disposition of women, might not so readily do. Nor, if a man be led by a very lofty spirit, so that either he does not feel the incitements to matrimony, or else easily dulls them, and can, otherwise, by deserving well, make himself a useful citizen of the universe, is he to be thought obligated by nature, so as altogether to cast fetters, as it were, upon his glorious efforts by the allurements of women. Now, as civil laws, except through the utmost unfairness, would not set out to prohibit from matrimony specific men who are fit for it; so, if it be definitely ascertained that some function can be much more conveniently performed by a bachelor than by a married man, of course nothing appears to prevent bachelors only from being admitted to that function; or, if they do not wish longer to go without a wife, to lose it. Precisely as, for example, an order can be given to a legate, or a general, or a soldier, not to take his wife with him when he goes abroad or upon some expedition.[4] Thus the civil authority can rightly make other dispositions on this point, for example, about the age at which people are to be united in marriage; about their status, as illustration, that no citizen marry a foreign woman, or no nobleman a commoner; likewise about the rites to be used in the marriage contract; or the contracting parties having to obtain the consent of others, as illustration, that no one should enter matrimony when his parents or guardians are unwilling, or even without consulting the magistracy, or the like. The force of civil laws of that kind can be the following, namely, that the wedlock in which some requisite prescript of the law is wanting may be without the effects of legitimate matrimony in

4. Cf. *JNG*, 6, 1, §8, referring to *Dig.*, I.xvi.4, §2; Tacitus, *Annales*, III chap. 33–34.

that state, as, for example, that the children are not to become full citizens, or are not to be admitted to the paternal inheritance or to definite civil dignities; or that such wedlock be reckoned merely as concubinage; or that it can even be altogether dissolved, despite its having been already consummated. For the mingling of bodies in itself does not by nature have the effect that those between whom that has taken place a number of times, or only once, are bound to cohabit for ever; and, for the firmness of the connubial pact, at all events in a civil court of law, it is required that what civil laws have bidden to be performed herein, should altogether be performed, as without these matters the pact would not be valid. From all of which it can be easily gathered what judgement is to be rendered about that most vexed question, whether, namely, parents can rescind the marriages of their children entered into without their knowledge and consent. Here it must be seen, before all else, whether the parent be living in the state or outside the state. For, if he live outside the state of which he is a subject, assuredly he will have over <278> his own family what amounts to supreme sovereignty, and so, whatever prescript he has laid down for his own about such a matter, will have the force of a civil law. When his son has contravened that law it will be possible for him to be punished by his father, or for the marriage contract also to be suspended, if, indeed, that point was expressly mentioned in advance, or, if he have removed himself from his father's sovereignty, it will be possible for him to be excluded from the family and the paternal inheritance. But if, now, there existed no order on his father's part regarding that matter, then he is understood to have left that matter to the free choice of his children, as those things which are not interdicted by the laws are taken for licit. Here, nevertheless, the duty of respect requires that when a matter of so great moment is being considered, children properly require the consent of the parent, who is not a little concerned as to those through whom his own stock is to be propagated or upon whom his goods are to devolve; in such wise, however, that, his consent not being requisite, the marriage none the less remains firm, since, forsooth, it should altogether have been promulgated beforehand in the way of a civil law, that the failure to secure the express consent of the father would have such force that the marriage would be rendered invalid thereby. But, once the marriage has been contracted validly, when, thereafter, his son's condition, perchance, displeases his father, it can no more be rightly rescinded than are antecedent licit deeds punished on the basis of a law passed afterwards. But, when the persons concerned live in states, the whole matter will have to be decided on the basis of civil laws. For it is theirs to define what amount of authority over their own children belongs properly to citizens, especially over those children who are of mature age.

5. For the rest, although it was both to the dignity of man not to be procreated like cattle by unregulated sexual intercourse, and it contributes very greatly to a decorous order in states for the cohabitation of males and females to be fortified, as it were, with the scrupulous observance of a pact; still it assuredly seems strange, that, among the more civilized nations, at least, a most sensitive modesty attaches both to the members destined for procreation, and to the act of generation itself, although that modesty seems to arise neither from some natural deformity of the members or an absurd shape; and the act itself is conformable to nature, and altogether necessary for the preservation of the human species, and suitable to produce a being of such dignity. Why should one blush at exercising this act any more than at eating or drinking, since without it the species can no more be preserved than individuals can be preserved without these others? Nor do those fully meet the case who here take refuge in the divine writings, where modesty of that sort is said to have manifested itself immediately after the fall. For the question none the less remains, why shame has fixed <279> its seat, as it were, especially in these parts, since the hand and the tongue of man are no less ready for the ministrations of disordered and evil desires. The most probable cause, therefore, of this circumstance which can be presented, seems to be this, namely, that, for the purpose of preserving the social life among men, so much stress had been laid upon having the propagation of offspring circumscribed by a respectable order, otherwise than is the case among beasts. Hence, by a certain innate modesty which affects minds almost more strongly than the interdict of the law, nature wished to fortify the innocence of acts tending to this end, both so that those members should be carefully covered, lest, by being always exposed to the eyes, they over-excite a lust circumscribed by no limit of time, and also that there should be a more careful abstention from illicit love, because the sensitiveness of modesty required the performance of even legitimate

love only in a hidden way and without onlookers. And this modesty is most effective between those directly generated and their generators, to such a degree that he who is not restrained by it, so as not to be ashamed to descend to that familiar commingling of bodies with a person of that sort so united to him, is judged to be a man of utterly brazen character, and one who would shrink back from no further crime.

6. From this we think the reason is to be drawn why wedlock is reckoned as being forbidden, by the very law of nature, in the direct line of ascent and descent; especially, since no case has arisen, or probably could arise in which the necessity of it would have to be admitted. For the case does not seem to be absolutely settled by the reason that either a son, as a husband, being superior by the law of matrimony, could not show such reverence to his mother as nature demands; or a daughter to a father, for, however much inferior by the law of matrimony she might be, she would, nevertheless, be prohibited because of this familiar intercourse from exhibiting the reverence of that relationship.[5] For, if you remove that natural modesty which I have mentioned, it would assuredly not be so absurd for it to be possible that a mother be united with a son under his own authority, and so owing her merely respect; since, also, otherwise the condition of sex, as far as regards the essentials of the matrimonial contract, makes her in due order subject to the free choice of the other, whoever it be that she marries, and filial respect can express itself in other things. And much less, if you remove the modesty of commingling, would a daughter be prohibited by matrimony from exhibiting respect to a father who was her husband; since it is by no means necessary that as wife she be taken to a share in the domestic sovereignty, much less that she would oppose her husband. But, in truth, although among brothers also and sisters, and the rest of persons united in a very close degree, this kind of modesty is assuredly found to be more lax than between parents and <280> children; nevertheless, the reason why we say, that, by the law of nature, marriages between these persons also have not been prohibited, is because, as the authority [*autoritas*] of the Sacred Scriptures teaches us regarding the origins of men, marriages were necessarily to be contracted between the children of the first husband and wife,

5. Reference to Grotius, *JBP,* II.v.12.

brothers, of course, and sisters. Now it does not seem probable that God would have brought about a case of such a kind that violence would altogether have had to be done to the law of nature; especially, since it would have been easy for him to have avoided that case by having created at the very first two pairs of husbands and wives. Nevertheless, the modesty in question counselled, that, after the necessity for this wedlock has passed away, the number of mankind being sufficiently enlarged, this grade of marriage should be prohibited by positive laws; especially, since their daily and unsupervised living together would have furnished a very ready occasion for lewdness and adulteries, if such loves could have formed marriages.[6] This reason is also to be extended to other grades of consanguinity and affinity, which positive laws further prohibit, or which are allowed to isolated individuals only by the special indulgence of the magistracy.

7. But, as touching polygamy, it is certain, indeed, that the form in which several men have one wife together, is utterly abhorrent from nature and the end of matrimony; but that one man should be united at the same time with several women, although it is now believed among Christians to have been forbidden by a divine law, is, nevertheless, in itself by no means repugnant to the law of nature. For it is not necessary that, just as a wife ought to grant the use of her body to no man but her one husband, so ought a husband to do the same to no other woman but his only wife. For the former regulation is necessary so as to secure certainty about offspring. But, in truth, that a man should spend upon appeasing the lust of one woman all the vigour which was sufficient to raise up offspring among a number of women, does by no means seem to be ordered by nature. But those reasons which have to do with jealousy between the wives, domestic discord, hatred on the part of stepmothers to be continued also among the offspring themselves, are valid only among those nations in whom the dispositions of women are too elevated. Such are most women to-day among Europeans, where he who is himself not beholden to his wife performs with vigour the office of a man. But, in truth, among the Asiatics

---

6. Ibid., §13. This argument originates from Moses Maimonides' interpretation of Leviticus 18. See Moses Maimonides, *The Guide of the Perplexed*, ed. Shlomo Pines (Chicago: University of Chicago Press, 1991), vol. II, pt. III, chap. 49, pp. 606–7.

and others,[7] where women are left merely the glory of obedience, several wives no more disturb domestic peace than elsewhere the preposterous lust for commanding [*imperandi libido*] on the part of a single virago. And yet it must altogether be the finding that polygamy, formerly allowed for very weighty reasons, has later been prohibited by positive <281> laws. But this feature also has been added to matrimony from the positive law of God, namely, that, on the violation through adultery of the essential condition of the contract, when the wife has granted the use of herself to a second person, it can be dissolved; for other inconveniences, however, which make cohabitation troublesome, it cannot be dissolved, even with mutual consent. Since, otherwise, the law of nature would not prevent any one from being able to divorce his wife on the ground of sterility, or ignoble faults and intolerable habits, especially if it has been inserted in the nuptial contract that there should be a faculty of divorce, if, indeed, something of the sort should be found in the wife, and otherwise what had been established by mutual agreement could be dissolved again by a contrary agreement, where positive law does not stand in the way.

8. By generation, furthermore, and birth there begins to exist a society between parents and children. For this supplies the occasion of acquiring over offspring a right, which is not merely valid against other non-parents, that, precisely in the way in which it is most natural for him who is the owner of the thing to be the owner of the fruits, so he who is the master of the body out of which the offspring was generated, has the first place in acquiring sovereignty over offspring; but also a right which is valid against the offspring itself. For, aside from the fact that nature herself has enjoined upon the parents the care of the children, it has enjoined upon the children reverence towards parents, for the reason, that, in taking up the infant, the parent, indeed, declares that he will fulfil the obligation laid upon him by nature, and will bring it up well, as far as in him lies. Here, although the infant, because it does not know the use of reason, cannot expressly promise the reciprocal offices enjoined by nature; none the less, by the nature of the

---

7. Pufendorf's knowledge of polygamy among non-European peoples came from travel books. Cf. the parallel passage in *JNG* (6, 1, §§16–17), where he refers to Christophe Richer, *De rebus Turcarum ad Franciscum Gallorum regem christianiss. libros quinque* (Paris, 1540), and to Girolamo Benzoni, *La historia del Mondo Nuovo* (Venice, 1565).

transaction, obligation towards the parent contracted in its own person, no less than if it had been contracted by an express agreement, manifests itself as soon as it can understand what the parent has done towards it. For it is presumed that, if the infant had had the use of reason at the time when it was taken up, it would have consented expressly to such sovereignty of its parent over it without which a suitable bringing up is impossible, and would have stipulated in its turn from the parent for a suitable bringing up. This agreement reasonably presumed is valid as though expressed, precisely as he, in whose absence and without whose knowledge, business has been transacted by a second person, is understood to have contracted the obligation to pay that other person what he spent for the first person's advantage; for it is presumed that he would have expressly consented to such a contract had he known his business needed the other's services. But, if the family live outside states, the quasi-civil sovereignty of the father over his already adult son is continued on the basis of a tacit <282> pact, equity and the law of gratitude also urging that the son should with his strength join him especially to whom he owes it that he is what he is; until, by the consent of his father himself, he be utterly released from that sovereignty.

9. Now, in truth, since to the procreation of offspring father and mother contribute equally, it is to be decided on the basis of the matrimonial pact which one shall duly have authority over the offspring, and to what degree.[8] For, if no pact intervenes between them, that offspring is the mother's; because, in such a status, the father cannot be known except on the evidence of the mother, at least with the certainty with which matters of fact are proved among men, and it is understood that no second person properly has here a closer right to the offspring than she, who, within her own body, carried and nourished it. Hence, even on the basis of the Roman laws, the issue which had been begotten without a marriage pact followed the venter.[9] But where life is passed outside of states, the marriage pact will show clearly enough to which one properly belongs sovereignty; for it cannot be that both parents should have equal sovereignty at the same time. In this pact,

8. Cf. Hobbes, *De cive,* chap. 9, §§1–6.
9. See Ulpian in *Dig.,* I.v.24: "The law of nature is that a child born out of lawful matrimony follows the mother."

since, in due order the husband takes the place of the lessor, the wife that of the lessee, and so the man has the purpose of getting offspring not so much for his wife as for himself, it is patent also, that, in due order, the father properly has sovereignty over the offspring. But if, however, it should happen outside the normal order, that the woman take the man to herself, and not the contrary; so that not only the man should properly have no sovereignty over his wife, but also that in the marriage pact the wife should be in the place of the lessor, the husband in that of the lessee, then, assuredly, the wife will also properly have sovereignty over the children. Examples of this thing occur in the case of women upon whom supreme sovereignty devolves. For they can assuredly take husbands to themselves, and are sometimes said to have done so, in such a manner that they concede the husband sovereignty neither over themselves nor over their issue. Here also you can refer what some say about the Amazons,[10] namely, that they sought after offspring not by irregular copulation, but each had her own definite husband dwelling in a different land, to whom they resorted only at a definite time, and to whom the male offspring was sent back. But, in states established by men, as men are in due order the heads of the family, so private sovereignty over children rests with the fathers, in such wise that the bidding of mothers has in itself about the force of counsel only, and obtains the force of obligation only on the basis of authority communicated by the father. As for this private sovereignty itself, however, over children, as in most states there has been left to parents, and ought also to have been left, so much as is required for the bringing up of the children; so, on the basis of the same laws, it <283> is to be judged what kind of authority parents have in regard to the other actions and things of their children, especially their adult children, and how far this extends.

10. For the rest, obligation has also been enjoined upon parents by the law of nature, that not merely shall they not destroy by abortion the offspring conceived within their flesh, nor expose it, nor put it to death after it has been brought into the light of day; but also that they shall supply it with nourishment (one or both of them, just as they have agreed in the

10. Cf. *JNG*, 6, 1, §9, with references to the ancient historians Marcus Junianus Justinus, Diodorus Siculus, and Jordanis.

marriage pact), until it can conveniently support itself, and, that, in proportion to their strength, they are to see that it is brought up and instructed to the good cultivation of the social life. In this latter function the principal part of the father's office consists, and therefrom the greatest necessity for gratitude is incumbent upon children; forasmuch as parents cannot impute to their children so much their mere generation, which is without annoyance or is compensated for by their own pleasure, as they can the bringing up which is both laborious and full of the most faithful solicitude, whereby, in proportion to each one's faculty, they are formed into useful members of human society. That this office be observed the more carefully, since, forsooth, it is among the principal supports of the social life, nature has implanted in parents a tender affection for their offspring, so that no one can be willing readily to neglect that office. But, if some parents, nevertheless, not only violating the law of nature but also overcoming common affection, are unwilling to nurture their offspring, and cast it forth, they cannot longer claim any right over it, nor can they demand from it longer any office due, as it were, to a parent. But he who has brought up an exposed infant succeeds to the rights of the parent, and to him the foster child owes the same offices which he does otherwise to those who have begotten him, nor can he go back under the authority of his natural parents, if his foster parent is unwilling.

11. Out of an antecedent war arises the society of slave-masters, that is to say, when I grant life to the man whom I could licitly have slain, and undertake to supply him with the things which make for its preservation, on condition that he be mine for ever, whatever services can be performed by him shall redound to my advantage, and that he obey absolutely my commands, as far as they can be effectively valid. For, in truth, just as the beasts, with whom we are perpetually at war, when conquered by the same right of war, indeed, are in a state of perpetual and absolute servitude to us; and yet, because they are not capable of obligation, they can be restrained by bodily bonds only, and when they have broken these, and run away, they return to natural liberty; so, with the man captured in war, whom I restrain with nothing but physical bonds, I am reckoned as having contracted as yet no pact, <284> and so, since passage is made from war to peace only by means of pacts, a state of war is understood to be still en-

during between us, nor is there any obligation upon him to serve. Hence such a man can licitly not merely run away, but even, when the chance has come to him, treat his captor as an enemy. And so the obligation to serve does not arise simply from granting him his life, but from the fact that confidence is placed in him by not having him bound or shut up in a work-house for slaves.[11]

12. Moreover, since an absolute authority over the slave has been acquired by the master, and the person of the slave has become the master's own, it is apparent also that the master properly has a right to all the things of the slave, not simply, what he has acquired after becoming a slave, but also what he had before slavery, if, indeed, the master has captured them along with him. For the things which have not fallen into the captor's hands along with their owner, enter the status to which they would have come upon the captive's death, unless the civil laws have otherwise disposed, so that there can be room for postliminy.[12] But, if the master grants the slave some private property of his own, the latter is reckoned as having proprietorship over it to the extent only that he can retain and defend it against any one else not his master. But, where it has happened that the master as a subject comes under the authority of a second person, it is manifest that the master's eminent domain, at least, over slaves, passes over to the other person, in such wise that the master as an intermediary cannot exercise more authority over the slave than seems best to the supreme master. Hence, if in any states the right of masters over slaves has been absolute, that particular right has not been given them by civil laws, but what they had previously had as heads of households outside states has been left them.

11. Pufendorf follows Hobbes in legitimating slavery as a result of war by supposing a tacit pact implied in the act of placing confidence in the captive by granting him corporeal liberty; see *De cive,* chap. 8, §§3–4. Apart from war as an occasion for slavery, the parallel section of *JNG* (6, 1) also mentions differences of wealth leading to a permanent attachment of poor people to wealthy families. Pufendorf conceives the resulting relationship as "labour for life" based upon a contract of "goods for work" (ibid., §4).

12. *Postliminium* (postliminy), lit. "return across the threshold," denotes the right of the returning prisoner of war to regain all his former rights (Hans Kreller, "Postliminium," in *Paulys Real-Encyclopädie der classischen Altertumswissenschaften,* XXII, pp. 863–73).

13. Now the society in question is dissolved when the right of the master over the slaves is extinguished. This happens, (1) If the master has given him his freedom. (2) When he has driven him away. This act differs from manumission, not in effect, but in method. For liberty is here given by way of a punishment, because, since the possession of such a wicked man is troublesome, it is judged to be far more damaging to the slave himself to be possessed of his own right, than if he should be a slave to a master. (3) If the slave be captured, the new servitude abolishes the old. (4) If the master die, and have not transferred his right to another, the slave is understood to be free, because there remains to him no obligation towards any one to be his slave. But whether he can conduct himself as a free citizen also in a state will have to be decided on the basis of civil laws. That also happens, moreover, if the master has no heir at the time of his natural or civil death. For a slave of that sort cannot be regarded as derelict and so <285> dragged off by any one into servitude, just as goods regarded as derelict fall to the man who takes possession of them. For the rest of things, whether they be inanimate or animate, as brutes, are defended by no right, so as to prevent their being claimed by anybody at all, unless a right to them has been acquired already for a second person. But, to a man, one can assert for oneself no right, except in so far as it arise from the former's own consent, or past deed regarding the latter. And so, when that right which the victor has acquired over the slave in a special way from war has been extinguished, there returns natural liberty, even if, perchance, servitude corresponds better with his character. For the inclination of character in itself, as some absurdly think, gives no one the right of dragging off into slavery a man against his will, and it is not licit for me forthwith to impose upon a second person by violence that which is, perchance, to his own best advantage.[13] (5) Where a slave, neither on the basis of an antecedent misdeed, nor by way of punishment, is thrown into chains, or in any way at all deprived of the physical freedom of his body, he is set free from that obligation arising out of the pact wherein the master did not wish longer to bind him by throwing physical chains upon him; and so it will be permissible for a

13. On Pufendorf's discussion of the ancient idea of the slave by nature, see bk. I, Def. 3, note 13.

slave of that sort here to do what we have said was permissible to captives in bonds, who have never given their word of honour.

14. Now, in truth, through neither of these two societies could a peace, in itself secure and stable, fall to the lot of men, because, as men multiplied, families grew to a very large number, which, due to their slight strength, were destined not to be sufficient to defend themselves against any violence, and to clash more frequently in wars with one another, the more numerous they became. To be sure, if a family, by the multiplication of offspring and the acquisition of slaves, has become so numerous that it cannot be subjugated without the uncertain cast of the dice of war, it will be able to furnish to its members the same security as that which otherwise states are wont to furnish.[14] But, in truth, unless the head of the family still lives and has, by the consent of the principal divisions, at least, of the family, so tied it together, as it were, that it is bound to remain one family for the future also; upon his death it will break up into as many families as there are sons who compete with one another for the inheritance, and so their divided strength will be rendered weak. For the prerogative of primogeniture is not of such avail that all sons born of the same parent are bound to be under the sovereignty of the first-born, unless they have submitted themselves to that subjection either through the disposition of the father or on their own agreement; which agreement is the more necessary, the farther the members of the family have separated from the common stock. <286>

15. In order, therefore, that the security of men should be fully provided for, as far, indeed, as the condition of human affairs permits; and, where it could not be prevented that one of two persons be at all hurt unjustly by the other, that this much, at least, be achieved, namely, that he could not be so hurt with impunity; it was necessary, finally, that a number of families be united. And when they entered into a mutual pact with one another in regard to procuring the common welfare, and conferred upon him to whom

---

14. There is almost verbatim agreement with Hobbes, *De cive,* chap. 9, §10. Nevertheless, for Pufendorf the distinctive characteristic of the state does not consist in the greater number of people and the attendant defense capability, but in its special purpose, which differs from that of household and family and determines the extent of its respective authority (*JNG,* 6, 2, §10). Only civil authority possesses the right of life and death (ibid., §6; 8, 3, §1).

they entrust the administration of that common welfare, the right to command that which will seem to contribute to this end, having contracted at the same time the obligation to do his bidding, the state arises.

16. From the end of the state, moreover, it is easy to gather what ought to be the character and extent of the sovereignty whereby it is kept together. For since, as was said above, it is not sufficient for the state that each one whatsoever of those who are going to coalesce into a state should pledge his good faith that he will observe the laws of nature towards his fellow-citizens, it is necessary that he to whom the whole of the state is entrusted for administration should have the faculty to affect with some evil or punishment the man who has refused to do what the former has laid down to be observed as being expedient for the public.[15] For then, and not till then, do I not have a plausible ground for fearing my fellow-citizens, when an equal or more severe evil awaits the man who is going to affect me with wrong. But, since they who cannot protect themselves against outsiders, cultivate peace among one another to no avail, nor can they whose strength has not been united protect themselves against outsiders; it follows that in a state there ought necessarily to be in the hands of some one person the authority to unite and arm as many citizens in any peril or occasion, as shall seem to be needed for the common defence, in view of the enemy's force, and again, to make peace with the enemy, as often as it shall be profitable to do so. This power will rest with the same one also who has the authority to exact punishments, since no one can of right force citizens to arms and to the expense of war, except the one who can also punish the recalcitrant. The same person will no less have the decision about the deeds of those in whose case there is a dispute as to whether they ought to suffer punishment. For, if the authority to judge were with one person, and the authority to execute the judgement with another, nothing would be done. For he who could not execute the decisions rendered would pass judgement to no pur-

---

15. Like Hobbes, Pufendorf sees the essential characteristic of sovereignty in the power of executing the law by inflicting punishment. Cf. the parallel passage in *JNG* (7, 4, §3) that is very close to *De cive,* chap. 6, §4. For Jean Bodin, on the contrary, legislative power forms the core of sovereign authority under which all its other rights are to be subsumed (Jean Bodin, *Les six livres de la République* [Paris, 1583; repr. Aalen: Scientia, 1961], I.10, pp. 221, 223).

pose; or if he himself should execute them on the right of a second person, he himself would not have the authority to punish, but the other person, whose minister only he would be. Also, since not all transactions can be performed directly by one man or a council, the same will have the faculty of delegating the care and execution of definite <287> transactions to definite men, who, however, will borrow all their authority [*autoritatem*] from him. Finally, since mutual offices between citizens cannot be rightly performed or exacted, unless it be defined how far the separate offices are due, it will belong to the same supreme authority to promulgate definite rules which they call civil laws, by which shall be declared, what right or what obligation one citizen has towards another, what they ought to furnish one another, or what they can exact from others, and on what score; in a word, what is necessary, through civil sovereignty, for them to do, or avoid doing, to one another.

17. As for the rest, just as he who confers upon a second person sovereignty over himself, contracts at the same time the obligation not to resist his bidding, since, forsooth, that would imply that some one has the right to command, in such a way, however, that the other person retains the authority to resist; so we must consider how far this obligation not to resist extends. Here this much is certain, namely, that, since every authority is understood to have been conferred upon some one, without violation of the right and authority of a superior, citizens also are reckoned as neither having been able to renounce, by having set up or recognized civil authority, the sovereignty of God over them, nor to have renounced it, and so ought to reject and not execute those orders of the supreme authority, which, it is well established, are openly opposed to the mandate of God. But if, now, on that account the supreme authority should set out to bring force to bear against my life, whether I may for that reason rightly oppose force to it, is a difficult question which arises. We are of the opinion that a distinction should here be made between those things which are properly enjoined by the Christian religion as such, and those which flow from natural religion, whose practice in large part consists in the exercise of the law of nature. In regard to the former, it is not ours to define what may be permissible when force is directed against one; since from the same Scriptures out of which that religion is drawn, any one whatsoever can determine for himself, how

much it ought to be worth to him to have done or professed nothing contrary to his own religion. But we do not think the case exists that the supreme civil authority should order something to be professed which was
contrary to the main theoretical precepts of nature;[16] especially since by
that religion the people is in the highest degree bound to obedience towards
the civil authority. It is an act of madness for this bond to be broken by the
one whom it most concerns to have it strong. But that one should sin even
against the practice of natural religion, which consists pretty much of the
observance of the law of nature, because death had been threatened him
by the civil authority, we think can scarcely be possible. For, where violence
is brought to bear against our life, so that we are to do something otherwise
forbidden by the law of nature, the <288> mere execution of that act will
be ours, and its guilt can be imputed not against us, but against the supreme
authority itself, and so the sin in this case will not rest with us, but with it
alone; hence there appears no reason for resisting. But if, however, the execution of the act be of such a kind that either it cannot be undertaken at
all without one's own sin, or be judged to be in itself more bitter than death,
where no reason is shown, or at least no reason is plausibly pretended, either
in consequence of my own misdeed or for the public good, why there is
brought upon me especially such a great necessity to perform that matter
which could be done by another, or which it is absurd to do at all; it is, of
course, apparent that what is being done is that I, who am an innocent
man, without any pretext of right or public good, am to be ruined because
of the mere whim of the sovereign, and his spirit of hostility towards me.
Now when the sovereign is found to be of that spirit towards me, certainly
he treats me no longer as a subject but as an enemy, and he himself is understood to have remitted the obligation by which I was held bound to his
sovereignty. In this case, since I pass from being a subject into being a free
enemy, the sovereign assuredly retains no right to keep me from being privi-
leged to employ against him, for the sake of defending myself, all means
commonly observed against an enemy, especially when there is no oppor-

16. The "main theoretical precepts of nature" are the theoretical propositions of
natural religion, that is, that God exists, is the founder of the universe, rules over the
world and the human race, and has no attribute involving any imperfection (*Off.*, 1, 4,
§§2–5).

tunity for flight, except in so far as some consideration is to be taken of my fellow-citizens, namely, that in this way they be not involved in great disorder. In our opinion the same judgement is to be rendered, if, apart from the case mentioned, the sovereign, without misdeed on our part, should set out to destroy us in our innocence. Here, although it is best for the sake of our fellow-citizens to seek safety by flight or by hiding; nevertheless, where there is no opportunity for flight or hiding, it will be permissible to defend our safety against the one who treats us no longer as subjects.[17] In this case even a third person who has no obligation towards him can properly undertake our defence. But, in truth, when the sovereign has determined to inflict a punishment upon us because of some offence, although we are not bound to bring punishment voluntarily upon ourselves, but to avoid it by flight or hiding; nevertheless, the reason why we cannot here defend ourselves by force is that the one who is in authority is using his own right, and for that reason to hurt him in any respect would assuredly be a wrong.

18. Now, as a supreme sovereignty of that kind is found in every state whatsoever, and that group in which it is not found is not to be reckoned as a state, so it is self-evident that it has no one upon earth to whom it is beholden, or who can bring it to order by legitimate authority. Not in the state itself, for that is implied; nor outside the same, because, due to the natural equality of men, no one can pretend <289> any right of sovereignty over a second person, unless he has acquired that by some antecedent act or consent of the person himself, such as we presuppose has not intervened here. From this it follows that this authority is also absolute, that is to say, that those acts which it has judged to be expedient to its own end it can perform of its own free choice, in such wise that it is not compelled to borrow, as it were, from a second person the authority to perform them, nor to recognize the rescinding of the same by a second person. And much less can he who enjoys that sovereignty be brought to face one in a civil court, or have some punishment inflicted on him because of some deed of

---

17. Otherwise *JNG*, 7, 8, §5: "Nay, if flight be not possible, a man should be killed rather than kill, not so much on account of the person of the prince, as for the sake of the whole commonwealth, which is usually threatened with grave tumults under such circumstances."

his.[18] For we can neither be judged nor punished except by him who has sovereignty over us. For the evils inflicted by those who are our equals outside the state, because of a wrong done them, do not properly have the character of punishment, since they proceed from the right of war, which obtains among those whom the force of human tribunals does not bind. From this also it is not difficult to gather how far he who rejoices in supreme authority on earth is obligated by laws. For that all men are equally obligated by natural and divine positive laws as such, is beyond doubt, and upon their violation action will be brought against prince and private person alike before the divine judgement-seat. But, when the question is raised as to just what efficacy there be in the obligations which are contracted by the supreme authority towards other men, then a distinction is found to exist between those things which are owed to outsiders and those which are owed to subjects. For that supreme authority does not prevent outsiders, indeed, from acquiring a perfect right against him on the basis of his obligation; and, by the strength of that right, since there does not exist a common tribunal among men, when he refuses, they can compel him by arms to pay his debt. But whatever obligation he has contracted towards his own subjects, provided only he has preserved the right of supreme sovereignty unimpaired, will be merely imperfect, that is, on its violation he will have to stand before the divine judgement-seat, indeed, but his subjects will be able to bring against him an action neither in a human court of law, forasmuch as there is none here, nor to apply force to him, because of the very sovereignty established over them, which becomes of no avail, when subjects are as much allowed to employ force against the bearer of authority for the violation of a law of nature, as he is to do so against them. Therein, however, monarchs are found to be in a far better condition than either aristocrats or individuals belonging to a free people. For here, since the supreme authority inheres in the whole council as such, if any individuals have been at fault in regard to the council, it will certainly be possible for

18. Cf. *JNG*, 7, 6, "On the Characteristics of Supreme Sovereignty," §§1ff. Supremacy, unaccountability, and indivisibility are the basic characteristics of the common early-modern concept of sovereignty. See Jean Bodin, *République* (bk. II, Observ. 5, note 15), I.8 (pp. 124, 131), I.10 (p. 221); cf. Hobbes, *Leviathan,* chap. 18, §§4–5, and Grotius, *JBP,* I.iii.7.

them to be judged and punished in a civil court of law, according to the laws of the state, because of having violated any obligation at all, by the rest <290> of the council, the majority of which has the force of all together; a condition which does not obtain in the case of monarchs.

19. Just as that supreme authority which we have spoken of, in any group not subject to a second person, which, indeed, constitutes a single moral body, is as though in the common subject; so, as the special forms of a commonwealth vary, it inheres now in one person, now in a certain few, now in the whole people. And in democracies, indeed, no one will readily call in doubt that the supreme authority, in the way in which we have described it, is in the whole people, in such wise that its acts can be rendered invalid by no one else, nor can it be brought to order or punished. For, when gatherings or assemblies of the people have degenerated into a confused mob of seditious men, the major part of the people can by its own right restrain and punish those disturbers, because, in the form of such a commonwealth, the major part has the force of the whole, and those fewer seditious men do not have some special right before those more numerous good citizens to look after the commonwealth. That such authority can be unlimited in a few, and so in one also, as though in the nearest subject,[19] is no less certain. For, assuredly, nothing prevents also a people conquered in war from being able so to subject itself to the victor for the purpose of avoiding destruction, that it leave itself absolutely no authority in regard to sovereignty; and a people otherwise free, and not pressed by any such necessity, from utterly abdicating its own sovereignty, and being able to confer it upon a second person, so as to leave itself no right therein. For, although it should seem necessary by the law of nature that a man should not merely as an individual exercise care for his own welfare, but also while living in society, and so, as he has the considerations of his own welfare intertwined with those of securing the welfare of others, he should see to defending it by common counsel; nevertheless, the latter injunction has never been so laid upon a man by nature, that, if it should seem more

19. "Nearest subject" [*subjectum proximum*] or "proper subject" [*subjectum proprium*] denotes the specific unit that holds sovereignty (that is, the monarch in a monarchy or popular assembly in a democracy) in contradistinction to the commonwealth as "common subject" [*subjectum commune*]. The distinction is taken from Grotius, *JBP,* I.iii.7.

suitable to him, he could not transfer that right and that care to another absolutely and irrevocably; at least, if it be probable that the second person is going to conduct that sphere of activity aright, a presumption which devolves as a regular thing upon all who take that function upon themselves. Yes, and that it be not merely licit, but even necessary, as said above, because that common welfare cannot be rightly administered except by one counsel.

Now such supreme authority is understood to be enjoyed by any person to whom the people has so conferred sovereignty over itself, that it has not reserved the right to hold, by itself or by its deputies, assemblies with the authority of inquiring into the acts of the sovereign, and of both making them invalid, and bringing him to order; or when, at the very outset, the prince is not bound to secure <291> the express consent of the people regarding the acts of sovereignty, without which consent they will be invalid. Here, however, it is not to be supposed that, if some princes do not wish their acts to be valid except they be approved by a definite council established by themselves, this council has forthwith an authority greater than that of the prince. For, if any acts be here rescinded, they ought to be understood as being rescinded by the will of the prince himself, who in this way wished to take precautions, partly not to decide upon something without adequate consideration, partly so as all the more conveniently to rid himself of the importunate solicitations of men to whom he grants something which he knows will be disapproved by that council.[20] Just as also the estates in a pure kingdom take nothing from the supreme authority of the prince, forasmuch as they have the authority [*autoritatem*] of counsellors only, so that the needs of the people be the better known. But, if some disadvantages seem to follow from having that supreme authority remain in the hands of one person, these do not make it impossible for one person to be so constituted; and, of course, they will be no more severe than those

---

20. *JBP,* I.iii.18: "They are greatly mistaken, however, who think that a division of sovereignty occurs when kings desire that certain acts of theirs do not have the force of law unless these are approved by a senate or some other assembly. For acts which are annulled in this way must be understood as annulled by the exercise of sovereignty on the part of the king himself, who has taken this way to protect himself in order that a measure granted under false representations might not be considered a true act of his will."

which attend other forms of commonwealths, since life will have to be lived everywhere by individuals under absolute authority, which not merely monarchs, but also aristocrats, and the whole people can sometimes abuse.[21]

20. Hence, those indulge in an extremely perilous error who from an original hatred towards monarchs, or else one drawn from a definite class of writings, contend that necessarily and always the supreme authority is with the people in so far as it is contradistinguished from its head, so that it can and ought to take cognizance of the deeds of kings and visit them with punishment.[22] Nor are they more sane who imagine some mutual subjection, in such wise that princes should be subject, indeed, to no one, as long as they rule according to the laws and in a civil fashion, but on their abusing authority should be subjected to the coercion of the people, and therefore are to be deposed from office before action is taken against them. For what if a king should assert, and perchance, with truth, that he has used his authority rightly, and the people should deny it; who will be arbitrator? Especially, since, in general, so great is the obscurity of civil acts

21. According to Pufendorf, sovereign authority in a democracy is even less able to be circumscribed than in a monarchy or aristocracy: "Indeed, in democracies the distinction between absolute and circumscribed sovereignty is apparently not so clearly discoverable. For although in every democracy there must exist certain institutions established by custom, or sanctioned by written laws, . . . yet since that council in which is vested the supreme sovereignty is composed of the entire body of citizens, and so no one outside it secures any right from its decisions, nothing will prevent the same people being able to abrogate and modify them at any time" (*JNG*, 7, 6, §8).

22. Pufendorf here turns against the doctrine of double majesty (*maiestas realis* and *maiestas personalis*) that had been influenced by the monarchomachs. That doctrine had been applied to the German *Reichsstaatsrecht* (imperial constitutional law) by a school of constitutional thinking established by the Dutch Calvinist Dominicus Arumeus, who taught in Jena from 1602 (see Friedrich Hermann Schubert, *Die deutschen Reichstage in der Staatslehre der frühen Neuzeit* (Göttingen: Vandenhoeck und Ruprecht, 1966) pp. 473ff). See Pufendorf's criticism of that doctrine in *JNG*, 7, 6, §§4 and 6: "It is a better course to discuss the reasonings of those who delight to exalt above kings that real, as they imagine it, majesty of the people. They claim that all kings are created by the people, and that it is in accordance with nature for the creator to be superior to his creation. . . . Furthermore, he who constitutes a person is superior to him only when it always lies within his power to stipulate how long the other should hold the position in which he is placed. But sometimes at the first it is a matter of free choice, whom you may wish to set up, and yet, after the appointment has once been made, it becomes a matter of necessity to bear it."

that the common people can rarely recognize their fairness or necessity, or frequently, as a result of a disturbed state of emotions, is unwilling to do so, and it is in the highest degree expedient for the commonwealth that the course of its counsels be not open to a large number. As confusion of that kind utterly subverts the purpose of sovereignties, so no people without exception in giving sovereignty to some one is presumed to have wished to introduce it. For the people which altogether wished to inquire into the acts of princes has expressly reserved to itself the authority of holding assemblies upon that matter in its own right, and has <292> prescribed definite formulae in accordance with which those acts were to be demanded. Yes, and where there is such a prince he has by no means supreme sovereignty, and merely holds the position of a magistrate properly so called, whatever may be the title with which he shines; just as the magistrate also can make no decision about public affairs, or at least of the weightier kind, except with the express consent of the people, or of its deputies or estates, sitting in council by their own right, and not by a right dependent upon some one else.

21. No more can they be tolerated who say, that, when the king has degenerated into a tyrant, he can be stripped of his sovereignty and punished by the people. For the same difficulty as the one above will return, namely, as to just what actions cause one to be rightly called a tyrant. Any one who is taken with dislike of the prince or of the present state of affairs will apply to the prince the unpopularity of that word, an unpopularity which arose from the vanity of the Greeklings.[23] Nor has any one hitherto clearly defined just what acts would make one a tyrant who is to be brought to order by his own subjects. For it is the common view that private vices do not make one a tyrant, nor a somewhat careless administration of the commonwealth. Are too heavy tributes demanded? Yes, but a subject not admitted to the counsels cannot judge whether the necessity of the state demands them. Are severe punishments imposed? Yes, but if they come in accordance with the laws, or after an antecedent misdeed, no one can justly

---

23. Pufendorf, like all early modern theorists of sovereignty, excludes the question of legitimacy from the theory of forms of states that are to be distinguished from each other by their bearer of sovereignty (*JNG,* 7, 5, §1). Cf. Bodin, *République* (see bk. II, Observ. 5, note 15), II.1, pp. 252ff, and especially Hobbes, *De cive,* chap. 7, §2.

complain, even if, perchance, clemency were better applied. Are certain great men, or others, without wrongdoing on their part, removed from the midst because of private enmities, a thing generally held to be most odious? Yes, but if the excuse of a misdeed or of machinations against the commonwealth or the status of the prince is given, or if the ordinary form of trials is observed, although, perchance, those who are removed may be quite certain of their own innocence, and a few others besides; nevertheless, how can that be clearly established to others, especially since the presumption of justice stands always on the side of the prince? Are promises not kept, or privileges previously granted (by which some part of supreme sovereignty is not given away) violated? Yes, but if the prince should offer as the ground either a misdeed, or a necessity, or a notable advantage to the commonwealth, he will be regarded as having acted in his right, and the subject will not have the faculty of judging clearly about it. From these cases other difficulties also which attend this view can easily be judged.

22. That no one should believe, however, that we grant a boundless licence to princes, and deliver over to them their subjects, from whom we have taken away every faculty of fighting back, like cattle to their pleasure, we are altogether of the opinion that, if, indeed, even <293> an absolute prince should assume a mind utterly hostile towards his subjects, and openly seek their destruction without the pretext of a cause which has at least the appearance of justice, his subjects can rightly employ against him also the means customarily used against an enemy, for the sake of defending their own welfare. And that, because, in this case, he is reckoned to have yielded up the obligation with which they had been bound, since the situation would involve that some one wished at the same time both to be a prince and to act as an enemy towards all his subjects.[24] However, it is scarcely possible for it to happen that a prince should assume such a mind

24. Cf. Grotius, *JBP,* I.iv.11, who refers to the doctrine of resistance in William Barclay, *De regno et regali potestate adversus Buchananum, Brutum, Boucherium et reliquos monarchomachos libri sex* (Paris, 1600): "In the fourth place, says the same Barclay, the kingdom is forfeited if a king sets out with a truly hostile intent to destroy a whole people. This I grant, for the will to govern and the will to destroy cannot coexist in the same person. The king, then, who acknowledges that he is an enemy of the whole people, by that very fact renounces his kingdom."

towards the whole people, unless, perchance, he be exercising sovereignty over more than one nation, so that by destroying or crushing one he may make conditions more pleasant for the other. But it can easily happen that a prince be such towards individuals, or a certain few. Since he is likewise ejecting these from the number of his subjects, it will be permissible for them to use the defence otherwise licit against an enemy, observing, however, the advice which we have given above about this case. It will not be permissible, however, for the rest of his subjects on this account to put off obedience, or to defend the innocent by violence, whether the prince present some pretext or not. For, aside from the fact that it is not permissible for them to inquire into the deeds of the prince which he exercises on the basis of his judicial authority, as it were, and it often happens that an accused person falsely proclaims his innocence in order to stir up ill-will against the prince, the doing of injury to a fellow-citizen does by no means absolve the rest from their obligation towards the prince; because each one of the subjects for his own person stipulates for himself the care and protection of the same, and does not lay it down as a condition, "If he is going to treat each and all of the citizens as subjects." Nor does fear lest he be dealt with in the same way himself suffice to break an obligation, forasmuch as this fear is an uncertain one, since there may have been special causes for hatred in that man's case which are not found in me. But, as long as the obligation of the subject towards the prince stands, it will be permissible neither to inquire into the acts of the latter, nor for any cause or on any pretext oppose violence to him.

23. These matters having been thus distinctly set forth, it will be easy to answer the arguments which are commonly brought against the absolute authority of princes. Most of them collapse of their very selves, if it be observed that the following are by no means the same thing: "A people has authority to bring even absolute kings to order, if, indeed, these have not ruled according to its liking"; and, "A people properly has the right, in a case of extreme necessity, namely, when the prince has become an enemy, to defend its welfare against him." For the reasons which establish the latter proposition do by no <294> means likewise lead to the former as their conclusion, and yet these propositions are confused by many. Thus, when it is said that the people, although it has yielded itself to servitude, has still not lost every right of asserting its liberty or security; if, indeed, this be

understood of such a right as that whereby a man can provide for his own welfare against the extremity of unjust force, which, when it is successful, is followed by liberty (for towards a master, after he has once turned into a foe, that is to say, when he has released me from my obligation, there is no longer a bond, although, perchance, he may afterwards wish to change his mind), we gladly concede. Apart from this case, a people which has delivered itself over into slavery has no more properly the right to assert its own liberty than have I to snatch back by violence the thing which I have already handed over to a second person on the basis of a pact. For this civil servitude is not, as some dream, so abhorrent from nature, that, even if a man at some moment, for the sake of avoiding a greater evil, shall have regarded it as necessary to consent thereto, he can afterwards, on a favourable opportunity, nature herself giving him the right, throw it off again. And, although this servitude may be repugnant to the genius of some definite people, either from the beginning, or afterwards as their minds have changed, nevertheless, it will by no means be permissible for this cause only to take away from the prince the right acquired; any more than it is permissible to take away from the purchaser a thing acquired by a pact, even if the seller has afterwards discovered that the agreement was not to his profit. Moreover, between a private master and a prince there is a great difference. For, when the former abuses his property, he is rightly restrained by the magistracy, because the latter properly has the right of eminent domain over those same goods. But, in truth, who would say that the people has eminent authority over the goods of princes, among which is also the right of sovereignty? For the sayings of the good princes which are here adduced, as of Trajan, Antoninus, &c., namely, that the commonwealth belongs to the people and not to themselves, mean nothing else, by that popular form of expression, than that sovereignty is to be administered not so much for the good of the sovereigns, as for the good of the subjects. From this it is no more permissible to infer that the people has properly a right over princes, than that children have a right over parents or their goods, because their authority, also, is commonly said to be for the sake and good of their children.[25] But this we gladly concede, namely, that, since the people has itself no right to destroy itself, or to rage unjustly against its

25. Cf. Grotius, *JBP,* I.3.8.

own body, it could not have given the king also such a right. For no king
of sane mind ever wished to claim such a right for himself. But, in truth,
just as a people had the right to administer the commonwealth in an absolute fashion at the free choice of several, even if, per-<295>chance, this
displease some few; so there is no doubt but it was able to confer the same
right upon the king, that, namely, what a number had previously been able
to do, henceforth the king alone should be able to do.

Now it properly follows that he who is not beholden to render accounts
cannot be punished by men. For, assuredly, absolute princes can be punished neither for not running the state to suit the people (for that is what
the case implies), nor for private misdeeds, a thing confessed by all. But,
after they have assumed the person of enemies, the evils which, perchance,
are inflicted upon them by the right of war do not have the character of a
punishment properly so called.[26] To cite the Roman consuls or any other
magistrates (using the word properly) is distinctly out of place, for they
outranked the people to a much slighter degree than do absolute princes.
Hence, what is surprising about their command [*imperium*] having been
greatly restricted, when as a matter of fact, the people had an authority
superior to theirs? But it is extremely dangerous to say that the people
pledged their faith to the king to the effect that they would obey as long as
he performed the office of a good prince; and that a manifest tyrant (let no
one be deceived in understanding that expression) does himself render invalid whatever has taken place between himself and the people in setting
up sovereignty, and thus releases the people from the obligation to obey.
For, although we concede the latter position (if by tyrant be understood
he who of set purpose and hostile mind devises the ruin of the people),
still the obligation of subjects does not at all depend on the goodness of
the prince, provided only he does not assume a hostile mind; unless we are
willing to give the people the authority to put down its princes whenever
it so pleases. For he whose sovereignty is for any cause displeasing imme-

---

26. Having forfeited his title of sovereignty, such a prince returns to the status of a
private citizen "against whom a man may use any defence he would against private citizens, in case they undertake to inflict grave injuries upon others" (*JNG,* 7, 8, §8). Cf.
Grotius, *JBP,* I.iv.12.

diately ceases to appear to be a good prince. Nor has it been as yet defined by what acts some one loses the name of a good prince; also, whether a bad prince is made so by one or by a few bad acts, or by more bad acts than good acts, or by bad acts without any intermixture of good acts. He who wishes to give the fault-finding common people the faculty of passing judgement on these matters will doubtless deserve uncommonly well of the tranquillity of the human race! And so, when, by an express agreement between the people and the prince, a form has not been set up in accordance with which goodness on his part is to be required, and the people has not reserved to itself the authority to examine into his acts and to bring him to order; whether the prince be good or bad, provided only he be not an enemy of the people, will make no difference as far as the obligation to obey is concerned.

Nor does what is brought forward about a wife have anything to do with the case, namely, that, although the man be set over her, she <296> is, nevertheless, by no means bound to endure the denial of the conjugal debt, the violation of the marriage pact, adulteries, and other grave injuries, but can look out for herself by securing a divorce. For if, indeed, husbands and wives live as subjects in a state, they have, of course, a superior who decides their controversies on the basis of the civil law. But, where life is spent outside a state, or husbands and wives are superior to civil laws, what they have agreed to between themselves is to be regarded. For, if a wife has subjected herself to the sovereignty of her husband, she cannot leave him, unless he puts on the character of an enemy. But, if no transaction has intervened between them beyond the marriage pact, then, as though also on a pact between equals, if one has been the first not to abide by it, the other will no longer be bound. Yet subjects do by no means bargain with an absolute prince in this latter fashion.

Finally, it is in vain that examples taken from the Sacred Scriptures are adduced, where the Israelites are said to have shaken off the yoke of the Moabites, the Ammonites, and the Philistines, after it appeared to God that they had paid enough punishment for their idolatry.[27] For either they were

27. Judges 3:12ff; 11:1–33.

still in a state of war, and had not yet subjected themselves to those peoples or their kings by a pact; or else they accepted the express mandate of God in that matter, which mandate no one will be able to allege for himself, except those to whom it was especially given.

The End
Glory to God

BIBLIOGRAPHY OF
WORKS CITED IN THE
INTRODUCTION AND NOTES

Works of Samuel Pufendorf

Briefwechsel. Edited by Detlef Döring. Vol. 1 of *Gesammelte Werke,* edited by Wilhelm Schmidt-Biggemann. Berlin: Akademie Verlag, 1996.

De jure naturae et gentium libri octo. Translated by C. H. and W. A. Oldfather. Carnegie Institution Classics of International Law, edited by James Brown Scott, 17. Oxford: Clarendon Press; London: Humphrey Milford, 1934.

Dissertationes academicae selectiores. Uppsala, 1677.

Elementa jurisprudentiae universalis. Edited by Thomas Behme. Vol. 3 of *Gesammelte Werke,* edited by Wilhelm Schmidt-Biggemann. Berlin: Akademie Verlag, 1999.

Eris Scandica und andere polemische Schriften über das Naturrecht. Edited by Fiammetta Palladini. Vol. 5 of *Gesammelte Werke,* edited by Wilhelm Schmidt-Biggemann. Berlin: Akademie Verlag, 2002.

Kleine Vorträge und Schriften: Texte zu Geschichte, Pädagogik, Philosophie, Kirche und Völkerrecht. Edited by Detlef Döring. Frankfurt am Main: V. Klostermann, 1995.

The Law of Nature and Nations. Translated by Basil Kennett. 5th ed. London, 1739.

The Political Writings of Samuel Pufendorf. Edited by Craig L. Carr. Translated by Michael Seidler. New York: Oxford University Press, 1994.

Samuel Pufendorf's "On the Natural State of Men." The 1678 Latin edition and English translation. Translated, annotated, and introduced by Michael Seidler. Studies in the History of Philosophy 13. Lewiston, N.Y.: Edwin Mellen, 1990.

The Whole Duty of Man, According to the Law of Nature. Translated by Andrew

Tooke, 1691. Edited by Ian Hunter and David Saunders. Indianapolis: Liberty Fund, 2003.

Other Works

Aristotle. *Analytica priora et posteriora.* Edited by W. D. Ross. Oxford Classical Texts (Scriptorum Classicorum Bibliotheca Oxoniensis). Oxford: Clarendon Press, 1964.

———. *Ethica Nicomachea.* Edited by William D. Ross. Vol. 9 of *The Works of Aristotle.* 2nd ed. Oxford: Clarendon Press, 1931.

———. *The Metaphysics.* Translated by Hugh Tredennick. Vols. 17 and 18 of *Aristotle.* Loeb Classical Library. Cambridge, Mass.: Harvard University Press, 1933; repr. 1980.

———. *Politics.* Translated by H. Rackham. Vol. 21 of *Aristotle.* Loeb Classical Library. Cambridge, Mass.: Harvard University Press; London: William Heinemann, 1944.

———. "Rhetorica ad Alexandrum." Translated by Harris Rackham. In vol. 16 of *Aristotle.* Loeb Classical Library. Cambridge, Mass.: Harvard University Press, 1965.

Augustine. *The City of God Against the Pagans.* Translated by George E. McCracken. 7 vols. Loeb Classical Library. Cambridge, Mass.: Harvard University Press; London: Heinemann, 1957–1972.

———. *Sermones.* Vol. 38 of *Patrologia Latina.* Edited by Jacques Paul Migne. Paris: Garnier, 1865.

Barbeyrac, Jean. *Le droit de la nature et des gens.* 2 vols. Amsterdam, 1706.

Barclay, William. *De regno et regali potestate adversus Buchananum, Brutum, Boucherium et reliquos monarchomachos libri sex.* Paris, 1600.

Barudio, Günter. *Das Zeitalter des Absolutismus und der Aufklärung (1648–1779).* Frankfurt: Fischer, 1981.

Behme, Thomas. *Samuel von Pufendorf, Naturrecht und Staat: Eine Analyse und Interpretation seiner Theorie, ihrer Grundlagen und Probleme.* Veröffentlichungen des Max-Planck-Instituts für Geschichte 112. Göttingen: Vandenhoeck und Ruprecht, 1995.

Benzoni, Girolamo. *La historia del Mondo Nuovo.* Venice, 1565.

Bodin, Jean. *Les six livres de la République.* Paris, 1583; repr. Aalen: Scientia, 1961.

Browne, Thomas. *Religio medici.* In vol. 3 of The Harvard Classics. New York: Collier, 1965.

Cauer, Friedrich. "Branchidai." *Paulys Real-Encyclopädie der classischen Alter-tumswissenschaften.* Edited by Georg Wissowa. Stuttgart: Metzler, 1893. III.1, cols. 809ff.

Charron, Pierre. *De la sagesse livres trois.* Bordeaux, 1601.

Cicero, Marcus Tullius. *De re publica.* Edited by Konrat Ziegler. Leipzig: Teubner, 1969.

———. *On Duties.* Edited by Miriam T. Griffin. Cambridge: Cambridge University Press, 1991.

———. "Pro Sexto Roscio" [*For Sextus Roscius*]. In vol. 1 of *M. Tulli Ciceronis Orationes.* Edited by Albert Curtis Clark. Oxford: Clarendon Press, 1961.

———. *Tusculan Disputations.* Translated and annotated by A. E. Douglas. Warminster, Eng.: Aris & Phillips, 1985.

Commentaria in Aristotelem Graeca. Edited by "consilio et auctoritate Academiae Litterarum Regiae Borussicae" [the counsel and authority of the Royal Prussian Academy of Letters]. 23 vols. Berlin: Reimer, 1882–1909.

Cujas, Jacques. *Observationum libri XXVIII.* Cologne: Hieratus; Oberursel: Iunghenius, 1618.

Diogenes Laertius. *Vitae philosophorum.* Edited by Miroslav Marcovich. 3 vols. Stuttgart: Teubner, 1999–2002.

Dionysius of Halicarnassus. *The Roman Antiquities.* Translated by Earnest Cary, on the basis of the version of Edward Spelman. 7 vols. Cambridge, Mass.: Harvard University Press; London: Heinemann, 1937–50.

Ehrenberg, Victor. "Phoibidas." *Paulys Real-Encyclopädie der classischen Alter-tumswissenschaften.* Edited by Georg Wissowa. Stuttgart: Metzler, 1893. XX.1, cols. 347–48.

Gentili, Alberico. *Hispanicae advocationis libri duo.* Translated by Frank Frost Abbott. Classics of International Law 9. New York: Oxford University Press, 1921.

Gerhard, Johann. *Loci theologici.* Edited by Eduard Preuss. Berlin, 1865.

Gratian. *Decretum Gratiani.* Vol. 187 of *Patrologia Latina.* Edited by Jacques Paul Migne. Paris, 1891.

Grotius, Hugo. *Commentary on the Law of Prize and Booty.* Translated by Gwladys L. Williams. Edited by Martine Julia van Ittersum. Indianapolis: Liberty Fund, 2006.

———. *De jure belli ac pacis libri tres.* Translated by Francis W. Kelsey. Edited by James Brown Scott. 2 vols. Carnegie Institution Classics of International Law 3. Oxford: Clarendon Press, 1925.

———. *The Free Sea.* Translated by Richard Hakluyt. Edited by David Armitage. Indianapolis: Liberty Fund, 2004.

———. *Opera omnia theologica.* 3 vols. Amsterdam, 1679; repr. Stuttgart–Bad Cannstatt: Frommann-Holzboog, 1972.

Häusser, Ludwig. *Geschichte der rheinischen Pfalz.* 2 vols. 1845; repr. Heidelberg: Winter, 1924.

Haythonus. *De Tartaris liber.* In *Novus Orbis regionum ac insularum veteribus incognitarum, una cum tabula cosmographica, [et] aliquot alijs consimilis argumenti libellis.* Edited by Simon Grynaeus. Basel, 1532.

Herberstein, Sigmund Freiherr von. *Rerum moscoviticarum commentarii.* Basel, 1571; repr. Frankfurt: Minerva, 1964.

Hobbes, Thomas. *De cive.* Vol. 2 of *The English Works.* Edited by William Molesworth. London, 1841.

———. *De cive.* Vol. 2 of *Opera philosophica quae Latine scripsit omnia.* Edited by William Molesworth. London, 1839; repr. Aalen: Scientia, 1961.

———. *The Elements of Law Natural and Politic.* Edited by Ferdinand Tönnies. With a new introduction by M. M. Goldsmith. London: Cass, 1969.

———. *Leviathan.* Vol. 3 of *The English Works.* Edited by William Molesworth. London, 1839.

Homer. *Odyssey.* Translated by Stanley Lombardo. Introduction by Sheila Murnaghan. Indianapolis: Hackett, 2000.

Hunter, Ian. *Rival Enlightenments: Civil and Metaphysical Philosophy in Early Modern Germany.* Cambridge: Cambridge University Press, 2001.

Isocrates. *Against Callimachus.* Translated by Larue van Hook. In vol. 3 of *Isocrates.* Loeb Classical Library. Cambridge, Mass.: Harvard University Press; London: Heinemann, 1961.

Ittersum, Martine Julia van. *Profit and Principle: Hugo Grotius, Natural Rights Theories and the Rise of Dutch Power in the East Indies, 1595–1615.* Leiden: Brill, 2006.

Justinian. *Digests.* Vols. 2–11 of *The Civil Law, Including the Twelve Tables, the Institutes of Gaius, the Rules of Ulpian, the Opinions of Paulus, the Enactments of Justinian, and the Constitutions of Leo.* Translated by Samuel Parsons Scott. Cincinnati: Central Trust Company, 1932.

———. *Institutes.* Vol. 2 of *The Civil Law, Including the Twelve Tables, the Institutes of Gaius, the Rules of Ulpian, the Opinions of Paulus, the Enactments of Justinian, and the Constitutions of Leo.* Translated by Samuel Parsons Scott. Cincinnati: Central Trust Company, 1932.

Kreller, Hans. "Postliminium." *Paulys Real-Encyclopädie der classischen Altertumswissenschaften.* Edited by Georg Wissowa. Stuttgart: Metzler, 1893. XXII, cols. 863–73.

Krieger, Leonard. *The Politics of Discretion: Pufendorf and the Acceptance of Natural Law.* Chicago: University of Chicago Press, 1965.

Leibniz, Gottfried Wilhelm. *Nouveaux essais sur l'entendement humain.* Edited by André Robinet and Heinrich Schepers. In vol. 6 of *Sämtliche Schriften und Briefe.* 2nd ed. Berlin: Akademie Verlag, 1990.

Leonhard, Rudolf. "Donatio." *Paulys Real-Encyclopädie der classischen Altertumswissenschaften.* Edited by Georg Wissowa. Stuttgart: Metzler, 1893. V.2, cols. 1533–40.

Livy. *Ab urbe condita.* Edited by Patrick G. Walsh. Oxford: Clarendon Press, 1999.

Lucretius. *On the Nature of Things (De rerum natura).* Edited and translated by Anthony M. Esolen. Baltimore: Johns Hopkins University Press, 1995.

Luther, Martin. *Werke.* Weimarer Ausgabe. Department I: 60 vols. Dept. II: 6 vols. Dept. III: 12 vols. Dept. IV: 15 vols. Weimar: Böhlau, 1883–2005.

Maimonides. *The Guide of the Perplexed.* Edited by Shlomo Pines. 2 vols. Chicago: University of Chicago Press, 1991.

Michael of Ephesus. *Michaelis Ephesii in librum quintum Ethicorum Nicomacheorum commentarium.* Edited by Michael Hayduck. *Commentaria in Aristotelem Graeca* 22.3. Berlin: Reimer, 1901.

Ovid. *Metamorphoses.* Translated by Alan D. Melville. Oxford: Oxford University Press, 1986.

———. *Ovid's Heroines: A Verse Translation of the Heroides.* Translated by Daryl Hine. New Haven, Conn.: Yale University Press, 1991.

Philo Judaeus (Philo of Alexandria). *De legibus specialibus.* Edited by Leopold Cohn. Vol. 5 of *Philonis Alexandrini opera quae supersunt,* edited by Leopold Cohn and Paul Wendland. Berlin: Reimer, 1906; repr. 1962.

Plato. *Symposium.* Edited and with an introduction, translation, and commentary by Christopher J. Rowe. Warminster, Eng.: Aris & Phillips, 1998.

Pliny the Elder. *Natural History.* Translated by Harris Rackham. Loeb Classical Library. Cambridge, Mass.: Harvard University Press; London: Heinemann, 1967–69.

Plutarch. *The E at Delphi [De E apud Delphos].* In vol. 5 of *Plutarch's Moralia.* Translated by Frank Cole Babbitt. Loeb Classical Library. Cambridge, Mass.: Harvard University Press, 1957.

———. *The Education of Children.* Translated by Frank Cole Babbitt. In vol. 1 of *Plutarch's Moralia.* Loeb Classical Library. Cambridge, Mass.: Harvard University Press, 1949.

———. "Lycurgus." In vol. 1 of *Plutarch's Lives: In Eleven Volumes.* Translated by Bernadotte Perrin. London: Heinemann, 1967.

———. *On the Eating of Flesh* [*De esu carnium*]. In vol. 12 of *Plutarch's Moralia.* Translated by Harold Cherniss and William C. Helmbold. Loeb Classical Library. Cambridge, Mass.: Harvard University Press, 1957.

———. *Table-Talk* [*Symposiacon*]. Vol. 8 of *Plutarch's Moralia.* Translated by Paul A. Clement and Herbert B. Hoffleit. Loeb Classical Library. Cambridge, Mass.: Harvard University Press, 1969.

———. "Theseus." In vol. 1 of *Plutarch's Parallel Lives.* Translated by Bernadotte Perrin. Loeb Classical Library. Cambridge, Mass.: Harvard University Press, 1914.

Quintilian. *Declamationes XIX maiores.* Edited by Lennart Håkanson. Stuttgart: Teubner, 1982.

———. *The Orator's Education* [*Institutio oratoria*]. Edited and translated by Donald A. Russell. 5 vols. Loeb Classical Library. Cambridge, Mass.: Harvard University Press, 2001.

Richer, Christophe. *De rebus Turcarum ad Franciscum Gallorum regem christianissimum libri quinque.* Paris, 1540.

Röd, Wolfgang. *Geometrischer Geist und Naturrecht: Methodengeschichtliche Untersuchungen zur Staatsphilosophie im 17. und 18. Jahrhundert.* Munich: Bayerische Akademie der Wissenschaften, 1970.

Roy, Hugo de. *De eo quod justum est et circa id philosophiae, theologiae et jurisprudentiae syncretismo libri tres.* Hildesheim, 1653.

Schaab, Meinrad. *Geschichte der Kurpfalz.* 2 vols. Stuttgart: Kohlhammmer, 1988–92.

Schubert, Friedrich Hermann. *Die deutschen Reichstage in der Staatslehre der frühen Neuzeit.* Göttingen: Vandenhoeck und Ruprecht, 1966.

Selden, John. *De jure naturali et gentium, iuxta disciplinam Ebraeorum.* London, 1640.

———. *De successionibus in bona defuncti, ad leges Ebraeorum, liber singularis; accedunt eiusdem De successione in pontificatum Ebraeorum, libri duo.* London, 1636.

———. *Mare clausum seu De dominio maris.* London, 1635.

Seneca, Lucius Annaeus. *De beata vita.* Edited by Pierre Grimal. Paris: Presses universitaires de France, 1969.

————. *De constantia sapientis* [*On the Steadfastness of the Wise Man*]. Edited by Louis Delatte. La Haye: Mouton, 1966.

————. *De ira libri tres* [*On Anger*]. Vol. 1. In *Seneca's Dialogs I–XII*. Edited by William Hardy Alexander. 3 vols. Berkeley: University of California Press, 1943–45.

————. *On Benefits*. Translated by Aubrey Stewart. London, 1905.

————. *17 Letters*. Translated by Charles Desmond Nuttall Costa. Warminster, Eng.: Aris & Phillips, 1988.

Sprenger, Gerhard. "Der Einfluss der Naturwissenschaften auf das Denken Samuel Pufendorfs." In *Samuel Pufendorf und seine Wirkungen bis auf die heutige Zeit*. Edited by Bodo Geyer and Helmut Goerlich. Baden-Baden: Nomos, 1996.

Tacitus. *The annals of Tacitus* [*Annales*]. Edited and with a commentary by Francis Richard David Goodyear. 3 vols. Cambridge: Cambridge University Press, 1972–96.

Tamm, Ditlev. "Pufendorf und Dänemark." In *Samuel v. Pufendorf 1632–1982*. Edited by Kjell Å. Modéer. Ett rättshistoriskt symposion i Lund 15–16 januari 1982. Stockholm: Nordiska Bokhandolen i Distributien, 1986.

Thomas Aquinas. *The "Summa theologica" of St. Thomas Aquinas*. Translated by Fathers of the English Dominican Province. 22 vols. London: Burns, Oates & Washburne, 1912–36.

Ulpian. *Ulpiani liber singularis regularum. Pauli libri quinque sententiarum. Fragmenta minora*. Edited by Paul Krüger. Collectio librorum iuris anteiustiniani 2. Berlin: Weidmann, 1878; repr. Hildesheim: Weidmann, 2001.

Valle, Pietro della. *The Travels of Pietro della Valle in India*. From the English translation of 1664, by George Havers. New York: Franklin, 1964.

Vázquez, Fernando. *Illustrium controversiarum aliarumque usu frequentium libri tres*. Lyon, 1595–99.

Velleius Paterculus. *Compendium of Roman History*. Translated by Frederick W. Shipley. Cambridge, Mass.: Harvard University Press, 1967.

Virgil. *Aeneid*. Edited by George P. Goold. In *Virgil: Eclogues, Georgics, Aeneid*. 2 vols. Loeb Classical Library. Cambridge, Mass.: Harvard University Press, 1999.

Vitoria, Francisco de. "De Indis." *Vorlesungen* (*Relectiones*). Latin and German. Edited by Ulrich Horst, Heinz-Gerhard Justenhoven, and Joachim Stüben. 2 vols. Vol. 2 (Stuttgart: Kohlhammer, 1997), 370–541.

Weigel, Erhard. *Analysis Aristotelica ex Euclide restituta*. Edited by Thomas Behme. Vol. 3.3 of Clavis Pansophiae. Edited by Charles Lohr and Wilhelm Schmidt-Biggeman. Stuttgart–Bad Cannstatt: Frommann-Holzboog, 2008.

———. *Arithmetische Beschreibung der Moral-Weissheit von Personen und Sachen.* Edited by Thomas Behme. Vol. 3.2 of Clavis Pansophiae. Edited by Charles Lohr and Wilhelm Schmidt-Biggemann. Stuttgart–Bad Cannstatt: Frommann-Holzboog, 2004.

———. *Dissertatio metaphysica posterior de modo existentiae qui dicitur duratio.* Jena, 1652.

———. *Universi corporis Pansophici caput summum.* Edited by Thomas Behme. Vol. 3.1 of Clavis Pansophiae. Edited by Charles Lohr and Wilhelm Schmidt-Biggemann. Stuttgart–Bad Cannstatt: Frommann-Holzboog, 2003.

Welzel, Hans. *Die Naturrechtslehre Samuel Pufendorfs: Ein Beitrag zur Ideengeschichte des 17. und 18. Jahrhunderts.* Berlin: De Gruyter, 1958.

———. *Naturrecht und materiale Gerechtigkeit.* Göttingen: Vandenhoeck und Ruprecht, 1980.

INDEX

abandonment: of children, 111; of property, 67, 78–80, 82–83

abortion, 28–29

absolute estimate of moral actions, 247–48. *See also* moral sphere

absolute or pure promises, 120

absolute rule: answers to arguments against, 394–98; defined, 387–88; imperfect mutuality of obligation regarding, 113–14; limited rule vs., 390–91; tyrants, legitimacy of overthrowing, 392–94

acquisition of property, 64–80; burdensome modes of, 68–70; derelict or abandoned property, 67, 78–80; by donation, 64, 66–70; illegitimate modes of, 73–78; increments and fruits of things acquired by owner, 70–71; industry, things produced by, 70–71; lucrative modes of, 66–68; occupation as original mode of, 62–64; production of a thing out of materials owned by another, 71–73; by succession, 64–66 (*see also* inheritance); time, elimination of fault in acquisition through passage of, 74–76; in trust, 66–67; in war, 68, 69–70, 74

actual imputation vs. imputability, 286

Adam, naming of things by, 361

adopted children, 380

adultery, 208, 303, 352, 356

adventitious obligation, 109

advice or counsel, 105

advocates, restitution owed by, 355

Aelian-Sentian law, 232

Aeneid (Virgil), 49n5, 330n6

affections: of moral actions, 233–34; of sovereigns and sovereignty, 387–89

affirmative law, 227–28, 260–61

agents: relative estimate of moral actions from status and condition of, 258

Agesilaos (Spartan king), 189n50

agio, 195

Alexander the Great, 183, 185, 292

alienation of property, right of, 79–80

allowed actions, 308

alluvium, 71

ambassadors, 227, 347

Ammonites, 397

Analysis Aristotelica (Weigel), x, 8n4, 9n5, 10n7, 24n1, 235n1, 284n1

animals: human dominion over, 57–60; nonownability of wild animals, 82; nonsocial life as life of, 320–22; obligation to, 142

antecedent conscience, 301

Antoninus, 295

aptitudes, 88, 93

Aquila, law of, 95

Aquinas. *See* Thomas Aquinas

arbitration, 144–45, 147, 358–59

aristocracy: esteem for, 97; monarchy preferred over rule by, 388; moral personage by virtue of, 41; titles, 86

407

This book is set in Adobe Garamond, a modern adaptation by Robert Slimbach of the typeface originally cut around 1540 by the French typographer and printer Claude Garamond. The Garamond face, with its small lowercase height and restrained contrast between thick and thin strokes, is a classic "old-style" face and has long been one of the most influential and widely used typefaces.

Printed on paper that is acid-free and meets the requirements of the American National Standard for Permanence of Paper for Printed Library Materials, z39.48-1992. ∞

Book design by Louise OFarrell
Gainesville, Florida
Typography by Apex CoVantage
Madison, Wisconsin
Printed and bound by Thomson-Shore,
Dexter, Michigan